Cambridge Middle East Studies

Editorial Board

Charles Tripp (general editor)
Julia Clancy-Smith
F. Gregory Gause
Yezid Sayigh
Avi Shlaim
Judith E. Tucker

Cambridge Middle East Studies has been established to publish books on the nineteenth- to twenty-first-century Middle East and North Africa. The series offers new and original interpretations of aspects of Middle Eastern societies and their histories. To achieve disciplinary diversity, books are solicited from authors writing in a wide range of fields including history, sociology, anthropology, political science, and political economy. The emphasis is on producing books affording an original approach along theoretical and empirical lines. The series is intended for students and academics, but the more accessible and wide-ranging studies will also appeal to the interested general reader.

A list of books in the series can be found after the index.

D1522305

26.82

Alamance Community College
Library
P. O. Box 8000
Graham, NC 27253

Religion and State in Syria

While Syria has been dominated since the 1960s by a determinedly secular regime, the uprising that began there in 2011 has raised many questions about the role of Islam in the country's politics. This book, which is based on the author's extensive fieldwork in Syria's mosques and schools and on interviews with local Muslim scholars, is the first comprehensive study of the country's little-known religious scene and its most influential actors, the ulama. It demonstrates that with the eradication of the Muslim Brothers after the failed insurrection of 1982, Sunni men of religion became the only voice of the Islamic trend in the country. Through educational programmes, the establishment of charitable foundations, and their deft handling of tribal and merchant networks, they took advantage of popular disaffection with secular ideologies to increase their influence over society. In recent years, with the Islamic resurgence, the Alawi-dominated Ba'thist regime was compelled to bring the clergy into the political fold. This ambiguous relationship was exposed in 2011 by the division of the Sunni clergy among regime supporters, bystanders, and opponents. This book affords an entirely new perspective on Syrian society as it stands at the crossroads of political and social fragmentation.

Thomas Pierret is a Lecturer in Contemporary Islam at the University of Edinburgh. He has edited two volumes on contemporary Islam and publis'   ·ies for
the *I*   rising
in 2(*New*
York   zeera
Eng'

Alamance Community College
Library
P. O. Box 8000
Graham, NC 27253

Religion and State in Syria

The Sunni Ulama from Coup to Revolution

THOMAS PIERRET
University of Edinburgh

CAMBRIDGE
UNIVERSITY PRESS

CAMBRIDGE UNIVERSITY PRESS
Cambridge, New York, Melbourne, Madrid, Cape Town,
Singapore, São Paulo, Delhi, Mexico City

Cambridge University Press
32 Avenue of the Americas, New York, NY 10013-2473, USA

www.cambridge.org
Information on this title: www.cambridge.org/9781107609907

© Presses universitaires de France 2011
© Cambridge University Press 2013

This publication is in copyright. Subject to statutory exception
and to the provisions of relevant collective licensing agreements,
no reproduction of any part may take place without the written
permission of Cambridge University Press.

First published in French as *Baas et islam en Syrie: la dynastie Assad face aux
Oulémas* by Presses universitaires de France 2011
First English edition 2013

Printed in the United States of America

A catalog record for this publication is available from the British Library.

Library of Congress Cataloging in Publication data
Pierret, Thomas.
  [Baas et islam en Syrie. English]
  Religion and state in Syria: the Sunni ulama from coup to revolution / Thomas Pierret.
    pages   cm – (Cambridge Middle East studies; 41)
  Includes bibliographical references and index.
  ISBN 978-1-107-02641-4 (hardback) – ISBN 978-1-107-60990-7 (paperback)
  1. Syria – Politics and government – 20th century.   2. Syria – Politics and
  government – 21st century.   3. Ulama – Political activity – Syria.   4. Hizb al-Ba'th
  al-'Arabi al-Ishtiraki (Syria)   I. Title.
  DS95.5.P5413   2012
  322'.1095691–dc23   2012016897

ISBN 978-1-107-02641-4 Hardback
ISBN 978-1-107-60990-7 Paperback

Cambridge University Press has no responsibility for the persistence or accuracy of URLs
for external or third-party Internet websites referred to in this publication and does not
guarantee that any content on such websites is, or will remain, accurate or appropriate.

To the martyrs of the Syrian revolution
To Mériam and Loueï

Contents

Acknowledgements

The last lines of this book were written in February 2012, at a time when the bloody suppression of the popular uprising in Syria had been ongoing for almost a year. During these past months, I have thought unceasingly of my many friends and acquaintances who live in, and in some cases have been forced to flee, this country that is so dear to me. It is to them that I address my greatest thanks – although, to my regret, the future is still too uncertain to allow me to mention the full names of people currently in Syria. At the top of the list are my guardian angels, the religious students who guided me through the mosques of Damascus and Aleppo: Mostafa, Bara', 'Ammar, Faris, Ali, Mahmud, Muhammad, and many more – may God protect you. Sheikh Ahmad Mouaz al-Khatib has not only been incredibly helpful and generous, but he also taught me much about human values. I also had the chance to meet astute observers such as 'Abd al-Rahman al-Hajj Ibrahim, Mohamad Berro, and Isam Abdulmola. Finally, I express my gratitude to the protagonists of this book, who agreed to receive me despite the difficult context, and especially to all those who granted me more time and attention than mere courtesy could ever demand.

This book would never have seen the light of day without the support of several institutions whose respective directors provided me with invaluable encouragement and advice. My doctoral research was funded by the Fonds National de la Recherche Scientifique of Belgium and supervised by Professor Gilles Kepel at Sciences Po Paris (Chaire Moyen-Orient Méditerranée), as well as by Professor Felice Dassetto at the Université catholique de Louvain (Centre for Interdisciplinary Research on Islam in the Contemporary World). During my fieldwork in Syria, I appreciated the helpfulness of the staff and Fellows of the French Institute (IFPO). The transformation of my dissertation into a book was facilitated by a postdoctoral fellowship at Princeton University funded by the Belgian American Educational Foundation and supervised by Professor Michael Cook. The translation into English of the French manuscript was carried out during a visiting fellowship at the Zentrum Moderner Orient in Berlin under the supervision of Professor Ulrike Freitag. For their help in various circumstances, I am also indebted to Amin Aït-Chaalal, Andrew Arsan, Francis Balace, Annabelle Böttcher, François Burgat, Baudouin Dupret, Jean-Pierre Filiu, Michael Gilsenan, Bernard Haykel, Steven Heydemann, Raymond Hinnebusch, Amaney Jamal, Gudrun Krämer, Brigitte Maréchal, Tarek Mitri, Élizabeth Picard, Bernard Rougier, and Ghassan Salamé. The insightful and friendly comments of Mohammad Al Attar, Souhail Belhadj, Cécile Boëx, Farid El Asri, Thomas Hegghammer, Steffen Hertog, Boris James, Stéphane Lacroix, Paulo Pinto, Laura Ruiz de Elvira, Kjetil Selvik, Ward Vloerberghs, and Odai Al Zoubi greatly enriched the content of this book. Sincere thanks also to Benedict Young of Babel Editing for his outstanding job in correcting my translation of the original French text. For reasons that are too numerous to be mentioned here, I cannot overstate my gratitude to Benjamin White.

Last but not least I thank my close friends, my parents, and my sister for their unceasing support during all these years. Above all, I thank Mériam for her patience and for being by my side from the first lines of this project until its completion. This book is dedicated to her as well as to our son Loueï, who has brought so much joy in our life in the midst of this tragic Syrian revolution.

A Note on Conventions

TRANSLITERATION

Arabic words are transliterated according to a simplified version of the *International Journal of Middle East Studies*' system (no special characters, diacritic signs, or long vowels). Arabic words in unabridged English dictionaries are not italicised. Other Arabic words are italicised only in the first instance.

NAMES

Arabic names are transcribed according to the preceding system unless a different transcription is dominant in English-language texts (e.g. Hussein, not Husayn; Abdullah, not 'Abd Allah).

ELECTRONIC SOURCES

Consultation date of Internet sources has been omitted, but all cited documents have been stored electronically by the author. Full URLs are provided only when the title of a page is not mentioned in the footnotes. When the title is mentioned, typing it in a search engine will allow the reader to find the text despite possible URL change or original website closure.

Introduction

At a time when the Syrian regime is facing an unprecedented wave of popular unrest, the political stance of the ulama is of utmost importance. In the 1960s and 1970s, as urban, religious, and Sunni elites, the ulama numbered among the main opponents of the Ba'thist regime, which was led by sons of peasants who were often members of the Alawite community and were driven by secular and socialist ideals. In the early 1980s, moreover, the bloody suppression of the Islamist insurgency, in which many sons and followers of the ulama were directly involved, led to dozens of clerics being driven into exile.

Three decades later, as the flame of revolt flares up, the influence of the clergy over Syrian society has increased considerably. This situation results from the population's growing religious fervour, and from official policies which, although still extremely repressive even by regional standards, have nevertheless relaxed in the last two decades. Potentially, then, the ulama could now constitute a more significant threat to the regime than they did in the past; but in fact the reality is more complex, both because of the clerics' understandable fears of state repression and because of the rapprochement between state and clergy that has taken place over the previous decade. This deepening partnership has been part of a broader trend whose consequences are now unfolding before our eyes: the Ba'th's alliance with its former enemies, the urban elites, has led it to turn its back on its original social base, peasants and the poor; and the latter have provided most of the manpower in the current uprising.

At the same time, though, it would be an oversimplification to say that nearly half a century after the Ba'thist coup of 1963, the ulama are, once again, on the 'wrong' side of a revolution. Indeed, some of the few major demonstrations witnessed thus far in the central districts of Damascus have originated in mosques that symbolise old traditions of clerical resistance to the Ba'th. In other words, just like the quietism of many clerics, the rebellious attitude of some of their colleagues has its origin in the long-standing processes that this book sets out to recover.

Damascus, 31 March 2007. Night is falling on the Sheikh 'Abd al-Karim al-Rifa'i mosque, a huge, futuristic building erected at the entrance to the upscale subdivision of Tanzim Kafr Suse and named in honour of one of the great figures of the Islamic 'renaissance' that occurred in the early days of the Ba'thist regime. Four years later, almost to the day, the first anti-regime demonstrations of central Damascus would start from here. But we are not there yet. In this twelfth day of Rabi' al-Awwal 1428 (hegira year), Muslims celebrate the Prophet's birthday (Mawlid) and a traffic jam is paralysing the streets that lead to the al-Rifa'i mosque.

Thousands of the faithful take their places for the evening on the carpets of the building, which is decorated for the occasion with light bulbs, banners, and green pennants. In a corner of the mosque, seated before a large model of the green-domed tomb of Muhammad, a choir of students from the mosque (mostly students of scientific university faculties) sings the glory of the Messenger. Faced with an apathetic crowd, impassive ulama, merchants, and other notables are seated on plastic chairs or, the most important of them, in leather armchairs. Periodically, they get up to hug a distinguished visitor who has gone through the crowd via a cordoned-off passage. Three or four times during the evening, prophetic anthems are interrupted by the exhortations of the clerics.[1]

Are we witnessing here some formal event? Nothing seems to indicate it. No state official is attending the ceremony. In addition, while we are just two months away from the plebiscite that will renew the mandate of President Bashar al-Asad, the only reference to state power heard in the speeches is particularly negative, since it takes the form of a warning. This comes from Sheikh Usama al-Rifa'i (b. 1944), the preacher of the mosque and the eldest son of the scholar who gave it his name. This

---

[1] For a description and analysis of the meanings of the celebration of the Mawlid in Syria, see Thomas Pierret, 'Staging the Authority of the Ulama: The Celebration of the Mawlid in Urban Syria', in *Ethnographies of Islam*, ed. Paulo Pinto, Thomas Pierret, Kathryn Spellman, and Baudouin Dupret (Edinburgh: Edinburgh University Press, 2012), 93–104.

former political exile concludes his speech by attaching the legitimacy of the regime to the embrace of an Islamic agenda:

I must warn the leaders in our country ... that their power ... springs from the umma. Thus, since this umma has come back to its religion ... those leaders have no other choice but to reflect the desire of their people and to raise the flag of Islam. Indeed, their [future] position depends on their return to God ... and to the desire of the umma ... If they don't reflect this desire, they will lose their credibility and in the end, they will lose everything in this world ... and God will replace them with better people.[2]

The simple fact that a former exile can talk this way at a public event attests to the profound changes that have permeated the relationship between the regime and Muslim clerics since the bloody suppression of the Islamist insurgency of 1979–82. After it was repressed and, in certain cities, decimated, the clergy took advantage of the disaffection with Ba'thist ideology and the eradication of the Muslim Brothers, which granted it a monopoly on the representation of the Islamic trend, to patiently reconstitute its forces and increase its margins of freedom within the framework of an ambiguous partnership with the state.[3] Remarkably, the most prominent Syrian ulama of the early twenty-first century are not all traditional clients of the regime but also figures who, like Usama al-Rifa'i, have long suffered from state repression.

From these observations, this book intends first to correct a number of misconceptions about Syria. The first of these is that the regime, because of its secular character and the fact that it is dominated by members of the Alawite minority, never enjoyed any kind of religious legitimacy among Sunnis.[4] I will show that, at least until 2011, the political leadership managed to establish ambiguous, but nevertheless robust, partnerships with religious figures who had genuine credibility in the eyes of many Muslims.

---

[2] Quoted in Thomas Pierret and Kjetil Selvik, 'Limits of "Authoritarian Upgrading" in Syria: Private Welfare, Islamic Charities, and the Rise of the Zayd Movement', *International Journal of Middle East Studies* 41, no. 4 (2009), 595–614, at 609.

[3] As will appear throughout this book, the idea according to which there is no clergy in Sunni Islam is an ideal, not a social reality.

[4] The dominant Sunni tradition has always considered Alawites as infidels. The only prominent Sunni Muslim scholar who issued a pro-Alawite fatwa in the twentieth century was Mufti of Jerusalem Amin al-Husseini, who did so for very political (nationalistic) reasons. See Yvette Talhamy, 'The Fatwas and the Nusayri/Alawis of Syria', *Middle Eastern Studies* 46, no. 2 (2010), 175–94.

Understanding state–ulama relations in Syria also means getting rid of another piece of common wisdom on local politics, a tendency to overestimate the regime's capacity for social engineering ('manipulation'). From this perspective the gradual rebuilding of the power of the clergy after 1982 is seen as the result of official policies which reportedly 'encouraged' the development of a quietist version of Islam, thus creating a genie that became harder to keep contained.[5] Actually, the case of Usama al-Rifaʿi and his network illustrates the fact that the Syrian government has been forced to take into account religious forces whose wide social roots result from long-term processes that go back to a time prior to the advent of the Baʿth and have been only partially affected by the interventions of the latter. In fact, the regime has not encouraged the re-Islamisation of society: it has only worked for limiting its political implications. This leads us to the second axis of my main argument, which refers to a broader debate on the fate of Sunni clerics in the contemporary era.

In the twentieth century, the Syrian ulama not only faced the challenge of secularist authoritarianism but also structural changes that, as in the rest of the Muslim world, seemed to irreparably undermine their power bases. These perils, which stemmed from the construction of the modern state that had started in the previous century,[6] included the secularisation of law,[7] the expansion of state control over religious institutions, and the modernisation–democratisation of education.

The first of these developments often excluded clerics from the judicial institutions in favour of specialists in positive law. The second, which led to the subsuming of religious endowments (*waqf*, pl. *awqaf*) under state control,[8] the bureaucratisation of religious personnel,[9] and the institutionalisation of its training under the aegis of the state,[10] was likely to put

---

[5] See in particular the articles published in 2005–6 by the Syrian correspondent of *al-Hayat*, Ibrahim Hamidi.

[6] Moshe Maʿoz, 'The Ulama and the Process of Modernisation in Syria during the Mid-Nineteenth Century', *Asian and African Studies*, no. 7 (1971), 77–88.

[7] Bernard Botiveau, 'Le mouvement de rationalisation du droit en Syrie au cours de la première moitié du XXe siècle', *Bulletin d'études orientales* 35 (1983), 123–35.

[8] Randi Deguilhem, 'Le *waqf* en Syrie indépendante', in *Le Waqf dans le monde musulman contemporain (XIXe–XXe siècles)*, ed. Faruk Bilici (Istanbul: Institut Français d'Études Anatoliennes, 1994), 123–44.

[9] Annabelle Böttcher, *Syrische Religionspolitik unter Asad* (Freiburg im Breisgau: Arnold-Bergstraesser-Institut, 1998).

[10] Bernard Botiveau, 'La formation des oulémas en Syrie: la faculté de shariʿa de l'Université de Damas', in *Les Intellectuels et le pouvoir: Syrie, Égypte, Tunisie, Algérie*, ed. Gilbert Delanoue (Cairo: CEDEJ, 1986), 67–91.

an end to their economic autonomy and take away their monopoly on the training of their successors.[11] As for the transformation of the education system, it produced a new type of literate elite that saw the worldview of the ulama as outdated.[12] Even when they displayed a religious sensibility, as was for instance the case with the leaders of the Muslim Brothers, some of these intellectuals derided the traditional Islamic scholarly corpus, whose mastery is the basis of the authority of the ulama, as archaic and dispensable. Instead of following the opinions of their predecessors, they claimed the right to direct interpretation of revealed texts.[13] Combined with the development of print and other mass media, which made some form of religious knowledge accessible to almost everyone, this development seemed to constitute 'a major assault on the ulama as interpreters of Islam'.[14]

Although the Syrian clergy has indeed faced all these dangers, the outcome of the battle has been far from uniformly negative. At the dawn of the twenty-first century, the process of bureaucratisation having remained very superficial, the ulama retain broad financial independence through their partnership with the private sector. In addition, they continue to exercise, if not a monopoly, at least a leading role in the training of future men of religion. The reason for that is partly that they have adapted to new teaching methods through the establishment of modern private institutes, which have enabled them to produce young clerics on a much larger scale than traditional methods. More unexpected was the fact that the old structures that were threatened by the dynamics of modernisation (the master–disciple relationship, study circles) were transformed, thanks to the flexibility given to them by their informality, into a powerful instrument of defence of the influence of the clerics. It is by relying on these structures that the ulama have integrated into their networks these graduates of secular schooling who were at one time perceived as the main threat to their

[11] For Egypt, see Gilles Kepel, 'Les oulémas, l'intelligentsia et les islamistes en Égypte: système social, ordre transcendantal et ordre traduit', *Revue française de science politique* 35, no. 3 (1985), 424–45.

[12] For Egypt, see Gregory Starrett, *Putting Islam to Work: Education, Politics, and Religious Transformation in Egypt* (Berkeley: University of California Press, 1998).

[13] For the early Egyptian Muslim Brothers, see Richard Mitchell, *The Society of the Muslim Brothers* (London: Oxford University Press, 1969), 211–14, 238.

[14] Francis Robinson, 'Technology and Religious Change: Islam and the Impact of Print', *Modern Asian Studies* 27, no. 1 (1993), 229–51, at 249. For a similar argument regarding modern media, see Dale Eickelman and Jon Anderson, *New Media in the Muslim World: The Emerging Public Sphere* (Bloomington: Indiana University Press, 2003).

authority. In fact, far from systematically becoming a rival of the *'alim* (sing. of ulama), the 'pious engineer' often became his disciple, when he had not himself attained the status of 'alim after having complied with the rules of acquisition of knowledge that were defined by his elders.

Central here is the notion of tradition in the sense of a heritage whose content and rules of transmission are regarded as relatively intangible. If the Syrian ulama can still control the training of their successors, despite the institutionalisation of specialised Islamic teaching, if they can include a pharmacist, it is because they have imposed among a large number of their co-religionists the idea that mastery of religious knowledge requires more than a diploma or self-teaching through books: it necessitates the study of the traditional scholarly corpus under the supervision of the custodians of that heritage – that is, themselves.

The fundamental cause of the ulama's success in promoting this conception is not only the force of their arguments, or the docility of their flocks, or state repression against the supporters of a modernised approach to religious knowledge. It is rather the fact that the ulama were the first, and leading, actors to respond to the main sociological consequence of the modern Islamic 'awakening', that is to say, the exponential increase in demand for religious education.

The rapid growth of a literate population wishing to study the Quran, the hadith, and fiqh has brought new customers to the old networks of religious scholarship, thus entailing the latter's development to an extent unprecedented in history. To this was added the now familiar phenomenon of sheikhs who have exploited the potential of mass media (newspapers, essays, tapes, radio and television, Internet) to reach an even wider audience. Social change was thus transformed from a threat into an opportunity.

STATE OF THE LITERATURE

This book aims to advance our knowledge of the still under-studied Sunni religious elite in Syria, but also to enrich the literature on Muslim scholars in the modern period; hence the reflection on the broader transformations of religious authority in Muslim societies.[15]

---

[15] See Marc Gaborieau and Malika Zeghal (eds.), 'Autorités religieuses en islam', *Archives de sciences sociales des religions* 49, no. 125 (2004), 5–210; Gudrun Krämer and Sabine Schmidtke, *Speaking for Islam: Religious Authorities in Muslim Societies* (Leiden: Brill, 2006); Frédéric Volpi and Bryan Turner (eds.), 'Authority and Islam', *Theory, Cultures & Society* 24, no. 2 (2007), 1–240.

Most of the bibliography on modern Syrian Islam concerns the Muslim Brothers,[16] on the one hand, and the reformist and Sufi currents during the period from the nineteenth to the mid-twentieth centuries,[17] on the other.

Regarding more contemporary issues, existing works focus on Sufism,[18] official religious policies, institutions and discourses,[19] pro-regime ulama such as the late Grand Mufti Ahmad Kaftaru, and Saʿid Ramadan al-Buti,[20]

[16] To mention only the most important publications: Johannes Reissner, *Ideologie und Politik der Muslimbrüder Syriens: Von den Wahlen 1947 bis zum Verbot unter Adib ash-Shishakli* (Freiburg im Breisgau: Klaus Shwarz, 1980); Hans Günter Lobmeyer, *Opposition und Widerstand in Syrien* (Hamburg: Deutsches Orient-Institut, 1995).

[17] Norbert Tapiéro, *Les Idées réformistes d'al-Kawakibi, 1265–1320=1849–1902: contribution à l'étude de l'Islam moderne* (Paris: Les Editions Arabes, 1956); David Dean Commins, *Islamic Reform: Politics and Social Change in Late Ottoman Syria* (New York: Oxford University Press, 1990); Itzchak Weismann, *Taste of Modernity: Sufism, Salafiyya, and Arabism in Late Ottoman Damascus* (Leiden: Brill, 2001); on Sufi traditions, see the numerous works by Itzchak Weismann that are mentioned throughout this book.

[18] Frederick de Jong, 'Les confréries mystiques musulmanes du Machreq arabe: centres de gravité, signes de déclin et de renaissance', in *Sufi Orders in Ottoman and post-Ottoman era in Egypt and the Middle East* (Istanbul: ISIS Press, 2000), 197–234; Eric Geoffroy, 'Soufisme, réformisme et pouvoir en Syrie contemporaine', *Egypte/Monde arabe*, no. 29 (1997), 11–21; Paulo Pinto, 'Sufism and the Political Economy of Morality in Syria', *Interdisciplinary Journal of Middle Eastern Studies* 15 (2006), 103–36; see also, on the cult of saints in Aleppo, Julia Gonnella, *Islamische Heiligenverehrung im urbanen Kontext am Beispiel von Aleppo (Syrien)* (Berlin: Klaus Schwarz, 1995).

[19] Böttcher, *Syrische Religionspolitik*; Olivier Carré, *La Légitimation islamique des socialismes arabes: analyse conceptuelle combinatoire des manuels scolaires égyptiens, syriens et irakiens* (Paris: FNSP, 1979); Andreas Christmann, 'An Invented Piety? Subduing Ramadan in Syria State Media', *Yearbook of the Sociology of Islam* 3 (2001), 243–63; Mordechai Kedar, *Asad in Search of Legitimacy: Message and Rhetoric in the Syrian Press under Hafiz and Bashar* (Brighton: Sussex Academic Press, 2005), 78–131; Eyal Zisser, 'Syria, the Baʿth Regime and the Islamic Movement: Stepping on a New Path?', *The Muslim World*, no. 95 (2005), 43–65, at 50; Joshua Landis, 'Syria: Secularism, Arabism and Sunni Orthodoxy', in *Tailor-Made Islam: Religion, Identity and Nation in Middle Eastern Schoolbooks*, ed. Eleanor Doumato and Gregory Starrett (Boulder: Lynne Rienner, 2006), 177–96; on the (limited) place of Islam in official Baʿthist history, see Stéphane Valter, *La Construction nationale syrienne* (Paris: CNRS Éditions, 2002).

[20] Böttcher, *Syrische Religionspolitik*; Leif Stenberg, 'Young, Male and Sufi Muslim in the City of Damascus', in *Youth and Youth Culture in the Contemporary Middle East*, ed. Jørgen Bæck Simonsen (Aarhus: Aarhus University Press, 2005), 68–91; Andreas Christmann, 'Islamic Scholar and Religious Leader: A Portrait of Muhammad Saʾid Ramadan al-Buti', *Islam and Christian–Muslim Relations* 9, no. 2 (1998), 149–69; Sandra Houot, 'Le Cheikh al-Bouti: exemple d'une éthique de la médiation aux fins de résolution du conflit', *Maghreb – Machrek*, no. 198 (2009), 53–64.

reformist intellectuals,[21] the use of the Internet by clerics,[22] and female preachers.[23]

Western bibliography on Syrian Islam therefore suffers from two major deficiencies that I am willing to address in this book: first, by focusing on major figures of official Islam or the Muslim Brothers, it ignores the significant portion of the local religious elite that belongs to neither of these categories; second, by focusing on personalities or groups viewed in isolation, it does not offer an overall analysis of the structuring of the clergy and of the challenges it faces.

With regard to the Sunni world as a whole, the literature on contemporary ulama also remains limited because research has long been inhibited by the fact that modernisation theories have popularised the idea that this social category was on the decline. Certainly, this idea has undergone welcome revisions.[24] However, most of the existing literature is characterised by profound imbalances. The first is a focus on the 'mass-media sheikhs', whether they rely on print or broadcasting,[25] to the detriment

[21] Paul Heck, 'Religious Renewal in Syria: The Case of Muhammad al-Habash', *Islam and Christian–Muslim Relations* 15, no. 2 (2004), 185–207; Muhammad Shahrur, Andreas Christmann, and Dale F. Eickelman, *The Qur'an, Morality and Critical Reason: The Essential Muhammad Shahrur* (Boston: Brill, 2009).

[22] Sandra Houot, 'Culture religieuse et média électronique: le cas du cheikh Muhammad al-Buti', *Maghreb – Machrek*, no. 178 (2003), 75–87; Ermete Mariani, 'Les oulémas syriens à la recherche d'une audience virtuelle', in *La société de l'information au Proche-Orient*, ed. Yves Gonzalez-Quijano (Lyons: Gremmo, 2007), 93–116; Andreas Christmann, 'Les cheikhs syriens et l'Internet', in *La Syrie au présent*, ed. Youssef Courbage, Baudouin Dupret, Mohammed Al-Dbiyat, and Zouhair Ghazzal (Paris: Actes Sud, 2007), 421–8.

[23] Hilary Kalmbach, 'Social and Religious Change in Damascus', *British Journal of Middle Eastern Studies* 35, no. 1 (2008), 37–57; Aurelia Ardito, 'Les cercles féminins de la Qubaysiyya à Damas', *Le Mouvement Social*, no. 231 (2010), 77–88.

[24] Andrée Feillard, *Islam et Armée dans l'Indonésie contemporaine: les pionniers de la tradition* (Paris: L'Harmattan and Association Archipel, 1995); Malika Zeghal, *Gardiens de l'islam: les oulémas d'Al Azhar dans l'Egypte contemporaine* (Paris: Presses de la Fondation nationale des sciences politiques, 1996); Muhammad Qasim Zaman, *The Ulama in Contemporary Islam: Custodians of Change* (Princeton: Princeton University Press, 2002); Nabil Mouline, *Les Clercs de l'islam: autorité religieuse et pouvoir politique en Arabie saoudite, XVIIIe–XXIe siècle* (Paris: PUF, 2011). See also Meir Hatina (ed.), *Guardians of Faith in Modern Times: 'Ulama in the Middle East* (Leiden: Brill, 2009).

[25] In addition to the aforementioned works on al-Buti, see, among many others: Hava Lazarus-Yafeh, 'Muhammad Mutawalli al-Sha'rawi: A Portrait of a Contemporary 'Alim in Egypt', in *Islam, Nationalism and Radicalism in Egypt and the Sudan*, ed. Gabriel Warburg and Uri Kupferschmidt (New York: Praeger, 1983), 281–97; Serif Mardin, *Religion and Social Change in Modern Turkey: The Case of Bediuzzaman Said Nursi* (Albany: State University of New York Press, 1990); Jan-Peter Hartung, *Viele Wege und ein Ziel: Leben und Wirken von Sayyid Abu l-Hasan 'Ali al-Hasani Nadwi (1914–1999)* (Würzburg: Ergon, 2004); Bettina Gräf and Jakob Skovgaard-Petersen, *Global Mufti: The Phenomenon of Yusuf al-Qaradawi* (New York: Columbia University Press, 2009).

of their less visible but extremely important colleagues who work to preserve the classical scholarly tradition,[26] or maintain direct daily contact with the faithful through educational and charitable activities. A second deficiency is that the majority of the publications concern individuals or particular doctrinal trends rather than the entire religious elite in a particular context.[27] A third problem is that possibilities of comparison between countries are limited by the fact that there are very few in-depth social–historical studies on the second half of the twentieth century,[28] and that two of them concern cases, namely Egypt and Saudi Arabia, that are characterised by an exceptionally high level of integration of the ulama into state institutions.

What precedes constitutes an incised outline of this book. The argument to be developed revolves around the thesis developed above – that is, the fact that the resources of tradition allowed the Syrian ulama to overcome the challenges of social change and Ba'thist authoritarianism. Whereas previous works on the modern ulama have stressed that they were able to take advantage of the Islamic revival that started in the 1970s, I push the argument further by asserting that in Syria at least, 'traditional' religious leaders have in fact *pioneered* that movement. The book is also a monograph that provides an overall picture of the transformations of the learned religious elite in twentieth- and early twenty-first-century Syria. It therefore explores its history, social basis, structures and organisations, daily social practices, and doctrinal controversies (in particular between the traditionalist and Salafi trends), without forgetting, of course, their relations with the economic and political–military elites.

DEFINITION OF THE TOPIC

From a historical point of view, the status of Sunni 'alim has always been acquired through a process of reputation building rather than through institutional arrangements: since there is no Muslim equivalent of Christian ordination, the right to wear the white turban – the symbol of

---

[26] For a rare example of an analysis of modern practices of writing and publication related to the Islamic scholarly heritage, see Zaman, *The Ulama*, 38–59.

[27] See for instance, among the growing literature on the Salafi trend, Bernard Rougier (ed.), *Qu'est-ce que le salafisme?* (Paris: PUF, 2008); Roel Meijer (ed.), *Global Salafism: Islam's New Religious Movement* (New York: Columbia University Press, 2009).

[28] The main exceptions are the books of Feillard, Zeghal, and Mouline. Zaman is mostly concerned with discourses and political behaviour.

religious knowledge – depends on the informal assent of elder scholars and followers.

In modern times, the boundary that separates the ulama from the rest of society has undergone a dual process of clarification and confusion: clarification, because the state has tried to delineate the class of Muslim clergy through legal and administrative devices;[29] confusion, because the modernisation of education entailed the emergence of new, secularly trained literate elites claiming religious authority in the name of the Sunni Islamic ideal according to which there should be no clergy in Islam.

However, I will show in this book that in Syria at least, contemporary changes have had relatively few consequences for the definition of the status of 'alim. In the twenty-first century, what distinguishes the latter from other believers is not a mere difference in degree of religious expertise, but rather a difference in kind: as Muhammad Qasim Zaman puts it, 'it is a combination of their intellectual *formation*, their *vocation*, and, crucially, their *orientation* viz., a certain sense of continuity with the Islamic tradition, that defines the ulama as ulama'.[30] Evidence of this includes the fact that books from the 'heritage' (*turath*) remain the basis of their training, and the critical editions of these books (*tahqiq*) are nowadays the subject of numerous doctoral dissertations, when they do not become full-fledged professional specialisations in themselves.

It is from the same point of view that we must understand the Muslim scholars' frequent mention of the hadith that states: 'the ulama are the heirs of the prophets (*warthat al-anbiya'*)'. For instance, on the occasion of a meeting convened by the Ministry of Awqaf (religious endowments) in honour of the Sheikh of the Umayyad Mosque, 'Abd al-Razzaq al-Halabi (1925–2012),[31] Sheikh Husam al-Din al-Farfur (b. 1951), one of al-Halabi's disciples, was suddenly racked with sobs during his speech:

To present our sheikh, I will say only one thing: look at this Muhammadian face! Look at this Muhammadian face! Look at the faces of the people of knowledge, these heirs of the prophets, and you will know who they are! ... When I look at our sheikhs here, I feel like I am in the midst of the remains of our pious ancestors [*baqiyat al-salaf*].[32]

[29] For the example of Iran, see Arang Keshavarzian, 'Turban or Hat, Seminarian or Soldier: State Building and Clergy Building in Reza Shah's Iran', *Journal of Church and State* 45, no. 1 (2003), 81–112.
[30] Zaman, *The Ulama*, 10.
[31] 'Sheikh of the Umayyad Mosque' is an informal title that is given to the scholar who teaches after the dawn prayer under the 'Eagle's Cupola' (*qubbat al-nasr*).
[32] Observation by the author, Umayyad Mosque, Damascus, 14 April 2008.

Such discourse is not merely self-laudatory, but reflects the aforementioned 'sense of continuity with the Islamic tradition' that constitutes the identity of the ulama. This identity is the lowest common denominator that unites people whose social practices otherwise vary considerably: some of them teach future scholars in study circles and sharia institutes; others apply their expertise to the writing of treatises or the promulgation of fatwas; others target a larger audience through mosque lessons or the mass media; and others, adopting a discursive practice that is similar to that of 'modern' intellectuals, involve themselves in the ideological debates of their time.

Belonging to the *mashyakha* (a collective substantive for 'sheikhs') is a social identity that has to be performed, and which in some cases is done only intermittently. An extreme – but revealing – example is that of Mahmud Abu al-Huda al-Husseini (b. 1960), who briefly served as director in Aleppo's Directorate of Awqaf in 2010. Because he is the son and grandson of ulama, al-Husseini explains, he did not need to study religious sciences at university, and so turned to medicine.[33] In his surgery, *Dr* Mahmud welcomes patients in perfectly 'lay' dress. Likewise, at an Islamic conference in Damascus, *Dr* Mahmud is dressed in an impeccable suit and tie and is presented in the programme as an 'Islamic thinker [*mufakkir*] and researcher [*bahith*]'. One Friday, however, when I greeted him by saying, 'How are you, Doctor?' as he was descending from his pulpit at the 'Adiliyya mosque wearing a white turban, one of his followers kindly suggested: 'Here, you'd better call him "Sheikh".' Doing so would also be appropriate at the morning lesson where *Sheikh* Mahmud, wearing the green headdress that symbolises his prophetic descent, tells his disciples of the exemplary lives of the masters of the Shadhili Sufi tradition.

Al-Husseini's case illustrates the shifting, but nevertheless clear, character of the 'horizontal' boundaries of the ulama class – that is, those that separate them from the rest of society. The 'vertical' segmentation is a more difficult issue: when does a cleric leave the status of neighbourhood sheikh to become an 'alim, or, better, a 'great 'alim'? Although it is subsumed within the concept of *'ilm* (sacred knowledge), the fame of the ulama results from a complex combination of various elements that are only partially related to the mastery of religious sciences: biological and scholarly genealogy, moral qualities, interpersonal skills, involvement in community work, and political stance.

[33] Interview with Mahmud Abu al-Huda al-Husseini, Aleppo, 9 March 2006.

This study is not limited to the ideal–typical and somewhat normative figure of the 'great 'alim'. Indeed, because the boundaries of the latter category are far from clear, they allow for the inclusion of individuals who do not possess the qualities outlined above, but who have been able nonetheless to avail themselves of various means of promotion, such as inheriting a private religious institute from one's father, or paying allegiance to an influential party (state, family, congregation, private institution) in exchange for a well-located mosque or an executive position in an administration, a school, or a charity. The group formed by adding together these various cases is much larger than that of the high dignitaries of the Catholic Church. For instance, a biographical dictionary of the Damascene ulama records an average of 4.5 deceased per year between 1942 and 1991.[34]

It would be pointless to try to define precisely a category that is based on a criterion as fuzzy as 'fame'. However, in order to allow for quantitative comparisons, I have made indicative counts of the leading clerics living in Damascus (120 individuals) and Aleppo (61) in the first decade of the twenty-first century.[35] The most reliable way to determine the central figures of a particular social field is to identify those most frequently involved in organisations and initiatives (leagues, committees, petitions, delegations) of which one can make sure (through qualitative enquiry) that they are genuinely representative of the religious elite. The count also includes holders of high positions in the official religious administration, the faculty of sharia and private Islamic institutes, preachers at cathedral-mosques, members of international Islamic organisations, masters of literate Sufi brotherhoods, as well as any figure whose significant influence was noticed during fieldwork.

On the basis of the recurrent participation of some individuals in the organisations and initiatives mentioned above, I have also established short lists of the 'greatest' ulama (thirty-two for Damascus, twenty-four for Aleppo). This status does not necessarily reflect the outstanding 'knowledge' or popularity of these individuals, but rather their degree of centrality in the local religious field.

It must be noted that there is no such thing as a unified 'Syrian' religious scene; there is only a juxtaposition of local clergies. This is the main reason for my decision to concentrate on the country's two largest cities,

---

[34] Nizar Abaza and Muti' al-Hafiz, *Tarikh 'ulama' Dimashq fi al-qarn al-rabi' 'ashar al-hijri* [History of the ulama of Damascus in the fourteenth century AH] (Damascus: Dar al-Fikr, 1986–91).

[35] The difference in size between the two counts reflects the 'parochialisation' of Aleppo's clergy throughout recent decades, a phenomenon that will be analysed in this book.

Damascus and Aleppo – in addition to the fact that once-vibrant centres of Islamic scholarship such as Homs and Hama never recovered from the repression of the early 1980s insurgency.

An illustration of the regional fragmentation of the Syrian religious scene can be seen in the absence of biographical collections of the 'Syrian' ulama: all existing biographical dictionaries are focused on particular cities.[36] Likewise, the religious elites of Damascus and Aleppo know very little about each other. Even when the fame of some ulama is considerable in their hometown, it rarely spreads outside it; for example, recordings of lessons by Damascene sheikhs are rare on the Aleppian market, and vice versa. Nationwide reputation is the privilege of a handful of high-ranking religious officials and internationally renowned academics. Even the Syrian Muslim Brothers, founded in 1946 as a nationwide organisation, split in the late 1960s between the Damascus branch of the thereafter Aachen-based Superintendent 'Isam al-'Attar (b. 1926) and the rival chapter of Aleppo, which the Egyptian mother organisation recognised as the legitimate leadership of the movement.[37]

This situation does not only result from the well-known rivalry between Syria's two largest urban centres, which is itself part of a broader geographical, historical, and cultural divide between the north and the south of the country; institutional and political factors are also relevant. Unlike at al-Azhar in Egypt, attendance at the young faculty of sharia at the University of Damascus (est. 1954) is not considered a necessary step in the training of the country's scholars. A significant proportion of them prefer foreign universities, private institutions, or informal training in their city's study circles. In addition, the Ba'thist regime has opposed the establishment of any effective representative body for the country's most eminent religious scholars.

---

[36] For Damascus, see Abaza and al-Hafiz, *Tarikh 'ulama Dimashq*; Hasan al-Humsi, *al-Du'at wa-l-da'wa al-islamiyya al-mu'asira al-muntaliqa min masajid Dimashq* [The preachers and contemporary Islamic call stemming from the mosques of Damascus] (Damascus: Mu'assasat al-Iman, 1991); Nizar Abaza, *'Ulama' Dimashq wa a'yanuha fi al-qarn al-khamis 'ashar al-hijri (1401–1425)* [The ulama and noteworthy people of Damascus in the fifteenth century AH (1980–2004)] (Damascus: Dar al-Fikr, 2007). For Aleppo, see 'Abd al-Rahman al-Uwaysi, *Nukhba min a'lam Halab al-shahba' min anbiya' wa 'ulama' wa awliya'* [Elite of the great figures of Aleppo-the-Grey among the prophets, the ulama and the saints] (Aleppo: Dar al-Turath, 2003); Ahmad Taysir Ka'ayyid, *Mawsu'at al-du'at wa-l-a'imma wa-l-khutaba' fi Halab (al-'asr al-hadith)* [Encyclopaedia of the imams and preachers in Aleppo (the modern period)] (Aleppo: Dar al-Qalam al-'Arabi, 2008); 'Adnan Katibi, *'Ulama' min Halab fi al-qarn al-rabi' 'ashar* [Ulama from Aleppo in the fourteenth century AH] (Aleppo: n.p., 2008).

[37] Umar Abdallah, *The Islamic Struggle in Syria* (Berkeley: Mizan Press, 1983), 107–8.

Islamic media, which are crucial to the formation of a unified national religious sphere, have been remarkably weak. No independent (let alone religious-leaning) newspaper has been allowed since 1963, and the last two private Islamic monthlies (the unofficial organ of the Muslim Brothers *Hadarat al-Islam* and the Salafi–reformist *al-Tamaddun al-Islami*) were suspended in 1981, to be replaced by the Ministry of Awqaf's *Nahj al-Islam*. Access to broadcast media has long been restricted to a limited number of pro-regime religious figures, a situation that only started to change after 2000, thanks in particular to private satellite channels such as the Kuwaiti al-Risala and the Jordanian al-Sufiyya.[38]

SOURCES

This book is based on field research that was conducted for the most part between 2005 and 2008. The research involved interviews with Muslim scholars, Islamic-leaning intellectuals and activists (including leaders of the Muslim Brothers living abroad), and students of religion. I also carried out numerous observations – either directly or through video CDs I found on the market – of the Friday sermon (*khutba*),[39] exhortation (*wa'z*), mosque lesson (*dars*), Sufi gathering (*hadra*), and celebrations such as the Mawlid described in the first pages of this introduction.

The relevant written sources mainly comprise scholarly treatises and hagiographies. The latter remain a vibrant genre because, for reasons that will be explained in this book, there is usually no 'alim without masters. Indeed, the training of the Muslim man of religion consists not only in acquiring knowledge through study, but also in accumulating social and symbolic capital through association with respected ulama: however, this association is effective only if it is 'advertised'. In order to remind his peers and followers that he is well and truly the heir of some illustrious sheikh, a cleric might use discursive means ('As my master used to say …'), pictures (a portrait hanging in one's office or displayed on one's website, a photomontage combining master and disciple), or hagiography, through which he honours his mentor and thereby claims his legacy.

---

[38] For more details on the Islamic media in Syria, see Thomas Pierret, 'Sunni Clergy Politics in the Cities of Ba'thi Syria', in *Demystifying Syria*, ed. Fred Lawson (London: Saqi, 2009), 70–84, at 80–1.

[39] In Damascus and Aleppo, Friday preachers are generally free to write their own sermons provided they abide by certain 'red lines'. In the other governorates, where the Ministry of Awqaf used to impose either ready-made sermons or general guidelines, rules started to relax somewhat during the last decade. See Böttcher, *Syrische Religionspolitik*, 101.

The enduring enthusiasm for the 'lives of the saints' in Syria is well illustrated by a recent tradition, the 'Assembly of loyalty and persistence in the pact' (*majlis al-wafa' wa-l-thibat 'ala al-'ahd*), which has been held at the al-Tawba mosque in Damascus every month since 2003. As the sheikh of the mosque explained, this initiative aimed to reaffirm Muslim solidarity at a time when a blow had been struck at the heart of the umma by the US–British invasion of Iraq.[40] During this celebration, participants successively display their allegiance to God through silent and simultaneous reading of the thirty parts (*ajza'*) of the Quran, to the Prophet through a similar reading of the hadith collection of al-Bukhari, and to the modern saints (*salihin*, 'pious') by listening to the biography of a twentieth-century Syrian scholar who worked for the survival of Islam.

The purpose of hagiographies is not historical but exemplary, with the result that they are more concerned with moral qualities than factual rigour. For the very opposite reason, autobiographies are not found among modern Syrian ulama, but only among Islamic activists.[41]

The daily press is an extremely poor source because of its monopolisation, since 1963, by the Ba'thist state. However, during the last ten years, information websites have helped improve the coverage of Syria's social and political life. For the period from 1948 to 1963, I relied on the comprehensive bi-weekly survey of the Syrian press made by the Office Arabe de Presse (OFA), which I consulted at the Institut Français du Proche-Orient in Damascus.

As far as official documents are concerned, I was denied access to the archives of the Ministries of Social Affairs and Awqaf.

ORGANISATION OF THE BOOK

The book begins with a prologue devoted to the limits of the institutionalisation of Islam by the Syrian regime. The Ba'th Party has in fact refused to incorporate the ulama into the state apparatus, thus allowing them to preserve relative economic and institutional autonomy.

The first chapter, which starts under the French Mandate and ends on the eve of the Islamist insurgency of 1979–82, examines the reorganisation

---

[40] Interview with Hisham al-Burhani, Damascus, 4 August 2007.

[41] Sa'id Hawwa, *Hadhihi tajribati … wa hadhihi chahadati* [This is my experience … this is my testimony] (Cairo: Maktaba Wahba, 1987); Ali al-Tantawi, *Dhikrayat* [Memories] (Jeddah: Dar al-Manara, 1989); Ma'ruf al-Dawalibi, *Mudhakkirat* [Memoirs] (Riyadh: 'Ubaykan, 2006).

of the religious scenes of Aleppo and Damascus around influential 'founding sheikhs'. The latter derived their charisma from new forms of social activism in the name of Islam, which was perceived as threatened by Westernisation. Through this activism, these scholars reaffirmed their relevance in a changing society and helped preserve the identity of their corporation despite the modernisation of religious education.

The second chapter begins by discussing the role of the ulama in the 1979–82 insurgency, as well as the human and institutional costs of the ensuing crackdown. It then examines the strategies deployed by the regime to promote loyal religious partners. Finally, it highlights the limitations of these strategies and explains why the state could not prevent the former victims of repression from returning to the fore in the first decade of the new millennium.

The third chapter deals with the definition of orthodoxy by the Syrian ulama. It shows that with the help of the state, the conservative clergy overcame the challenges addressed to them by the Salafi and reformist currents. However, the guardians of tradition themselves were transformed in the course of this confrontation, which continues to intensify today because of new information technologies.

The fourth chapter examines the strategic alliance between the ulama and the private sector, which has funded their mosques, schools, and charities. This alliance has secured the financial independence of the clergy vis-à-vis the state and allowed it to benefit from the recent economic liberalisation, particularly through its crucial role in the development of the charitable sector.

The fifth chapter analyses the involvement of the Syrian Muslim scholars in the political field and their relations with the Muslim Brothers. It shows that despite their radical hostility to the ideology of the Ba'th, clerics differ from political activists in their approach to politics: whereas the latter behave as a true opposition force and accordingly work towards the opening up of the political system, even the most intransigent ulama tend to focus on sectoral interests rather than on the structural transformation of the regime.

The sixth chapter addresses the ambitious reforms of the Syrian religious administration that were launched in 2008, as well as the behaviour of the ulama during the uprising that started in March 2011.

Prologue: Aborted Institutionalisation (1946–1979)

Unlike Mustafa Kemal in Turkey and Abdel Nasser in Egypt, the Syrian Ba'thists did not seek to integrate the ulama into the state apparatus: on the contrary, they deliberately excluded them from it. As a result, the clergy has enjoyed relative economic and institutional autonomy in spite of the suffocating surveillance by the *mukhabarat* (intelligence service).

INSTITUTIONAL DEVELOPMENT AND KEMALIST-LIKE MODERNISATION (1946–1963)

While a modern centralised state emerged in Egypt in the early nineteenth century, state regulation of religious activities is relatively new in Syria. The Arab provinces of the Ottoman Empire were hardly affected by the attempts of the Sublime Porte to establish a formal religious hierarchy (*ilmiyye*),[1] while the Awqaf administration that was established in the 1840s was only concerned with economic issues.[2] Therefore, by the outbreak of the First World War, there were only a handful of state-appointed clerics in Syrian cities (mufti, judges, and preachers at the Great Mosque).[3]

Faced with the need to build the structures of the young Republic of Syria, the first post-independence regimes chose to manage Islam by

[1] Amit Bein, *Ottoman Ulema, Turkish Republic: Agents of Change and Guardians of Tradition* (Stanford: Stanford University Press, 2011).
[2] Böttcher, *Syrische Religionspolitik*, 17–24.
[3] Linda Schatkowsky-Schilcher, *Families in Politics: Damascene Factions and Estates of the 18th and 19th Centuries* (Wiesbaden: Steiner, 1985), 115.

17

establishing formal institutions and regulations.[4] At the request of the Congress of Ulama that was held in Damascus in 1938,[5] President Taj al-Din al-Hasani (1941–3), the son of an eminent scholar and a turbaned 'alim himself, instituted a status of 'grand 'alim': this involved the payment of a monthly salary that aimed to help beneficiaries 'not to be in need and have to accept zakat and donations'.[6] In 1947, local muftis were placed under the authority of a 'Grand Mufti' (*al-mufti al-'amm*). Two years later, a law gave the government ownership of all mosques in the country, even those built with private funds. The same law defined the status of religious officers and officially established the Awqaf Administration. The latter included national and local clerical councils in charge of appointing the muftis and the staff of the mosques.[7] In 1961, a new law established the current Ministry of Awqaf.

In parallel with this institutional development, the first military rulers of Syria were concerned with social modernisation according to the Kemalist model. During his brief tenure in 1949, Colonel Husni al-Za'im not only submitted the awqaf to state control and promulgated a secular legal code (which did not, however, apply to personal status),[8] but also encouraged the abandonment of 'Oriental' fashions.[9] He treated the ulama with a studious lack of consideration, and was especially critical of their turbans. According to the hagiographer of the Damascene Sufi Sheikh Yahya al-Sabbagh (1868–1961), this behaviour was the cause of his ultimate downfall:

Under President Husni al-Za'im, oppression and corruption were rising, and official receptions were an insult to religious knowledge and the ulama. One of al-Za'im's decisions was to forbid scholars to wear the turban.

---

[4] For more information on the development of official religious institutions in Syria, see Böttcher, *Syrische Religionspolitik*; Thomas Pierret, 'The State Management of Religion in Syria: The End of Indirect Rule?', in *Comparing Authoritarianisms: Reconfiguring Power and Regime Resilience in Syria and Iran*, ed. Steven Heydemann and Reinoud Leenders (Palo Alto: Stanford University Press, 2012), 83–106.

[5] *Bayan mu'tamar al-'ulama' al-awwal al-mun'aqad bi-Dimashq 11–13 rajab 1357* [Communiqué of the First Congress of Ulama Held in Damascus, 6–8 September 1938]' (www.islamsyria.com, 1 May 2006).

[6] 'Abd al-Rahman Habannaka, *al-Walid al-da'iya al-murabbi al-shaykh Hasan Habannaka al-Midani* [My father the preacher and educator Sheikh Hasan Habannaka al-Midani] (Jeddah: Dar al-Bashir, 2002), 65. In 1948, the title of 'grand 'alim' was renamed 'fatwa lecturer' (*mudarris fatwa*).

[7] The national councils were the Higher Awqaf Council and the Higher Ifta' Council (for the issuing of fatwas).

[8] Deguilhem, 'Le *waqf* en Syrie indépendante'.

[9] Patrick Seale, *The Struggle for Syria: A Study of Post-war Arab Politics, 1945–1958* (London: Oxford University Press, 1965), 58.

Sheikh Yahya woke up one day and asked his daughters if they had seen something in a dream. One of them said: 'I have seen the Greater Sheikh standing on the top of stairs,[10] and Husni al-Za'im standing at the bottom. Al-Za'im was with his henchmen, and they were getting smaller and smaller'.

Sheikh Yahya then started to say 'Allah Akbar' against Husni al-Za'im and his henchmen until the sunrise. In the morning came the news of the President's death.

People say: 'God has His men – when they want something, He wants it too.'[11]

Sheikh Yahya's miraculous tyrannicide did not, however, rid him of the 'enemies of the ulama'. In December 1949, Adib al-Shishakli, another officer inspired by Kemalism, organised the third coup of the year. In 1952, he brought about a revolution in the religious life of the country; in order to 'protect the men of religion from charlatans', a decree submitted the wearing of the – henceforth standardised – religious garb (white turban and dark *jubba*) to official authorisation, and provided for the arrest of violators.[12] After al-Shishakli's fall in 1954, however, and faced with unshakable opposition from the ulama, the clerical uniform was abandoned for good.[13] Although the habit prescribed by the 1952 decree remains widespread today, it is not the only type of clerical garb that is worn in Syria.

BA'THIST REVOLUTION AND THE END OF INSTITUTIONALISATION (1963–1979)

Unlike previous regimes, the Ba'th displayed a striking lack of interest in the development of the religious bureaucracy, preferring a strictly security-focused approach aimed at reducing the influence of clerics over the administration. Perceived as hostile by the regime, Grand Mufti Abu al-Yusr 'Abidin (1889–1981) was replaced by the subservient Ahmad Kaftaru (1915–2004), while in 1965 the clerical councils had their prerogatives transferred to the Minister of Awqaf.[14]

---

[10] The 'Greater Sheikh': Ibn 'Arabi.

[11] Usama Muhammad al-Mun'im al-Badawi, *al-Nafahat al-rabbaniyya fi hayat al-qutb sayyidi al-shaykh Yahya al-Sabbagh al-dimashqi* [Divine inspirations in the life of the pole, my master Sheikh Yahya al-Sabbagh the Damascene] (Damascus: n.p., n.d.), 45–6.

[12] *OFA*, 1–4 March 1952, no. 409, V.

[13] Interview with 'Isam al-'Attar, Aachen, 29 September 2007.

[14] Itamar Rabinovich, *Syria under the Ba'th, 1963–66: The Army–Party Symbiosis* (Jerusalem: Israel Universities Press, 1972), 143. The Higher Ifta' Council still exists, but it meets very rarely and does not seem to have any real power.

The latter decision was a major turning-point in the modern history of the Syrian ulama because it put an end to the existence of a formally defined 'high clergy' endowed with a sense of responsibility towards the state, like the senior ulama of al-Azhar in Egypt and the Committee of Grand Ulama in Saudi Arabia.[15] This would have at least two important consequences for the future: first, the re-establishment of a representative organ for the country's senior Muslim scholars would constitute one of the main aspirations of the Syrian religious elite in the following decades; second, the structure of the clergy would be very different from what it is in Egypt and Saudi Arabia. Since there has been 'no powerful establishment Islam aligned with the regime',[16] that is, no 'centre', there have been no 'peripheral ulama' either,[17] but only clerical factions with varying degrees of proximity to the state.

Accordingly, legal reform was neglected by the Ba'thist regime, and no new law on awqaf ever replaced the regulations issued in 1949 and 1961. The men of religion were neither incorporated into the unions and popular organisations the regime created to supervise various social groups (peasants, workers, women, teachers, artists, writers, and students) nor fully bureaucratised. The only employees of the Ministry of Awqaf who benefited from the full status of 'civil servants' (*muwazzafi al-dawla*) were the 200 to 300 members of the administrative staff.[18] As for the staff of the mosques, they were placed under a special – and especially disadvantageous – wage system.[19] In such circumstances, the ulama, including senior officials such as the muftis, continued to depend on the resources of the private sector.[20]

The most likely explanation of this policy is that the Ba'thists had neither the means nor the desire to 'nationalise' Muslim scholars. Their economic resources were limited and the urban elites were hostile to them. Moreover, the ideology of the party, especially the Marxist version adopted by the 'Neo-Ba'thists' who held power from 1966 to 1970, no longer had much to do with the Kemalism of al-Za'im and al-Shishakli: as positivist modernisers, the latter had dreamed of order and progress

---

[15] Zeghal, *Gardiens de l'islam*; Mouline, *Les Clercs de l'islam*, 192–222.

[16] Raymond Hinnebusch, *Authoritarian Power and State Formation in Baathist Syria* (Boulder: Westview Press, 1990), 278.

[17] For the concept of peripheral ulama, see Zeghal, *Gardiens de l'islam*.

[18] *Al-Majmu'a al-ihsa'iyya* [Statistical yearbook] (Damascus: Central Bureau of Statistics, 1962–78).

[19] See the salary scale in ibid.

[20] Hanna Batatu, 'Syria's Muslim Brethren', *Merip Reports*, no. 110 (1982), 12–20.

through the regulation of every dimension of daily life; as revolutionary modernisers, the Neo-Ba'thists intended to upset the foundations of society by establishing a socialist economy and a new infrastructure that would in turn generate a social order where there would be no place for the 'reactionary' ulama. For example, whereas al-Shishakli reserved the wearing of the green turban for the trustee of the descendants of the Prophet (*naqib al-ashraf*),[21] and whereas the 1961 law provided for the latter's election by a clerical council, the Neo-Ba'thists simply abolished the position in 1970.[22]

The confidence in the future of the Neo-Ba'thists is remarkably illustrated by the Minister of Education who, in the late 1960s, told a French researcher: 'Backward preachers and other men of religion can say whatever they want, it will not catch on, and we are not worried about it.' Referring to the recent reform of the public schools' textbooks of religious education, which blended Islam and Arab socialism, the Minister added: 'we have taken over religious teaching ... and we know it will profoundly transform the entire youth in the good sense'.[23]

For the more secularist wing of the party, religion itself was doomed to be swept away by the wind of revolution. In 1967, a famous article published in the army magazine proposed to store it in the 'museum of history' along with 'all the values that governed the old society'.[24]

Despite the Islamic 'awakening' (*sahwa*) that followed the Arab defeat of 1967, the religious policy of the Syrian regime did not change fundamentally in the first decade of the 'Corrective Movement' launched by Hafiz al-Asad in 1970. It is true that the new President inaugurated a detente with the Islamic trend by displaying outward signs of piety (an Alawite, he performed the prayers of the major Muslim holidays in the company of Sunni ulama) and increased the real expenditures of the Ministry of Awqaf.[25] However, this spending dropped by one-third during the second half of the 1970s, which was all the more remarkable given that other state agencies were thriving as a result of the tremendous economic growth caused by the oil boom: for instance, the actual expenditure of the Ministry of Culture and National Guidance was multiplied *sevenfold* between 1975 and 1980.[26]

---

[21] *OFA*, 1–4 March 1952, no. 409, V.
[22] Böttcher, *Syrische Religionspolitik*, 64.
[23] Carré, *La Légitimation*, 31.
[24] See Tabitha Petran, *Syria* (London: Ernest Benn, 1972), 197–8.
[25] Hanna Batatu, *Syria's Peasantry, the Descendants of Its Lesser Rural Notables, and Their Politics* (Princeton: Princeton University Press, 1999), 260.
[26] *Al-Majmu'a al-ihsa'iyya*, 1970–1980.

As in the 1960s, the religious policy of the Ba'th thus neglected the development of religious institutions and remained focused solely on the neutralisation of political threats. Waves of arrests continued to target the Muslim Brothers, but the authorities turned a blind eye to the expansion of the Islamic educational movements spearheaded by the ulama – to such an extent that some clerics reminisce about the 1970s as the 'Golden Age of Islamic call [da'wa]'.[27] As will be shown in the first chapter, the exclusion of the religious elite from the state apparatus had indeed enabled it to devote all of its energy to community work, with the result that it played a major role in setting in motion the Islamic 'awakening'.

[27] Interviews with al-Husseini and Ahmad Mu'adh al-Khatib, Damascus, 23 April 2008.

I

The Era of the 'Founding Sheikhs' (1920–1979)

The state has become a Christian state.
The rule of Islam has come to an end.[1]
A Damascene 'alim commenting on the Western-inspired
reforms undertaken by the Egyptian authorities during their
occupation of Syria (1831–41)

During the twentieth century, as in other regions of the Muslim world, Syria witnessed the development of new forms of religious activism among the ulama. These were responses to Westernisation (which was felt in Syria well before the French invasion of 1920, as this chapter's epigraph shows) and the abolition of the Caliphate in 1924. In such a context, the challenges faced by those who claimed to be the guardians of Islam gave rise to a new conception of the social role of men of religion. Mere 'pastoral care', which Max Weber defines as the religious cultivation of the individual, was now combined with 'preaching' – that is, a form of collective religious instruction that is reminiscent of the prophetic stage.[2] The latter development underlies the modern success of the concept of da'wa ('call', 'invitation').[3] In the face of a threat which the Muslim clergy perceived as existential, da'wa was no longer defined as an individual effort but transformed into a collective and organised endeavour of social reconquest.

[1] Ma'oz, 'The Ulama', 81.
[2] Max Weber, *Economy and Society: An Outline of Interpretive Sociology* (Berkeley: University of California Press, 1978), 464.
[3] Saba Mahmood, *Politics of Piety: The Islamic Revival and the Feminist Subject* (Princeton: Princeton University Press, 2005), 57–64.

Despite the political upheavals that occurred in Syria in the years shortly before and after 1920 (the collapse of the Ottoman Empire, the short-lived rule of King Faysal, French occupation), the ulama's activities focused primarily on the educational realm – partly because access to the political scene remained difficult until the 1950s due to the hegemony of the great notables, but more importantly because of the intrinsically educational nature of the religious function, which led the clerics to see teaching as the foremost weapon in a *Kulturkampf* between the Islamic and secularist trends.

Through the study of the missionary and organisational involvement of the ulama who constituted the generation of the 'founding sheikhs' from the French Mandate to the Islamic uprising of the late 1970s, this first chapter sheds light on several fundamental dynamics. First, contrary to the widespread assumption that the ulama 'declined' in the twentieth century, their activism in the educational field has not only provided them with an opportunity to demonstrate their continued social relevance, but, combined with the emergence of new audiences as a result of mass literacy, has given them unprecedented influence over society. Accordingly, the ulama have well and truly reoriented the course of history by pioneering the Islamic revival witnessed during the last quarter of the twentieth century. Second, by taking control of new educational institutions – and in particular of seminaries specialising in the training of young clerics – they have put themselves in an ideal position to preserve traditional conceptions of religious knowledge in the face of modernism. In other words, educational work was crucial for the definition of the identity of both society and the religious elite itself. Third, studying the figures of the modern founding sheikhs and the contemporary hagiographic narratives devoted to them is essential to understanding the present structure of the Syrian religious scene. In many cases, indeed, the social identity of an 'alim is primarily defined by his affiliation to one of these 'founding fathers' and his group.

Thus, the historiographical centrality of the ulama who will be presented in this chapter does not primarily result from their exceptional expertise in the realm of Islamic sciences, but rather from their vocation as educator (*murabbi*): it is precisely this vocation that provided them with the numerous disciples who keep their memory alive and make them overshadow colleagues who, though possibly more brilliant, only addressed a limited, specialised audience.

It is important to stress that this chapter is not about what Western authors generally call 'Islamic reform' – that is, a project of doctrinal *aggiornamento*. Proponents of Islamic reform, such as those presented in the third chapter, generally see the scholarly corpus inherited from the Ottoman era as a corrupt and fossilised tradition that stands in contradiction to both scriptural sources and contemporary realities. However, most Syrian ulama reject that view, arguing instead that the scholarly tradition has been enriched, not corrupted, by centuries of glosses and commentaries. The 'renaissance' (*nahda*) with which the protagonists of this chapter are credited in Syrian hagiography was a purely revivalist movement, in the sense that it was focused on the revival of religious observance while being perfectly conservative in intellectual terms.

The Syrian ulama's 'praxeological' conception of Islamic revival concerns two levels of religious practices: individual observance and, upstream of this, proselytising. Thus, whereas they were only transmitters of existing doctrines, the founding sheikhs of the twentieth century were nevertheless innovators as far as modes of action (*manhaj*, pl. *manahij*) are concerned. Indeed, they created structures that were unknown during the previous centuries, such as primary and secondary schools, sharia institutes, and informal groups providing large numbers of lay people with sophisticated religious education.

THE NAHDA ('RENAISSANCE OF SACRED KNOWLEDGE')

Syrian historians look very poorly on the condition of the country's religious elite at the end of the Ottoman era, which they depict as a period of darkness and ignorance. The author of a history of the ulama of Damascus writes that 'this era was nothing but stasis and backwardness ... A small number of active scholars tried to awaken society ... but they could not work any miracles.'[4] Other recent accounts even talk of the outright disappearance of the ulama in some neighbourhoods of the city. A famous sheikh told his disciples that in the early 1920s, his quarter, the Midan, had become a shadow of the major religious centre it was in the previous century:[5] 'There was no longer any 'alim worthy of this name; there were very few students in religion and most of them were poor.'[6]

Such accounts form part of a narrative strategy in which decline prepares the way for a 'renaissance of sacred knowledge' (*al-nahdat al-'ilmiyya*;

---

[4] Humsi, *al-Du'at*, vol. I, 105–6.
[5] Schatkowski-Schilcher, *Families in Politics*.
[6] Interview with a student of Sheikh Hasan Habannaka (1908–78), Damascus, 29 November 2006.

known as the Nahda), initiated by the modern 'founding sheikhs', and
thereby legitimising their dazzling social climb. However, this climb was
in fact made possible by a real upheaval within the Syrian religious scene:
the disappearance of the clerical elite of the Ottoman era.

The End of the Old Religious Dynasties

In the aftermath of the 1963 coup, the Ba'thist government symbolically
put an end to the dominance of the old 'houses of knowledge' (*buyut 'ilm*)
over the religious field by dismissing Grand Mufti Abu al-Yusr 'Abidin,
whose ancestors had been prominent in Damascus since the tenth century.[7]
However, by choosing his successors from among the newcomers – 'Abd
al-Razzaq al-Humsi (1963–4), a member of the Damascene petty merchant bourgeoisie, and Ahmad Kaftaru (1964–2004), the son of a Sufi
master born in Kurdistan – the new regime simply assented to a sociological process that had been under way for several decades. Proof of this lies
in the fact that the majority of the clergy, who were hostile to Kaftaru's
appointment as the Grand Mufti because of his pro-Ba'th stance, did not
support any challenger of noble descent, but instead the son of a humble
shopkeeper, Hasan Habannaka (1908–78).

In fact, the sociological renewal of the Syrian religious elite in the twentieth century did not result from state policies, but rather from cultural
transformations that had begun before the First World War. The origin
of these transformations was the emergence of Western-inspired educational institutions in the Near East such as the Syrian Protestant College
(1866), later known as the American University of Beirut, Maktab 'Anbar
(1893), the first state-run high school in Damascus,[8] and the Institute of
Medicine and Pharmacology (1903), which would become the University
of Damascus.[9] These institutions, like more remote universities such as
Darülfünun in Istanbul and La Sorbonne in Paris, were offering diplomas
that were henceforth more valued by social elites than religious training. Consequently, illustrious families that had for centuries dominated

---

[7] Sharif al-Sawwaf, *Mu'jam al-usar wa-l-a'lam al-dimashqiyya* [Dictionary of Damascene
families and notables] (Damascus: Bayt al-Hikma, 2004), vol. II, 625–33.

[8] Randi Deguilhem, 'Idées françaises et enseignement ottoman: l'école secondaire Maktab
'Anbar à Damas', *Revue des mondes musulmans et de la Méditerranée*, no. 52–3 (1990),
199–206.

[9] Abdul-Karim Rafeq, 'The Syrian University and the French Mandate (1920–1946)', in
Liberal Thought in the Eastern Mediterranean: Late 19th Century until the 1960s, ed.
Christoph Schumann (Leiden: Brill, 2008), 75–98.

the ranks of muftis and judges – al-Ghazzi, al-Shatti, al-Hamzawi, al-Ustuwani, and al-Kizbari – vanished from the religious scene and turned to activities such as medicine, the (modern) judiciary, academia, and politics.[10] It thus comes as no surprise that in the 2000s, among the Damascene families displaying a religious vocation, only two (al-Khatib and al-Burhani) had been known as houses of knowledge before the First World War.[11]

The vanishing religious dynasties were replaced by scholars stemming from three main backgrounds: petty and middle-class craftsmen–merchants, and – though to a lesser extent – rural immigrants and foreigners. For centuries, Damascus had been a haven for refugees and migrants from various parts of the Muslim world: Palestinians during the Crusades; Kurds in the following centuries; Caucasians from the eighteenth century onwards; Albanians in the first half of the twentieth century; and, starting from the French invasion of Algeria in the 1830s, North Africans, who came to exert remarkable influence over the Damascene religious scene. Two Algerians – Emir 'Abd al-Qadir (1807–82) and Tahir al-Jaza'iri (1852–1920)[12] – were among the founding figures of the local reformist trend, whereas some of their fellow countrymen imported new Sufi traditions such as the Shadhiliyya, which was popularised among the Syrian ulama by Muhammad al-Hashimi (1880–1961).[13] Moroccans played an even more visible role: Badr al-Din al-Hasani (1850–1935), the son of a scholar from Marrakesh, was the unrivalled leader of the Damascene clergy under the Mandate; and Makki al-Kittani (1890–1973), whose father left the Sherifian Sultanate following the French occupation in 1912, became the president of the League of Ulama (the political arm of the Syrian clergy from 1946 to 1963) and the representative of his adopted country in the World Islamic League.[14]

Although both al-Hasani and al-Kittani were the sons of renowned scholars and direct descendants of the Prophet, the acknowledgement of these foreigners' symbolic primacy by the local ulama can hardly be explained without taking into account the void created at the top of the clerical hierarchy by the disappearance of the old religious dynasties. One

---

[10] Schatkowski-Schilcher, *Families in Politics*, 169–74; al-Sawwaf, *Mu'jam al-usar*.
[11] Al-Sawwaf, *Mu'jam al-usar*, vol. I, 326–40.
[12] On these figures, see Commins, *Islamic Reform*; Weismann, *Taste of Modernity*.
[13] See Itzchak Weismann, 'The Shadhiliyya–Darqawiyya in the Arab East', in *La Shadhiliyya: une voie soufie dans le monde*, ed. Éric Geoffroy (Paris: Maisonneuve et Larose, 2004), 255–70, at 262–4.
[14] Abaza and Hafiz, *Tarikh 'ulama' Dimashq*, vol. II, 909–13.

century earlier, indeed, Emir 'Abd al-Qadir had failed to acquire a similar status despite political, economic, and intellectual resources that were incomparably superior.[15]

The 'secularisation' of the old clerical elite was also witnessed in the other Syrian cities, probably the most remarkable example being that of the Atasi family, which gave Homs all of its muftis from 1553 to 1984, and gave Syria its last Sunni President, the Ba'thist physician Nur al-Din (1929–92).[16] Outside the capital, however, the religious career retained its prestige until a later period, a situation that probably resulted from the remoteness of the higher teaching institutions. In Aleppo, where a university was established only in 1958, in the late twentieth century there were still a dozen prominent ulama whose ancestors had been first-rank clerics at the time of the French Mandate.[17]

The sociological renewal of the Syrian religious elite had two major consequences, among many others. First, since the newcomer ulama were not members of the families that had been in control of awqaf for centuries, the clergy was little affected by the dismantling and de facto nationalisation of these endowments in the middle of the twentieth century. Second, the ulama were gradually excluded from the judiciary, including religious courts. Under the Mandate, holding a degree in secular law (*qanun*) was made compulsory for judges.[18] At a time when studying at the university was the privilege of a tiny elite, this decision made judicial positions unattainable to most ulama, who were from relatively low social backgrounds. When the two last Damascene ulama who had worked as religious judges died in the early twenty-first century, they were more than ninety years old.[19]

Narratives of Re-foundation and Transition

The narrative provided by contemporary Syrian clergy about their own history starts under the Mandate: in Damascus, a 'renaissance of sacred

---

[15] Schatkowski-Schilcher, *Families in Politics*, 217.

[16] Basil al-Atasi, *Tarikh al-usra al-atasiyya wa tarajim mashahiriha* [History of the al-Atasi family and the biographies of its famous men], unpublished document, undated.

[17] Mustafa al-Zarqa (1904–99), Zayn al-'Abidin al-Jadhba (1910–2005), Abdullah Siraj al-Din (1924–2002), Ibrahim al-Salqini (1934–2011), Ahmad al-Hajji al-Kurdi (b. 1939), Nur al-Din 'Itr (b. 1939), Bashir al-Idlibi (b. 1940), Abu al-Fath al-Bayanuni (b. 1940), Isma'il Abu al-Nasr (b. 1947).

[18] After the creation of the faculty of sharia in 1954, religious judges were required to hold degrees in both law and sharia.

[19] Murshid 'Abidin (1914–2007) and Bashir al-Bani (1911–2008).

knowledge' sees the emergence of the founding sheikhs, most of whom claim to be disciples of the 'supreme hadith scholar' (*al-muhaddith al-akbar*) Badr al-Din al-Hasani; as for Aleppo, it witnesses a golden age that begins in 1922 with the modernisation of the Khusrawiyya madrasa, of which more will be said in this chapter.

There is an important difference between the two cities, however: whereas Aleppian historiography sees Khusrawiyya as the product of the harmonious integration of the local scholarly tradition with the process of renewal, its Damascene counterpart presents Sheikh al-Hasani, an almost entirely self-taught scholar,[20] as the author of a re-foundation that completely overshadows the previous generations of ulama. Such 'amnesia' might seem paradoxical on the part of men of religion who consider that true religious knowledge is necessarily a *heritage* that has been transmitted from one generation to another since the origins of Islam.

Actually, this historiographical break is aimed at constructing the legitimacy of newcomers who cannot claim any family ties with the religious elite of the Ottoman era. Regardless of Badr al-Din al-Hasani's genuinely prominent role during his lifetime, the use that was made of his image by later generations of scholars largely explains his centrality in modern Damascene hagiography – his name was given to a street of the Old City and, in 1997, to one of the largest religious institutes of the capital.[21]

THE CHALLENGES OF EDUCATIONAL MODERNISATION

As far as formal schooling was concerned, twentieth-century Syrian Muslim scholars involved themselves in the field of general education, with little success, as well as in the training of young clerics, which was at the centre of a power struggle between modernist and traditionalist agendas.

[20] Itzchak Weismann, 'The Invention of a Populist Islamic Leader: Badr al-Din al-Hasani, the Religious Educational Movement and the Great Syrian Revolt', Arabica 52, no. 1 (2005), 109–39, at 113–15.

[21] Formerly known as the Madrasa al-Aminiyya, this institute was established in 1959 under the name of Ma'had Ihya' al-'Ulum al-Shar'iyya (Institute for the revivification of religious sciences). For al-Hasani's biography and the construction of his image by his hagiographers, see Weismann, 'The Invention'; for his last hagiography to this date and a survey of previous writings on him, see Mahmud al-Bayruti, *al-Shaykh Muhammad Badr al-Din al-Hasani wa athr majalisihi fi al-mujtama' al-dimashqi* [Sheikh Muhammad Badr al-Din al-Hasani and the influence of his teachings on Damascene society] (Damascus: Dar al-Bayruti, 2009).

Al-Gharra"s Aborted Project of Communal Islamic Schooling

The Syrian ulama played a pioneering role in the creation of modern primary schools from the 1870s onwards – this is unsurprising given the fact that they had traditionally been responsible for the ancestor of such schools, the *kuttab*.[22] Starting from the Mandate, however, they became engaged in unequal competition with the state: indeed, education constituted 'the one major exception' to the general neglect that characterised the social policies of the Syrian bourgeois republic.[23]

In this context, the importance of the attempt by the Damascene al-Jam'iyyat al-Gharra' (The noble association) to create a network of Muslim communal schools on the model of Christian congregations lies less in its – limited – long-term impact than in the place it occupies in the contemporary narrative of the deeds of the founding sheikhs.[24]

Al-Gharra', which sought to curb the cultural influence of missionary schools and public institutions reformed under the aegis of the coloniser, was founded in 1924 by two disciples of Badr al-Din al-Hasani, Ali al-Daqr (1877–1943), a wealthy merchant, and Hashim al-Khatib (1886–1958), who before the First World War had been one of the leaders of the anti-reformist journal *al-Haqa'iq*.[25] Al-Daqr provided the association with much of its economic and human resources: an eloquent preacher and a gifted teacher, he was very popular among his merchant colleagues (his exhortations against tobacco have become legendary),[26] and he attracted many disciples. Many of the latter were recruited in the rural periphery of Damascus (Hauran, Beqaa, and northern Transjordan) by trade agents working with al-Daqr.[27] Some of them were sent back to their homeland in order to preach to the locals and – so certain hagiologists claim – to foil the colonial authority's attempt to 'Christianise' the

---

[22] See Reissner, *Ideologie und Politik*, 81–3; Weissmann, 'The Invention', 129.

[23] Raymond Hinnebusch, *Syria: Revolution from Above* (London: Routledge, 2001), 25.

[24] See for instance Nizar Abaza, *al-Shaykh Ali al-Daqr: rajul ahya Allah bihi al-umma* [Sheikh Ali al-Daqr: the man through whom God reawakened the umma] (Damascus: Dar al-Fikr, 2010).

[25] On first years of al-Gharra', see Reissner, *Ideologie und Politik*, 86–8; Weismann, 'The Invention', 127–32. On the Islamic opposition to French educational policies, see Elizabeth Thompson, *Colonial Citizens: Republican Rights, Paternal Privilege, and Gender in French Syria and Lebanon* (New York: Columbia University Press, 2000), 106, 109. Thompson describes the Islamic associations that emerged during the Mandate as 'populist', which might wrongly suggest that they were party-like mobilisation structures.

[26] Usama al-Rifa'i, 'Durus min hayat al-shaykh 'Abd al-Karim al-Rifa'i' [Lessons from the life of Sheikh 'Abd al-Karim al-Rifa'i], no. 1 (www.sadazaid.com, 17 April 2008).

[27] Abaza, *al-Shaykh Ali al-Daqr*, 47.

Syrian countryside.[28] Other disciples constituted the core of al-Gharra''s schoolteachers.

Despite the departure of al-Khatib, who in 1931 founded his own education association, the popular influence of al-Gharra' continued growing – in 1935, it was managing eleven primary and secondary schools – and one of its sheikhs even secured a seat in the parliamentary elections of 1943.[29]

After independence, however, fortune abandoned al-Gharra', which was facing competition from a rapidly expanding public education system as well as problems of funding. Indeed, no charismatic figure – i.e., no effective fundraiser – ever emerged among al-Daqr's descendants, who have remained in control of al-Gharra' from the founder's death in 1943 until the present day.[30] As a result, most of the schools of the associations were closed in the late 1950s. Moreover, having failed to co-opt al-Gharra''s leaders within the religious administration, the authorities of the United Arab Republic (1958–61) ordered the closure of the Institute of Religious Studies, al-Gharra''s training school for young clerics.[31]

This Islamic seminary was born in 1937 from the institutionalisation of al-Daqr's study circles. The first of its kind in Damascus, it paved the way for the ulama to prove themselves more successful than in the realm of general education. The ulama's prominent role in the setting up of modern Islamic seminaries would prove to be crucial for the future of the clergy, since it put them in a position to mitigate those potential consequences of the institutionalisation of specialised religious teaching that they deemed threatening to their identity.

The Training of the Ulama: Modernisation and Its Challenges

The 'Great Transformation'[32] of religious teaching that spread throughout the Muslim world starting from the second half of the nineteenth

---

[28] Usama al-Rifa'i, exhortation given at the Mawlid at Sheikh Ali al-Daqr mosque, Damascus, 3 May 2008 (observation).

[29] Reissner, *Ideologie und Politik*, 87; Abaza and Hafiz, *Tarikh 'ulama' Dimashq*, vol. II, 590.

[30] After Ali's passing away, al-Gharra' was successively chaired by his sons Ahmad (1908–77) and 'Abd al-Ghani (1916–2002), a renowned grammarian. See Iyyad Khalid al-Tabba', *'Abd al-Ghani al-Daqr* (Damascus: Dar al-Qalam, 2003).

[31] Abaza, *al-Shaykh Ali al-Daqr*, 117–27, 130–1. The institute was reopened in the early 1970s. Along with a primary school, it is all that is left of al-Gharra' today.

[32] Dale Eickelman, *Knowledge and Power in Morocco* (Princeton: Princeton University Press, 1985), 165.

century seemed to challenge the very foundations of the training of ulama as it had been conceived until then.[33] This training had tradition-ally taken place within informal study circles (*halqat*, sing. *halqa*); in Syria, the method would retrospectively come to be called 'free teaching' (*al-ta'lim al-hurr*). Such study circles were held either in mosques, private houses, or madrasas. The latter were not institutions characterised by dis-tinct procedures of knowledge transmission but were, in the literal sense of the Arabic word, 'places for teaching'. Indeed, unlike medieval Western universities, pre-modern madrasas had no precise curriculum and did not issue diplomas:[34] they merely provided a salary to a limited number of teachers as well as material support for boarders thanks to the revenues of a waqf.[35] Studying in a madrasa was therefore in no way compulsory for would-be ulama, whose aim was not to be associated with particular institutions, but rather with the most prestigious masters wherever they were teaching. Madrasas could be important in the career of scholars, but only because of the prestigious and well-paid teaching positions that were attached to some of them.[36]

The non-institutionalisation of classical Islamic teaching was the result of a personalised and fixist conception of the transmission of religious knowledge. Instead of a diploma, students were awarded an individual licence (*ijaza*) by a master according to criteria that were left to the lat-ter's discretion. Through this licence, the teacher was personally attesting that the disciple was affiliated with his own scholarly genealogy (*silsila*). By the same token, he was authorising him to teach the treatises of the scholarly heritage (turath) on which he had commented (*sharh*) in his study circle. The ijaza could also certify to the memorisation of certain important 'contents' (*mutun*, sing. *matn*) by the student.

[33] See for instance Gilbert Delanoue, 'L'enseignement religieux musulman en Égypte du XIXe au XXe siècle: orientations générales', in *Madrasa: la transmission du savoir dans le monde musulman*, ed. Nicole Grandin and Marc Gaborieau (Paris: Arguments, 1997), 93–100.

[34] Jonathan Berkey, *The Transmission of Knowledge in Medieval Cairo: A Social History of Islamic Education* (Princeton: Princeton University Press, 1992); Michael Chamberlain, *Knowledge and Social Practice in Medieval Damascus, 1190–1350* (Cambridge: Cambridge University Press, 1994), 69–90; Dale Eickelman, 'The Art of Memory: Islamic Education and Its Social Reproduction', *Comparative Studies in Society and History* 20, no. 4 (1978), 485–516.

[35] For late Ottoman Aleppo, see 'Adnan Katibi, *al-Ta'lim al-shar'i wa madarisuhu fi Halab fi al-qarn al-rabi' 'ashar al-hijri* [Religious teaching and its schools in Aleppo in the four-teenth century AH] (Aleppo: n.p., 2006), 25–66.

[36] For late Ottoman Damascus, see Abaza and Hafiz, *Tarikh 'ulama' Dimashq*, vol. I.

An example of such training is given in the biography of the Damascene sheikh Adib Kallas (1921–2009), which is typical of the pre–Second World War era:

> He read *al-Arba'in al-nawawiyya* with Sheikh Muhammad Salih al-Farfur, and the principles of *fiqh* in *Nur al-idah*. After the dawn prayer, he was with his sheikh to study *Hashiyat Ibn 'Abidin* ... He memorised the *Alfiyyat* of Ibn Malik ... then he completed his knowledge by studying with the fount of knowledge Sheikh Muhammad Abu al-Yusr 'Abidin, the Mufti of Syria ... Sheikh Muhammad Salih al-Farfur issued him with a general *ijaza* in the sciences of religion and Arabic language, among others, and he also received an *ijaza* from Sheikh Abu al-Yusr 'Abidin.[37]

Such a system reflected a belief in the necessity of a personally guaranteed connection with the previous generations of scholars, and through them with Islam's founding figures.[38] Its underlying rationale was less a concern for the integrity of the teachings' contents (except, of course, for the Quran and Sunna) than a ritual conception of the transmission of knowledge, the latter being assimilated to godly blessing (*baraka*).[39] This model also concealed issues of power: the power of the student, who could pride himself on having studied with such-and-such renowned master – thus making what Dale Eickelman calls an 'iconic' use of his *ijaza*;[40] and, of course, the power of the ulama who exerted strict control over access to religious knowledge.

From the Mandate period on, this education model was challenged in Syria by so-called 'organised' (*nidhami*) – that is, institutionalised – Islamic teaching, which was inspired by Western schools. The new system was based on principles that were diametrically opposed to those of its predecessor: the student was attached to a formal institution rather than to the person of an individual master; and the goal was no longer to inculcate an unchanging inherited corpus but rather, as a result of the spread of utilitarianism, to convey global mastery of a set of disciplines forming a coherent curriculum. Accordingly, classical treatises were gradually replaced with modern textbooks, and acquisition of knowledge was certified with a diploma (*shahada*) that was granted following a standardised procedure of examination.

---

[37] Ahmad Kallas, 'Tarjamat al-'allamat al-murabbi al-zahid al-faqih al-shaykh Muhammad Adib Kallas' [Biography of the savant, educator, ascetic and *faqih*, Sheikh Muhammad Adib Kallas]' (www.alfatihonline.com, 2007).

[38] William Graham, 'Traditionalism in Islam: An Essay in Interpretation', *Journal of Interdisciplinary History* 23, no. 3 (1993), 495–522.

[39] Chamberlain, *Knowledge and Social Practice*, 125.

[40] Eickelman, 'The Art of Memory', 504.

Because it was based on an ideal of the depersonalisation of knowledge, this genuine revolution seemed likely to presage the irremediable decline of the ulama, who would be dispossessed from their personal monopoly on the transmission of 'ilm by the new educational institutions. Moreover, bureaucratic procedures of certification would deprive them of the ability to directly designate their successors from among their favourite disciples, a system that had facilitated the social reproduction of the great scholarly families. More fundamentally, the liberation of knowledge from 'mnemonic domination'[41] seemed to threaten the very identity of the ulama. Whereas they had until then been defined by their function of preserving and transmitting Islam's sacred tradition, they now seemed destined to become mere juridical experts specialising in a particular sort of law – that is, sharia.

But in Syria at least, things did not take place as the modernisation theory would suggest. When asked about his training in Damascus in the early 2000s, a young Syrian 'alim stressed that in parallel with the formal teachings he was receiving at the al-Fath Islamic Institute, he was assiduously attending lessons taught according to what he calls the 'sheikhist method' (*al-manhaj al-mashyakhi*), that is, informal study circles during which ancient treatises were explained and at the end of which students were issued an *ijaza*:

> It was said that the best teacher of Hanafi fiqh was Sheikh Adib Kallas, then I attended his lessons. As for Shafi'i fiqh, it was Sheikh Sadiq Habannaka. I also went to Sheikh Rushdi al-Qalam, for the *usul al-fiqh* [foundations of fiqh], fiqh, and Arabic language. And so on. I have been issued with many ijazat: by Sheikh Adib Kallas, for the books *al-Hidaya* and *Ta'lil al-Mukhtar*; by Sheikh 'Umar al-Sabbagh, for *al-Lubab fi sharh al-kitab*, and many more.[42]

Similar accounts are commonplace among young Syrian clerics. The following pages will both illustrate this persistence and analyse its causes.

Institutionalisation and Reformism

Except for the pioneering work of Sheikh 'Abd al-Qadir al-Qassab (1847–1941), who opened the first modern Islamic institute of Syrian history in Dayr 'Atiya (Qalamun mountains, north of Damascus) in 1898,[43] the

---

[41] Eickelman, *Knowledge and Power*, 168.
[42] Interview with an anonymous source, Damascus, May 2008.
[43] This seems to be an anomaly in view of the Qalamun's disadvantaged and isolated nature. The most plausible explanation lies in the personality of al-Qassab, who had

institutionalisation of the training of the country's ulama really started in Aleppo in the early 1920s. Here it built upon traditional madrasas, of which there was still a vibrant culture in the city – whereas, for reasons that remain unclear, they had undergone a marked decline in Damascus during the nineteenth century.[44]

Thus, it was in the imposing sixteenth-century Khusrawiyya madrasa that in 1922 the local Directorate of Awqaf opened an Islamic seminary for secondary-level education. The school, which would later be called 'Aleppo's al-Azhar', produced every figure who would go on to be prominent among the ulama of northern Syria in the second half of the twentieth century.[45]

The first director of the Khusrawiyya was the reformist scholar Raghib al-Tabbakh (1876–1951), a journalist, former member of the Committee of Union and Progress, and a correspondent of the Nadwat al-Ulama of Lucknow.[46] Therefore, the school he set up began as a hybrid of the old and new systems of teaching: in addition to the use of benches, it had an entrance exam and a stable curriculum spread over six years, at the end of which a diploma was issued in the name of the institution. At the same time, however, the school kept in touch with the local scholarly tradition by hiring the city's most revered ulama, maintaining the gloss of classical texts as part of its programme, and by including the signature of each teacher on the diploma by way of individual ijaza. In 1942, however, al-Tabbakh further modernised the Khusrawiyya by adding courses in natural sciences and foreign languages.[47]

It was also in 1942 that the first state-run Islamic seminary was opened in Damascus. The Faculty of Sharia (al-Kulliyyat al-Shar'iyya, not to

---

taught for twenty-seven years at al-Azhar, where he had witnessed the first reforms of the mosque–university (Abaza and Hafiz, *Tarikh 'ulama' Dimashq*, vol. I, 543–4). Another factor might have been the influence of European missionary schools, which were widespread in the region because of its large Christian population (Mériam Cheikh, 'Pour une histoire de l'émigration syrienne vers l'Amérique latine. Le cas du Qalamoun: territoire d'émigration, lieu de mémoire', master's thesis, Université de Provence, 2005).

[44] Katibi, *al-Ta'lim al-shar'i*, 36–66; Bayruti, *al-Shaykh Muhammad Badr al-Din al-Hasani*, 35–7.

[45] On the creation of this school, see Jean Gaulmier, 'Note sur l'état présent de l'enseignement traditionnel à Alep', *Bulletin d'études orientales* 9 (1942), 1–27; Katibi, *al-Ta'lim al-shar'i*, 67–78.

[46] Majd Makki, 'al-Shaykh Muhammad Raghib al-Tabbakh' (www.islamsyria.com, 24 July 2007). The Nadwat al-Ulama is a reformist seminary that was founded in 1894 by Deobandi ulama. See Jan-Peter Hartung, 'Standardising Muslim Scholarship: The Nadwat al-Ulama', in *Assertive Religious Identities: India and Europe*, ed. Satish Saberwal and Mushirul Hasan (New Delhi: Manohar, 2006), 121–44.

[47] Katibi, *al-Ta'lim al-shar'i*, 75–6, 78.

be confused with the faculty of sharia that was founded in 1954 at the University of Damascus) was created at the instigation of the reformist sheikh Kamil al-Qassab (1853–1954), a former student of Muhammad 'Abduh. Like its Aleppian counterpart, this secondary school offered a combination of religious and secular lessons, the first being taught by ulama and the second by effendis.[48]

In the 1950s, state-run seminaries were renamed 'Sharia high schools' (*thanawiyyat shar'iyya*).[49] In 1972, their curriculum was reformed in order to make their diploma equivalent to that of the literary section of general secondary schools, thus making their students eligible for admission into all of the Syrian universities' faculties of humanities.[50] In addition to the fact that it strongly increased the proportion of secular disciplines in the programme, this reform entailed the generalisation of the use of modern textbooks at the expense of classical treatises.[51]

A project of modernisation also inspired the founders of the country's first higher faculty of sharia (*kulliyyat al-shari'a*), which was created within the University of Damascus in 1954.[52] The founders – Mustafa al-Siba'i (1915–64), Mustafa al-Zarqa (1904–99), Muhammad al-Mubarak (1912–82), and Ma'ruf al-Dawalibi (1909–2004) – were the leaders of the reformist wing of the Muslim Brothers.[53] The first two being non-conformist Azharites, the others graduates in sociology and law from the Sorbonne, they were all the more inclined to give free rein to their modernist inclinations given that they were not working within an age-old mosque–university such as al-Azhar (which until then had been the only available option for young Syrian ulama who had the privilege to continue studying at a higher level), but in the recently created Syrian university.

Tellingly, most of the teachers appointed in the first academic year were effendis with a profile very similar to that of the founders,[54] whereas

---

[48] Abaza and Hafiz, *Tarikh 'ulama' Dimashq*, vol. II, 657–67. In this context, 'effendi' refers to someone who combines traditional, informal religious training with secular education. As a result, he is characterised by Islamic-leaning opinions while displaying a Westernised lifestyle symbolised by the suit and tie.

[49] Katibi, *al-Ta'lim al-shar'i*, 80.

[50] *OFA*, 2–4 May 1972, no. 762, IV.

[51] Katibi, *al-Ta'lim al-shar'i*, 82.

[52] See Botiveau, 'La formation des oulémas'; Böttcher, *Syrische Religionspolitik*, 131–43.

[53] Al-Dawalibi was a sympathiser, but not a formal member, of the Muslim Brothers. On these figures, see the third chapter and Itzchak Weismann, 'Democratic Fundamentalism? The Practice and Discourse of the Muslim Brothers Movement in Syria', *The Muslim World* 100 (2010), 1–16.

[54] 'Adnan al-Khatib, the future president of the State Council, and 'Abd al-Karim al-Yafi had been trained in France. Mustafa al-Barudi would be appointed as the Minister

there was only one representative of the traditional mashyakha, Grand Mufti Abu al-Yusr 'Abidin.[55] Even the minbar of the faculty mosque was not entrusted to a 'sheikh' but to the future superintendent of the Muslim Brothers 'Isam al-'Attar, a high school professor of literature. As for the curriculum, the 'modernity' of which was extolled by Professor al-Mubarak, it included matters such as economy and the 'current situation of the Muslim world'.[56]

Through this approach, al-Siba'i and his companions anticipated the 1961 modernist reform of al-Azhar by Nasser.[57] In both cases, the goal of higher Islamic education was no longer conceived as the training of ulama in the traditional sense of the term – that is, to pass down the Islamic scholarly heritage – but rather, taking a utilitarian perspective, to train modern experts in Islamic law who would have a grasp of modern realities. Accordingly, from the very first year on, the curriculum of the Syrian faculty included the comparative study of the Islamic schools of laws, including non-Sunni ones. This choice was linked to a will to develop a unified and modernised Islamic law that could constitute an alternative to secular law in a context where Syria had just adopted a European-inspired civil and penal code (1949).

This initial orientation was confirmed in the late 1960s by the dean, Wahba al-Zuhayli, who, much in line with the philosophy of the faculty's founders, stressed the need to teach Islamic law 'in relation with public and private positive law' and to avoid 'any dissipation in theoretical issues whose study is vain'.[58]

From the point of view of their founders, institutions such as state-run secondary seminaries and the faculty of sharia were aimed at bringing about the emergence of a new kind of 'alim who would replace traditional sheikhs – the latter, according to the faculty's first dean, Mustafa al-Siba'i, being 'completely out of touch with the problems of the modern Muslim society'.[59] However, this reformist project would soon be faced with several obstacles, the first of which was the Ba'thist coup of 1963.

of Information in 1961. See Ahmad al-'Alawna, *Dhayl al-a'lam* [Continuation of the great men] (Jeddah: Dar al-Manara, 1998), 139; Raghda' Mardini, 'Rahil al-'allama al-mawsu'a al-duktur 'Abd al-Karim al-Yafi' [Death of the eminent scholar, the encyclopaedia Dr 'Abd al-Karim al-Yafi] (www.odabasham.net, 18 October 2008); Sawwaf, *Mu'jam al-usar*, vol. I, 120.

[55] *OFA*, 11–14 December 1954, no. 681, V.
[56] *OFA*, 29 March–1 April 1958, no. 1003, V.
[57] Zeghal, *Gardiens de l'islam*, 114–28.
[58] Botiveau, 'La formation des oulémas', 77; Böttcher, *Syrische Religionspolitik*, 132, 136–8.
[59] Quoted by 'Adnan Zarzur, *Mustafa al-Siba'i: al-da'iya al-mujaddid* [Mustafa al-Siba'i: the preacher and renovator] (Damascus: Dar al-Qalam, 2000), 150.

One of the consequences of the advent of a 'progressive' regime was to generate a context that was more favourable to traditional conceptions of religious authority – this is only an apparent paradox. As Gregory Starrett explains, the dilemma faced by the ulama is that 'the thinner the tradition spreads itself over social, political and economic problems – the more useful the tradition is – the more control over it they have to concede to others'.[60]

In any case, the opposite of Starrett's assertion is also true: by making Islam irrelevant to most aspects of social life, Ba'thist secularism indirectly reinforced those who value religious tradition for itself – the ulama – rather than as something necessarily *useful*. As shown above, the reformist project of the faculty of sharia at the University of Damascus was driven by the aim to set up a modern, *applicable* fiqh. Conversely, the same project was severely weakened when the gradual consolidation of the Ba'thist regime ruined any hope for the restoration of Islamic law.

From the mid-1960s, the new political situation forced the founders of the faculty of sharia into exile, depriving it of its most influential reformist members. Afterwards, the faculty was exposed to the growing influence of a new generation of Azharites of traditionalist persuasion, the most famous of whom was Sa'id Ramadan al-Buti (b. 1929), a staunch critic of the Muslim Brothers, who was dean of the faculty from 1977 to 1983.[61]

As a result of this transformation, the students of the faculty have been socialised in an intellectual environment where 'free teaching' is still highly valued, not as a mere auxiliary of formal studies but as a distinct approach that is seen as superior because it provides direct access to the scholarly heritage. Such a view is expressed for instance by Sheikh Hisham al-Burhani (b. 1932), a Shadhili Sufi master and Hanafi *faqih* (specialist in fiqh) who taught at the university and holds study circles at the al-Tawba mosque:

The real *shari'a* [is] not taught at the university but in the mosque, with a shaykh. At university the students learn *about* the shari'a, by means of modern books explaining the mechanics of the science of fiqh, Sunna and other fields. With the shaykh in the mosque one studies the shari'a itself, by means of reading fiqh.[62]

[60] Starrett, *Putting Islam to Work*, 186.
[61] Other prominent members of this generation were Mustafa al-Khann (1922–2008) and Mustafa al-Bugha (b. 1938) – two disciples of the Damascene sheikh Hasan Habannaka, like al-Buti – and Nur al-Din 'Itr (b. 1939), the spiritual heir of the Aleppian scholar Abdullah Siraj al-Din.
[62] Quoted by Maurits Berger, 'The Shari''a and Legal Pluralism: The Example of Syria', in *Legal Pluralism in the Arab World*, ed. Baudouin Dupret (The Hague: Kluwer Law International, 1999), 113–24, at 115.

Attending the mosque lessons of Sheikh al-Burhani helps to understand that 'studying the sharia' – instead of 'studying about the sharia' – is not only a matter of different texts, but also of immersion in sacrality: sacrality of a blessed hour, that which lasts from the dawn prayer to the sunrise; sacrality of the place, in this case an Ayyubid building where the al-Burhani family has been teaching for four generations; and, last, sacrality of the atmosphere created by the invocations and prayers that give rhythm to the lesson.[63] Of course, nothing prevents a student from limiting himself to university classes if he has no ambition to pursue a clerical career. However, the quotation above shows that recognition by the elders necessarily requires attending informal study circles, without which the aspirant 'alim would be perceived as merely having notions 'about' the sharia, rather than direct knowledge of it.

In addition to the weakening of its reformist orientation, the faculty of sharia suffered from deep-rooted mistrust by the Ba'thist regime. Indeed, despite the departure of the historical leaders of the Muslim Brothers in the 1960s, active members of the movement continued to teach in the faculty until the late 1970s,[64] and several of the deans who headed the institution until the 1980s had known sympathies with the Brothers.[65] More generally, the faculty managed to remain relatively autonomous in its recruitment policy. Competence almost always took precedence over proximity to the regime, as shown by the brilliant international careers of many of its professors.[66] Another illustration of the regime's inability to mould the faculty in its image was the resounding failure of a project announced by the Ba'th in 1980, which aimed to force the institution to graduate 'a majority of students armed with nationalist progressive thought within a period of six years'.[67] Despairing of turning the faculty into a breeding-ground for 'Ba'thist ulama', the regime curbed its development by preventing it from granting doctorates until 1998 and by delaying the opening of a sister faculty in Aleppo until 2006.[68]

---

[63] Observations by the author, 2006–8.

[64] Muhammad Adib Salih (b. 1926), the editor of the Muslim Brothers' journal *Hadarat al-Islam*, and 'Adnan Zarzur (b. 1939), the biographer of Mustafa al-Siba'i (interview with Muhammad al-Hawari, Aachen, 11 August 2008).

[65] Fawzi Fayd Allah (b. 1925), Wahba al-Zuhayli (b. 1932), 'Abd al-Rahman al-Sabuni (b. 1929), and Ibrahim al-Salqini (b. 1934–2011).

[66] Mustafa al-Khann, Mustafa al-Bugha, Wahba al-Zuhayli, Ibrahim al-Salqini, Ahmad al-Hajji al-Kurdi, and Muhammad 'Ajjaj al-Khatib.

[67] Olivier Carré and Gérard Michaud, *Les Frères musulmans: Égypte et Syrie, 1928–1982* (Paris: Gallimard, 1983), 141.

[68] E-mail from a professor of the faculty of sharia in Damascus, 3 March 2009.

For reformist principles to achieve hegemonic status would also have required that conservative clergymen stand idly by. They did not, of course.

Private Institutes: The Strongholds of Tradition

Most of the dozen private Islamic seminaries of Damascus and Aleppo were established between independence and the advent of the Ba'thist regime, with the authorities only issuing a couple of licences after this period. The founders of these schools were generally members of the petty and middle traditional bourgeoisie, being the sons of – or indeed themselves working as – shopkeepers, craftsmen, and merchants. In Damascus they had been trained in traditional study circles, whereas in Aleppo they had studied at the Khusrawiyya.

The goal of such seminaries was to institutionalise the age-old study circles and so enable them to absorb the growing number of pupils in an age of mass literacy. Expanding and rationalising the structures of specialised religious teaching allowed the ulama to train clerics on an 'industrial' scale, and therefore to provide society with unprecedented levels of religious supervision.

For some scholars, however, private religious institutes were also a reaction to modernist 'aberrations'. Such was the case of Abdullah Siraj al-Din (1924–2002), the son of a respected merchant–'alim of Aleppo and a teacher at the Khusrawiyya, who used to tell his disciples that the founding director, Raghib al-Tabbakh, had died from despair caused by the 'disastrous' consequences of the modernisation of the school![69] Combined with the 'interference of influential parties' (i.e., the government) in the management of the Khusrawiyya, these reforms had led, according to Siraj al-Din, to the 'weakening of the level of the students', and therefore to a situation in which 'mosques were entrusted to people who were not worthy of them'. In 1962, in order to counter this trend by preserving the 'ancient method', he opened al-Ta'lim al-Shar'i (Religious teaching), an institute that is better known under the name of the medieval madrasa that houses it, al-Sha'baniyya.[70]

Whatever the intentions of their founders, private sharia institutes (*ma'ahid shar'iyya*) have constituted an obstacle to the spread of reformist principles. Indeed, unlike both the public and the private sharia high

[69] Nur al-Din 'Itr, *Safahat min hayat al-imam shaykh al-islam al-shaykh Abdullah Siraj al-Din al-Hussayni* [Pages from the life of the Imam Sheikh of Islam, Sheikh Abdullah Siraj al-Din al-Husseini] (Aleppo: Dar al-Ru'ya, 2003), 35.
[70] Fayyad 'Absu, 'al-Madrasa al-Sha'baniyya' (www.alkeltawia.com, 2 August 2008).

schools (thanawiyyat shar'iyya), whose curriculum is set by the Ministry of Education, these institutes decided their own programmes, which were more in line with the traditional system – and which were not recognised by the state, meaning that their students were not admitted to the faculty of sharia. At the al-Fath institute of Damascus, which was founded by Sheikh Salih al-Farfur (1901–86) in 1956, teachers used to pledge to 'spread knowledge as they took it'.[71] The teachings of these institutes originated in the lessons of the founding master, a principle symbolised by the general lesson – a commentary on a classical treatise – that he would give for students of all levels.[72] To stress their attachment to 'tradition', these schools also imposed a uniform on their students composed of a dark robe (*dishdasha*) and a white turban.

Over the years, the private Islamic seminaries have been forced to undergo some degree of modernisation, for instance by using a growing number of textbooks and, in Damascus, by giving up the uniform. In most cases, however, their organisation has remained inspired by age-old conceptions of religious authority. Indeed, the bureaucratic structure of these schools is often a mere legal and administrative screen for a *jama'a* (pl. *jama'at*), an informal group whose hierarchy relies on the master-disciple relationship. Consequently, although sharia institutes are run by boards of administrators who are elected by the members of the association that is in charge of fundraising, the main administrative and educational positions are held by the founding sheikh's closest disciples.[73] The same principle governs the further renewal of the hierarchy: whoever aims at making a career in such an institute has no other choice than to become the follower of one of its influential figures.

It should be noted that a similar rule prevails as far as the allocation of mosques is concerned: indeed, although officers of religious rites are appointed by the Ministry of Awqaf, the support of a 'patron' from within the clergy is often essential, because the Ministry requires the candidate to produce a letter of reference from an established scholar, and because the money of the merchants who support the latter might serve to 'orient' the choice made by the administration and the security services.[74]

---

[71] Abaza and Hafiz, *Tarikh 'ulama' Dimashq*, vol. III, 512.
[72] Habannaka, *al-Walid al-da'iyya*, 162; Muti' al-Hafiz, *Dar al-Hadith al-Ashrafiyya bi-Dimashq: dirasa tarikhiyya wa tawthiqiyya* [Dar al-Hadith al-Ashrafiyya in Damascus: a historical and documentary study] (Damascus: Dar al-Fikr, 2001), 293–6.
[73] See for instance the accounts of the foundation of the Damascene institutes al-Tawjih al-Islami and al-Fath: Habannaka, *al-Walid al-da'iyya*; Abaza and Hafiz, *Tarikh 'ulama' Dimashq*, vol. III, 507–20.
[74] Interview with a Damascene cleric, Damascus, 14 April 2008.

This situation, combined with the authorities' concern for not antagonis-
ing certain neighbourhoods, explains the numerous cases of hereditary
transmission of mosque positions, the most impressive example being
that of the aforementioned al-Burhani family at the al-Tawba mosque in
Damascus.

Concretely, 'becoming the disciple' of a renowned sheikh consists in
attending his study circles and spending as much time as possible in his
company.[75] Given that many of the aforementioned jama'at are headed
by Sufi masters, it also often consists in pursuing mystical training under
the aegis of the master.[76] In certain religious schools, it is compulsory for
pupils to attend the weekly collective *dhikr*[77] through which the school
community reasserts its spiritual affiliation with the founding sheikh.[78]

Beyond the fact that this model is seen as intrinsically good by the
ulama, its persistence is tied to issues of power. From the start, Syrian
clerics have been aware of the fact that the rational–legal mode of domination that characterises modern institutions could potentially undermine the master–disciple relationship, which is personal, permanent,
and based on absolute obedience.[79] The Damascene Salafi writer Ali al-
Tantawi (1909–99), who was hostile to such a conception of authority,
reminded his readers that

the bond between the sheikh and his disciples is much stronger than the bond
between the members of an association and its leaders ... The explanation for
this is a principle that is contrary to both Islam and reason, that is, the idea that
'the disciple in the hands of a sheikh should be like a corpse in the hands of a
corpse-washer'.[80]

As for conservative Syrian ulama, they chose to combine these two modes
of domination in order to benefit from the efficiency and rationality of
bureaucratic structures without giving up the Sufi model that ensures
their personal authority over their followers and the cohesion of their

[75] Interview with Muhammad Khayr al-Tarshan (b. 1967), a prominent young sheikh of
the al-Fath institute (Damascus, 13 April 2008).
[76] See for instance the biographies of the teachers of the Kaftaru Academy: www.abunour.
net/.
[77] A Sufi ritual that consists in the vocal or silent repetition of the name of God.
[78] This is the case for two institutes related to the Naqshbandi tradition, al-Da'wa wa-l-Irshad
in Damascus and al-Kiltawiyya in Aleppo (Böttcher, *Syrische Religionspolitik*, 156; interview with a former student of the Kiltawiyya, Aleppo, 8 November 2006).
[79] See Rachida Chih, 'Sainteté, maitrise spirituelle et patronage: les fondements de l'autorité
dans le soufisme', *Archives des Sciences Sociales des Religions* 49 (2004), 79–98.
[80] Al-Tantawi, *Dhikrayat*, vol. VII, 155.

group. For instance, Ali al-Daqr's grandson explains that it was the concern for 'keeping his students attached to his person' that had led the founder of al-Gharra' to initiate them in a Sufi tradition.[81]

Because it gives the master discretionary power over the promotion of the disciple within the group's hierarchy, the Sufi model induces a situation of structural favouritism that benefits the sheikh's biological heirs and most loyal students. Of course, favouritism is not alien to – theoretically meritocratic – modern education institutions. What is peculiar in the case of Syrian private seminaries, however, is its systematic nature, with the result that these institutions are often the fiefdom of the families of the founding sheikh and of his closest companions.

Such is the intellectual environment in which many Syrian ulama were socialised during the second half of the twentieth century. Given the lack of interest of the Ba'thist regime in the development of state-run religious institutions, Islamic seminaries were not affected by the 1967 nationalisation of private schools. Moreover, the competition from state-run sharia high schools such as the Khusrawiyya has been limited: because their graduates are admitted to all faculties of humanities, they do not only attract future men of religion, but also the sons and daughters of conservative families who desire to see their children studying in sexually segregated classes. As a result, by 2008 more than half Aleppo's imams and preachers who were born after 1950 had graduated from private seminaries, and only one-fourth of them had studied in state-run religious schools.[82] In Damascus, private institutes had trained only 40 per cent of the corresponding group,[83] but the reason for this was not the competition from the public system of religious education (sharia high schools/ faculty of sharia): it was, instead, the astonishing fact that no less than 40 per cent of the ulama of the capital were in fact graduates of *secular* faculties, in particular Arabic literature and secular law.[84]

---

[81] Interview with Mundhir al-Daqr, Damascus, 7 February 2007.

[82] Calculation based on a population of 251 clerics. The proportions remain identical if calculated on the basis of the 28 most prominent ulama of the city born after 1950. Source of biographical data: Ka'ayyid, *Mawsu'at al-du'at*.

[83] Based on a population of seventy-two people born after 1950. In the absence of a systematic census such as the one made in Aleppo by Ka'ayyid, we include in the sample group the most prominent members of the Damascene clergy. Source of biographical data: miscellaneous.

[84] Based on a population of the eighty-five most prominent members of the Damascene clergy. The proportions remain identical if calculated on the basis of the forty-one most prominent ulama of the city. Source of biographical data: miscellaneous. Unlike in Egypt, where it is possible to study Arabic literature at al-Azhar, in Syria it is a purely secular course of study.

Such a figure starkly contrasts, for instance, with the Egyptian and Saudi cases, where formal religious training has become the rule for the grand ulama.[85] It is relatively easy to explain regarding the sons of ulama, who constitute half of the group in question, since it is considered to be obvious that they have benefited from first-rate religious teachings within their family. However, it seems more difficult to make sense of the profile of someone like hadith scholar Na'im al-'Arqsusi (b. 1951), the son of a barber and a 'mere' graduate in Arabic literature, whose lessons attract thousands of listeners in the gigantic al-Iman mosque and are broadcast by the Kuwaiti satellite channel al-Risala. Such a phenomenon has nothing to do with the emergence of self-taught ulama but rather results from the fact that traditional study circles remain a way to acquire knowledge that is not only necessary but also *sufficient* to be recognised as an 'alim. Before I analyse the causes of this situation, I will present the founders of private seminaries who dominated the religious scenes of Damascus and Aleppo during the 1960s and 1970s.

Portraits

The three most prominent founders of private Islamic seminaries in Damascus were Hasan Habannaka, Ahmad Kaftaru, and Salih al-Farfur. Like the other founding sheikhs, they recruited their right-hand men within their neighbourhoods. Indeed, since they were generally not prolific authors, mosque-based lessons and sermons were the main instruments of their call to Islam. Consequently, their jama'at often emerged as clerical factions attached to particular urban territories: Habannaka was the sheikh of the Midan, the city-off-the-walls that spread over three kilometres southward, Kaftaru that of the slopes of the Qasiun mountain (Rukn al-Din, Salhiyye), and al-Farfur that of the Old City and its northern extension, al-'Amara.

Because of their political influence, I will here sketch portraits of Habannaka and Kaftaru. For the same reason, I will also present the Aleppian sheikh Muhammad al-Nabhan, who, after Siraj al-Din, founded the other private sharia institute of the capital of the north.

Hasan Habannaka, the Rebellious Sheikh of the Midan
The son of a petty merchant and a shopkeeper himself, Habannaka studied with Ali al-Daqr, who entrusted him with the management of one of

---

[85] Mouline, *Les Clercs de l'islam*, 238.

his schools.[86] In 1946, with the help of his brother Sadiq (1920–2007), he founded his own institute, al-Tawjih al-Islami (The Islamic orientation). This institution is most notable for having trained some of the most eminent Syrian ulama of the late twentieth century, who pursued their studies at al-Azhar and then achieved international fame: Habannaka's son 'Abd al-Rahman (1927–2004), who wrote religious textbooks for Saudi schools;[87] the 'Imam of usul al-fiqh', Mustafa al-Khann (1922–2008), who taught in Syrian and Saudi universities;[88] Mustafa al-Bugha (b. 1938);[89] and the famous Sa'id Ramadan al-Buti (b. 1929).[90] Habannaka also established the Council of Quran Readers (Majlis al-Qurra'), which is composed of the readers with the highest *sanad* (position in the chain of transmission) in Damascus.[91] It would go on to be headed successively by two of his closest followers, Hussein Khattab (1920–88) and Krayyim Rajih (b. 1926), the most charismatic preachers of their generation in the Syrian capital.[92]

Basking in the glow of his participation in the anti-French Great Revolt of 1925, Habannaka quickly converted his religious authority into political influence. He played an important role in the mobilisation of the Midan against the projected reform of the Personal Status Law imposed by the French in 1938, and in 1952 he was the most vocal opponent of al-Shishakli's decision to impose a uniform on clerics.[93] The unofficial leader of the Damascene ulama, he secured their majority support in the 1964 election of the Grand Mufti but, as already mentioned, eventually lost to the Ba'th's favourite, Ahmad Kaftaru. In the following years, Habannaka's group, known as *jama'at al-Midan* (the Midan group), spearheaded the opposition to the regime's leftist radicalisation.[94]

---

[86] Habannaka, *al-Walid al-da'iyya*, 83.

[87] 'A'ida al-Jarrah, '*Abd al-Rahman Hasan Habannaka al-Midani, al-'alim al-mufakkir al-mufassir: zawji kama 'araftuhu* ['Abd al-Rahman Hasan Habannaka al-Midani, the scholar, thinker, and exegete: my husband as I have known him] (Damascus: Dar al-Qalam, 2001).

[88] Son of the mayor ('*umda*) of the Midan. See Muhi al-Din Dib Mastu, *Mustafa Sa'id al-Khann: al-'alim al-murabbi wa shaykh 'ilm usul al-fiqh fi bilad al-Sham* [Mustafa Sa'id al-Khann: the scholar, educator, and sheikh of usul al-fiqh in Bilad al-Sham] (Damascus: Dar al-Qalam, 2001).

[89] Son of the trustee of the butchers of the Midan. See Mustafa al-Bugha, 'Interview' (www.alkeltawia.com, 9 July 2008).

[90] On this important figure see Chapter 2.

[91] Habannaka, *al-Walid al-da'iyya*, 15–17.

[92] Majd Makki, 'Hussein Khattab: shaykh qurra' al-Sham' [(Hussein Khattab: sheikh of the Quran readers of Damascus]) (www.islamsyria.com, 10 July 2007); Yahya al-Hakami al-Fifi, 'Muhammad Krayyim Rajih' (www.islamsyria.com, 10 July 2007).

[93] Habannaka, *al-Walid al-da'iyya*, 21–8, 50; interview with 'Isam al-'Attar, by telephone, 4 August 2009.

[94] See Chapter 5.

Habannaka's rebellious stance led to a brief imprisonment in 1967, and his institute, which at that time was teaching about 500 pupils, was closed down for good.[95] However, thanks to his personal prestige and his close relations with the Saudi kingdom, he succeeded the late Makki al-Kittani as the Syrian representative at the Muslim World League in 1973, a position that passed to his son 'Abd al-Rahman upon his death five years later.[96] In the meantime, donations from Midani merchants and the Saudi government allowed the sheikh to leave his mark on the landscape of the Midan through the foundation of some of the largest mosques in the Syrian capital.[97]

Ahmad Kaftaru, the Grand Mufti of the Ba'th

Ahmad Kaftaru was a latecomer in the field of advanced Islamic teaching, opening his own private institute, al-Da'wa wa-l-Irshad (Islamic call and guidance), in 1975, more than a decade after his accession to the top of the country's official religious hierarchy.

Kaftaru was the only Damascene founding sheikh whose spiritual gene-alogy does not pass through Badr al-Din al-Hasani. When he emerged on the religious scene in the 1940s, it was as the successor to his father Amin (1877–1938), a native of Kurdistan and a sheikh of the so-called Kaftariyya branch of the Naqshbandi Khalidi Sufi tradition. As will be shown in the following pages of this chapter, most of the founders of mod-ern Syrian jama'at were followers of the Naqshbandiyya Khalidiyya. The spread of this Sufi tradition in nineteenth-century Syria was not the cause of the subsequent emergence of modern jama'at, which were responses to twentieth-century problems, but the Naqshbandiyya Khalidiyya had *elective affinities* with these new religious organisations: of the two most fashionable Sufi traditions amongst modern Syrian ulama, it was the most populist in orientation;[98] the other, the Shadhiliyya Darqawiyya, is more elitist and thus less suitable for the management of large popular movements.

Since Kaftaru's Sufi dimension has already been studied in depth, as has the higher Islamic institute he established after 1980,[99] I intend here to

---

[95] Habannaka, *al-Walid al-da'iyya*, 228–302.
[96] Ibid., 204–7; Jarrah, *'Abd al-Rahman Hasan Habannaka*, 19.
[97] Manjak, al-Hasan, Abdullah bin Rawaha (Habannaka, *al-Walid al-da'iyya*, 188–91).
[98] Itzchak Weismann, 'The Forgotten Shaykh: 'Isa al-Kurdi and the Transformation of the Naqshbandi–Khalidi Order in Twentieth Century Syria', *Die Welt des Islams* 43 (2003), 273–93.
[99] See Böttcher, *Syrische Religionspolitik*; and Stenberg, 'Young, Male and Sufi Muslim'.

set out aspects of his biography that have not received enough attention: the nature of his audience; and how early on he adopted a strategy of alliance with the state.

By no means a creation of the Ba'thist regime, Kaftaru first achieved celebrity due to the lessons in *tafsir* (explanation of the Quran) that he gave in mosques and, from the mid-1950s onwards, on national radio, thus becoming one of the first Syrian 'media sheikhs'. According to a famous Indian 'alim who attended one of his lessons at the Umayyad Mosque in 1951, the key to his success was a mixture of a populist style and a modern approach:

I appreciated the way he applied the Quranic verses to everyday life, comparing them to current realities, and not confining himself to scholarly interpretations and generalisations. He adapted his speech to the cultural level of ordinary people, speaking the local dialect.[100]

Another of Kaftaru's idiosyncratic features was the interest in Muslim–Christian dialogue that he displayed as early as the mid-1950s, an orientation that fitted perfectly with the dominant nationalist discourse of the time.[101] This relatively modern attitude explains why, although Kaftaru had not been educated beyond primary school, he nevertheless exerted his magnetism far beyond 'popular' circles. The core of his following included sons of renowned houses of knowledge,[102] as well as university graduates,[103] who at the time were a tiny privileged minority. The presence of such figures in the brotherhood was not only the result of the nature of Kaftaru's discourse but also of the social characteristics of the neighbourhoods that constituted his stronghold. The latter were traditionally home to migrant populations, including Kurds, but from the Mandate period they had also welcomed well-off Arab families from the southern quarters of the city.[104]

This invites us to qualify the thesis that the Kaftariyya was headed by a Kurdish elite that eventually forged an alliance of minorities with

[100] Abu al-Hassan Ali al-Nadwi, *Mudhakkirat sa'ih fi al-sharq al-'arabi* [Memories of a tourist in the Arab East] (Beirut: Dar Ibn Kathir, 1975), 232.
[101] *OFA*, 28 December 1954–3 January 1955, no. 782, V.
[102] Al-Ustuwani, al-Khani, al-Bani.
[103] Religious judges Bashir al-Bani (1911–2008) and 'Abd al-Ra'uf al-Ustuwani (1913–68), Paris-trained physician 'Arif al-Taraqji (1912–92) (Abaza and Hafiz, *Tarikh 'ulama' Dimashq*, vol. II, 816–17; Abaza, *'Ulama' Dimashq wa a'yanuha*, 241–2).
[104] See for instance the case of Kaftaru's grandson-in-law Muhammad Habash, whose parents left the Midan for the north of the city in the 1960s (*al-Thawra*, 9 November 2007).

the Alawite-dominated Ba'thist regime.[105] Although there were indeed Kurds in Kaftaru's entourage – such as his political and media right-hand man Marwan Shaykhu (1940–2001) – the most prominent clerics of his Islamic centre have been Arabs, starting with his three main spiritual successors, Bashir al-Bani, Rajab Dib, and Ahmad Rajih. Nor is Kaftaru's marital strategy marked by ethnic endogamy, as exemplified by the fact that his second wife was a daughter of an old Damascene family, the al-Jabri.

As for Kaftaru's strategy of alliance with the state, it developed well before the coup of 1963 and the subsequent rise of the Alawite officers. Rejecting the adage 'the misery of the ulama is at the gates of the princes' (*ba's al-'ulama' 'ala abwab al-umara'*), the Kurdish sheikh argued that men of religion should advise the 'powers-that-be' (*mutasaddir al-umur*), whether 'pious' or not, provided they were 'patriotic' (*watani*).[106] That was, as he said to his Indian visitor in 1951, the fastest way to bring about the implementation of reforms in line with Islamic precepts:

The surest way to eliminate corruption and enforce the religion in society … is to influence the men of government … through personal meetings with them and by establishing relationships of trust. What can be achieved in one year by preaching, can be done in less than a week through these people.[107]

These were not empty words. In the 1947 parliamentary election he went against the other ulama, who were supporting their colleagues who were running as candidates, by calling on people to vote for professional politicians who, he rightly believed, had greater chances of success. The voices of his flock therefore went to the highest bidder, in this case Jamil Mardam Bey, who promised to abolish state-regulated prostitution (a French heritage).[108] In 1951, the year his Indian visitor noted down his words, Kaftaru was appointed Mufti of Damascus.

The schism between Kaftaru and the rest of the Islamic trend occurred in 1957: during a parliamentary election in the district of Damascus,

---

[105] Annabelle Böttcher, 'Official Islam, Transnational Islamic Networks, and Regional Politics: The Case of Syria', in *The Middle East and Palestine: Global Politics and Regional Conflict*, ed. Dietrich Jung (New York: Palgrave Macmillan, 2004), 125–50, at 132.

[106] Humsi, *al-Du'at*, vol. I, 309–11; 'Imad 'Abd al-Latif Nadaf, *al-Shaykh Ahmad Kaftaru yatahaddath* [Sheikh Ahmad Kaftaru speaks] (Damascus: Dar al-Rachid, 2005), 203.

[107] Al-Nadwi, *Mudhakkirat sa'ih*, 247–8.

[108] Humsi, *al-Du'at*, vol. I, 308. The Mardam Bey government failed to fulfil that promise (*OFA*, 17–19 November 1948, no. 70, VI). Regulated prostitution was eventually abolished in 1961.

he backed the Ba'thist candidate Riyad al-Maliki against the Muslim Brother Mustafa al-Siba'i. By doing so, Kaftaru had once again shown a pragmatism that many viewed as opportunism: on the eve of the union with Egypt, the influence of the Ba'th in the army was such that to some extent it was the real centre of power in the country.[109] In 1964, a year after the coup of Michel 'Aflaq's party, Kaftaru was rewarded for his support by being made Grand Mufti of the Republic.

Muhammad al-Nabhan: Tribalism and Apocalypse

In 1964, two years after the foundation of the Sha'baniyya in Aleppo by Abdullah Siraj al-Din, Muhammad al-Nabhan (1900–74), another graduate of the Khusrawiyya, opened a private institute named Dar Nahdat al-'Ulum al-Shar'iyya (the house of the renaissance of religious sciences), which is better known under the name of the neighbouring mosque, al-Kiltawiyya.[110]

Exceptionally for the modern history of religious education in Syria, the Kiltawiyya was created especially to 'teach the sons of peasants and tribesmen'.[111] This choice resulted from al-Nabhan's own social profile: he was born into a wealthy family of the Khudayrat, one of the clans (*'asha'ir*) settled in Bab al-Nayrab, a neighbourhood that forms an interface between the city of Aleppo and the surrounding Bedouin and Shawaya tribes.[112] Although he allied himself with urban merchants (in particular the rich Badinjki family of Bab al-Nayrab),[113] al-Nabhan stood out from his colleagues due to his strong affinity with the countryside. Whereas his peers, following the example of Siraj al-Din, generally combined their religious vocation with trade – the urban occupation *par excellence* – the founder of the Kiltawiyya 'preferred agriculture', and kept a farm on which he worked with his own hands. Moreover, he chose to become affiliated with the Shafi'i *madhhab* (school of law), which prevails in the Syrian countryside, rather than the Hanafi school, to which the urban religious elite of Aleppo had traditionally belonged.[114]

[109] On this episode, see Zarzur, *Mustafa al-Siba'i*, 344–6.
[110] Katibi, *al-Ta'lim al-shar'i*, 98–103.
[111] 'Al-Shaykh Mahmud 'Ubayd al-Qadiri' (www.alkeltawia.com, 2009).
[112] Jacques Hivernel, 'Bab al-Nayrab, un faubourg d'Alep, hors la ville et dans la cité', *Études rurales*, no. 155–6 (2000), 215–37.
[113] 'Amir Rashid Mubayyid, *Mi'a awa'il min Halab* [One hundred prominent figures from Aleppo] (Aleppo: Dar al-Rifa'i, 2004), vol. I, 417–18.
[114] Faruq al-Nabhan, *al-Shaykh Muhammad al-Nabhan: shakhsiyyatuhu – fikruhu – atharuhu* [Sheikh Muhammad al-Nabhan: his personality – his thought – his influence] (Aleppo: Dar al-Turath, 2004), 104.

Every Thursday, al-Nabhan toured the villages to spread the Word, an endeavour that was facilitated by his tribal connections; there were thus many provincials, peasants, and tribesmen among his early close adherents.[115] Concerned about the insufficient number of clerics in the villages, al-Nabhan invited the youth to go and study at the Sha'baniyya. However, he quickly realised that the rural candidates' lack of background knowledge was impeding their success in the difficult entrance exam, a situation that convinced him to open the Kiltawiyya.[116]

There was much more to al-Nabhan than a simple desire to train men of religion for the countryside. Above all, he displayed a great capacity to adapt to the increasingly diverse audiences being created by the spread of literacy, as shown by the fact that he held weekly lessons for the tribes of Bab al-Nayrab, as well as for merchants, high school and university students, schoolteachers, and women – the latter having traditionally been excluded from mosque teaching.[117] Benefiting from his tribal and Sherifian origins – he had people call him 'al-Sayyid', a title for a descendant of the Prophet which had fallen into disuse among twentieth-century Sunni Syrians[118] – he became one of the most popular disciples of the famous Naqshbandi master of northern Syria, Muhammad Abu al-Nasr (1875–1949).[119]

Al-Nabhan's charisma is rooted in an exuberant conception of sainthood, and he is credited with miracles such as meetings with the Prophet, the Companions, and Ibn 'Arabi. He reportedly justified these supernatural powers with the following words: 'I am omnipotent, unbound, I am

---

[115] 'Abd al-Rahim al-Hut (1904–92), the first director of the Kiltawiyya and the uncle of its present director, Mahmud al-Hut, was born in another branch of the Khudayrat; Muhammad al-Shami (1923–80), his political counsellor, was a member of the Darawisha clan; Adib Hassun (1915–2008), his main spiritual heir, was born in the village of Yaqid al-'Ads; Najib Salim (1917–74), whose sons would play a leading role within al-Nabhan's group, was al-Nabhan's deputy in his hometown of Ariha. See ''Abd al-Rahim al-Hut, awwal mudir al-Kiltawiyya' ['Abd al-Rahim al-Hut, first director of the Kiltawiyya] (www.keltawia.com, 19 May 2008); Katibi, *'Ulama' min Halab*, 375–80, 612–8; Abdullah al-Janabi, 'al-Shaykh Najib Salim' (www.islamsyria.com, 7 April 2007).

[116] 'Al-Shaykh Mahmud 'Ubayd al-Qadiri'.

[117] 'Al-Shaykh Muhammad al-Nabhan: manhajuhu wa da'watuhu' [Sheikh Muhammad al-Nabhan: his method and preaching] (www.alkeltawia.com, 18 December 2007).

[118] City-dwellers have traditionally disregarded tribes, whose lifestyle they see as rough and violent. However, this contempt has generally gone hand in hand with admiration for the purity of their Arab genealogy.

[119] On Abu al-Nasr, see Itzchak Weismann, 'The Hidden Hand: The Khalidiyya and the Orthodox–Fundamentalist Nexus in Aleppo', *Journal of the History of Sufism* 5 (2007), 41–58, at 55.

the Muhammadian heir.'[120] Moreover, some of his disciples claim that his decision not to appoint a successor had to do with millenarianism: his true successor was none other than the Mahdi, for whom he was 'preparing the way' (*umahhid li-l-mahdi*).[121]

Regardless of their authenticity, such statements illustrate the kind of religiosity that prevails among al-Nabhan's followers, a religiosity that certain people deem 'superstitious'; certainly it contrasts with the much more sober discourse found among the ulama of the Sha'baniyya school.[122] Nevertheless, al-Nabhan was in no way seen as a heretic or even as marginal by his peers. On the contrary, his popularity made him one of the main political leaders of the local clergy.[123] Although he always maintained close relations with power holders, he acquired a reputation for intransigence in the defence of Islam against 'impious' politicians. His disciples say that in the early 1950s, when rumour had it that Rushdi Kikhiya, the head of the People's Party (an Aleppo-based bourgeois nationalist organisation), was in favour of a secular state, al-Nabhan harangued the crowd at the market, saying: 'If nobody kills Kikhiya, I will do it myself!'[124] The political leader soon came to the Kiltawiyya, hagiographers claim, and repented of his ungodly plan before al-Nabhan. Although the truthfulness of this story is open to doubt, since al-Nabhan was himself a member of the People's Party,[125] his fearless character was confirmed by a non-hagiographic source. A Syrian Muslim Brother from Hama, Sa'id Hawwa (1935–89), wrote that in 1973, the first scholar he invited to sign his petition against the secular draft constitution was the sheikh of the Kiltawiyya because, according to him, 'none in Syria was more courageous than Sheikh al-Nabhan'.[126]

In 1970, al-Nabhan won a victory against 'impiousness' that symbolised the reconquest of the public sphere by religion. Next to Aleppo's university there was a restaurant called Montana, where alcohol was served. The sheikh raised funds among his followers to buy out the restaurant, and then equipped it with a minaret and turned it into a mosque, al-Furqan.

---

[120] 'Al-Shaykh Muhammad al-Nabhan: min karamatihi' [Sheikh Muhammad al-Nabhan: some of his miracles] (cb.rayaheen.net, 26 July 2007).

[121] 'Al-Shaykh Muhammad al-Nabhan: khilafatuhu [Sheikh Muhammad al-Nabhan: his succession] (alsayed-alnabhan.com, 19 December 2007).

[122] See in particular the hagiography of Siraj al-Din by his son-in-law: 'Itr, *Safahat*.

[123] Interview with Ali Sadr al-Din al-Bayanuni, London, 15 April 2009.

[124] 'Min shama'il al-sayyid al-Nabhan' [Some of the innate qualities of Sayyid al-Nabhan] (www.alkeltawia.com, 19 December 2007).

[125] *OFA*, 12–15 March 1955, no. 705, VII.

[126] Hawwa, *Hadhihi tajribati*, 107.

The latter, which for some time remained known as 'the Montana mosque', eventually gave its name to the entire neighbourhood.[127]

Al-Nabhan's fame spread not only throughout northern Syria (in 1977 a group of his followers from the Madjadme clan founded Dar al-Arqam, an offshoot of the Kiltawiyya, in the city of Manbij),[128] but also to the Iraqi province of al-Anbar, and more particularly to the city of al-Falluja. The latter being an old trading partner of Aleppo, to which it is connected via the Euphrates, al-Nabhan's da'wa was spread there by Iraqi merchants on their return from Syria. In the 1960s the sheikh himself visited Iraq, where his local disciples founded seven sharia institutes.[129] The 'Nabhaniyya' came to exert a major influence on al-Falluja's religious scene, as shown by the fact that among its members were Jamal Shakir, the sheikh of the city's Great Mosque in the early 2000s, and Abdullah al-Janabi, the leader of the first anti-American uprising in the spring of 2004. After al-Falluja's destruction by the coalition at the end of that year, both of them took refuge in Aleppo.[130]

Despite the rivalries that later divided the spiritual heirs of al-Nabhan, the cult that surrounds him is still alive and well today. He remains present for those who gather every Friday afternoon at the Kiltawiyya for the dhikr: through the white marble grave that has pride of place in a glass-walled room in the middle of the complex, and also through recordings of the lessons of the master, to which the audience listens with rapt attention.[131]

CO-OPTING THE 'LITERATE YOUTH': INFORMAL EDUCATION MOVEMENTS

After independence, Syria witnessed an acceleration of cultural change that deeply worried the clergy.[132] Up to that point, anti-religious ideas had had little influence beyond a narrow social elite; but now, with the expansion of public education, they were growing in popularity. Many schoolteachers had a distinctly secular profile, as shown by the fact that

[127] 'Adnan Katibi, *Tarikh al-ifta' fi Halab al-shahba'* [History of *ifta'* in Aleppo-the-Grey] (Aleppo: Maktabat al-Turath, n.d.), 309–10; interview with a former resident of the neighbourhood, Damascus, 6 March 2007.

[128] Ka'ayyid, *Mawsu'at al-du'at*, vol. I, 289.

[129] Al-Nabhan, *al-Shaykh Muhammad al-Nabhan*, 223.

[130] Interviews with anonymous sources, Aleppo, November 2006; Jamal Shakir, 'Interview' (www.alkeltawia.com, 16 July 2008).

[131] Observations by the author, Aleppo, November 2006.

[132] On the political reactions of the ulama to these transformations, see Chapter 5.

they constituted the most loyal urban supporters of the Ba'th Party, starting with its two founders, Michel 'Aflaq and Salah al-Din al-Bitar. Talking
of this period, a contemporary Damascene 'alim recounts that

> atheism was exerting tyrannical domination over high school teachers ... I heard
> Dr Amin al-Masri[133] ..., who was teaching at the Tajhiz[134] ..., say that when he
> entered the teachers' room, he felt like a stranger because most of his colleagues
> were atheists.[135]

According to the biographers of Muslim scholars of that time, this situation entailed the loss of 'any respect and consideration for the ulama
in the minds of the masses and the youth', with the result that 'mosques
were empty, except for a handful of old men who were only coming for
prayers'.[136] Of course, one recognises here the 'declinism' that is characteristic of modern Syrian hagiography, where the hero initiates a 'renaissance' that is necessarily preceded by doldrums. Nevertheless, the ulama
of the post-independence era had good reason to think that they were
going through a period of crisis: for instance, the parliamentary elections of 1947 and 1949 witnessed the success of several members of the
Muslim Brothers, whose tense relations with the clergy have already been
mentioned, while none of the sheikhs running as candidates obtained a
seat in the capital.[137]

Although the creation of the aforementioned religious institutes was
part of a reaction to this feeling of decline, it only partially addressed
the problem. By definition, such institutes were destined for a limited
number of specialists, with the result that students of secular schools
were doomed, the Damascene sheikh 'Abd al-Karim al-Rifa'i (1901–73)
lamented, 'to be eaten alive by the demons' – that is, to become athe-
ists.[138] In order to ward off this peril, al-Rifa'i pioneered an approach
that would soon be imitated by many of his peers. According to him, it
was futile to try to divert young Syrians from public schools and secular disciplines: their faith would be best preserved through an informal

---

[133] Amin al-Masri (1914–77): member of the Muslim Brothers who went into exile in
1965 and then taught at the faculty of sharia in Mecca (Muhammad Lutfi al-Sabbagh,
'Muhammad Amin al-Masri', *Majallat al-Jami'at al-Islamiyya fi al-Madinat
al-Munawwara* 39 (n.d.), 17).
[134] A public high school in Damascus.
[135] Al-Rifa'i, 'Durus min hayat', no. 2.
[136] 'Al-Shaykh 'Abd al-Karim al-Rifa'i wa masiratuhu al-da'wiyya' [Sheikh 'Abd al-Karim
al-Rifa'i and his journey through da'wa], no. 4 (www.sadazaid.com, 5 April 2008).
[137] See Chapter 5.
[138] 'Al-Shaykh 'Abd al-Karim al-Rifa'i wa masiratuhu', no. 1.

movement devoted to education and proselytising (*haraka tarbawiyya wa da'wiyya*) and relying on 'mosque work' (*'amal masjidi*).[139] Such a movement should be not an alternative but a complement to secular schooling. From the early 1950s, Jama'at Zayd (Zayd's group), named after al-Rifa'i's mosque, Zayd bin Thabit al-Ansari, was the first and predominant Damascene organisation to address the growing demand for religious education that was spreading among the educated youth.[140] As a consequence, it went on to play a key role in the 'Islamic revival' (*al-sahwa al-islamiyya*) of the 1970s.

The Engineer and the Mosque

Born into a poor family of the Qabr 'Atke neighbourhood, al-Rifa'i pursued a traditional religious training with Ali al-Daqr and then became a teacher in the schools of al-Gharra' – in other words, nothing predestined him to reach out to the modern-educated youth.[141] Moreover, his present-day disciples never describe him as a visionary ideologue (his only writings are a concise handbook of dogmatic theology and a prayer booklet),[142] or as a charismatic orator, which he obviously was not: Sa'id Ramadan al-Buti wrote that 'without the great knowledge and wisdom with which God had honoured him ... one could have thought he was a poor wretch'.[143] In fact, al-Rifa'i's capacity to transcend the cultural gap between him and the pupils of high schools and universities was rather the result of his moral qualities – that is, his patience towards a youth whose faith had been shaken by secular ideologies,[144] and an open-mindedness that led him to surround himself with young counsellors who were culturally close to the target audience.[145]

What al-Rifa'i wanted to revive was not the traditional use of the mosque, as an open space for daily prayers and a limited number of weekly lessons. His aim, on the contrary, was to 'turn the mosque into a

---

[139] Sa'id Ramadan al-Buti, foreword to 'Abd al-Karim al-Rifa'i, *al-Ma'rifa fi bayan 'aqidat al-muslim* [Knowledge in the statement of the doctrine of the Muslim] (Damascus: al-Ghazali, 1990), 8–9.

[140] For a non-hagiographic account of the movement's activities in the mid-1950s, see Hawwa, *Hadhihi tajribati*, 53.

[141] 'Al-Shaykh 'Abd al-Karim al-Rifa'i wa masiratuhu', no. 3.

[142] Al-Rifa'i, *al-Ma'rifa*; al-Rifa'i, *al-Awrad al-mukhtara* [Selected litanies] (Damascus: al-Ghazali, 1992).

[143] Foreword to al-Rifa'i, *al-Ma'rifa*, 7–8.

[144] 'Al-Shaykh 'Abd al-Karim al-Rifa'i wa masiratuhu', no. 4.

[145] Hawwa, *Hadhihi tajribati*, 53.

university',[146] that is, to offer free but methodically organised teachings within myriad study circles.

In al-Rifa'i's movement, the halqa underwent a change of nature: whereas it had traditionally been a temporary gathering constituted by students around a master in order to study a particular matter or book, it was now a stable group of a dozen members of similar age and intellectual level that met at least once a week.[147] It was the fundamental organisational unit of the movement, like the 'family' (*usra*) of the Muslim Brothers, or the 'cell' (*khaliya*) of the Communist Party. In addition to its flexibility and discretion – which would prove a crucial asset in an authoritarian context – this structure allowed the delegation of authority while exerting closer control over each follower. A 'head of circle' (*ra'is halqa*) chosen among the advanced disciples was entrusted with bringing his subordinates up to the required standards of religious knowledge and watching over their daily behaviour – he even had the right to 'punish whoever was disrespectful to his parents'.[148] The circle was not merely a repressive device, however: it was also a venue for dialogue and collective support in case of personal problems.[149] And, of course, it had a major function in the organisation of teachings.

Students were attracted to the mosque by the supplementary lessons in secular disciplines, in particular natural sciences, that were given by school-teachers affiliated with al-Rifa'i. Such lessons were not only a recruitment device (they were offered free of charge but, of course, reserved for those who also attended the mosque's religious classes), they were also part of a drive to 'conquer elites'. Indeed, supplementary lessons were not only provided during the first phase of the new follower's membership: heads of circles were made responsible for identifying their students' weaknesses and orienting them towards the appropriate courses.[150] Implementing this policy with young people who came mostly from the middle classes – that is, from relatively privileged cultural backgrounds – inevitably led to an

---

[146] Sariya al-Rifa'i, 'Min fiqh al-da'wa' [From fiqh of da'wa] (www.sadazaid.com, 10 May 2006). This expression, which was used by one of al-Rifa'i's sons in a recent article, might well be apocryphal. Its possible origin could be a description of the – very similar – group of the Alexandrine sheikh Ahmad al-Mahallawi (b. 1925) by the famous Egyptian 'alim Muhammad al-Ghazali: 'I have seen the mosque turned into a university, and I have seen the mosque filled with educated people' (quoted by Zeghal, *Gardiens de l'islam*, 219).

[147] 'Al-Shaykh 'Abd al-Karim al-Rifa'i wa masiratuhu', no. 7.

[148] Ibid.

[149] Interview with a former member of Zayd, Damascus, 17 May 2006.

[150] 'Al-Shaykh 'Abd al-Karim al-Rifa'i wa masiratuhu', no. 6.

increase in the proportion of Islamic-leaning elements in the best university faculties (medicine, pharmacology, engineering), and all the more so given that the Muslim Brothers had adopted a similar approach after the advent of the Ba'th put political life into deep freeze.[151]

Zayd's religious teachings began with the basics, that is, with memorisation of the Quran. The exponential growth of literacy in the twentieth century had increased the numbers of those who aspired to become *hafidh* (one who has memorised the whole of the Quran). In promoting memorisation, however, al-Rifa'i was not only responding to a new social reality: he also proved flexible enough to break with part of the scholarly tradition in order to make the status of hafidh more easily accessible. Until that time, obtaining such an ijaza required memorising *ten* different ways to read the Quran (*qira'at*).[152] For a motivated student, this was a matter of four to five years of learning. Given the fact that only one of these readings (Hafs) is commonly used in Syria, one might reasonably suspect that such restrictive conditions were a device aimed at drastically reducing the number of memorisers. Sheikh al-Rifa'i put an end to this situation by enjoining his right-hand man, 'Sheikh of the Quran' Muhi al-Din Abu al-Hasan al-Kurdi (1917–2009), to issue an ijaza to anyone who had memorised the reading of Hafs.[153]

This was a break with tradition, but not with the traditionalist paradigm. It was, on the contrary, an attempt to incorporate a larger number of people within this model. Al-Rifa'i's hagiography makes it clear that 'his action was aimed at reminding Muslims that the Quran did not reach us through written text only but also through a chain of transmission that goes back to the Prophet'.[154] Tellingly, Quran memorisation was taught by advanced disciples within their respective circles, but the ijaza was issued by one person only: Sheikh al-Kurdi, who had the highest sanad within the movement. During his very long life, al-Kurdi thus signed hundreds of pre-printed ijazat for new memorisers as part of what would be called the 'Quranic renaissance'.[155]

Profoundly inspired by Sufi conceptions – al-Rifa'i himself had been initiated into the Naqshbandi tradition[156] – Jama'at Zayd promoted a comprehensive conception of education (*tarbiya*). Understood as both

[151] Interview with Haytham al-Malih, Damascus, 13 May 2008, and al-Hawari.
[152] Qira'at differ from each other in terms of pronunciation and the division of the suras.
[153] 'Al-Shaykh 'Abd al-Karim al-Rifa'i wa masiratuhu', no. 8.
[154] Ibid.
[155] *Hayat al-qari' al-jami' al-shaykh Muhi al-Din Abu al-Hasan al-Kurdi* [Life of the Quran reader Muhi al-Din Abu al-Hasan al-Kurdi] (Damascus: Markaz Zayd, 2006), VCD.
[156] Rifa'i, 'Durus min hayat', no. 2.

moral and spiritual, it was based on a mimetical relationship between the disciple and his master, who was supposed to be not only an expert, but first and foremost a 'model that is close to God and brings people closer to God' (*qidwa rabbaniyya*).[157] Such principles constituted the foundations of the informal hierarchy of the movement.

Although Zayd's structure was very similar to that of the Sufi brotherhoods, it nevertheless stood out from them by also being a social movement in the modern sense:[158] its members were not only in a posture of *consumption* (of spiritual goods), but also of *mobilisation*, each follower – not only the leaders – bearing responsibility for achievement of the group's aims. Indeed, al-Rifa'i had ambitions that were broader than bringing the literate youth back to the path of Islam: by providing graduates of secular disciplines with informal, 'traditional' religious training, he allowed them to officiate in the mosques as volunteers while remaining involved in a mundane activity as a 'pious example' (*qidwat saliha*). The sheikh reportedly used to repeat:

I do not want to grant you diplomas that will allow you to be hired by the Ministry of Awqaf or to teach religion in schools. I want to train a physician who leads the prayer in front of the *mihrab*, an engineer who preaches on Friday, a merchant who calls to God in his shop.[159]

Provided they had the required aptitudes, disciples could aspire to more than becoming part of the 'lower clergy': by attending advanced study circles with prominent scholars, they themselves had the opportunity to be recognised as ulama by their elders. Al-Rifa'i's hagiographers write that 'he wanted a physician that would be a faqih at the same time, and an engineer that would be a hadith scholar too'.[160] Zayd's leadership was therefore composed of both formally trained ulama (al-Rifa'i's first two successors were Azharites)[161] and graduates of secular faculties. Of the four most

[157] Sariya al-Rifa'i, 'al-Qidwat al-rabbaniyya asas al-da'wat al-islamiyya [The rabbanian model is the foundation of da'wa] (www.sadazaid.com, 5 April 2008).
[158] Social movements are 'sustained and intentional efforts to foster or retard social changes, primarily outside the normal institutional channels encouraged by authorities': George Ritzer and J. Michael Ryan (eds.), *The Concise Encyclopedia of Sociology* (Chichester and Malden, MA: Wiley-Blackwell, 2011), 565.
[159] 'Al-Shaykh 'Abd al-Karim al-Rifa'i wa masiratuhu', no. 18.
[160] Ibid., no. 4.
[161] Muhammad 'Awad (1936–2009), a weaver who resumed his studies at his master's instigation, and Shawkat al-Jibali (1932–89), a Palestinian refugee (interview with a former member of Zayd, Damascus, 29 July 2007; Mundhir al-Jibali, 'al-Da'iya al-shaykh Shawkat al-Jibali' [The sheikh and preacher Shawkat al-Jibali] (www.sadazaid.com, 19 April 2008).

prominent figures of Zayd today, three – including Na'im al-'Arqsusi, the aforementioned hadith specialist, and Usama al-Rifa'i, the founder's elder son and the movement's scholarly reference point – have no other diploma than a licence in Arabic literature.[162] As for the second-rank leadership, it includes many engineers, physicians, and pharmacists.

Al-Rifa'i's efforts helped redefine the boundaries of the ulama: on the one hand, it widened these boundaries through the integration of 'lay' elites; on the other, it rigidified them in a traditionalist fashion – at a time when the ijaza system was threatened by the institutionalisation of specialised religious teaching, Zayd was successfully promoting the idea that genuine sacred knowledge was not found in schools, but in the study circles of the ulama. Importantly, this definition was defended and promoted through the foremost representatives of 'modernity': the graduates of secular institutions.

Study circles were also the main setting for the movement's efforts at political awareness building (*taw'iya*). Followers were encouraged to read modern Islamic writers such as the Syrian Sa'id Ramadan al-Buti, the Indian Abu al-Hasan Ali al-Nadwi, the Pakistani Abu al-A'la al-Mawdudi (founder of the Jamaat-i-Islami), and Fathi Yakan (an ideologue of the Lebanese Muslim Brothers), and their ideas were discussed within the halqa. A senior member of Zayd explains that such readings were intended to make up for the absence of ideological production within the movement itself:

I subscribe to the educational method of Sheikh 'Abd al-Karim al-Rifa'i, but he was not a thinker [*mufakkir*]. From that point of view, my main influences were [the Muslim Brothers] Mustafa al-Siba'i, Hasan al-Banna, and Sayyid Qutb. I was also reading the journal of the Syrian Muslim Brothers, *Hadarat al-Islam*, and that of the Kuwaiti branch, *al-Mujtama'*.[163]

A former member describes Zayd's approach as being 'halfway between traditional Sufi brotherhoods and the Muslim Brothers', because its goal was 'the development of the individual in terms of religious knowledge, spirituality, and some [social and political] thought [*shwayyet min al-fikr*]'.[164] The supervised readings of modern Islamic authors were thus

---

[162] The third is Nadhir Maktabi (b. 1949). Sariya al-Rifa'i (b. 1948), 'Abd al-Karim's second
        son, graduated from al-Azhar but, tellingly, his own disciples present him as a less out-
        standing scholar than his brother Usama (interview with his son 'Ammar, Damascus, 17
        June 2007).
[163] Interview with an anonymous source, Damascus, 10 May 2008.
[164] Interview with an anonymous source, Damascus, 16 July 2006.

aimed at inculcating in followers an 'Islamic' understanding of the realities of their time, but the mere fact that they took place did not mean that Zayd was a political organisation.

During the liberal era, al-Rifa'i forbade his students to become affiliated to political parties or to run for election. This was not inspired by an outward rejection of the political game, however, since the sheikh himself maintained 'cordial' relations with some politicians, and overtly lent his support to conservative and Islamist electoral candidates. Al-Rifa'i's position was driven by a concern for *functional distinction*, the idea that Zayd's fundamental mission – education – would be endangered if it had to be carried out in concert with direct political involvement, which involves taking tactical rather than morally principled stances.[165]

After 1963, al-Rifa'i eschewed any cooperation with the Ba'thist regime despite pressures that culminated in a street attack on him in 1965.[166] During that period, he reportedly addressed his disciples by comparing their role with that of the first Muslims – that is, as the only source of light in an era of darkness:

My children, if those people accuse you of 'reaction' because you go to the mosque, then you should raise your head up, because your return is the return to Truth and to the principles of Islam[167] ... that have cleansed Muslim society from the stains of pre-Islamic barbarity [*jahiliyya*], which our enemies try to restore. Tell them: 'we are the ones who held the lantern of Guidance on the day the entire Umma held the bludgeon of tyranny, and we told people: "this is the Way".'[168]

In such a context, the mosque was not seen as a mere venue for education, but also as an alternative social space where followers should spend most of their free time (an average of thirty hours a week),[169] in order to recreate the embryo of an 'authentically' Islamic society.[170] For instance, Zayd set up its own recreational centre in order to allow its members to do sports without 'mixing with the evil society'.[171] It is difficult here not to draw a parallel with the Turkish *cemaat* such as the Nurcu,[172]

---

[165] 'Al-Shaykh 'Abd al-Karim al-Rifa'i wa masiratuhu', no. 19; interviews with al-Malih and al-Hawari.
[166] Interview with al-Malih.
[167] In Arabic, the words 'reaction' (*raj'iyya*) and 'return' (*ruju'*) share a common root.
[168] 'Al-Shaykh 'Abd al-Karim al-Rifa'i wa masiratuhu', no. 10.
[169] Interview with a former member of Zayd, Damascus, 17 May 2006.
[170] Interview with Usama al-Rifa'i, Damascus, 5 March 2007.
[171] 'Al-Shaykh 'Abd al-Karim al-Rifa'i wa masiratuhu', no. 11.
[172] A Turkish word deriving from the Arabic *jama'at*.

Sufi-inspired 'communities' that emerged in reaction to Kemalist secularism, which Thierry Zarcone describes as 'a reconstruction of the Umma,
a micro-society governed by sharia'.[173]

The Expansion of the 'Educational Method'

In the 1960s, al-Rifaʿiʿs movement expanded beyond its cradle in Qabr
ʿAtke and established itself in the newly built middle-class quarters of
the north-east of Damascus,[174] as well as in neighbouring villages where
missionaries were sent every Friday.[175] Zayd subsequently spread to
the western bourgeois districts of the capital,[176] and to the environs of
the university, with the result that it controlled a total of several dozen
mosques. This rapid expansion was facilitated by al-Rifaʿiʿs popularity
among merchants, who called for his disciples to animate the mosques
whose construction they had financed.[177] The sheikh's privileged relations
with the private sector allowed him to found several charities,[178] and also
to build three giant mosques equipped with special rooms to accommo-
date study circles.[179]

The movement's remarkable expansion at the local level contrasted
with its inability to spread to the rest of the country.[180] However, Zayd's
educational method was widely emulated by other clerical groups and, as
already mentioned, by the Muslim Brothers.[181]

A sister organisation to Zayd emerged in Aleppo in the mid-1960s.
Jamaʿat Abi Dharr – here also, the name refers to the mosque of the
founder – was founded by Ahmad ʿIzz al-Din al-Bayanuni (1913–75),
the son of ʿIsa (1873–1943), a prominent ʿalim who, like al-Nabhan,
had been a disciple of the Naqshbandi sheikh Abu al-Nasr.[182] A founding member, in 1935, of what would later become the local branch of

[173] Thierry Zarcone, *La Turquie moderne et l'islam* (Paris: Flammarion, 2004), 146.
[174] Al-Qusur, al-Qassaʿ, Abbasids, al-Tijara, al-ʿAdawi, and Mezraʿa.
[175] 'Al-Shaykh ʿAbd al-Karim al-Rifaʿi wa masiratuhu', no. 9.
[176] Mezze, al-Malki, and Baramke.
[177] Interview with a leader of Zayd, Damascus, 11 April 2008.
[178] See Chapter 4.
[179] Al-Iman (Mezraʿa), al-Hamza wa-l-ʿAbbas (Abbasids), and the mother-mosque, Zayd
      bin Thabit. All of them were inaugurated in 1969–70.
[180] The only exception was the al-Qassab institute of Dayr ʿAtiya (Qalamun), which was
      taken over by Zayd in the late 1970s ('al-Shaykh ʿAbd al-Karim al-Rifaʿi wa masir-
      atuhu', no. 16).
[181] 'Al-Shaykh ʿAbd al-Karim al-Rifaʿi wa masiratuhu', no. 13; interviews with al-Hawari
      and Muhammad al-Zuʿbi, Damascus, 8 May 2007.
[182] On ʿIsa, see Weismann, 'The Hidden Hand', 55.

the Muslim Brothers,[183] Ahmad 'Izz al-Din eventually distanced himself from this movement because of diverging aspirations. As a graduate of a teacher-training college, he held himself responsible for bridging the gap between 'the ulama and the sheikhs' with whom he had grown up, and 'the new, secularly trained generation'.[184] In 1968, harassment by the authorities forced him to resign from his position as a secondary school Arabic teacher.[185] From then on, he devoted himself entirely to writing booklets of religious education,[186] as well as to the development of Jama'at Abi Dharr, whose method and social profile were very similar to Zayd's.[187] In 1975, when al-Bayanuni's sons inherited the leadership of the organisation from their deceased father, they commanded several thousand disciples and sympathisers.[188]

CONCLUSION

From the late nineteenth century onwards, the development of secular schooling led the families that had hitherto dominated the Syrian clergy to turn away from religious careers. As a result, newcomers of petty/middle-bourgeois and foreign origin came to constitute a growing proportion of the ulama. Some of these newcomers were later represented by their hagiographers as the fathers of a 'renaissance of knowledge' following a period of ignorance and impiety.

This 'renaissance' was not about doctrinal innovation, but was rather a revivalist movement focusing on the encouragement of religious observance through new modes of preaching. The most prominent sheikhs of that period were thus first and foremost educators and leaders of men, the founders of institutions and jama'at, informal structures modelled on Sufi brotherhoods and inspired by a collective and organised project of social transformation – in other words, of social movements.

This innovation significantly changed the ulama's logic of identification. The traditional Sufi orders were not cohesive entities but mere spiritual traditions whose leadership underwent a constant process of

---

[183] 'Abd al-Majid al-Bayanuni, *Ahmad 'Izz al-Din al-Bayanuni: al-da'iya al-murabbi (1913–1975)* [Ahmad 'Izz al-Din al-Bayanuni: the preacher and educator (1913–1975)] (Damascus: Dar al-Qalam, 2006), 56.

[184] Ibid., 9–10.

[185] Ibid., 45–50.

[186] For instance *al-Iman bi-l-llah* [Faith in God] (Cairo: n.p., 1987).

[187] Interview with Abu al-Fath al-Bayanuni, Aleppo, 20 April 2008.

[188] Interviews with Abu al-Fath al-Bayanuni and a former member of Abi Dharr, Damascus, 15 July 2006.

fragmentation due to the fact that there were always several candidates for succession from the same master. Therefore, in terms of collective identity, one belonged to the group formed by the followers of a particular living sheikh rather than to the 'Naqshbandiyya' or the 'Shadhiliyya'.[189] On the contrary, although they are not immune to internal rivalries, as will be seen in the second chapter, modern jama'at constitute more tangible identification groups, either because they possess an institutional basis or because their members share the method of action developed by the founding sheikh.

In the face of Westernisation and secularisation, the Syrian ulama proposed three kinds of answers. In the style of Christian congregations, the Damascene association al-Gharra' set up general Muslim communal schools. However, faced with the unmatchable capacities of the state in the educational realm it faltered in the late 1950s.

A second strategy consisted in institutionalising the training of young clerics in order to reinforce religious supervision over society. The creation of private Islamic institutes in the mid-twentieth century also allowed conservative clerics to ensure the survival of the traditional conception of religious teaching. The latter was indeed threatened by the bureaucratic and utilitarian ideals governing the state-run seminaries and the faculty of sharia set up at the instigation of reformist scholars. Under the Ba'th, the guardians of tradition were facilitated in their endeavour by the regime's lack of interest in specifically clerical training, which translated into a refusal to nationalise private institutes.

The institutionalisation of specialised religious teaching in Syria thus followed a singular path. In Egypt, this institutionalisation was imposed on the conservative ulama by a modernising state;[190] in Saudi Arabia, it was engineered by the ulama themselves as a result of their proximity with the political leadership;[191] in Ba'thist Syria, the conservative clergy were allowed to play a prominent role in that process *because the state did not want to be involved in it.*

Although some of the founders of private Islamic seminaries acquired considerable popularity and even political influence, they lacked the means to attract the graduates of secular schooling: the latter, when they were not actively anti-religious, were more naturally attracted to

---

[189] Paolo Pinto, 'Mystical Bodies: Ritual, Experience and the Embodiment of Sufism in Syria', Ph.D. thesis, Boston University, 2002, 64.

[190] Zeghal, *Gardiens de l'islam.*

[191] Mouline, *Les Clercs de l'islam,* 179.

the sophisticated intellectuals heading the Muslim Brothers than to the conservative mashyakha.

Such was the challenge taken up by the advocates of a third strategy, known as 'mosque work', which consisted in providing informal religious training to lay people, and more particularly to secondary school and university students. Mosque-based teaching had always existed, but the novelty here was its methodical organisation – study circles were turned into cells – that nevertheless coexisted with a traditional, Sufi-inspired conception of the transmission of religious knowledge.

By skilfully exploiting the resources of tradition in order to adapt to a changing society, informal education movements constituted the biggest challenge faced by the advocates of secularism. Indeed, by entrenching themselves in specialised religious institutes and turning them into the strongholds of Islam, some ulama were de facto acknowledging the process of secularisation, in the sense of an increasingly clear separation between the 'religious' and the 'secular'.[192] Such an implicit admission of defeat was rejected by the founders of movements such as Jama'at Zayd, whose goal was to make the life-blood of a changing society – its physicians, pharmacists, engineers, and schoolteachers – the spearhead of re-Islamisation. The social profile of these groups was therefore very similar to that of more strictly political movements such as the Muslim Brothers, with the result that they were inevitably dragged into conflict with the regime during the 1979–82 uprising.

[192] For this process in Pakistan, see Zaman, *The Ulama*, 84.

2

Landscapes after the Battle (1979–2007)

In 1975, the Syrian authorities arrested Marwan Hadid (1934–76), a Muslim Brother from Hama who had advocated armed struggle for a decade. Hadid, who would soon die in custody, had just published a pamphlet in which he denounced the 'cowardice' of the ulama, telling them that their attitude would not protect them from the blows of the regime, or from the wrath of the Almighty:

Here is what I fear for you: that if the worshippers of God launch the struggle against His enemies, you behave as spectators, without fighting, and therefore the enemies of God will crush you while you are in your homes, and then you will go to Hell.[1]

Hadid's prophecy proved to be partially correct. When the uprising erupted, only a minority of the sheikhs wholeheartedly sided with the armed opposition, but all of them suffered to varying degrees from state repression, except the most loyal supporters of the regime. Indeed, since it was increasingly unwilling to integrate the religious elite into the state apparatus, the regime chose instead to redraw the country's religious map by supporting loyal, but privately funded, clerical networks.

This policy was not entirely successful, however, which highlights the limits of state action in the religious field. Whereas the post-uprising reshuffling has proved durable in Aleppo, where certain clerical networks were bled dry by state repression, in Damascus the end of the twentieth

---

[1] Marwan Hadid, 'Nida' ila al-'ulama' al-'amilin wa-l-muslimin al-mukhlisin wa-l-jama'at al-islamiyya' [Call to the active scholars, the sincere Muslims, and the Islamic groups] (www.almaqdese.net [written in 1975]).

century saw an impressive comeback by religious forces that had been apparently eliminated after 1982, but nevertheless managed to revive thanks to the depth of their social roots. As a result, the regime had no choice but to reach out to these former enemies.

THE ULAMA IN THE UPRISING

I am not proposing to give a detailed account of the 1979–82 Islamist uprising, which has already been studied in depth.[2] Let us start with a brief reminder, however. This episode is often wrongly reduced to a struggle between the regime and the 'Muslim Brothers'. This misconception has a double origin: first, the official propaganda of the early 1980s used the term *ikhwan* (brothers) to describe all its Islamic opponents; second, the (real) Brothers in exile managed to monopolise the representation of the Islamic opposition thanks to the support of their international networks and the anti-Syrian Arab regimes (Iraq, Jordan).

In reality, the Muslim Brothers did not seriously engage in violent action until the crisis turned into open warfare in June 1980. Moreover, they fared poorly in that realm because of their lack of preparation.[3] Most of the military operations were actually carried out by the Fighting Vanguard (al-Tali'a al-Muqatila), a splinter group founded by followers of Marwan Hadid. After Hadid's death, his supporters organised attacks against a growing number of state officials and pro-regime figures, including religious scholars such as Muhammad al-Shami (1923–80), the right-hand man of Sheikh al-Nabhan; Rashid al-Khatib (1912–81),[4] the preacher of the Umayyad Mosque; and Salah 'Uqla (d. 1985), a sheikh of the al-Gharra' association, who survived his wounds for a couple of years.[5]

The first major operation of the Fighting Vanguard, and the starting-point of the uprising, was the June 1979 massacre of eighty-three Alawite cadets at Aleppo Artillery School. Thereafter the pace of attacks

[2] Lobmeyer, *Opposition und Widerstand*; Jamal Barut, 'Suriyya: usul wa ta'arrujat al-sira' bayn al-madrasatayn at-taqlidiyya wa al-radikaliyya' [Syria: origins and twists and turns of the conflict between the traditional and radical schools], in *al-Ahzab wa-l-harakat wal-jama'at al-islamiyya* [Islamic parties, movements, and groups], ed. Jamal Barut and Faysal Darraj (Damascus: Arab Center for Strategic Studies, 2000), 255–324.

[3] 'Umar 'Abd al-Hakim (aka Abu Mus'ab al-Suri), *al-Thawra al-islamiyya al-jihadiyya fi Suriyya* [The jihadi Islamic revolution in Syria] (n.p.: n.p., n.d.), 106–7.

[4] Ayman al-Sharbaji (leader of the Fighting Vanguard in Damascus in the early 1980s), 'Mudawwinat' [Log book], no. 29 (www.sooryoon.net, 18 November 2010).

[5] Abaza, *'Ulama' Dimashq*, 124–5.

accelerated, and security forces were pitted against demonstrators in increasingly violent incidents in the towns of the north. In June 1980, hundreds of Islamist detainees were executed in the prison in Palmyra in retaliation for a failed assassination attempt against the head of state. The next month, the parliament voted in Law No. 49, which provided for the death penalty merely for membership of the Muslim Brothers. The year 1981 was marked by the executions of hundreds of people by security forces in northern cities as well as by deadly bombings in the capital. The last act took place in Hama, where the February 1982 uprising ended with the partial destruction of the city and the killing of thousands of its inhabitants. Subsequently, violence decreased gradually as sweeps led to the dismantling of the last armed Islamist cells.

The ulama were secondary protagonists in the crisis itself, but their role upstream of the events was not negligible. Indeed, they had been the primary educators of the 'generation of the awakening' (*jil al-sahwa*) that was now rising against the Ba'th. The ulama gave birth to the insurgents from a spiritual standpoint, and also sometimes from a biological one, as illustrated by the tragic examples of sheikhs Ahmad Ikbazli (1908–88), a Kurd from Damascus, and Muhammad al-Hajjar (1920–2007), the son-in-law of Ahmad al-Bayanuni, both of whom lost three sons in the events.[6]

The Jama'at: Cradles of the Armed Groups

The Islamist opposition recruited extensively among the study circles of the ulama, particularly those whose da'wa was aimed at young educated members of the middle class, which constituted the majority of Islamic militants at the time.[7] Educational groups provided the Fighting Vanguard with some of their leading figures: the Damascene branch of the organisation was headed by Ayman al-Sharbaji, an engineer and former student of Muhammad al-Zu'bi (b. 1933), the sheikh of the jama'a based in the al-Daqqaq mosque of the Midan;[8] in Aleppo, the main leaders of the

---

[6] Ikbazli died in Damascus and al-Hajjar in Medina. See Majd Makki, 'al-Shaykh Ahmad Raf'at Ikbazli Zadeh' (www.odabasham.net, 22 January 2011); Majd Makki, 'al-Shaykh Muhammad al-Hajjar' (www.islamsyria.com, 25 January 2007).

[7] Lobmeyer, *Opposition und Widerstand*, 394.

[8] Interview with an anonymous source, Damascus, 28 July 2007. Al-Zu'bi inherited the mosque from his father 'Abd al-Rahman (1902–69), a disciple of Ali al-Daqr who was born in the Hauran. Muhammad graduated in sharia and secular law from the University of Damascus (interview with al-Zu'bi).

Islamic militants were Husni 'Abu (a teacher of Islamic education) and
'Adnan 'Uqla (an engineer), who were not only the followers but also the
sons-in-law of Sheikh Tahir Khayr Allah (1922–89),[9] the preacher at the
al-Rawda mosque in the wealthy neighbourhood of Mogambo.

These figures are emblematic of a broader phenomenon, which an
Islamic intellectual describes as the fact that the educational jama'at were
no less than the 'cradle' of radical Islam at the time.[10] These groups played
a crucial role in the development of many young Syrians into opposition
activists: first, by building the political consciousness of their members,
with the result that their ranks were especially susceptible to the ferment
that overcame so many of the Muslim youth at the time of the Iranian
revolution; second, because the similar sociological profiles of their members facilitated movements between educational and political–military
groups. In his log book, the leader of the Fighting Vanguard in Damascus
explains that in 1980 his quest for new recruits led him to reconnect with
former brothers-in-arms who, following the death of founder Marwan
Hadid, had abandoned clandestine action to focus on the education of
teenagers in a mosque in the Midan.[11]

From 1979, the base of the jama'at radicalised in a context of increasing violence between militant Islamists and the state. Sheikh Muhammad
al-Zu'bi remembers:

I was aware of the fact that among my disciples, who were about five hundred at
the time, twenty or so were influenced by the ideas of Sayyid Qutb and wanted
to join the Muslim Brothers. Therefore, I gathered all my students in the mosque,
each halqa before me in single file, with the heads of halqa in front. I told them:
'Here we teach the Quran and its exegesis, the hadith and its explanation, and
the elements of fiqh upon which the ulama have agreed. He who does not like
this, he can leave'.[12]

This call to order did not prevent defections, nor did the wait-and-see
policy adopted by the leadership of Zayd, some of whose followers eventually joined the armed groups under the influence of a second-rank
leader of the movement. According to a witness:

With violence intensifying, members were asking their sheikhs what was their
position regarding the Fighting Vanguard. The sheikhs wanted neither to openly

[9] Thomas Mayer, 'The Islamic Opposition in Syria, 1961–1982', *Orient* 24, no. 4 (1983),
   589–609, at 594.
[10] Interview with an anonymous source, Damascus, May 2008.
[11] Al-Sharbaji, 'Mudawwinat', no. 16.
[12] Interview with al-Zu'bi.

oppose the regime nor to defend it. Consequently, they decided to prohibit merely asking the question, under penalty of expulsion from the group! This resulted in a split: the most menial obeyed and the others were poached by a teacher from one of Zayd's mosques in [the bourgeois neighbourhood of] Malki, who had joined the insurgents. When the regime realised this, the sheikhs of the movement had no choice but to go into exile.[13]

The case of Zayd partially invalidates the Marxist analysis proposed by Hanna Batatu, who explains the quietism of religious actors such as the al-Gharra' association by their degree of proximity to the trading community of Damascus, which had been favoured by the regime.[14] Yet the fact that Zayd was the most popular religious group among the merchants of the capital did not prevent it from being dragged into the conflict. In fact, the relevant factor here was not the economy, but culture, since the secularly educated youth of the jama'at, not the students of the sharia institutes, was the part of the population that was the most receptive to modern Islamist ideology.

An economic approach nevertheless remains relevant, to explain the comparatively milder state repression in Damascus, where, for the reasons expounded by Batatu, the opposition gathered less support among the population.[15]

The Scars of Repression

With the exception of Hama, where such senior religious figures as the Rifa'i Sufi master Mahmud al-Shuqfa (1898–1979) and the Mufti of the city Bashir al-Murad (1920–82) were killed by security forces, few Syrian ulama lost their lives during the events. However, many of them had to take the path of exile.

In the first weeks of the uprising, the authorities had given leaders of educational groups the responsibility of negotiating with the armed groups,[16] but they rapidly came to suspect them of double dealing. During the wave of protest that swept Aleppo in March 1980, Tahir Khayr Allah and the leader of Jama'at Abi Dharr, Abu al-Nasr al-Bayanuni, narrowly escaped arrest by fleeing to Jordan. Dozens of their followers were then

[13] Interview with an anonymous source, Damascus, July 2007.
[14] Batatu, *Syria's Peasantry*, 261.
[15] Batatu, 'Syria's Muslim Brethren', 16.
[16] Al-Tahir Ibrahim, 'al-Jama'at al-islamiyya bayn al-ihtiwa' wa-l-ilgha' [Islamic groups between restraint and self-effacement], *Majallat al-'Asr*, 28 June 2007; 'Abd al-Hakim, *al-Thawra al-islamiyya*, 104.

interned in the prison in Palmyra, where they perished in the massacre of June 1980.[17] That same month the Damascene ulama were received by President al-Asad, who expressed his anger at the involvement of some of their followers in the armed uprising.[18] The following year, several sheikhs of Zayd – including al-Rifa'i's two sons as well as his *khalifa* (appointed successor), Muhammad 'Awad – took refuge in Jeddah.

The case of the al-Bayanuni family illustrates a fact that contributed to increased repression against the Aleppian clergy: its proximity with political Islam in the strict sense. Indeed, Abu al-Nasr al-Bayanuni was the brother of Ali Sadr al-Din (b. 1938), one of the main executives of the Muslim Brothers. Likewise, the respected hadith scholar 'Abd al-Fattah Abu Ghudda (1917–97) was a leading figure in the movement. Although he had left Syria in 1967, he had retained many students there, especially among the teachers of the Sha'baniyya institute: as a consequence, although the founder of the madrasa, Abdullah Siraj al-Din, had always been strictly apolitical, he was forced to take refuge in Medina from 1980 to 1983,[19] while the most respected teachers of his school never came back to their homeland.[20]

Exile deprived the religious landscape of Aleppo of many of its other pillars: in addition to the aforementioned Muhammad al-Hajjar, the grand Shadhili master of northern Syria 'Abd al-Qadir 'Isa (1920–91) took up residence in Turkey, and Fawzi Fayd Allah (b. 1925), the former dean of the faculty of sharia at the University of Damascus, settled in Kuwait.[21] Not all of them were subject to arrest warrants: sometimes they were seeking only to protect themselves from the unpredictable fist of the state.[22]

The repression of the uprising accelerated the 'turban drain' that had affected Aleppo since the 1960s, a decade which, in addition to the departure of Abu Ghudda, witnessed that of Mustafa al-Zarqa, another leading member of the Muslim Brothers, Muhammad Ali al-Sabuni (b. 1930), who became a renowned Quran exegete in Saudi Arabia, and Abu al-Fath al-Bayanuni (b. 1940), Ahmad's son and Abi Dharr's reference in matters of fiqh.

[17] Anonymous source, written message to the author, 15 July 2006.
[18] Sharbaji, 'Mudawwinat', no. 19.
[19] 'Itr, *Safahat*, 94, 103.
[20] Abdullah 'Alwan, Muhammad 'Awwama, Ahmad Qallash, Zuhayr al-Nasir, Mahmud Mira (interviews with anonymous sources, Aleppo, February–March 2006).
[21] Muhammad Yasir al-Qudmani, *Muhammad Fawzi Fayd Allah* (Damascus: Dar al-Qalam, 2002).
[22] Interview with al-Hawari.

This phenomenon was not only related to the political context but also to the narrowness of the local labour market. Indeed, the Ba'thists' centralist policies and distrust of the northern metropolis prevented the establishment of any institution of higher Islamic education, be it public or private, until the opening of the faculty of sharia in 2006. Such a context often led the brightest young scholars to migrate to the University of Damascus (Ibrahim al-Salqini, Nur al-Din 'Itr, Ahmad al-Hajji al-Kurdi), and also to foreign countries, particularly the Gulf monarchies.[23] As a result, at the time of my fieldwork in Syria, there were at least thirty senior Aleppian clerics holding Ph.D.s in religious sciences who were established abroad, compared to a dozen for Damascus.

REGAINING CONTROL OF THE RELIGIOUS FIELD: THE 'WEAK STATE STRATEGY'

The Ba'th of the 1980s was the most authoritarian regime Syria had ever experienced. While state terror definitively eradicated the remnants of the Muslim Brothers and the Fighting Vanguard,[24] al-Asad's personality cult reached unprecedented levels – the President was now said to rule 'for eternity'. This regime only acquired the trappings of totalitarianism, however, after the project of creating a 'new man' disappeared for good under the rubble of Hama. Society was no longer expected to transform itself in a 'progressive' fashion, but to obey.[25] Although in the short term, the new phase of al-Asad's rule was synonymous with further exclusion of the ulama from the state, the regime's gradual post-ideological turn nonetheless held out the prospect of future reintegration.

The regime relied on a two-pronged strategy to regain control of the religious field. Its first component was, of course, coercion. During the dark 1980s, the most benign religious activities were subject to drastic limitations. Many mosques kept their doors closed between prayers,

---

[23] Among many examples: al-Salqini was the dean of the faculty of Islamic studies in Dubai from 1989 to 2004; al-Kurdi has worked for the Kuwaiti religious administration since 1993; Faruq al-Nabhan (b. 1940), the grandson of Muhammad, chaired the Dar al-Hadith in Rabat from 1977 to 2000; 'Abd al-Majid Ma'az (b. 1944) spent most of his career at Saudi universities.

[24] The only political Islamic movement that managed to retain a limited underground presence in Syria after that period was the Islamic Liberation Party (Hizb al-Tahrir al-Islami), a non-violent group founded in the 1950s that calls for the immediate restoration of the Caliphate.

[25] Lisa Wedeen, *Ambiguities of Domination: Politics, Rhetoric, and Symbols in Contemporary Syria* (Chicago: University of Chicago Press, 1999).

which prevented the holding of lessons, dhikr assemblies, and celebrations of the Mawlid.

The second pillar of the state's strategy was more surprising. Although one might have expected a revival of the process of institutionalisation of the religious field, what actually occurred was exactly the opposite. While discouraging the intensification of religious observance in society (in 1982, for instance, a decree banned the wearing of headscarves in schools),[26] the authorities could not afford to ignore it, especially the growing demand for religious education. In order not to entirely abandon the latter to private networks such as the elusive but influential Qubaysiyyat, a female upper-class movement relying on home-based study circles,[27] the regime relied on 'subcontractors' selected from among the most loyal clerical factions.

The Withering Away of the Religious Bureaucracy

The regime's campaign to defeat the Islamic uprising involved unprecedented budgetary outlays on the part of the Ministry of Awqaf, whose real expenditures tripled between 1980 and 1984.[28] However, the bulk of the new financial resources were used to increase the meagre salaries of clerics and subsidise the construction of mosques,[29] rather than develop the religious bureaucracy.

The only state-run religious structure that was created at this time was the network of organisations known as the Hafiz al-Asad Institutes for the Memorisation of the Quran (Ma'ahid Hafiz al-Asad li-Tahfiz al-Qur'an).[30] Although they were placed under the close scrutiny of the mukhabarat, these 'institutes' were not part of a process of bureaucratisation: in reality they were informal study circles organised in mosques under the supervision of volunteers, with only the director (usually the imam of the mosque) receiving a small stipend. Asked about the role of the state administration in the management of his 'institute', one of these directors answered:

'Institutes Hafiz al-Asad', it's just a name written on student identification cards and the copper plate that hangs on the wall of the mosque. As for the rest

---

[26] Zisser, 'Syria, the Ba'th Regime', 43.
[27] See Ardito, 'Les cercles féminins'.
[28] *Al-Majmu'a al-ihsa'iyya*, 1980–90.
[29] Batatu, *Syria's Peasantry*, 260.
[30] See Böttcher, *Syrische Religionspolitik*, 117–19.

(recruiting teachers, organising courses and summer schools), *we* [i.e. the Sufi brotherhood based in the mosque] take care of it.[31]

In addition, we have seen in the previous chapter that circles for the memorisation of the Quran were not a creation of the state, but had multiplied since the 1950s through private initiatives. The 'foundation' of the Hafiz al-Asad Institutes was therefore a mere official labelling of pre-existing structures in order to symbolically underline the President's reverence for the Holy Book.

An even more striking illustration of the regime's unwillingness to develop its religious bureaucracy despite – or, actually, because of – the bloody warning of 1979–82 is the fact that the size of the administrative staff of the Ministry of Awqaf was reduced by no less than two-thirds during the two decades that followed the uprising.[32] This decision was presumably due to the regime's lack of confidence in its religious functionaries. Indeed, during the 1970s, suspensions, resignations, and forced transfers were common within the Ministry of Awqaf,[33] while several cases of defection were recorded during the uprising – the most notable being, in Aleppo, those of Abi Dharr's leader Abu al-Nasr al-Bayanuni, who was also the director of the city's sharia high school, and Abdullah al-Salqini (b. 1936), the brother of Ibrahim, who went into exile in 1982 after two years as the head of the local religious administration.[34]

Lacking economic and symbolic resources, the post-uprising Syrian regime had few transformative capabilities and was thus less able than ever to shape a religious bureaucracy in its own image. In such circumstances, strengthening the Ministry of Awqaf was likely to lead, as in Egypt from the 1970s, to the development of a powerful religious lobby inside the state apparatus.[35] Such a phenomenon would have been particularly destabilising in a political configuration dominated by a secular-minded Alawite military elite. This is probably why the regime decided to rely on private organisations in managing the religious field.

---

[31] Interview with an anonymous source, Aleppo, July 2006.
[32] There were 296 statutory civil servants in 1978, 237 in 1984, and 103 in 2000 (*al-Majmu'a al-ihsa'iyya*, 1979–85; figures given by the Minister of Awqaf, all4syria. info, 19 August 2009). On the ministry's structural lack of human resources, see Böttcher, *Syrische Religionspolitik*, 60–84.
[33] Böttcher, *Syrische Religionspolitik*, 80–3.
[34] Interview with Ali Sadr al-Din al-Bayanuni.
[35] See Zeghal, *Gardiens de l'islam*.

The Time of the 'Subcontractors'

In the drive to reassert its authority over the religious scene, the regime naturally turned to clerical networks that had shown unfailing loyalty during the crisis. In Damascus, the brotherhood of Grand Mufti Ahmad Kaftaru and the group of Sheikh Salih al-Farfur were allowed to develop private higher Islamic institutes, while Sa'id Ramadan al-Buti, a renowed academic and writer, was endowed with the delicate task of conferring religious legitimacy on the regime. In Aleppo, most key religious positions were granted to disciples of Muhammad al-Nabhan.

The Kaftaru and al-Farfur Families between State Support and Succession Quarrels

Rather than strengthen the perceivedly unreliable faculty of sharia at the University of Damascus, the regime allowed two Damascene clerical factions to establish private higher Islamic institutes for which the Syrian state bore no funding responsibilities: in 1982 the Kaftariyya created the Abu al-Nur Islamic Centre,[36] which in 2004 was renamed the Sheikh Ahmad Kaftaru Academy (Mujamma' al-Shaykh Ahmad Kaftaru), and in 1991 followers of Salih al-Farfur opened a 'section of specialisation' within the al-Fath institute.[37]

By doing this, the state did not 'encourage' anything, but simply entrusted the most loyal religious forces with the task of responding to a genuine social demand. By the 1970s, the Kaftariyya, al-Fath, and the Sha'baniyya in Aleppo had developed plans to set up colleges that would cater for the graduates of private secondary Islamic institutes, who were not admitted to the faculty of sharia and therefore had to continue their studies abroad, at al-Azhar or the Islamic University of Medina.[38]

Despite the fact that the degrees they awarded were not recognised by the state, with the result that their holders were not allowed to teach in public schools, the new higher institutes were successful, enrolling respectively 8,000 and 4,300 students in 2008.[39] With salaries up to ten times those of public schools, they also allowed their managers to become the

---

[36] Böttcher, *Syrische Religionspolitik*, 147–225.

[37] Interview with Husam al-Din al-Farfur, Damascus, 28 June 2006.

[38] 'Nubdha 'an ma'had al-Fath al-islami' [Note about the al-Fath Islamic Institute] (www.alfatihonline.com, n.d.); Böttcher, *Syrische Religionspolitik*, 151–63; 'Absu, 'al-Madrasa al-Sha'baniyya'.

[39] Leif Stenberg, 'Préserver le charisme: les conséquences de la mort d'Ahmad Kaftaro sur la mosquée-complexe Abu al-Nur', *Maghreb – Machrek*, no. 198 (2008), 65–74, at 68; 'Aqsam al-ma'had' [Sections of the Institute] (www.alfatihonline.com, 2008).

employers of renowned scholars from other networks, in particular disciples of Hasan Habannaka. Through a partnership with the University of Karachi, Abu al-Nur also distinguished itself by distributing doctorates of convenience, a practice that became widespread among pro-regime ulama and greatly contributed to the devaluation of this degree among the Syrian religious elite.

The state's partnership with the Kaftariyya and al-Fath naturally had consequences for the political and religious institutions of the country: while the brotherhood of the Grand Mufti continued to monopolise 'Islamic' parliamentary seats in Damascus and access to media,[40] the director of al-Fath, 'Abd al-Fattah al-Bazam (b. 1943), the son of Salih al-Farfur's right-hand man, was appointed Mufti of the capital in 1993.[41]

On the ground, fellow students of al-Bazam were given mosques formerly controlled by Zayd in the bourgeois neighbourhood of Malki. However, more than al-Fath, which has been especially influential in the countryside around Damascus through its training of clerics, it is the Kaftariyya that sought to 'reconquer' the religious-minded educated urban youth.

Until the mid-1990s, the freedom of action given to Kaftari ulama and the restrictions paralysing other factions gave the former a near-monopoly on the 'mosque work' in the capital at a time when demand for religious education was booming. In a highly repressive context, the brotherhood of the Grand Mufti offered their followers the opportunity to learn the religious sciences without attracting the suspicion of the mukhabarat. This is made clear in the testimony of Bassam, the son of a merchant:

> I was born in the district of al-Qusur, where mosques are controlled by people of Zayd, but I grew up in the context of the 'events'. When I wanted to study religion, my father sent me to Kaftaru. He was afraid for me and was convinced that it was the only way to get [me] to safety.[42]

In spite of state support, however, the Kaftariyya failed to significantly expand outside its historic stronghold, the north of the city. In 2007, a

---

[40] Marwan Shaykhu, who sat in Parliament from 1973 to his death in 2001, also presented Islamic programmes on the national radio and television (Abaza, 'Ulama' Dimashq, 226). The other Kaftari MPs were Muhammad Habash (since 2003), 'Abd al-Salam Rajih, and, in Latakia, Zakariya Salwaya (since 2007).

[41] 'Al-Sirat al-dhatiyya li-l-duktur al-shaykh 'Abd al-Fattah al-Bazam' [Curriculum vitae of Dr Sheikh 'Abd al-Fattah al-Bazam] (www.alfatihonline.com, n.d.). Al-Bazam occupied this position in company with Bashir 'Id al-Bari (b. 1935), who was appointed in 1984 (Böttcher, Syrische Religionspolitik, 84).

[42] Interview, Damascus, May 2008.

sheikh of the Midan told me that he was engaged in a struggle with a Kaftari scholar who was trying (in vain) to take his mosque in order to create the first beachhead for the brotherhood in the area.[43] The group has established only a marginal presence in other major Syrian cities,[44] but it has had some success in Lebanon.[45]

Among both the al-Farfur and Kaftaru clans, the growth of the family patrimony since the 1980s has exacerbated sibling rivalries. Two years before the death of Salih al-Farfur in 1986, al-Fath was entrusted to his son Husam al-Din (b. 1951), to the detriment of the elder son, 'Abd al-Latif (b. 1945). Although he enjoys strong support within the mukhabarat, 'Abd al-Latif has few friends among the religious elite and administration. This imbalance probably explains the conflicting official decisions regarding his own project for an Islamic institute of graduate studies, which was opened in 1990 but was forced to close six years later.[46]

The problem of the succession was even more acute within the Kaftariyya, where the legacy not only included an institution, but also a Sufi brotherhood. Zahir Kaftaru, the eldest son of the master, was the designated successor, but he was killed in 1979 in what was reported as a land dispute.[47] Second in order of succession, his brother Mahmud (b. 1945) was pushed aside in 1999 over embezzlement in the management of the centre, and the leadership thus fell to his younger brother Salah al-Din (b. 1957). However, the document in which the Grand Mufti and his chief disciples formally endorsed this decision made no reference to any spiritual succession, but only to 'the affairs of the mosque and academy'.[48] In fact, Salah al-Din, who only wore the jubba and turban when he was preaching on Fridays, was not a real 'alim, nor did he claim to be one: he was behaving more as a manager, and displaying political ambitions which will be discussed later. It was not Salah al-Din who inherited his father's popular lessons in tafsir, but the senior scholars of the Academy, who are also the leading Sufi educators of the group; and

---

[43] Interview, Damascus, March 2007.

[44] In 2007, there were only three Kaftari clerics in Aleppo, none of whom was a prominent figure (Ka'ayyid, *Mawsu'at al-du'at*).

[45] Annabelle Böttcher, 'Au-delà des frontières: réseaux soufis au Moyen-Orient' (naqchbandi.org, n.d.).

[46] Böttcher, *Syrische Religionspolitik*, 109–10; interviews with anonymous sources, Damascus, November 2006 and May 2008.

[47] Although the assassination occurred *in tempore suspecto*, none ever claimed that Islamic militants were responsible for it.

[48] *Mujamma' al-shaykh Ahmad Kaftaru* [Sheikh Ahmad Kaftaru Academy] (Damascus: Kaftaru Academy, 2006), 26–30.

indeed the late Grand Mufti himself continued to lecture, virtually and posthumously, through extensive video recordings.[49]

In other words, the disappearance of the founder of the Kaftariyya led to a disjunction between its administrative leadership, which was embodied by Salah al-Din Kaftaru, and its spiritual authority, which none of the Grand Mufti's prominent disciples monopolised. Besides the fact that it weakened the position of Kaftaru the younger, as will be shown in the last chapter, this situation favoured the emergence of centrifugal elements, especially among those who could avail themselves of the spiritual legacy of the founding sheikh without relying materially on his son.

The Political Emergence of Sa'id Ramadan al-Buti

It is commonly assumed that the main role of official religious institutions in Muslim countries is to produce an interpretation of Islam that legitimises the powers that be. However, this idea needs to be seriously qualified in the case of Syria. Although it might sound counterintuitive, the Grand Muftis have promulgated very few fatwas under the Ba'th, and none of them have dealt with sensitive political issues.[50] In contrast to what has been witnessed in Egypt, for instance, Grand Muftis have never been asked to give legal sanction to a controversial decision by the regime.[51] Kaftaru neglected his role as jurisconsult to such an extent that when he died the position of Fatwa Secretary (*amin al-fatwa*) had been vacant for a decade.[52] Clerics do run 'fatwa desks' in the local branches of the religious administration, but their function is to provide citizens with a service rather than to impose a standardised interpretation of fiqh, since the state does nothing to curb the widespread practice of informal *ifta'* (the issuing of fatwas). In reality, the function of the Grand Mufti of Syria is not to monopolise legal interpretation, but has more to do with protocol (officiating during official religious celebrations) and public relations (reception of foreign delegations, tours abroad).[53]

---

[49] Stenberg, 'Préserver le charisme', 70–1.

[50] Lina al-Humsi, *al-Muftun al-'ammun fi Suriyya* [The Grand Muftis in Syria] (Damascus: Dar al-'Asma', 1996), 115; Böttcher, *Syrische Religionspolitik*, 52–62.

[51] Jakob Skovgaard-Petersen, *Defining Islam for the Egyptian State: Muftis and Fatwas of the Dar al-Ifta* (Leiden: Brill, 1997).

[52] Interview with 'Abd al-Qadir al-Za'tari, who was appointed as Fatwa Secretary in 2005, Aleppo, 9 November 2005.

[53] See Muhammad Habash, *al-Shaykh Ahmad Kaftaru wa manhajuhu fi al-tajdid wa-l-islah* [Sheikh Ahmad Kaftaru and his method for renewal and reform] (Damascus: Dar Abu al-Nur, 1996).

The non-exploitation of official ifta' for political ends has apparently been due to two factors: first, the reluctance of a secularist regime to lock its policies into an Islamic legal framework that could gradually become binding; and second, the lack of moral authority by the Grand Muftis, whose legitimacy has been contested from the outset because of the circumstances of their appointment.

For that reason, when al-Asad was desperately in need of Islamic legitimacy during the uprising, he had to seek it outside the official religious institutions, in the person of Sa'id Ramadan al-Buti (b. 1929). The latter's ascent to the pinnacle of Syria's informal religious hierarchy reflects a broader process which I have already illustrated with the example of Kaftaru's radio programmes: the emergence of Muslim scholars whose reputation is based on the use of mass media, through which they reach an audience on a hitherto unimaginable scale.

Al-Buti is the son of Mulla Ramadan (1888–1990), a renowned Kurdish scholar who chose to live in Damascus after fleeing the Kemalist repression of the 1930s.[54] Despite his ethnic background, al-Buti the elder was an active supporter of Habannaka's candidacy for the position of Grand Mufti in 1964. It was in Habannaka's institute that his son Sa'id began his religious studies, before earning a doctorate in theology at al-Azhar in 1965. Upon his return to Syria, he joined the faculty of sharia at the university, of which he was dean from 1977 to 1983.

Alongside his brilliant academic career, al-Buti became famous as a writer. To understand the success of his books, one must take into account that he has occupied a strategic position at the intersection of two modes of intellectual production, 'ilm ('sacred knowledge') and *fikr* (modern 'thought'), not only in Syria, but in the Arab world at large. Indeed, alongside the Egyptians Muhammad al-Ghazali and Yusuf al-Qardawi, al-Buti is one of the few doctors from al-Azhar to have made a substantial contribution to the corpus of the Islamic 'awakening', with the result that he was extremely popular among the youth that populated the ranks of jama'at such as Zayd and Abi Dharr in the 1970s.[55]

Although he did not neglect religious sciences in the strict sense, and has demonstrated his talents at clarifying them for a broad audience,[56]

---

[54] For his biography, see Christmann, 'Islamic Scholar'; Ali al-Atasi, 'al-Faqih wa-l-sultan: Shaykh al-Buti namudhijan' [The faqih and the sultan: the example of Sheikh al-Buti] (www.arraee.com, 19 November 2004).

[55] Interviews with former members of these groups, Damascus and Aleppo, 2006–7.

[56] See in particular Sa'id Ramadan al-Buti, *Fiqh al-sira al-nabawiyya* [Fiqh of the life of the Prophet] (Damascus: Dar al-Ghazali, 1968).

he distinguished himself even more by his refutations of the ideologies 'imported' from the West. Besides scientism and Marxism,[57] the 'godless' doctrine on which he concentrated his attacks was nationalism. Although he evoked 'the warmth of [his] Kurdish belonging',[58] and worked to introduce the literature of his native language to Arab readers,[59] his approach was purely cultural, not political. Nostalgic for the Ottoman Empire, he described nationalism as a virus introduced into the empire by the imperialist powers and Freemasonry in order to destroy it.[60] Thanks to his mastery of Turkish, he became fascinated by the personality of the anti-Kemalist Islamic leader and thinker Sa'id Nursi (1878–1960), whom he popularised among the Syrian public through a text entitled *The Miracle of the Islamic Revolution in Turkey*.[61]

Given all this, it might seem improbable that al-Buti would one day become a strategic ally of a secularist regime championing nationalism and socialism. However, he also had poor relations with the Muslim Brothers. Although he frequented the latter's intellectual circles in the 1950s and regularly contributed to their monthly *Hadarat al-Islam*, he was perceived as a detractor, with the consequence that the Islamist movement unsuccessfully tried to prevent his recruitment by the faculty of sharia in the mid-1960s.[62] Besides the fact that al-Buti, a traditionalist, was fiercely hostile to the Salafi doctrine that was permeating the Damascus

---

[57] Sa'id Ramadan al-Buti, *Kubra al-yaqiniyyat al-kawniyya* [The great convictions of the universe] (Damascus: Dar al-Fikr, 1969); al-Buti, *Naqd awham al-jadaliyya al-maddiyya al-diyaliktikiyya* [Refutation of the illusions of dialectical materialism] (Damascus: Dar al-Fikr, 1986).

[58] Sa'id Ramadan al-Buti, 'Risala maftuha ila al-akrad al-bartiyyin' [Open letters to the Kurds of the [Iraqi] parties] (www.bouti.net, April 2003). In this letter, al-Buti criticises the Kurdish leaders of Iraq for supporting the US invasion.

[59] Andreas Christmann, 'Transnationalising Personal and Religious Identities: Muhammad Sa'id Ramadan al-Buti's Adaptation of E. Xani's "Mem u Zin"', in *Sufism Today: Heritage and Tradition in the Global Community*, ed. Catharina Raudvere and Leif Stenberg (London: I. B. Tauris, 2009), 31–46.

[60] Sa'id Ramadan al-Buti, 'Hakadha nasha'at al-qawmiyya' [This is how nationalism was born], *Hadarat al-Islam* 3, no. 6 (1963), reprinted in *Shawqi Abu Khalil: buhuth wa maqalat muhaddat ilayhi* [Festschrift in honour of Shawqi Abu Khalil] (Damascus: Dar al-Fikr, 2004), 169–82.

[61] First published in *Hadarat al-Islam* in 1963, this article was reprinted in the best-seller *Min al-fikr wa-l-qalb: fusul al-naqd fi al-'ulum wa-l-ijtima' wa-l-adab* [From thought and heart: chapters of critique in the realms of sciences, society, and literature] (Damascus: Dar al-Farabi, 1972), 287–319.

[62] Interviews with al-Hawari and al-Malih; Sa'id Ramadan al-Buti, 'Mustafa al-Siba'i', in *Shakhsiyyat istawqafatni* [People who attracted my attention] (Damascus: Dar al-Fikr, 1999), 198.

branch of the Muslim Brothers,[63] the main cause of this dispute was his rejection of political activism in the name of Islam.[64]

In his aforementioned article on Nursi, for instance, al-Buti made it clear that he was not an admirer of Nursi's early career as a political leader, but rather of his later role as a thinker and writer. Under no circumstances does al-Buti's posture consist in advocating a separation of religion and state. It is rather motivated by a desire to keep men of religion away from political bargains, which are by their very essence unprincipled. It also draws on the idea that Islam should be 'the common element that unites' all political forces, not the preserve of one of them.[65]

Al-Buti's opposition to political Islam thus largely pre-dated the drift towards violence that was observed in the 1970s. However, it was the uprising that convinced him to cross the Rubicon: in 1979 he appeared on television to condemn the attack on the Artillery School of Aleppo, which according to him did not come under the category of jihad, nor even of rebellion, but of mere 'banditry'.[66] Fourteen years later, al-Buti theorised his long-standing opposition to Islamic political and military activism in his famous book *Jihad in Islam*.

In the meantime, the scholar developed close relationships at the highest levels of the government and mukhabarat, which was facilitated by the 1980 appointment of Muhammad al-Khatib (b. 1930), a former classmate at the institute of Sheikh Habannaka, as Minister of Awqaf.[67] Al-Buti was not treated as a common informer, however, since he was given the privilege of direct access to the President. Al-Asad, who rarely devoted more than a few minutes to a visitor and was said to see his own family very little, granted him lengthy personal meetings.[68] Such a mark of esteem was a reflection of the immensity of the favour done by al-Buti to the regime: the scholar who had publicly come to its rescue was not a 'Ba'thi sheikh' bereft of any credibility, but the son of a respected 'alim, a brilliant academic, and a successful writer whose star shone beyond the borders of the country.

---

[63] See Chapter 3.
[64] Interview with al-Hawari.
[65] Sa'id Ramadan al-Buti, *al-Jihad fi al-islam: kayfa nafhamuhu wa kayfa numarisuhu* [Jihad in Islam: how we understand it, how we practise it] (Damascus: Dar al-Fikr, 1993), 65–6, 83.
[66] Christmann, 'Islamic Scholar', 163; Houot, 'Le Cheikh al-Bouti', 54.
[67] Interview with an anonymous source, Damascus, May 2008; Mastu, *Mustafa Sa'id al-Khann*, 31.
[68] Interview with al-Hawari.

By contributing to the stifling of the Islamic uprising, al-Buti became a sort of 'papal' figure within the Syrian religious scene. He did not achieve this status by asking for those things that, when considered ill-gotten, definitely sully the whiteness of a turban. His proximity to the state did not make him rich, and he rejected offers of senior positions in the religious administration (until 2008), as well as proposals to represent 'moderate' Islam within the National Progressive Front.[69]

Instead, al-Buti acquired his centrality thanks to a freedom of expression that was denied to most of his colleagues. In the 1980s, he exerted a de facto monopoly on 'intellectual' (*fikri*) Islamic discourse, which was banned from mosques at that time. Bassam, who eagerly attended his lessons for years, explains that 'he was the only sheikh who could afford to openly discuss the ideas of Hasan al-Banna or Yusuf al-Qardawi'.[70] Moreover, in addition to the lessons he was giving in the largest mosques of the capital, al-Buti started to present religious programmes on national television. However, this was a privilege for which he could hardly be blamed by his colleagues: was he not doing his duty by making the voice of Islam heard on prime time, twenty years after the army magazine proposed putting religion 'in the museum of History'?

The other factor that made al-Buti the 'Pope' of Syrian Sunni Islam was his self-appointed role as intercessor. Following in this the traditional political posture of the ulama, he requested the leniency of the prince in exchange for the loyalty of his subjects.[71] This strategy is illustrated by a speech he gave in front of Hafiz al-Asad on the occasion of a Ramadan reception in the early 1990s. Thousands of Islamist prisoners had just been released, and al-Buti did not fail to praise the magnanimity of the President before inviting him to continue on this path:

Mr President … I wish that God makes your extraordinary wisdom (I chose my words carefully), your great calm and the dedication your family and friends know well, into a solid pillar for the protection of this religion …

I am convinced that those who have been released these days are the vanguard of those who burn to be always behind you … and I know that the small number of those who still await their release are impatient to stand with their brothers in this trench in order to be devoted soldiers behind you.

---

[69] The ruling coalition composed of the Ba'th and small left-wing/nationalist parties. See Sandra Houot, 'De la religion à l'éthique: esquisse d'une mediation contemporaine', *Revue du monde musulman et de la Méditerranée*, no. 85–6 (1999>), 31–46, at 37.

[70] Interview, Damascus, May 2008.

[71] On the ulama's traditional function as brokers between the state and the population, see Kepel, 'Les oulémas', 427–8.

As for your soldiers outside this country, they are our Syrian brothers who ... perhaps have been prevented from seeing the truth in the past ... perhaps have been deceived by conspirators ... but today – I can personally testify to that – they repudiate their old ideas and raise their heads, proud of this country and its leadership.[72]

What al-Buti could 'testify' to he had learned by touring Saudi cities and meeting exiled Syrian scholars, whom he promised could return home – provided of course they kept a low profile.[73] His mediation was key to the return in the mid-1990s of figures such as Hisham al-Burhani ('on presidential decree', the latter insists),[74] and the Muslim Brothers' spiritual leader 'Abd al-Fattah Abu Ghudda.[75]

Al-Buti also portrayed himself as the chaplain of the presidential palace, implying that he had brought the spark of – Sunni – faith into the heart of Hafiz al-Asad. Indeed, he recounted that, at the President's request, he had provided him with the collection of litanies (*awrad*) of Imam al-Nawawi, a purely Sunni reference-point, in order for him to read it with his family.[76]

It goes without saying that all of this has not been enough to win al-Buti unanimous support in Islamic circles. Jihadis, unsurprisingly, hate him,[77] and he has been fiercely criticised by the Muslim Brothers as well as by pro-democracy Islamist intellectuals.[78] Among the conservative ulama, some of those who had the freedom to speak have not spared him either. The Saudi-based son of his master Hasan Habannaka wrote of him:

He was a precocious and brilliant student, but he recently started to glorify and praise the leaders of the Ba'th Party, which gave rise to much criticism. I consider him as a mistaken *mujtahid* who is not a help to this world. Some of his friends advised him to reconsider his positions but he has not responded to their request.[79]

---

[72] Sa'id Ramadan al-Buti, *Hadha ma qultuhu amama ba'd al-ru'asa' wa-l-muluk* [Here is what I said in front of some presidents and kings] (Damascus: Dar al-Farabi, 2002), 73–5.

[73] Interview with Ali Sadr al-Din al-Bayanuni.

[74] He had been based in the Emirates since the mid-1970s for professional then political reasons (interview with al-Burhani).

[75] Zisser, 'Syria, the Ba'th Regime', 52–3; Ali Sadr al-Din al-Bayanuni, 'Ziyara khassa', Al Jazeera TV, 26 November 2005.

[76] 'Ma'a al-Buti fi hayatihi wa fikrihi' [With al-Buti in his life and thought], no. 2, al-Sham TV, 25 August 2009.

[77] See for instance this article by London-based Syrian jihadi scholar 'Abd al-Mun'im Mustafa Halima (a.k.a. Abu Basir al-Tartusi), 'Hadha huwa al-Buti fa-ahdharuhu' [Here is the true face of al-Buti, be wary of him] (www.tawhed.ws, 9 February 2001).

[78] Zisser, 'Syria, the Ba'th Regime', 50; see Chapter 3.

[79] Habannaka, *al-Walid al-da'iya*, 133.

Nevertheless, the transactional system centred around the figure of the Kurdish scholar has proved profitable for all parties involved: the regime has acquired an effective apparatus of religious legitimisation, al-Buti has become nothing less than the backbone of the relationship between the state and the clergy, and the latter has gradually won spaces of freedom while letting al-Buti assume the thankless task of praising the ruler for his 'leniency'.

Bab al-Nayrab Sets Out to Conquer Aleppo

By the dawn of the twenty-first century, there were manifest structural differences between the clergy of Aleppo and that of Damascus. The first was that its members in the former were on average significantly younger: in 2006, more than two-thirds of the most prominent religious figures of Aleppo were under sixty years old, as against less than one-third in Damascus.[80] The second difference was that, whereas the upper echelons of the Damascene clergy were almost exclusively occupied by autochthons (93 per cent), in Aleppo, one-third of the most prominent clerics were of rural or provincial origin.[81]

Such figures reflect not only the vacuum that was created in Aleppo by the repression of the uprising but also the social characteristics of the clerics whom the regime entrusted with the reconstruction of the local religious field: they were in their thirties in the 1980s, and were related to the Nabhaniyya, whose rural roots have already been mentioned. Comparable networks no longer existed in Damascus at that time: from the Mandate on, al-Gharra' had allowed sons of peasants from the Hauran to achieve prominence within the religious elite of the capital,[82] but the decline of the association from the 1950s had put an end to this 'chain migration'.

While posing as an intransigent defender of Islam against the state, Muhammad al-Nabhan had nevertheless forged close relations with the Ba'thist regime. When he founded his Kiltawiyya institute in 1964, one year after the coup of 8 March, the Ministry of Awqaf was headed by his disciple and personal lawyer Ahmad Mahdi al-Khudr. Moreover, his

---

[80] Population: respectively 25 and 35.

[81] The proportion of sons of ulama is roughly the same in both cities, that is, about half. The reason is that non-native scholars are not necessarily newcomers, a number of them being the scions of clerical families from second-rank cities.

[82] 'Abd al-Rahman al-Zu'bi (1902–69), Ahmad Ghabjuqa (1910–98), Khalid al-Jibawi (1912–2003), Ahmad Nasib al-Mahamid (1912–2000), Salah 'Uqla (d. 1985), Nayif al-'Abbas (1916–87).

right-hand man Muhammad al-Shami was skilfully making use of his contacts among the political and security authorities in aid of the brotherhood.[83] As has already been mentioned, his proximity to the regime proved fatal, as the Fighting Vanguard assassinated him in 1980.

Two years after the death of al-Shami, his son Suhayb (b. 1949) was appointed as the head of the local Directorate of Awqaf, a position he occupied for a quarter of a century. Widely accused of having exploited this position to accumulate a considerable personal fortune,[84] al-Shami became the emblem of one of the state's favourite strategies to control the clergy: corruption. By allowing certain men of religion to enrich themselves through illegal means, the regime made them vulnerable to possible judicial action. For instance, charges of corruption were used to wreck the career of Abdullah Dakk al-Bab, the former Awqaf director in Damascus and head of the Sheikh Badr al-Din al-Hasani institute, who was sentenced to hard labour in 2007.[85] As will be shown in the last chapter, a similar fate befell Salah al-Din Kaftaru two years later.

Let us now come back to 1980s Aleppo, where al-Shami the younger built a vast clientele thanks to his privileged relations with the mukhabarat, handing out freedom to clerics who pledged allegiance to him. He took advantage of this situation to promote men of his generation, drawn largely from the Nabhaniyya and wearing the latter's distinctive turban, which is coiled in the so-called 'Pakistani' (crossover) manner.[86] He appointed them to key positions in the religious administration,[87] as well as to the pulpits of the largest mosques in the well-off western neighbourhoods of the city.[88] Symbolically, for example, he gave the al-Rawda mosque of the now exiled Sheikh Tahir Khayr Allah to his protégé Muhammad Abdullah al-Sayyid (b. 1956).[89] The Nabhaniyya

---

[83] Hawwa, *Hadhihi tajribati*, 112.

[84] Böttcher, *Syrische Religionspolitik*, 73–4.

[85] Nizar 'Arrabi, *Murafa'at wa ahkam* [Pleadings and judgments] (Damascus: Dar Tlass, 2007).

[86] There are two other major distinctive turbans in Aleppo: that of the Sha'baniyya institute, which is coiled simply, and that of the disciples of the Shadhili sheikh 'Abd al-Qadir 'Isa, which has a kind of frontal bump.

[87] Ahmad Taysir Ka'ayyid (b. 1955), the director of religious inspection until the end of the 1990s, his successor Muhammad al-Hamad (b. 1967), the Mufti of Manbij Ahmad 'Isa Muhammad (b. 1953).

[88] 'Ammar bin Yasir (Nabih Salim, b. 1950), al-Rahman (Khalid Sayyid Ali, b. 1952), al-Ridwan ('Abd al-Hadi Badla, b. 1958). Mahmud al-Hut (b. 1956), the director of the Kiltawiyya and the holder of its minbar, is also one of Aleppo's most popular preachers.

[89] Ka'ayyid, *Mawsu'at al-du'at*.

therefore dominated the local clergy, in terms of both visibility and number: although its Kiltawiyya institute had initially been established to train clerics for the countryside, it became the main training centre for the city's mosque personnel.[90]

In 1990, Suhayb al-Shami's links with the regime grew even stronger thanks to the election to parliament of his brother 'Abd al-'Aziz (1957–2007), whose seat automatically fell to his younger brother Anas when he died,[91] and of one of his fellow disciples from the Madjadme tribal clan, the Mufti of Manbij, Ahmad 'Isa Muhammad. During electoral campaigns, Nabhani candidates have shared a list with notables from the Bab al-Nayrab neighbourhood, the cradle of Sheikh al-Nabhan's jama'a, including tribal chiefs from the al-Barri family, which is part of the Djes clan.

The accession of the clans of Bab al-Nayrab to parliamentary representation was itself a reflection of the influence they had gained within the security and political apparatus of the city.[92] Indeed, after the Islamic uprising – whose sociological centre of gravity was the traditional urban middle class – the regime quite logically allied with elites that were seen as 'aliens' by city-dwellers. Increasing state support for the disciples of Muhammad al-Nabhan may be considered, to some extent, as the religious dimension of this strategy.

In order to counterbalance the influence of al-Shami, the mukhabarat has also backed a rival branch of the Nabhaniyya, that of the Hassun family. As we have already seen, al-Nabhan did not appoint a successor. At his death, Muhammad al-Shami symbolically put the turban of the deceased master on the head of his grandson, Faruq al-Nabhan.[93] However, the latter spent the rest of the century in Morocco, since he was hired by Hassan II in 1977 to lead the Dar al-Hadith institute in Rabat. Meanwhile, a rival of al-Shami, Adib Hassun (1915–2008), recruited numerous disciples by claiming the spiritual legacy of al-Nabhan.[94] In 1977, Hassun even opened his own sharia institute, al-Furqan, which

[90] In 2008, one-third of Aleppo's imams and preachers born after 1950 had graduated from the Kiltawiyya, against one-fourth for each of the Khusrawiyya and Sha'baniyya (population: 251; calculation based on Ka'ayyid, *Mawsu'at al-du'at*).

[91] See www.elaph.com, 18 September 2007.

[92] Hivernel, 'Bab al-Nayrab', 230–1.

[93] Nabhan, *al-Shaykh Muhammad al-Nabhan*, 131.

[94] Adib Hassun, *Ala' al-rahman 'ala al-'arif al-Nabhan* [Benedictions of the merciful upon the knower of God al-Nabhan] (Aleppo: n.p., n.d.), 112–13.

was closed seven years later by the authorities at the instigation of Suhayb al-Shami.[95]

A son of Adib Hassun, Ahmad Badr al-Din (b. 1949) distinguished himself as a gifted and sophisticated preacher – it was to him that, in the early 1970s, al-Nabhan entrusted the minbar of the al-Furqan mosque, the former restaurant close to the university – as well as being possessed of considerable political acumen. Like al-Shami's brother, in 1990 he began a career as an 'independent' member of parliament, which was a prelude to his ascent to the highest levels of the Syrian religious hierarchy: he was appointed Mufti of Aleppo in 1999 and Grand Mufti of Syria six years later.[96] The time had come for revenge: two months after Hassun's appointment as the successor of Kaftaru, al-Shami was dismissed from his position as the head of Aleppo's Awqaf Directorate.[97]

Hassun was the first non-Damascene to hold the office of Grand Mufti since its inception in 1947, a choice that resulted from the political context of the first years of this century. Kaftaru had passed away in September 2004; that is to say, at the very moment that the Lebanese issue plunged Syria into diplomatic crisis. The leading candidates for the succession were pillars of the powerful religious establishment of the capital (al-Buti, al-Zuhayli, al-Bazam, and Husam al-Din al-Farfur),[98] and therefore constituted potentially troublesome partners in such a delicate period. Al-Asad therefore waited ten months, eventually appointing Hassun by decree.

The reason for the President's use of his legislative prerogatives to circumvent the 1961 law, which provides for the election of the Grand Mufti by a committee of scholars, was easy to understand: Hassun simply had no chance of being elected by his peers, not only because Damascenes would have been the majority within the caucus, but also because of his personality. With a relatively narrow social base, Hassun was absolutely 'safe' in political terms, which was the main reason for his appointment. However, it is not his obvious docility that has most irritated his peers, but the apparently sincere enthusiasm with which he has executed his mission – embodying the smiling face of 'enlightened' (*tanwiri*) Syrian Islam in order to improve the image of his country abroad.

---

[95] Katibi, '*Ulama' min Halab*, 615; interview with an anonymous source, Aleppo, November 2006.
[96] Katibi, *Tarikh al-ifta'*, 307–15; *al-Nahar*, 17 July 2005.
[97] *Al-Thawra*, 10 September 2005; interview with an anonymous source, Aleppo, July 2007.
[98] Salah al-Din Kaftaru, 'Interview', *al-Mar'at al-Yawm*, 16 April 2005.

Kaftaru had certainly done likewise, but had confined himself to inter-religious dialogue. Hassun, who enlisted the help of a Christian personal adviser,[99] has gone further. Reaching out to Judaism while expressing support for secularism (*'ilmaniyya*), he managed to convince the French Jewish intellectual Marek Halter that 'peace runs through Damascus':

> Even the Grand Mufti of Syria, Ahmad Badr al-Din Hassun, said he was a secularist. According to him, this implies respect for other religions. He invited me, a Polish Jew ... to address the faithful during the Friday prayer in one of the most famous mosques in the Muslim world, the Umayyad Mosque in Damascus.[100]

In January 2010, on the occasion of another meeting with a representative of Judaism, Professor Marc Gopin from George Mason University, Hassun took a step too far. During the reception, Hassun reportedly said: 'If the Prophet Muhammad had ordered me to declare that Jews and Christians are unbelievers, I would have replied that he himself was an unbeliever.'[101] The somewhat confused denials by the Grand Mufti did not deflect the wrath of his colleagues: whereas until then criticisms had been relayed by word of mouth,[102] they were now expressed openly. While Muhammad Abu al-Huda al-Ya'qubi (b. 1962), the teacher of dogmatic theology at the Umayyad Mosque of Damascus, openly called on Hassun to resign,[103] the Grand Mufti was publicly reproached by the two most prominent Arab Sunni Muslim scholars of our time, Sa'id Ramadan al-Buti and Yusuf al-Qardawi.[104]

NEW POLICIES, NEW PARTNERS

During the 1990s, the Syrian regime's opposition to the Oslo Accords allowed it to develop relations with foreign Islamist forces that were no longer only Shiite (Iran, Hizbullah), but also Sunni (Hamas, Islamic Jihad, the Jordanian Muslim Brothers).[105] In parallel, religiosity was becoming ever more visible in Syrian society, with the consequence that it was increasingly trivialised and depoliticised: in the early twentieth

---

[99] all4syria.info, 28 December 2009.
[100] *Libération*, 14 January 2008.
[101] *Al-Quds al-'Arabi*, 19 January 2010; *al-Watan* (Damascus), 20 January 2010.
[102] Informal discussion in the souk of Aleppo, April 2008.
[103] Sermon of Friday 29 January 2010 (www.youtube.com/watch?v=9oRnPg_HG1k).
[104] Sa'id Ramadan al-Buti, 'Tawdih li-mas'ala hamma' [Clarification on an important issue] (www.naseemalsham.com, 6 February 2010); al-Qardawi in his weekly program *al-Shari'a wa-l-hayat* [Sharia and life] on Al Jazeera TV, 10 February 2010.
[105] Zisser, 'Syria, the Ba'th Regime', 57–9.

century, for example, wearing the headscarf was no longer inconceivable among deputies of the National Progressive Front and wives of ministers. Taking note of these developments and seeking to give assurances to the conservative public, Bashar al-Asad began his presidency by permitting the wearing of headscarves in schools and the opening of prayer-rooms in universities.[106]

In the mid-1990s, most mosques were again allowed to organise activities between prayers, while some exiled ulama started to come back to their homeland. During the next decade, the regime sought to diversify its partnerships within the clergy, a strategy of which al-Buti was the first victim. Although he had led the prayer at the funeral of Hafiz al-Asad in 2000, an occasion on which he shed much-remarked-upon tears,[107] and publicly legitimated the dynastic succession of the head of state, the Kurdish scholar entered a period of relative disgrace: despite repeated attempts, he was no longer granted personal meetings with the President.[108]

As for the Kaftariyya, it also lost its previous centrality: although its members continued to occupy leading official positions such as the Awqaf portfolio (Ziyad al-Ayyubi, 2004–7), the young President's drive to strengthen his shaky rule in a context of regional turmoil (the al-Aqsa Intifada, the invasion of Iraq, the Lebanese crisis) led him to reach out to clerical networks that had been marginalised by his father.

One target of the new religious policy of the regime was the heirs of Hasan Habannaka. In 2004, his son 'Abd al-Rahman was allowed to come back from a forty-year exile to die in his homeland. In the second half of the decade, Mustafa al-Bugha was honoured by private visits from the President, who hinted at the possibility of reopening the al-Tawjih al-Islami institute, which had been closed since 1967.[109] In 2007, al-Bugha's son Hasan was appointed dean of the faculty of sharia.[110]

However, courting the disciples of Habannaka was only a temporary solution to the regime's problems of religious legitimacy. Indeed, although they were still in control of the main mosques of the Midan, the fact that they had no private institute like al-Fath or the Kaftaru

---

[106] Ibid., 43; interview with students at the University of Aleppo, 9 November 2006.

[107] See the footage from Syrian national television (www.youtube.com/watch?v= VqOciIkv_tg).

[108] *Al-Ba'th al-shi'i fi Suriyya 1919–2007* [The Shiite renaissance in Syria] (n.p.: n.p., 2008), 72.

[109] Interview with an anonymous source, Damascus, April 2008.

[110] *Al-Thawra*, 12 October 2007.

Academy was preventing them from training large numbers of young clerics who would be able to take over. The result was that in the early twenty-first century, the 'ulama of the Midan' were a small group composed of respected but ageing figures (Sadiq Habannaka, who died in 2007; Mustafa al-Khann, who passed away a year later; Krayyim Rajih, an octogenarian; and al-Bugha, ten years his junior), and a few younger clerics who were very popular among religious students but enjoyed little visibility (Muhammad Shuqayr, Rushdi al-Qalam). This is why, during the first decade of the twenty-first century, the regime turned to another old enemy, but a much more powerful one.

Jama'at Zayd: Back in Favour ... and in Force

In 1990, al-Buti described the da'wa of 'Abd al-Karim al-Rifa'i as a historical episode that had definitively come to an end because of the sheikh's heirs:

> Without a stupid discord [*fitna*] resulting from the negligence of the rules of religion by its leaders, this blessed work would have penetrated every mosque of Damascus, then it would have spread to every home and family, but it has huddled up until it became part of memory, as we can see today.[111]

At that time, indeed, most senior scholars of the movement were in exile and the activities of its mosques were frozen. Yet the group survived, thanks to a handful of figures who had been allowed to remain in Syria, such as Sheikh of the Quran Abu al-Hasan al-Kurdi, and Sheikh Shawkat al-Jibali, who was 'the guarantor of the unity of the da'wa of Zayd's mosques ... during this difficult time'.[112] In addition, although the movement lost several mosques in the bourgeois districts of al-Malki and Mezze, second-rank scholars of the group continued to officiate in its historical strongholds of the south-west and north-east of the city.

The relative leniency of the regime was a consequence of Zayd's roots in the Damascene merchant class, whose loyalty helped limit the scope of the 1979–82 crisis, a crucial factor in saving the regime.[113] Yet, even a 'soft eradication' of Zayd, that is to say the forced replacement of the staff of its mosques in favour of other groups, would have constituted a declaration of war against its merchant supporters. The latter were

---

[111] Al-Buti, foreword to al-Rifa'i, *al-Ma'rifa*, 9.
[112] Al-Jibali, 'al-Da 'iya al-shaykh Shawkat al-Jibali'.
[113] Patrick Seale, *Asad of Syria: The Struggle for the Middle East* (Berkeley: University of California Press, 1989), 326.

also key to the state's decision to authorise the return of the exiled sons of al-Rifaʿi in 1994, and the visits to Syria of the Medina-based khalifa Muhammad ʿAwad.[114]

Zayd therefore resumed its activities, recovering its former supporters, but also rallying followers of the Kaftariyya. Muhammad, an engineer, explains that he studied with the latter in the 1980s 'because there was nothing else', but joined Usama al-Rifaʿi on his return because of his 'knowledge' and 'political line', which he sees as more independent from the regime. At the same time, the movement resumed its territorial expansion towards the newly built bourgeois district of Tanzim Kafr Suse and parts of the suburbs.

In the early twenty-first century, Zayd has become an informal network of several dozen mosques, four of which are invested with special status because of their imposing size and the personality of their preachers, who form the collective leadership of the movement. The Zayd bin Thabit mosque, which followers call 'the sweet mother' (*al-umm al-hanin*), is headed by al-Rifaʿi's second son, Sariya (b. 1948), who is known as the 'Sheikh of the Merchants'.[115] The second mosque, named after Sheikh ʿAbd al-Karim al-Rifaʿi, was built in Tanzim Kafr Suse in the 1990s; it is occupied by the elder of the al-Rifaʿi brothers, Usama, the *primus inter pares* of the ulama of the group, whose boldness has been illustrated in the introduction. That two former exiles preach in the mosque of their father (Sariya), and in a mosque named after him (Usama), demonstrates that certain officers of religious rites are only formally state appointed in Syria: although the Zayd bin Thabit and al-Rifaʿi mosques are legally owned by the Ministry of Awqaf, like any other mosque, their use actually 'belongs' to the al-Rifaʿi family and its movement.

The third-largest mosque of Jamaʿat Zayd is al-Iman, next to the headquarters of the Baʿth Party in al-Mezraʿa (north-east), where crowds throng to attend the teachings of the hadith specialist Naʿim al-ʿArqsusi. The fourth is the nearby al-Hamza wa-l-ʿAbbas, in the mixed Christian–Muslim Abbasids district, whose preacher is the poet Nadhir Maktabi.

Generally speaking, the educational method of Zayd has changed little since the 1970s, the heirs of al-Rifaʿi having literally implemented their master's injunction to 'turn the mosque into a university'. Every morning, Usama al-Rifaʿi holds a lesson reserved for the elite of his followers (*al-khassa*), mostly members of the movement's mosque personnel and

---

[114] Interview with an anonymous source, Damascus, June 2007.
[115] See Chapter 4.

long-standing merchant disciples.[116] After the prayer, about two hundred of them descend to the mosque's basement, which has been fitted out to resemble university classrooms. Whereas the teachings that are provided during this advanced dawn lesson are based on classic texts, study circles for beginners now rely on textbooks specifically designed for that purpose.[117] At the same time, Zayd's teaching activities continue to escape any legal framework and therefore take place thanks to a tacit agreement with the authorities.

Although all the jama'at that emerged in Syria in the mid-twentieth century started as missionary efforts, those that developed large formal institutes (Kaftariyya, al-Fath) have moved to a more entrepreneurial model. On the contrary, Zayd remains a genuine 'movement' (*haraka*) in that it does not limit itself to offering educational services to its followers but personally entrusts every one of them with the mission to conduct da'wa – a vital principle for a group whose study circles are not run by salaried teachers, but by volunteers.

Zayd has also kept some of its early political orientation. Today, the leaders of the movement say they no longer provide anything other than religious education in the strict sense,[118] but, besides the fact that it is impossible to know what is really happening in the study circles, one does not have to look far to find that the group continues to promote the reading of moderate Islamist literature: Sada Zayd ('the Echo of Zayd'), the group's very lively website,[119] stands out among the Syrian electronic media for publishing articles by authors such as Mustafa al-Siba'i, Yusuf al-Qardawi, and former Saudi dissident Salman al-'Awda. The same website also features articles by members of Zayd on issues such as democracy and secularism.[120]

This leads on to the issue of Zayd's ambiguous relationship with the regime. In 2002, in order to broaden his support base among the religious elite, Bashar al-Asad made a private visit to Usama al-Rifa'i, a gesture of respect that is only granted to a Muslim scholar under exceptional circumstances. In January 2005, with the regime facing a serious foreign

---

[116] Observation by the author, 5 March 2007.
[117] *Al-Thaqafat al-islamiyya li-l-nashi'a* [Islamic culture for the youth] (Damascus: Dar Zayd bin Thabit, 2007).
[118] Interview with 'Ammar al-Rifa'i.
[119] www.sadazaid.com.
[120] 'Al-Dimuqratiyya: mawqif al-muslimin minha' [Democracy: what Muslims think of it] (www.sadazaid.com, 24 December 2006); Anas Zaghlul, 'al-'Ilmaniyya: mafhumuha wa haqiqatuha' [Secularism: concept and reality] (www.sadazaid.com, August 16, 2007).

policy crisis, the sermon of the celebration of the 'Id al-Kabir organised in the presence of the President was not given by a notoriously pro-regime cleric, as had usually been the case, but by the very popular 'Zaydi' Na'im al-'Arqsusi.[121]

The regime's gestures of good will towards Zayd were not merely symbolic. As its room to manoeuvre increased, the movement was able to launch new projects, such as charities, the Zayd Centre for Service to the Quran, a private sharia high school named in honour of the founding sheikh, and even, in 2008, the short-lived satellite channel al-Da'wa. At the same time, members of the movement made their way to senior executive positions within the Ministry of Awqaf.[122] However, the new official policies failed to turn the ulama of Zayd into sycophants of the regime, as shown by Usama al-Rifa'i's exhortation, quoted above.[123]

From a sociological standpoint, Zayd still recruits primarily among the students of secular teaching. Engineers, doctors, and pharmacists are overrepresented among the medium-ranked leadership of the group, many of them scions of Damascene clerical–mercantile families – a situation that is denounced even among the followers. Tellingly, graduates of Zayd's own sharia institute al-Furqan are assigned only a marginal role within the movement, a situation that arguably results from class discrimination since religious schools usually cater for teenagers from more humble backgrounds.[124] Instead of a robe and long beard, the typical follower of Zayd follows the fashion of the pious educated middle class: 'Western' clothes and three-day stubble.

Zayd's 'lay' character is also reflected by the dress of its scholars. Whereas 'Abd al-Karim al-Rifa'i used to wear a turban, his successors prefer the *hatta* (or *ghatra*), a simple piece of white cloth similar to the headgear of the Bedouin but without the *'agla* (circular headband). This Gulf fashion was adopted by many of the Syrian ulama who, like the leaders of Zayd, had spent several years in the Arabian peninsula. Within the movement, this choice is justified by a concern for modesty and the idea that, although not problematic in itself, the turban has lost much of its value in modern times due to the proliferation of those who wear it without being worthy to do so.[125]

---

[121] Syrian National Television, 20 January 2005 (VCD).
[122] Pierret and Selvik, 'Limits of "Authoritarian Upgrading"', 608.
[123] See also ibid., 608–9.
[124] Interview with an anonymous source, Damascus, June 2007.
[125] Interview with an anonymous source, Damascus, April 2008.

With the return of Zayd, the limited liberalisation initiated in the mid-1990s has led to a profound transformation of the Damascene religious scene. This new policy also prompted a shift in the media sphere in favour of a figure who was not politically ambiguous, but nevertheless owed his progress to his own merits rather than to state support.

Ratib al-Nabulsi, the Star of Radio Preaching

In 2010, a Syrian magazine published a ranking of the best-selling authors of the previous year. If proof is needed that the mass media had dramatically increased the audience of 'traditional' Islamic authorities, note that the winning quintet included no less than three ulama. Between the Algerian novelist Ahlam Mosteghanemi and the Lebanese astrologer Maguy Farah, there appeared the names of the three great media-sheikhs of the country: al-Buti; the prominent faqih Wahba al-Zuhayli; and Ratib al-Nabulsi (b. 1938), who is best known for his radio broadcasts.[126]

A professor of education at the University of Damascus, al-Nabulsi preaches in the Rukn al-Din mosque, which houses the shrine of his famous ancestor, the great Sufi 'Abd al-Ghani al-Nabulsi (1641–1731).[127] He attracts a large audience thanks to his unusual style. He is clean-shaven, a choice he explains by a desire not to 'raise a barrier' between people and himself.[128] Contrasted with the stormy tone of most Islamic preachers, his voice is a little monotonous. The language is simple but avoids any use of dialect. Supporting his remarks by many hadiths, al-Nabulsi deals mainly with the rules of everyday morality and, above all, the 'scientific miracle of the Quran' (*al-i'jaz al-'ilmi*), a popular genre that consists in showing how the Holy Book anticipated modern scientific discoveries.[129]

In the first decade of the twenty-first century, the daily broadcasts of his mosque lectures on Radio al-Quds (the media outlet of the pro-Syrian Popular Front for the Liberation of Palestine – General Command) made al-Nabulsi a real 'star' whose popularity was obvious to anyone taking a taxi or a minibus in Damascus at that time.

Thanks to his weekly programmes on Gulf-based Islamic satellite channels such as al-Risala and Iqra', al-Nabulsi also acquired pan-Arab

---

126 *Al-Iqtisadi*, January 2010.
127 'Sirat al-duktur Muhammad Ratib al-Nabulsi al-dhatiyya' [Curriculum vitae of Dr Muhammad Ratib al-Nabulsi] (nabulsi.com, 22 April 2006).
128 all4syria.info, July 13, 2010.
129 See Ratib al-Nabulsi, *Mawsu'at al-i'jaz al-'ilmi fi al-qur'an wa-l-sunna* [The encyclopaedia of scientific miracle in the Quran and Sunna] (Damascus: Dar al-Maktabi, 2007).

recognition. This was reflected by the fact that in March 2011, his website, by far the most popular of its kind in Syria, received the overwhelming majority (85 per cent) of its hits from Internet users based outside the country.[130]

This extraordinary success has its roots in the fact that al-Nabulsi's discourse is adapted to a broad part of the Syrian population in an era of mass literacy. Thanks to its simplicity and clarity, it is accessible to the bus driver, but because it never lapses into the popular, it remains acceptable for the university student. In addition, his lectures on the scientific miracle of the Quran offer an informative entertainment that provides the believer with rational arguments in order to reinforce his – possibly shaky – faith.

Opening Up in Aleppo: Old Religious Families and 'Conscious Preachers'

In 2002, tens of thousands of Aleppians accompanied the mortal remains of Sheikh Abdullah Siraj al-Din to his final resting-place, his beloved Sha'baniyya madrasa. During his final years, the scholar had acquired a reputation for sainthood among the people of the city, who had given him such titles as 'Sheikh of Islam' and, during the Kuwait crisis in 1991, 'Protector of Aleppo'.[131] Tellingly, his hagiology was built on features radically opposed to those that characterised the local religious scene in the post-insurrection period.

First, in a wounded city that had been deprived of many of its most eminent scholars, Siraj al-Din was famous for his exceptional knowledge of the Prophetic tradition (he had reportedly memorised no fewer than 80,000 hadiths), which he displayed in treatises on spiritual and ritual issues as well as in prayer booklets that were disseminated widely.[132] Second, whereas the Nabhaniyya, the regime's main local religious ally, had its roots in the countryside, Siraj al-Din epitomised the urban identity. From this point of view, a deep sociological divide persists between the Sha'baniyya, whose audience is 90 per cent city-dwellers (principally

---

[130] www.nabulsi.com. At the time of my enquiry in 2011, it was the only Syrian Islamic website to be ranked among the 100,000 most visited sites on the web. The number two, a website of al-Buti (www.naseemalsham.com), ranked well beyond the 400,000th position (stats: www.alexa.com).

[131] Informal discussions, Aleppo, 2006–7.

[132] For instance, al-Salat 'ala al-nabi: ahkamuha, fada'iluha, fawa'iduha [The prayer for the Prophet: its rules, its virtues, its benefits] (Aleppo: Dar al-Falah, 1990); ad'iyat al-sabah wa-l-masa' [Invocations of the morning and evening] (Aleppo: Dar al-Falah, n.d.).

the sons of merchants), and the Kiltawiyya, two-thirds of whose students come from rural areas.[133] Finally, the domination of the city's religious scene by young, ambitious clerics locked in fierce rivalry (al-Shami, Hassun) made Siraj al-Din's rejection of mundane affairs all the more remarkable: having always kept away from the conflicts of his peers, he spent the last decade of his life in almost total seclusion (*i'tizal*).[134]

The enduring popularity of the 'Protector of Aleppo' had highlighted a fact known to all, namely that although the favourites of the regime had certainly conquered the upper echelons of the local religious admin-istration, they did not have the hearts of the faithful. From as early as the 1980s, therefore, the authorities had been forced to make room for other figures. The first of these were the sons and followers of the Shadhili sheikh 'Abd al-Qadir 'Isa, who ended his days in Turkey; one of them, former schoolteacher Nadim al-Shihabi (b. 1937), returned from Medina in 1982 and became a very popular preacher in al-Fath, one of the larg-est religious complexes in the affluent neighbourhoods of the city.[135] His brother Muhammad (b. 1947) was appointed as the Fatwa Secretary of the city in 1989.[136] Another disciple of 'Isa, Ahmad al-Na'san (b. 1954), is the current Mufti of the neighbouring city of al-Bab.

In the 2000s, the regime also reached out to scions of great clerical families known for their political independence from and even hostility towards the Ba'th. In 2001, after more than three decades of exile, Abu al-Fath al-Bayanuni was allowed to settle in his hometown.[137] This was a highly symbolic decision, since he was not only the son of the founder of Jama'at Abi Dharr, but also the brother of the incumbent superintendent of the Muslim Brothers, Ali Sadr al-Din. Abu al-Fath was also the father of Bashar, a businessman who in 2010 would participate in the creation of the first sexually segregated mall in Syria.[138] This suggests that his return, like that of the al-Rifa'i brothers in Damascus, was perhaps not unrelated to the regime's strategy of rapprochement with the economic elites of the city.

Similar considerations explain the promotion of Ibrahim al-Salqini to the post of Mufti of Aleppo in 2005, after he refused to become Minister of Awqaf.[139] The son and grandson of prominent scholars, al-Salqini himself

---

[133] Calculation based on Ka'ayyid, *Mawsu'at al-du'a*.
[134] Interview with Ali Sadr al-Din al-Bayanuni.
[135] Interview with Nadim al-Shihabi and observation, Aleppo, 22 November 2006.
[136] Katibi, *Tarikh al-ifta'*, 404–6.
[137] Interview with Abu al-Fath al-Bayanuni.
[138] all4syria.info/content/view/31032/113/, 22 August 2010.
[139] Interview with Ali Sadr al-Din al-Bayanuni.

served as dean of the faculties of sharia in Damascus (1983–9) and Dubai (1989–2004).[140] During the first parliamentary elections of the Asad era in 1973, he was elected with the support of the Muslim Brothers.[141] He was also very popular with conservative businessmen (in particular Hamdi al-Za'im, who funded the construction of the Abu Hanifa mosque–cathedral), who relied on his arbitration to resolve their conflicts.[142]

Parallel to its rapprochement with such religious notables, the regime has tolerated the emergence of younger preachers who dare to address social and/or political issues. This move was designed to develop relatively safe partners to meet the expectations of the educated youth, which badly resented the deterioration in the quality of religious discourse that resulted from the 1980 crackdown on the most politicised clerics. The first of these figures, Mahmud 'Akkam (b. 1952), emerged in the mid-1980s. The son of a merchant, he is a former member of Jama'at Abi Dharr and still praises the latter's 'balanced' combination of exoteric teachings, Sufi education, and social–political consciousness building.[143] In 1983, having obtained a Ph.D. in Islamic sciences at La Sorbonne along with his friend Suhayb al-Shami (and thanks to a scholarship he owed to the efforts of the latter's father), 'Akkam was appointed director of the Khusrawiyya.[144] The modernity of the discourse he proposed was unparalleled in the local religious landscape at that time. Yasin, a schoolteacher of Islamic religion, narrates his encounter with 'Akkam:

When I was a teenager, I was a disciple of a Sufi sheikh who had a very narrow worldview. With him, our concerns were limited to prayer, dhikr, meditation, asceticism … I met Dr 'Akkam during my studies at the Khusrawiyya. His approach was completely different. We used to love him very much because he knew the Islamic sciences but also the culture of his time. He was courageous because the city was emerging from a difficult period and no one dared to speak as he did.[145]

'Akkam's distance from what he calls the 'traditional mashyakha' is also obvious in the titles of his books (for instance, 'On the philosophical categories of Islamic thought'),[146] as well as from the catalogue of his small

---

[140] Katibi, *'Ulama' min Halab*, 179–81, 548–52; 'al-Shaykh Ibrahim al-Salqini' (www.dr-salkini.com, n.d.).

[141] Interview with Ali Sadr al-Din al-Bayanuni.

[142] all4syria.info/content/view/31673/113/, 3 September 2010.

[143] Interview with Mahmud 'Akkam, Aleppo, 20 November 2006.

[144] Ka'ayyid, *Mawsu'at al-du'at*, vol. I, 344.

[145] Interview, Aleppo, November 2006.

[146] *Min maqulat al-fikr al-islami* (Aleppo: Fussilat, 2002).

publishing-house, Fussilat, which includes Arabic translations of books by John Esposito, Noam Chomsky, and Orhan Pamuk. He also displays this distance through his dress: on his website he poses in a turtleneck, and when he preaches he wears a hatta rather than a turban, leans on a sword (a warlike symbol that, for obvious reasons, has become extremely rare in Syria), and is wrapped in a black cloak, another idiosyncratic trait seen by many as reflecting his pro-Shiite orientation.

It was because of this Shiite connection that 'Akkam lost his status as mentor for a whole generation. One Friday in 1989, he organised the Prayer of the Absent for Ayatollah Khomeini: this act was frowned upon in a city that was notoriously pro-Iraqi, and which had moreover just suffered harsh repression by a regime allied to Iran. "Akkam was no longer with us,' one of his former admirers recalled.[147]

In spite of his declining popularity, 'Akkam remained a pillar of Aleppo's religious administration. In 2006, he was entrusted with the supervision of the new faculty of sharia of Aleppo, and then was appointed Second Mufti of the city – this was a way for the authorities to ensure that the independent-minded al-Salqini would not be the sole head of local Islam.

Meanwhile, the theme of preaching 'in tune with the realities of the age' ('asri) was taken up in Aleppo by a former admirer of 'Akkam, Mahmud Abu al-Huda al-Husseini (b. 1960). The rapid rise of this son and grandson of provincial ulama (his father was the preacher of the Grand Mosque of Manbij) illustrates the fluidity of Aleppo's religious hierarchy. While studying medicine, al-Husseini was initiated into the Shadhili path by the great Damascene master 'Abd al-Rahman al-Shaghuri (1912–2004). Al-Husseini was entrusted with the supervision of al-Shaghuri's circle of disciples in Aleppo, which grew rapidly thanks to his charisma. In 1994, due to his close ties to Suhayb al-Shami, al-Husseini obtained the chair of the 'Adiliyya mosque in the old souk; this was a highly symbolic promotion for a young Shadhili sheikh, because the mosque, a jewel of Ottoman architecture, was the former headquarters of 'Abd al-Qadir 'Isa himself.[148]

Over the next decade, the sheikh–physician al-Husseini displayed overt political ambitions. After the June 2005 Tenth Regional Congress of the Ba'th reaffirmed the prohibition on creating religious parties, he gave a sermon that expressed his profound disappointment: 'As long as

[147] Interview, Damascus, December 2006.
[148] Interview with al-Husseini.

the doors of democracy are open, we are obliged to express the spirit of Islam ... Why did they exclude from this project those whose minds are influenced by Islamic culture?'[149] The political field remained closed, and al-Husseini eventually turned to the local religious administration, of which he became the director in 2010.

With his sophisticated sermons – during which he used a data projector ('a world first', he says proudly) – al-Husseini attracted an audience of students from the best faculties (medicine, pharmacy, engineering). He was explicitly laying claim to the elitist character of his brotherhood, explaining that he was seeking to 'bring together exceptional profiles', on the grounds that 'five light bulbs give more light than fifty candles'.[150]

Although his brilliant career had required solid relationships within official circles, al-Husseini was not a sycophant of the regime. For example, he did not hesitate to subvert the wording of a famous secularist slogan while alluding to the widespread use of torture:

You know the slogan that says 'Religion is for God, and the homeland is for all'? Well I say, 'Religion is for God, and the homeland too'. To say this is in the interest of the people in this country because, on this earth, God does not whip those who do not believe in him.[151]

The 'rebellious' aspect represented by al-Husseini emerges in an almost caricatured form in the short career of his colleague Mahmud Gul Aghasi, better known as Abu al-Qa'qa' (1973–2007).[152] The way in which this young jihadi preacher became a major member of Aleppo's religious establishment illustrates the vulnerability of the local clergy to the manipulations of the mukhabarat.

Abu al-Qa'qa' was a Kurdish graduate from Damascus's faculty of sharia who came to fame in the late 1990s due to the incendiary sermons he delivered in the popular district of Sakhur, where he also set up a paramilitary movement called the Strangers of Sham (Ghuraba' al-Sham).[153] These were extraordinary acts in a context that still saw the active repression of most of his peers; the authorities tolerated him because he did not

[149] Friday sermon, 17 June 2005, quoted in 'Imams Hussainy and Habash on Democracy in Syria' (www.joshualandis.com, 20 June 2005).
[150] Interview with al-Husseini; mosque lesson, 15 October 2006 (observation).
[151] Lesson, 14 October 2006 (observation).
[152] On this figure, see Arnaud Lenfant, 'Les transformations du salafisme syrien au XXe siècle', in *Qu'est-ce que le salafisme?*, ed. Bernard Rougier (Paris: PUF, 2008), 161–78, 176; Bernard Rougier, *L'Oumma en fragments: contrôler le sunnisme au Liban* (Paris: PUF, 2011), 154–60.
[153] *Bilad al-Sham* ('the land of Sham') is an ancient Arabic designation for the Levant.

challenge the Syrian regime, only the USA and Israel, and also because, thanks to their collaboration with the firebrand preacher, the mukhaba-rat were able to monitor the jihadi networks, which grew considerably after the US invasion of Iraq.

Despite his militant beginnings, Abu al-Qa'qa' succeeded in trans-forming himself into a notable of local Islam. From late 2003, he calmed down, exchanged his Afghan *qamis* for a suit, and trimmed his beard. Three years later, he was appointed the director of the Khusrawiyya and received the pulpit of a mosque–cathedral in the upmarket quarter of Halab al-Jadida. Far from gentrifying, however, his sermons evolved in a populist direction, and he called on the President to act against corrup-tion and the state-related 'mafias' that oppress the poor. In September 2007, he was shot dead outside his mosque. It remains unclear whether the assassin was punishing him for his criticisms of the regime or aveng-ing the mujahidin he had reportedly betrayed to the mukhabarat.

CONCLUSION

Lacking both the will and the means to create a 'Ba'thist clergy' *ex nihilo*, the Syrian regime has traditionally relied on the principle of selection among existing clerical networks: whereas loyal groups were favoured, rebellious ones were marginalised, or destroyed.

Educational movements such as Zayd and Abi Dharr were especially targeted by state repression because some of their members rallied to the armed groups, but more fundamentally because they had prepared the ground for the 1979–82 uprising by instilling an 'Islamic' vision of cur-rent social and political realities in a significant section of the educated youth.

Once order was restored, the regime chose not to rely on its religious administration – which it in fact left to wither – but on subcontractors selected for their loyalty. In Aleppo, the years of conflict saw the regime largely opposed to the old urban society; subsequently, the regime has promoted the Nabhaniyya while building its allies among the tribes that are rooted, like the Nabhaniyya, in the 'rurban' neighbourhood of Bab al-Nayrab. In Damascus, the privileged partners of the state were the Kaftariyya, the al-Fath institute, and Sa'id Ramadan al-Buti.

The co-option of al-Buti was a master-stroke on the part of al-Asad, for he was an exceptionally prominent scholar who managed to pre-serve his credibility by portraying himself as a mediator rather than a mere apologist for power. Beyond his personal political strategy, the rise of al-Buti reflected the growing influence of the media sheikhs, of which radio star Ratib al-Nabulsi represents an ideal type for the early twenty-first century.

Despite apparent similarities in the state's response, the legacy of those bloody years differed in Damascus and Aleppo, which resulted in profound differences in the further development of their religious elites. In the capital, the regime had contented itself with the exile of the main ulama of Zayd, without trying to eliminate the lower echelons of its leadership. This relative leniency allowed for the subsequent reconstruction of the movement, beginning with the return of the al-Rifa'i brothers in the mid-1990s. The outcome was spectacular: at the start of the next decade, recognising the limits of his father's policies, Bashar al-Asad reached out to this former enemy in order to broaden his social base in a delicate period of presidential succession and regional tensions.

In Aleppo, on the other hand, the consequences of repression were irreversible. The influence of the Nabhaniyya within the city's religious scene has seemed far more profound and lasting than that of the Kaftariyya in the capital. The complete annihilation of Abi Dharr has deprived the ulama of a large movement that connected them with the educated youth. It is in light of this deficiency that one must interpret the popularity of preachers such as Mahmud 'Akkam, Mahmud Abu al-Huda al-Husseini, and Abu al-Qa'qa', whose 'modern' or militant rhetoric the public, by now, rarely hoped to see fulfilled. Overall, forty-five years of Ba'thism, with its combination of repression and centralisation, have significantly provincialised Aleppo's religious elite, which in the last thirty years has been dominated by a handful of young and ambitious individuals, while respected scholars have become rare.

3

(Re)defining Orthodoxy against Reformist Trends

Above all else, the ulama are men of religion; it is thus hardly surprising that the definition of orthodoxy should be foremost among their concerns, as is evidenced by the abundance of their written and oral production in this realm.

For the purpose of this analysis, I adopt a sociological rather than a theological perspective on the notion of orthodoxy. From a theological point of view, orthodoxy consists in fidelity to the 'true' meaning of the scriptural sources; from the sociological perspective adopted here, orthodoxy is defined as the religious doctrine that has hegemonic status at a particular place and time.

In Sunni Islam, where there is no universally accepted religious hierarchy, orthodoxy is defined through collegiality and mutual control: it consists in the relatively consensual interpretation of a scholarly corpus that each ʿalim has the responsibility to preserve while calling to order those of his peers who might diverge from the majority opinion. Such a system involves a considerable number of individuals, who in classical terminology are referred to as the 'mass' or the 'crowd' of scholars (*jumhur al-ʿulama'*). Although in modern times this 'mass' has certainly grown with the development of mass higher education, it is not an infinitely expandable category: to have influence on the debate requires that one have sufficient interest to take part in it, the intellectual capacity to master its terms, and enough social capital to make one's voice heard. In other words, the definition of Sunni orthodoxy is a matter of *elites* and not, as has been suggested, of the mass of the faithful.[1]

---

[1] Yadh Ben Achour, *Aux fondements de l'orthodoxie sunnite* (Paris: PUF, 2008), 266–7.

This leads us to the problem of the role of the state in the definition of orthodoxy – or, in other words, the problem of the relationship between the political and religious fields. Let us first remember, with Pierre Bourdieu, that the religious field is characterised by relative autonomy because it is constituted by actors engaged in a specific social activity, namely the management of the goods of salvation.[2] Therefore, many of the debates that shape the religious field (in Sunni Islam these include: Should one interpret God's attributes metaphorically or not? Should one stick to the opinions of the established schools of law? Is it licit to repeat the name of God out loud in Sufi rituals?) are generally irrelevant to political leaders. The latter thus intervene in the religious debate according to two kinds of – political – logic. In the first case, a specific religious discourse will be promoted or combated because of its direct political implications (progressivism vs. conservatism, quietism vs. militancy, sectarianism vs. tolerance). In the second, when what is at stake is obviously limited to the religious field, the executive's concern for maximising support within this field leads it to remain neutral, or, if that is impossible, to support the majority camp.

According to previous researchers concerned with modern Syrian Islam, the Ba'thist regime has not only favoured some especially loyal religious groups and personalities (a fact that is indisputable), but has also supported broader doctrinal trends. If it did so, these researchers claim, it is not because of these trends' explicit political content, but rather because they structurally reinforce state control over society: by preventing the personalisation of religious leadership, as Paulo Pinto argues regarding scripturalism, or, conversely, by propagating an authoritarian pattern of social relations, as Annabelle Böttcher argues with respect to Sufism.[3]

These analyses are problematic. The idea that the Ba'th has promoted a 'disembodied' conception of religious authority is undermined, for instance, by the state's alliance with the Nabhaniyya, which is known for exuberant worship of its founder. As will be shown in this chapter, the fact that some pro-regime ulama such as Kaftaru have felt compelled to produce a more 'rational' discourse on Sufism is not related to (even indirect) official encouragement, but to normative changes provoked in religious debate by the rise of Salafism and modernism.

[2] Pierre Bourdieu, 'Genèse et structure du champ religieux', *Revue française de sociologie* 12 (1971), 295–334, at 329. In Islam, a religion without sacraments, the management of the goods of salvation consists in showing believers the way to Paradise through the definition of orthodoxy and orthopraxy, as well as providing practical ways to achieve it through the organisation of religious education and worship.

[3] See Pinto, 'Sufism and the Political Economy', 116; Böttcher, 'Official Islam', 130.

The regime's support for Sufism against Salafism, meanwhile, is very real; however, we should not seek the causes of this in the intrinsic qualities of these two tendencies (in Syria, many Sufi ulama have been among the Ba'thist regime's deadly foes, whereas many of their Salafi colleagues have stayed away from politics), but rather in their respective positions within the country's religious field. In the following pages, I argue that, before 2001, apolitical Salafism was not repressed because it was perceived as a security threat by the regime, but rather because traditionalists have always constituted the vast majority of the clergy, with the result that they were able to orient official religious policies in a sense that suited them.

Thus far, for the purpose of clarity, I have presented the Syrian Sunni clergy as relatively homogeneous in terms of doctrine. Indeed, in line with their Ottoman predecessors, the vast majority of the Syrian clerics adhere to Ash'ari–Maturidi theology (moderate rationalism), follow one of the four Sunni schools of fiqh, and recognise Sufism as legitimate. However, in this chapter, I will stress the fact that this hegemony of the 'old orthodoxy' is not mere historical persistence, but the result of the victory won by its supporters over the 'heresies' that emerged in the twentieth century, such as Salafism. I will also illustrate the fact that this confrontation continues today, despite the almost complete disappearance of Salafi scholars from the country, due to the increasing dissemination of their precepts through new information technologies. Finally, I will show that the dominant tradition has not emerged unchanged from these controversies.

Of course, the Syrian religious debate cannot be reduced to an opposition between the old orthodoxy and Salafism. In the final section of the chapter, I present various reformist currents, and analyse the ambiguous strategies of their supporters vis-à-vis the dominant ulama.

THE EXPANSION AND DECLINE OF SYRIAN SALAFISM

Late Ottoman Syrian Islamic reformism consisted in two closely linked but nevertheless distinct trends. The first, the leading figure in which was the Damascene Jamal al-Din al-Qasimi (1866–1914), aimed at the reform of religious doctrines. This was 'Salafism' in the strict sense; it built upon the rediscovery of the neo-Hanbali tradition inaugurated by Ibn Taymiyya, which stood in opposition to the pillars of Sunni orthodoxy as crystallised throughout the Muslim world since the late Middle Ages. In contradistinction to Ash'ari–Maturidi theology, it advocated Ibn Hanbal's literalist reading of the scriptures, and in particular of God's attributes; it rejected the imitation of the four schools of fiqh (*madhahib*, sing. *madhhab*) and broadened the scope of *ijtihad* (the exercise of independent judgement) by returning to the scriptures;[4] and it criticised Sufism as being un-Islamic, either in certain of its actual expressions, or as a whole.

The second component of early Syrian reformism, mainly represented by 'Abd al-Rahman al-Kawakibi (1849–1902), in Aleppo, and Tahir al-Jaza'iri (1852–1920), in Damascus, was social–political and aimed to modernise Muslim societies. Like the previous trend, it was opposed by the vast majority of the ulama as well as by the authoritarian regime of Sultan 'Abd al-Hamid II (r. 1876–1909).[5]

The association of religious and social–political reforms was not purely contingent, since the neo-Hanbali ambition to 'purify' Islam had elective affinities with the modernism and rationalism that profoundly influenced the intellectual elites trained in the recently created secular schools. However, this relationship was not a necessary one either: later in the twentieth century, certain Syrian Salafis such as Nasir al-Din al-Albani (1914–99) departed from the aforementioned double agenda by narrowly focusing on issues of doctrine and worship.

Salafism and New Intellectual Elites in the Middle of the Twentieth Century

My aim here is not to recount the history of Syrian Salafism before the advent of the Ba'th,[6] but only to mention its main features. First, this doctrinal trend was not propagated by powerful jama'at such as those created by the sheikhs of the Nahda. Whereas the latter had turned to common people, their Salafi colleagues often displayed an elitist approach rooted in their superior social and cultural capital. Such was, for instance, the case for their leading figure at the time of independence, Bahjat al-Bitar

---

[4] What is at stake here is indeed broadening, not re-establishing, the practice of ijtihad. In the Sunni tradition as it developed from the late Middle Ages, the only legitimate form of ijtihad is the so-called *fatwa ijtihad*, which consists in issuing new rulings while remaining as close as possible to the opinions already produced by the founding figures of one of the four madhahib on specific issues (*furu'*, 'branches'). *Madhhab ijtihad*, which relies only upon the general rules (*usul*, 'foundations') of one school, is considered to be a prerogative of outstanding scholars. As for 'absolute ijtihad' (*ijtihad mutlaq*), which only draws upon the Quran and hadith, this is the form whose 'gates' have been well and truly closed by the dominant tradition for a millennium.

[5] See Commins, *Islamic Reform*; Weismann, *Taste of Modernity*, 273–304.

[6] For such an account, see Lenfant, 'Les transformations du salafisme'.

(1894–1976), who was appointed to important positions within the Saudi education and judicial systems.[7]

Second, although Salafi scholars remained a small minority among the Syrian clergy, their audience nevertheless expanded. This was the result of three factors: the spread of Egyptian Salafi journals (al-Manar, al-Fath), Wahhabi proselytising through Syrian–Saudi trade networks,[8] and the growth of a modern school system whose pupils were receptive to a rationalist religious discourse.[9] Besides those who were ulama by training, therefore, Salafism found many supporters among the new intellectual elites – lawyers, writers, academics, and senior civil servants.

These 'Salafi effendis' set up two associations, al-Tamaddun al-Islami (Islamic civilisation) (1932), a small club of notables that published a homonymous journal until 1981,[10] and al-Shubban al-Muslimun (Muslim youth) (1937), which in 1946 became the Damascene branch of the Muslim Brothers. Only in the capital would the latter be characterised by a Salafi orientation, the other chapters, in particular those in Aleppo and Hama, being more traditional in terms of religious doctrine.[11]

Whereas al-Tamaddun al-Islami had a good relationship with the conservative religious elite, with founder Ahmad Mazhar al-'Azma even being appointed as spokesman of the League of Ulama,[12] the Muslim Brothers remained sharply critical of the clergy's conservatism. Responding to the criticisms stirred up by his book The Socialism of Islam (1959), the Muslim Brothers's founder Mustafa al-Siba'i regretted that most of the ulama opposed 'any attempt at solving [contemporary] problems in the light of the principles and goals of Islam'. 'All they have to offer', he wrote, 'is to say "the return to Islam is what will save us from our problems" … but how? To what extent? And what does Islam think of the problems our ancestors have not known at the time of the Rightly Guided Caliphs?'[13]

[7] See Lenfant, 'Les transformations du salafisme'; David Commins, 'Wahhabis, Sufis and Salafis in Early Twentieth Century Damascus', in Guardians of Faith in Modern Times: 'Ulama' in the Middle East, ed. Meir Hatina (Leiden: Brill, 2009), 231–46, at 241–4.
[8] Interview with Zuhayr al-Shawish, Beirut, 23 February 2006.
[9] Itzchak Weismann, 'The Politics of Popular Religion: Sufis, Salafis, and Muslim Brothers in 20th-Century Hamah', International Journal of Middle East Studies 37, no. 1 (2005), 39–58, at 44.
[10] Ahmad Mouaz al-Khatib, 'al-Tamaddun al-Islami: passé et présent d'une association réformiste damascène', Maghreb – Machrek, no. 198 (2008), 79–92.
[11] Lenfant, 'Les transformations du salafisme', 164–7.
[12] Abaza and Hafiz, Tarikh 'ulama' Dimashq, vol. III, 436.
[13] Quoted by Zarzur, Mustafa al-Siba'i, 150.

One can gauge the magnitude of this challenge to the mashyakha if one remembers that the author of these lines was not a marginal figure, but a renowned intellectual, the head of an influential party, and the editor of a widely read Islamic journal, *Hadarat al-Islam*. Moreover, because many of its members had the required skills to work in modern state institutions, the reformist trend then occupied important positions in the Ministry of Education as well as at the university, where it founded the faculty of sharia and was well represented in the faculty of literature.[14]

Salafi influence on certain agencies of the young Syrian state manifested itself through the organisation, in 1960, of celebrations in honour of Ibn Taymiyya that were sponsored by the Higher Council for the Protection of Arts,[15] as well as in the names given to general public schools in Damascus (Jamal al-Din al-Qasimi, Bahjat al-Bitar, Ibn Taymiyya),[16] and by the decision taken in 1956 by the national radio to stop broadcasting the hymns in honour of the Prophet that were sung in the Umayyad Mosque after the Friday prayer. While the grand ulama voiced their indignation at the latter decision, the Salafi-leaning judge Ali al-Tantawi argued in the press that such hymns include 'nonsense' that offends both dogma and reason.[17]

Salafi Ulama under the Ba'th

In the 1950s, then, the Syrian Salafi trend had both the will and the means to challenge the traditionalist ulama's domination of the religious field. However, by provoking a massive exodus among the most influential advocates of Syrian Salafism – the Damascene Muslim Brothers – the Ba'thist takeover dealt it a blow from which it never recovered.[18] The paradoxical effect of the rise to power of a progressive regime was thus to entail a 'traditionalisation' of the religious elite by weakening its more modern fringe. As for the handful of Salafi clerics who remained in the country, they had neither the social and cultural capital of al-Siba'i and his like nor the popular roots of the founding sheikhs of the Nahda.

When a Saudi cleric visited Syria in 1978, he lamented that he only met two major Salafi ulama there, the Albanian-born Damascene hadith scholars

[14] *OFA*, 20–3 July 1963, no. 1526, V.
[15] *OFA*, 8–11 January 1960, no. 1252, V; 1–7 April 1961, no. 1299, V.
[16] Observations by the author, 2006–7.
[17] *OFA*, 11–14 February 1956, no. 794, V; 22–24 February 1956, no. 797, V.
[18] Lenfant, 'Les transformations du salafisme', 165.

Nasir al-Din al-Albani and 'Abd al-Qadir al-Arna'ut (1928–2004).[19] Both had discontinued formal education after primary school and made their livings as watchmakers. They had received their initial religious training with Hanafi scholars (al-Farfur, al-Burhani), before breaking with them to continue their quest for knowledge through self-teaching. Their main interest was to reappraise the authenticity of Prophetic traditions, an agenda they implemented in the critical editing (tahqiq) of ancient manuscripts.

Al-Arna'ut was a consensual figure who had excellent relations with certain Sufi scholars;[20] al-Albani, however, was highly controversial, in part because of his bold criticism of the canonical collections of hadiths, but above all because of his approach to fiqh. Whereas his Salafi predecessors had only meant to decompartmentalise the four schools of law and reassess their corpus in the light of scriptural sources, al-Albani made a clean sweep of the madhahib's instruments of reasoning (hence his detractors called his approach 'anti-madhhabism')[21] in favour of a literal interpretation of the Sunna. Not only did this approach lead al-Albani to issue non-conformist legal opinions such as the permissibility of praying with one's shoes on, it was tantamount to denying any relevance to the centuries-old legal corpus whose mastery had been the cornerstone of the ulama's authority.[22]

Al-Albani's ideas were subjected to an impressive number of rebuttals published by, among others, Sa'id Ramadan al-Buti, and also Nur al-Din 'Itr (b. 1939), the son-in-law of Abdullah Siraj al-Din and Syria's most revered hadith scholar today.[23] The confrontation soon departed from the realm of strict intellectual debate: as early as 1955, al-Albani appeared before a 'court' of ulama headed by the Grand Mufti, who urged him not

---

[19] For their biographies, see ibid., 168; Stéphane Lacroix, 'Between Revolution and Apoliticism: Nasir al-Din al-Albani and His Impact on the Shaping of Contemporary Salafism', in *Global Salafism: Islam's New Religious Movement*, ed. Roel Meijer (New York: Columbia University Press, 2009), 58–80.

[20] 'Sirat al-shaykh 'Abd al-Qadir al-Arna'ut' [The life of Sheikh 'Abd al-Qadir al-Arna'ut] (www.arnaut.com, 20 January 2005).

[21] Sa'id Ramadan al-Buti, *al-La madhhabiyya: akhtar bid'a tuhaddid al-shari'a al-islamiyya* [Anti-madhhabism: the dangers of an innovation that threatens sharia] (Damascus: Dar al-Fikr, 1970). See also Sa'id Ramadan al-Buti, *al-Salafiyya: marhala zamaniyya mubaraka la madhhab islami* [Salafiyya: a blessed historical period, not a school of fiqh] (Damascus: Dar al-Fikr, 1991).

[22] On al-Albani's method, see Lacroix, 'Between Revolution and Apoliticism'; Jonathan Brown, *The Canonization of al-Bukhari and Muslim: The Formation and Function of the Sunni Hadith Canon* (Leiden: Brill, 2007), 321–34.

[23] For a list of these rebuttals, see Jibril Fu'ad Haddad, *Albani and His Friends: A Concise Guide to the Salafi Movement* (n.p.: Aqsa Publications, 2004).

to 'use his sect to cause unrest among the people' by 'reciting a special prayer in unison' during the office at the Umayyad Mosque.[24] As the liberal era passed, the conservatives came to have more effective means of coercion at their disposal. Al-Albani's tours in the province were routinely hampered by the police at the request of local religious authorities, and in 1967 the 'defamation of the sheikhs of the Sufi brotherhoods' earned him eight months in prison.[25]

Faced with the hostility of the religious establishment, al-Albani embarked on a career as a fellow traveller of reformist organisations: in the 1950s, he began publishing a monthly column in the journal *al-Tamaddun al-Islami* and attended meetings of the Muslim Brothers, a prominent figure in which, Zuhayr al-Shawish, was his editor and employer. When the Aleppo branch of the Brothers turned against the Damascene leadership in the late 1960s, al-Shawish and al-Albani engaged in fierce scholarly controversies with 'Abd al-Fattah Abu Ghudda, the spiritual leader of the northern faction and himself a leading hadith specialist of Hanafi, anti-Salafi persuasion.[26]

However, al-Albani was fundamentally hostile to the utilitarian approach of the Muslim Brothers. He was concerned not with the modernisation of the umma, but only with the purification of its beliefs and rituals.[27] After the departure of his Muslim Brother friends in the mid-1960s, and due to the difficult environment, al-Albani moved into total apoliticism.

Al-Albani and his disciples thus played no role in the Islamic uprising. When he finally left for Amman in 1979, his departure took place in a context characterised by heavy security pressures on Islamic groups in general, but not by a specifically anti-Salafi policy on the part of the state. For instance, following a Prophetic custom they had resurrected in the late 1950s, the so-called 'Oratory of the Celebration Day' (Musalla al-'Id), Damascene Salafis remained permitted to organise a yearly outdoor prayer attended by several thousand people at the end of Ramadan.[28]

---

[24] *OFA*, no. 743, 10–12 August 1955, V.

[25] Ibrahim Muhammad al-'Ali, *Muhammad Nasir al-Din al-Albani: muhaddith al-'asr wa nasir al-sunna* [Muhammad Nasir al-Din al-Albani: hadith scholar of the century and defender of the Sunna] (Damascus: Dar al-Qalam, 2001), 26–7. His arrest was not related to the political unrest Syria witnessed that year (interview with al-Hawari).

[26] Lenfant, 'Les transformations du salafisme', 168; 'Isam al-'Attar, 'Muraja'at' [Recapitulations], no. 2; al-Hiwar TV, 26 November 2007; interview with al-Shawish.

[27] Al-'Ali, *Muhammad Nasir al-Din al-Albani*, 50.

[28] *OFA*, 3–5 July 1957, V; interviews with al-Hawari and al-Khatib.

Only in the mid-1990s did things become significantly more complicated for the Syrian Salafis. Al-Arna'ut, who had become their main point of reference after the departure of al-Albani, was barred from preaching, while his sympathisers were harassed by the police. The attacks of 11 September 2001 significantly aggravated the situation, with the Salafists thereafter identified as a global and soon a local threat, because jihadi networks were involved in various incidents from 2004 onwards. Although most of the followers of 'scholarly Salafism' (*al-salafiyya al-'ilmiyya*) were unrelated to violent groups, they were frequently arrested, and their Ramadan outdoor prayer was banned. Al-Arna'ut died in 2004 under quasi-house arrest and without leaving a successor. The situation was similar in Aleppo, whose would-be Salafi scholars migrated to the Gulf.[29]

The Invisible Enemy

In the 1990s, the evolution of official policies towards the Salafis seems to have resulted less from security concerns than pressure from members of the religious establishment who were concerned about the growing popularity of neo-Hanbali doctrines among the youth.[30] The post-September 11 environment encouraged traditionalist scholars to harden their stance towards their doctrinal rivals. Such was, for instance, the case at the al-Fath institute, a student of which recounted that

one professor of the institute has toured the classes to give lectures on Salafism and its destructive dangers ... Recently, several students were taken to the Palestine branch of the State Security. They were questioned and, although one of them was acquitted of the charge of Wahhabism by the mukhabarat, he was nevertheless expelled from the institute because he failed to prove himself innocent in the eyes of the sheikhs.[31]

Some figures of the religious establishment, and highly respected ones at that, openly encouraged state severity against the partisans of Ibn Taymiyya. In a sermon devoted to the defence of the Ash'ari–Maturidi

[29] Lenfant, 'Les transformations du salafisme', 172–7; interview with al-Khatib.
[30] Interviews with anonymous sources, Damascus, December 2005, April 2006, May 2008; 'Abd al-Rahman al-Hajj Ibrahim, 'al-Shaykh 'Abd al-Qadir al-Arna'ut' (www.islamweb.net, 20 March 2002).
[31] 'Bayna sufiyya Dimashq wa sufiyya Dar al-Mustafa bi-Tarim, wa lu'bat al-salibiyyin al-judud bi-tawatu' wa qasd ma'a al-mutasawwifa' [Between the Sufis of Damascus and the Sufis of Dar al-Mustafa in Tarim, and the game of the new Crusaders with the voluntary complicity of the Sufis], (www.alsoufia.org [2003]).

theological schools, al-Buti praised the 'determination of our leaders to clean the country of those who seek to sow discord'.[32]

Statements such as these, like the numerous lessons and articles devoted by Jama'at Zayd to the refutation of Salafi doctrines,[33] reflected the fact that despite the almost complete extinction of the Salafi wing of the Syrian religious elite, this current was becoming increasingly influential at a grassroots level. Now more than ever, it has become impossible to seal the country against the vehicles of Salafi conceptions – in particular, migrants returning from the Gulf and mass media such as the Internet and satellite channels.[34]

In the mid-2000s, the 'invisible enemy' of the Syrian religious establishment also made skilful use of an inexpensive medium, the video CD, to strike blows against the Sufi hegemony. A violent charge against the Sufi brotherhoods entitled *The Opium of the People* (*Afyun al-shu'ub*) spread across the country like wildfire. This collection of footage of Sufi ceremonies shows spectacular images of *darb al-shish* (body piercing with metal skewers) shot in the Euphrates valley, but also sequences that involve leading clerics such as al-Buti and Suhayb al-Shami, the director of Aleppo's Directorate of Awqaf. The latter are seen listening without flinching to the narration of extravagant miracles performed by a saint who was said to enjoy 'mastery of the universe' (*al-tasarruf bi-l-kawn*), or sing-along verses addressed to the Prophet ('You are the replica of the universes / In You there is the image of the Merciful') which, commentaries suggest, fall under associationism (*shirk*). The excitement generated by *The Opium of the People* convinced many Sufi brotherhoods to drastically curtail the dissemination of recordings of their ceremonies, or to edit out controversial sequences.[35]

THE OLD ORTHODOXY'S NEW CLOTHES

The episode just discussed illustrates both the topicality of the conflict between Salafis and Sufis and the apparently immutable nature of this

---

[32] Sa'id Ramadan al-Buti, 'al-Asha'ira wa-l-maturidiyya' [The Ash'aris and the Maturidis], (www.bouti.net, 3 December 2004).

[33] See, for instance, the following interviews with Usama al-Rifa'i on www.sadazaid.com: 'al-Bid'a bayn al-salafiyya wa ahl al-sunna wa-l-jama'a' [Innovation between the Salafis and the Sunnis] (27 August 2008); 'Ba'd al-masa'il allati hiya mathar jadal ma'a al-ikhwa al-salafiyyin' [Some questions that are a source of controversy with our Salafi brothers] (4 November 2008).

[34] Lenfant, 'Les transformations du salafisme', 173.

[35] Interview with the clerk of an Islamic VCD store, Damascus, May 2007.

age-old controversy. However, this latter impression should not obscure the fact that in modern times this struggle has led the old orthodoxy to undergo a number of changes aimed at neutralising Salafi criticisms – though not at achieving any kind of 'reform'.

The Persistent Rejection of Islamic Reform

Mainstream Syrian ulama have rejected not only Salafism, but the idea of Islamic reform as a whole. I gave a taste of this traditionalist stance in the first chapter when I referred to the purely revivalist nature of the last century's religious Nahda. In the narrative provided by the contemporary clergy about the late Ottoman period, the absence of any reference to Syrian reformists such as al-Qasimi is matched by fierce criticisms of their Egyptian counterparts. For instance, al-Buti and Usama al-Rifa'i have vilified Jamal al-Din al-Afghani and Muhammad 'Abduh as supporters of British imperialism and Freemasonry.[36]

Citing the example of the Companions of the Prophet, al-Buti asserted that the adaptation of Muslims to historical change does not go through any doctrinal reform, but rather through unwavering commitment to the permanent features of their religion:

Muslims who embraced Islam at the time of the Seal of the Prophets ... experienced throughout half a century more changes in their lifestyle than the so-called 'enlightened' Muslims over the last four centuries, without this leading to the change of a single commandment of Islam. Instead, the secret of their progress was the strength of their attachment to these commandments.[37]

From this perspective, the only theoretical dimension of religion that could legitimately be subject to a revival is 'Islamic thought' (*al-fikr al-islami*), as opposed to 'Islamic sciences' (*al-'ulum al-islamiyya*). 'Yes to the renewal of thought, no the the renewal of fiqh', said the prominent faqih Wahba al-Zuhayli.[38] To the extent that it is denied any legal, let alone theological, implication, 'thought' is understood here as a purely illustrative discipline. Al-Buti defined it as the 'cultural or educational attempts at presenting an aspect of the essence and reality of

---

[36] Al-Buti, *Kubra al-yaqiniyyat*, 222; Usama al-Rifa'i, 'Du'at al-istighrab' [The preachers of Westernisation], Friday sermon, 15 June 2007 (observation).

[37] Sa'id Ramadan al-Buti, 'Laysat al-mushkila ghiyab al-hadatha innama al-mushkila ghiyab al-hawiya' [The problem is not the absence of modernity but that of identity] (www.sadazaid.com, 8 August 2008).

[38] Wahba al-Zuhayli, 'Na'am li-tajid al-fikr la li-tajdid al-fiqh' [Yes to the renewal of thought, no to the renewal of fiqh] (www.islammemo.cc, 19 October 2006).

Islam'.[39] This reminder, he wrote, was called for by the disproportionate claims of contemporary 'thinkers' (*mufakkirin*) who unduly encroach on the expertise of the ulama and therefore substitute the eternal truths of Islam with considerations that are exaggeratedly influenced by the contingencies of the age.[40]

The main purpose of this strict delineation of the scope of intellectual innovation is the preservation of a certain definition of orthodoxy, and therefore of the status of its custodians. However, such discourse is not only defensive but also offensive, since it aims at reaffirming the superiority of the opinions of the ulama, which are supported by the intangible 'truths' of religion, over those of mere 'thinkers' who rely too heavily on personal interpretations.

The Impregnable Dominance of Ash'ari Theology

Clearly, the Syrian ulama have encountered few difficulties in ensuring the continued hegemony of the Ash'ari school of theology, a discipline commonly called *'aqida* (creed), *tawhid* (the oneness of God), or more rarely today *'ilm al-kalam* (the science of discourse), in the face of the neo-Hanbali challenge. The reason for this is that this highly theoretical discipline has been to some extent spared by the stresses that have affected fiqh and Sufism because of social change and modern rationalism.

In every major jama'a and Islamic institute of the country, the basic reference in theology remains *Jawharat al-tawhid* (Quintessence of the oneness of God), a seventeenth-century Ash'ari treatise. For al-Buti, the Ash'aris and the Maturidis constitute 'the largest group [*al-sawad a'zam*] of this umma', a feature that, from a traditional Sunni perspective, is in itself a proof of orthodoxy.[41]

As demonstrated above by his call for its repression, al-Buti has been among the most fervent enemies of the Salafi trend. Other major clerics have shown more flexibility. Usama al-Rifa'i, who was invited to deliver a eulogy at the funeral of 'Abd al-Qadir al-Arna'ut,[42] speaks of his 'Salafi brothers'.[43] However, he has no fundamental disagreement with al-Buti

---

[39] Al-Buti, *al-Jihad*, 11.

[40] Ibid., 11–12.

[41] Al-Buti, 'al-Asha'ira'.

[42] Quoted in Ahmad Mu'adh al-Khatib, 'al-Imam al-mazlum, nasir al-sunna al-'allama 'Abd al-Qadir al-Arna'ut' [The oppressed imam, the defender of Sunna, the savant 'Abd al-Qadir al-Arna'ut] (www.darbuna.net, 3 November 2006).

[43] Al-Rifa'i, 'Ba'd al-masa'il'.

over the fact that 'in matters of creed, the Sunnis [*ahl al-sunna wa-l-jama'a*] are the Ash'aris and the Maturidis'.[44]

An essentially apologetical discipline, theology has witnessed a revival as a result of the twentieth century's challenges – the rise of Salafism as well as the new ideologies 'imported' from the West. Al-Buti has become the leading expert in the 'theologisation' of modern ideological debates, or 'ideologisation' of Islam, which he has presented as a total intellectual system that is radically incompatible with the various brands of modern Western thought. At the faculty of sharia, where for years he headed the department 'doctrines and religions', he dealt with the various schools of Islamic theology in the same course as Marxism and existentialism.[45]

Defensive Revisions of Fiqh

In the realm of fiqh, although the reformists' calls to return to the scriptures have not gone completely unheeded, the revisions made by the conservative Syrian ulama have been essentially defensive in character. In particular, the development of comparative fiqh and the revival of hadith studies have not prevented the vast majority of the clergy from remaining faithful to the principle of one-school affiliation.

The Persistence of 'Madhhabism'

'Madhhabism' (*madhhabiyya*), following the rulings of one particular school of fiqh, results less from intellectual jingoism, as is often assumed, than from the practical dimensions of the transmission of knowledge in Islamic scholarship. Given the conceptions that govern such transmission, disciples are naturally trained in the school of their master. This does not prohibit them from studying with another school, but only in a subsidiary way, because in-depth mastery of more than one school is considered the privilege of outstanding scholars.[46]

Until the twentieth century, Damascus had one mufti for each Sunni school of law. The Hanbali and Maliki muftis were dismissed without being replaced, in 1966 and 1988 respectively,[47] decisions that coincided with

[44] Usama al-Rifa'i, 'al-Salafiyya wa ahl al-sunna wa-l-jama'a' [The Salafis and the Sunnis] (www.sadazaid.com, 4 June 2008).

[45] Sa'id Ramadan al-Buti, *al-'Aqidat al-islamiyya wa-l-fikr al-mu'asir* [The Islamic creed and contemporary thought] (Damascus: University of Damascus, 1982).

[46] See for instance the opinion of a leading Hanafi faqih of Aleppo: Ahmad al-Hajji al-Kurdi, 'Interview' (www.alkeltawia.com, 3 August 2008).

[47] 'Abd al-Ra'uf Abu Tawq (1914–98) and Fatih al-Kittani (b. 1920), Makki's son (interview with 'Abd al-Qadir al-Kittani, Damascus, 12 February 2007).

the quasi-extinction of these minority schools.[48] Historically, the majority of Syrian Sunnis have been of the Shafiʿi persuasion, but the Hanafi school spread to the urban centres with the development of the Ottoman administration, and was adopted in particular by high-ranking clerics.[49] Conversely, the disappearance of Ottoman institutions and the extinction of the old ulama families has led to a weakening of this school, although it is still represented in Damascus by the al-Fath institute and the al-Tawba mosque, which are controlled by clerics from the neighbourhoods where the Ottoman religious elite used to reside (the Old City, al-ʿAmara, al-ʿUqayba).[50] As for the Shafiʿi school, it dominates in the southern quarters and on the slopes of Mount Qasiun, which are the strongholds of Sheikhs al-Daqr, Habannaka, al-Rifaʿi, al-Buti, and Kaftaru. In the twentieth century it has experienced a resurgence, symbolised by the fact that the three Grand Muftis since 1963 have been Shafiʿi scholars.

The majority of clerics in Aleppo also follow the Shafiʿi school, despite the fact that Ottoman influence, and hence Hanafism, was stronger there than in Damascus. In addition to the 'natural' disappearance of old scholarly dynasties, state policies and repression have also played a role here, since they have weakened the Hanafi Shaʿbaniyya institute in favour of the Shafiʿi Kiltawiyya.

Wahba al-Zuhayli and Legal Comparativism

In the first chapter, I mentioned that the founders of the faculty of sharia in Damascus had an interest in the comparative study of the schools of fiqh. This agenda materialised in a project to create an encyclopaedia of fiqh, work on which was interrupted in 1961 before being taken up by the Egyptian and Kuwaiti religious administrations.[51]

Today, the leading proponent of this comparative approach is Wahba al-Zuhayli (b. 1932),[52] the son of a farmer from Dayr ʿAtiya (Qalamun).

---

[48] The centuries-old Hanbali community of Damascus still survives in Duma (Eastern Ghuta). Malikism is still represented by a few families of scholars of North African descent (al-Kittani, al-Yaʿqubi).

[49] Schatkowski-Schilcher, *Families in Politics*, 120.

[50] Philip Khoury, 'Syrian Urban Politics in Transition: The Quarters of Damascus during the French Mandate', *International Journal of Middle East Studies* 16, no. 4 (1984), 507–40, at 512.

[51] Mustafa al-Zarqa, *al-Fiqh al-islami wa madarisuhu* [Fiqh and its schools] (Damascus: Dar al-Qalam, 1995), 133–4.

[52] Badiʿ al-Sayyid al-Lahham, *Wahba al-Zuhayli: al-ʿalim al-faqih al-mufassir* [Wahba al-Zuhayli: the ʿalim, the faqih, the exegete] (Damascus: Dar al-Qalam, 2001).

His widely praised expertise has made him a pillar of the faculty and, as mentioned above, he was one of the candidates to succeed Grand Mufti Kaftaru. In his doctoral thesis, which he obtained at the University of Cairo, al-Zuhayli proposed a pioneering comparative analysis of the issue of war in eight Sunni and non-Sunni schools of law.[53]

Al-Zuhayli's work, the centrepiece of which has been reprinted twenty-three times so far,[54] is remarkable in the first place from a formal point of view: he has revitalised the genre of the legal treatise by combining a high degree of expertise with a modern, encyclopaedic presentation that makes it easy for the non-expert reader to solve daily fiqh-related problems.

In doctrinal terms, moreover, al-Zuhayli has moved away somewhat from the conservative mainstream by praising reformers such as Muhammad Ibn 'Abd al-Wahhab and al-Afghani,[55] as well as by proposing cautiously non-conformist legal positions. For instance, he contradicted the dominant opinion among his peers by approving *talfiq*, the possibility of following the opinion of the most flexible school of law on a particular issue, rather than the opinion of the school to which one is affiliated.[56] Like Yusuf al-Qardawi, and against al-Buti, he considers that it is not required for women to cover their faces.[57]

The most original aspects of al-Zuhayli's work, however, have been his attempts at making fiqh relevant to legal realms in which it remained underdeveloped. A member of the Fiqh Academy of Jeddah, he has been part of Saudi-backed projects aimed at providing an Islamic contribution to international norms, such as the Islamic Declaration of Human Rights adopted in 1983 by the Organisation of the Islamic Conference.[58] I will also discuss further his involvement in Islamic finance.

---

[53] Ibid., 87.

[54] Wahba al-Zuhayli, *al-Fiqh al-islami wa adillatuhu* [Fiqh and its scriptural evidences] (Damascus: Dar al-Fikr, 1984).

[55] Wahba al-Zuhayli, *al-Mujaddid Jamal al-Din al-Afghani wa islahatuhu fi al-'alam al-islami* [The renewer Jamal al-Din al-Afghani and his reforms in the Islamic world] (Damascus: Dar al-Maktabi, 1998); Wahba al-Zuhayli, *Ta'aththur al-da'wat al-islamiyya bi-da'wat al-shaykh Muhammad bin 'Abd al-Wahhab* [The influence of the da'wa of Sheikh Muhammad bin 'Abd al-Wahhab over Islamic da'wa] (Riyadh: n.p., 1994).

[56] Sa'id Ramadan al-Buti, 'Kayfa sarat ma'rifati li-l-ustadh al-duktur Wahba al-Zuhayli' [How I met Dr Wahba al-Zuhayli]', in *Wahba al-Zuhayli buhuth wa maqalat muhaddat ilayhi* [Festschrift in honour of Wahba al-Zuhayli] (Damascus: Dar al-Fikr, 2003), 24–43, at 33.

[57] Ibid. Many Syrian scholars are in favour of the face-veil (*niqab*), which, contrary to widespread belief, is not characteristic of the Salafi trend. For al-Buti's position, see *Ila kull fatat tu'min bi-llah* [To every girl who believes in God] (Damascus: Dar al-Farabi, 1973), 49.

[58] Al-Sayyid al-Lahham, *Wahba al-Zuhayli*, 31.

The Revival of Hadith Studies: An Anti-Salafi Weapon

In the second half of the twentieth century, Syria's most remarkable hadith scholars of anti-Salafi persuasion were three Aleppians: Abdullah Siraj al-Din, the founder of the Sha'baniyya; his son-in-law Nur al-Din 'Itr; and Muslim Brother 'Abd al-Fattah Abu Ghudda, who had been deeply influenced by the Deobandi school (Hanafi reformism) while travelling in South Asia.[59]

The situation in Damascus, however, was quite different: in 1958 an observer wrote that after the death of the Supreme Hadith Scholar Badr al-Din al-Hasani in 1935, the city 'lacked an imam known for his science of hadith'.[60] This situation, which was paradoxical in view of al-Hasani's seminal influence, was presumably related to the top priority of the era, which was the religious edification of the masses against Western 'cultural invasion' rather than specialisation in a field which, from the point of view of the conservatives, was relatively devoid of practical implications.[61]

Not until the early twenty-first century did the Syrian capital witness a dramatic upsurge in interest in hadith studies among the mainstream religious elite. This development, which was directly related to the struggle against the spread of Salafism, materialised in the revival and popularisation of practices that had long since fallen into obsolescence.

First, the memorisation of hadith collections, which had lost importance with the development of print, was revived on an unprecedented scale by the female Qubaysiyyat movement. In 2007, they opened a girls' school specifically dedicated to this purpose, the Madrasat al-Hadith al-Nuriyya, situated next to the Umayyad Mosque.[62]

The second of these practices was the ritual public hearing (*sama'*) of canonical collections of authentic hadith (*sahih*), which was abandoned in the nineteenth century under circumstances unknown to us.[63] It was reintroduced in 2007 by the young Sufi master and theologian Muhammad al-Ya'qubi, who was later imitated by Na'im al-'Arqsusi of Jama'at Zayd.

[59] Zaman, *The Ulama*, 55.
[60] Foreword to Nasir al-Din al-Albani, *al-Radd 'ala* al-Ta'aqqub al-hathith *li-l-Shaykh Abdullah al-Habashi* [Refutation of *The Winged Monitoring* of Sheikh Abdullah al-Habashi] (Damascus: al-Tamaddun al-Islami, 1958), 3.
[61] Badi' al-Sayyid al-Lahham, 'Juhud 'ulama' Dimashq fi al-hadith fi al-qarn al-rabi' 'ashar al-hijri Habashi' [The efforts of the ulama of Damascus in the realm of hadith in the fourteenth century AH] (www.alfatihonline.com, n.d.).
[62] *The National* (Abu Dhabi), 13 September 2008; interview with the husband of a leading 'sheikha' of the Qubaysiyyat, Damascus, May 2008.
[63] See Stefan Leder, *Spoken Word and Written Text: Meaning and Social Significance of the Institution of Riwaya* (Tokyo: University of Tokyo, 2002).

The value of such readings is the fact that they rely on copies that are presumed perfectly reliable by traditionalists. Indeed, their owners corrected them by listening to readings made by ulama who were themselves part of an oral chain of transmission that goes back to the compilers of the canonical collections. Accordingly, the sama' is followed by the enunciation of the links of this chain.[64]

These initiatives met with great success. On the occasion of al-'Arqsusi's reading of al-Bukhari's *Sahih* in 2008, the vast al-Iman mosque welcomed thousands of young people, including many religious students, but also those future engineers and physicians who form the sociological core of groups such as Zayd. Such massive attendance was all the more remarkable given that the complete recitation of al-Bukhari's collection requires around twenty days at a daily average of eight hours of reading.

Participation in the full cycle of reading was rewarded by an ijaza, on the condition that each participant bring with him a copy of the hadith collection to be corrected according to the reading. The problem, however, was that the ijaza system was designed centuries ago for small study circles where the master could easily check the regular attendance of his disciples, not for thousands of listeners. In the al-Iman mosque, the solution that was found was to give a barcode to each participant in order to check in and out each time he entered and left the mosque.[65]

The resurgence of this long-vanished tradition was clearly linked to the rise of Salafism. Al-Ya'qubi, a staunch traditionalist, started his 2007 reading of the *Sahih* of Muslim by telling the audience that, unlike him, 'neither Nasir al-Din al-Albani nor 'Abd al-Qadir al-Arna'ut had an ijaza in hadith relation'.[66]

In the exhortation he gave at the end of his own public reading the following year, al-'Arqsusi also evoked the Salafists – but implicitly, by referring to their controversial positions on the gestures of prayer. He also mimicked, in a rhetorical question, their own traditional objection ('You will ask, what is your scriptural evidence [*dalil*]?') before answering with the appropriate hadith. Unlike al-Ya'qubi, however, the sheikh of al-Iman adopted a conciliatory tone, insisting at length on the need to overcome doctrinal divisions:

Sahih al-Bukhari has brought us all together at the same table, despite our differences of schools and persuasion ... I will not go by the names of these

---

[64] Interview with religious students, spring 2008; observation of the final session of al-'Arqsusi's reading, 25 April 2008.

[65] Interview with religious students, spring 2008.

[66] Interview with a participant, Damascus, April 2008.

categorisations, I do not like them. Any other categorisation than 'worshipers of God' or 'Muslims' divides the umma.[67]

At the close of his remarks, the sheikh asked his thousands of listeners to take each other by the hand and to raise their arms as one to heaven as a sign of unity among Muslims, a request accepted with great enthusiasm by the audience.

For two reasons, the reinvented sama' tradition was also a successful attempt to reassert the essential role of the ulama. First, by spending days in a mosque to get an ijaza validating the mere hearing of the verbatim reading of a text that is easily available in any bookstore or on the Internet, thousands of young Syrians gave credence to the Muslim scholars' claim that true knowledge resides in their voices rather than in books, because they embody a guaranteed personal connection with the founding figures of Islam, in this case al-Bukhari and Muslim, and ultimately the Prophet Muhammad.

Second, as was made clear in the exhortations that followed the reading, the latter (re-)places the ulama at the core of the politics of Islamic identity. Indeed, as is the case for any religious or national identity, the construction of Muslim identity relies on the idea of continuity between a particular community and a founding moment (in this case, the first days of Islam). Through the ritual reading of hadith collections, Muslim scholars present themselves as the very embodiment of this continuity. Moreover, they show themselves able to substantiate that claim in a quasi-scientific way through the enunciation of the chain of transmission.

Making Sufism Immune to Salafi–Modernist Criticisms

Both Salafism and modernism have singled out Sufism in their attacks on the religious tradition. It was this that in 1968 led 'Abd al-Qadir 'Isa, the Shadhili sheikh of Aleppo, to publish his famous *Haqa'iq 'an al-tasawwuf* (Truths about Sufism), a modern apologia of Islamic mysticism that has been reprinted fourteen times so far.[68]

Under these circumstances, the relationship of the Syrian ulama to Sufism has undergone more significant changes than those we have just mentioned concerning theology and fiqh. Again, however, it is important to keep in mind that formal adjustments have sometimes served to

[67] Observation by the author, 25 April 2008.
[68] Weismann, 'The Shadhiliyya–Darqawiyya', 265; Pinto, 'Sufism and the Political Economy', 115.

conceal the endurance of core principles. It would therefore be risky to argue that modern times have seen the emergence of a 'neo-Sufism' in which the esoterism has given way to a scripture-based focus on the sole moral dimension of spirituality.[69]

A Pillar of Sunni Orthodoxy

In Syria, Sufism had been incorporated into Sunni orthodoxy even before the Ottoman era.[70] Almost four hundred years later, modern Salafis thus emerged in a context from which anti-Sufism was absent except, in the guise of Wahhabism, as an external threat. For the generations of scholars trained in this milieu, Sufism was neither a heterodox current nor a particular tendency within orthodox Islam, but an indispensable part of their curriculum, since any future 'alim had to 'take the path' (*akdh al-tariqa*) from a master.

For instance, the founding sheikhs of the Nahda were taught exoteric sciences by Badr al-Din al-Hasani, but in parallel they followed the spiritual teachings of representatives of the Tijaniyya (al-Daqr), the Shadhiliyya (al-Farfur), and the Naqshbandiyya (Habannaka, al-Rifa'i).[71] The example of these newcomers should not suggest that being a Sufi was the mark of 'subaltern' clerics. For example, Abu al-Yusr 'Abidin, the Grand Mufti of the pre-Ba'thist era and the scion of a prestigious family of scholars, was a Naqshbandi Sufi.[72]

In this same traditional system, Sufism was also a potential subject of specialisation for aspirant scholars who aimed at initiating disciples into a mystical path. The hagiographers of such a scholar would then call him an 'educator' (murabbi) or a 'Sufi' (*sufi*), a vocation that was not inconsistent with, for example, an expertise in fiqh.

In terms of principles, most major Syrian scholars continue to agree that Sufism is an essential component of Islam. Al-Buti, who has been a reference point for his peers in this domain as in many others, approvingly quoted these words of Imam Malik: 'The one who studies Sufism

---

[69] On this debate, see Rex O'Fahey and Berndt Radtke, 'Neo-Sufism Reconsidered', *Der Islam*, no. 70 (1993), 52–87, at 63.

[70] Éric Geoffroy, *Le Soufisme en Égypte et en Syrie sous les derniers Mamelouks et les premiers Ottomans: orientations spirituelles et enjeux culturels* (Damascus: IFEAD, 1995), 89–101.

[71] Interview with al-Farfur; interview with Qasim al-Nuri, Damascus, 29 November 2006; Rifa'i, 'Durus min hayat', no. 4.

[72] Abaza, *'Ulama' Dimashq*, 325.

without fiqh is an unbeliever, the one who studies fiqh without Sufism is an infidel, the one who studies fiqh and Sufism is in the right.'[73] What distinguishes 'good' Sufism from 'bad' Sufism' is thus compliance with sharia, a stance that is not reformist in itself – it is probably as old as the existence of literate Islamic mysticism – but rather seems to be compulsory in the discourse of ulama who are anxious to steer clear of the 'deviances' of certain popular brotherhoods.[74]

To further distinguish themselves from 'bad' Sufis, modern Syrian ulama such as Ahmad Kaftaru and the Muslim Brother Sa'id Hawwa proposed replacing the traditional Sufi lexicon with Quranic vocabulary. *Ihsan* ('doing good') and *rabbaniyya* ('to be close to God and to bring others to God') were thus preferred to *tasawwuf* ('Sufism').[75] For example, the followers of 'Abd al-Karim al-Rifa'i commonly call him a *rabbani* scholar – a term that, they acknowledge, is synonymous with 'Sufi'.[76] Whatever words are used to refer to it, however, Sufism still poses a much thornier problem: that of its content.

Moral or Esotericism?

Muslim scholars commonly distinguish between 'ethical' (*akhlaqi*) Sufism and 'esoteric' (*'irfani*) Sufism, which is also called 'ecstatic' (*dhawqi*, lit. 'gustative') or, pejoratively, 'philosophical' (*falsafi*). Ethical Sufism is found in the writings of authors such as Abu Hamid al-Ghazali (1058–1111), Abu al-Qasim al-Qushayri (986–1074), and Ibn 'Ata' Allah al-Iskandari (1250–1309); the esoteric or ecstatic form is found in particular in the writings of Ibn 'Arabi (1165–1240).

Syrian ulama generally give a definition of Sufism that refers exclusively to its ethical dimension, through the famous adage 'Sufism is all morality, so that he who surpasses you in morality surpasses you in Sufism'.[77] Corresponding writings are widely taught in mosque lessons, the most successful of which, in the early twenty-first century, was al-Buti's explanation of Ibn 'Ata' Allah al-Iskandari's *Aphorisms* (*al-Hikam al-'ata'iyya*). In contrast, very few ulama admit that they are

---

[73] Sa'id Ramadan al-Buti, fatwa on Sufism (www.bouti.net, n.d.).

[74] 'Al-Shaykh 'Abd al-Karim al-Rifa'i wa masiratuhu', no. 15.

[75] Böttcher, *Syrische Religionspolitik*, 168–81; Itzchak Weismann, 'Sufi Fundamentalism between India and the Middle East', in *Sufism and the 'Modern'*, ed. Martin Van Bruinessen and Julia Howell (London: I. B. Tauris, 2007), 115–28, at 124–6.

[76] Interview with Usama al-Rifa'i.

[77] Abu al-Kheir Chukri, 'Un soufi dans le siècle: autobiographie du cheikh Abu al-Kheir Chukri', *Maghreb – Machrek*, no. 198 (2008), 75–8, at 76.

versed in esoteric Sufism, and a broad discursive consensus prohibits even reading Ibn 'Arabi on the grounds that his books were altered after his death.[78]

Censorship of these texts, says Damascene Shadhili sheikh 'Abd al-Hadi al-Kharsa (b. 1945), is not absolute: it aims at 'protecting the rectitude of the faith of common people', but religious students are allowed to read them 'under the supervision of a knowledgeable teacher'.[79] One must remember here that Sufism is a fundamentally initiatory discipline, so it is only natural to conceal from the uninitiated ideas they are unable to understand. Moreover, esoteric Sufi concepts must be guarded against the 'malicious' use Salafis could make of them.

In an illustration of this strategy of concealment, Aleppian Shadhili master Mahmud al-Husseini reserves his explanation of Ibn 'Arabi's *Futuhat* for his advanced disciples, and for this purpose receives them at dawn in his own home, rather than at the mosque.[80] Grand Mufti Kaftaru, the champion of 'Quranic' Sufism, did exactly the same.[81]

Preserving Sufi beliefs and practices is not only a matter of perpetuating a revered tradition: it also directly affects the status, and thus the authority, of the ulama. Crucial here is a concept that is closely linked to Sufism: sainthood.

Sainthood: Baraka, Spiritual State, and Miracles

The Muslim saint (*wali*) is characterised by three exceptional qualities: baraka (blessing), an elevated spiritual state (*hal*), and the ability to perform miracles (*karama*).[82] In this section, I illustrate the persistence of these conceptions by showing their importance in the discourse and practices of Jama'at Zayd. I choose Zayd because this movement presents itself (and is widely perceived) as following a 'moderate approach' (*manhaj mu'tadil*), which means that it aims to strike a balance between 'extremist Sufis' (*ghulat al-tasawwuf*) and Salafis.[83] Sufi-related notions that are accepted within Zayd are therefore also acceptable for the majority of Syrian scholars, who are generally more traditional than the group led by the al-Rifa'i brothers.

---

[78] Al-Buti, *al-Salafiyya*, 204–5; 'Muhyi al-Din Ibn 'Arabi' (www.sadazaid.com, 2 November 2006).

[79] Lesson given at the home of al-Kharsa in the presence of the author, Damascus, 15 April 2007.

[80] Interviews with disciples, Aleppo, November 2006.

[81] Böttcher, *Syrische Religionspolitik*, 176.

[82] For recent Syrian cases, see Paolo Pinto, 'Performing Baraka: Sainthood and Power in Syrian Sufism', *Yearbook of Sociology of Islam* 5 (2004), 195–214.

[83] Interview with 'Ammar al-Rifa'i.

In Zayd's mosques, one does not see believers seeking to capture the baraka of their sheikh by grabbing his clothes, as is still the case elsewhere. This is not because Zayd's scholars are bereft of this precious gift, but because they are aware of Salafi criticisms that equate this form of *tabarruk* (seeking baraka) with the cult of personality, and therefore promote the supposedly more 'orthoprax' transmission of baraka through mere physical proximity.

Accordingly, at weddings held in the mosques of the group, the task of making the father of the bride and his future son-in-law repeat the terms of contract was systematically entrusted to the venerable Sheikh of the Quran Abu al-Hasan al-Kurdi (1917–2009). An amusing incident that occurred at the wedding of Na'im al-'Arqsusi's daughter and one of his disciples shows that what is at stake here is indeed baraka:

Al-'Arqsusi and the fiancé face each other, on their knees and holding each other's right hands in front of al-Kurdi, who is seated on a chair.

AL-KURDI: Usually I do repeat the formula but here we have a scholar, Sheikh Na'im, so it's not worth me doing so. Sheikh Na'im will make his son-in-law repeat. [He hands the microphone to al-'Arqsusi] Please. [laughter among the audience]

AL-'ARQSUSI (embarrassed): But ... we want your baraka, Sidi. Your words are the baraka and spirituality of this meeting ... It is to take your baraka.

AL-KURDI: It's not complicated, Sheikh Na'im, first you tell him ...

[al-'Arqsusi interrupts him and gives him the microphone back]

AL-'ARQSUSI (tongue-in-cheek): Tell me what I must say, I forgot [new laughter in the audience][84]

Like baraka, spiritual elevation, which is the main objective of Sufism, is acquired primarily through proximity to the saint.[85] Despite their focus on exoteric sciences, Zayd's leaders do not reject this principle, which they call 'the eloquence of the spiritual state' (*balaghat al-hal*).[86] One of them, an engineer, downplays the importance of reading in comparison to the value of associating with the ulama: 'Whatever books you study ... there are many things that will remain obscure to you and which you can only learn through the companionship [*suhba*] of virtuous men.'[87]

[84] *'Aqd qiran bint al-shaykh Na'im al-'Arqsusi* [Wedding of the daughter of Sheikh Na'im al-'Arqsusi], n.d. (VCD).

[85] See Paulo Pinto, 'Bodily Mediations: Self, Values and Experience in Syrian Sufism', in *Veränderung und Stabilität: Normen und Werte in Islamischen Gesellschaften*, ed. Johann Heiss (Vienna: Österreichischen Akademie der Wissenschaften, 2005), 201–24.

[86] *'Al-Shaykh 'Abd al-Karim al-Rifa'i wa masiratuhu'*, no. 17.

[87] Ghayyath al-Sabbagh, 'Suhbat al-akhyar al-salihin wa majalis al-'ulama' al-'amilin' [The companionship of the virtuous and pious, and the assemblies of the active ulama] (www.sadazaid.com, 10 June 2008).

Rather than physical miracles, such as the providential downpour al-Buti attributes to his father,[88] the ulama of Zayd prefer those of a psychological nature such as foreknowledge by the saint of the questions his disciples are about to ask.[89] When a miraculous recovery is mentioned in the hagiography of 'Abd al-Karim al-Rifa'i, it is in an allusive fashion: 'the sheikh loved the patient very much', the author writes, but 'what did actually happen? we do not know'.[90]

In addition, the leaders of the group encourage their followers to observe a certain restraint in the evocation of miracles: 'There is no harm in telling a couple of miracles', Usama al-Rifa'i has said, 'but it is pointless to spend all our time at that.'[91] The purpose of such restraint is not only to blunt Salafi and rationalist criticisms but also to promote a more worldly conception of sainthood. The same al-Rifa'i explains that his father did not see the saints of the past as models because of their miracles but 'because of their actions and efforts' in this world.[92]

In other words, whereas the saint of the past used to transform reality by the mere strength of his faith (one recalls how Yahya al-Sabbagh caused the death of dictator Husni al-Za'im by the sheer force of his litanies), the 'modern' one, following the example of al-Rifa'i senior, does this through patient educational work. As a result, he no longer symbolises, as he once did, the permanence of the social and cultural urban order of the city, which fell apart under the onslaught of Westernisation; instead, he has no choice but to become part of mundane history. By combining a special relationship to God and worldly action, the founding sheikh is thus both saint and hero.[93]

Supererogatory Rituals and the Problem of the Tariqa

Worship practices that focus on saints and the Prophet – such as visiting their tombs, seeking the Prophet's intercession (*tawassul*) and the help of the saints (*istighatha*), or celebrating the birth of Muhammad

---

[88] Andreas Christmann, 'Ascetic Passivity in times of Extreme Activism: The Theme of Seclusion in a Biography by al-Buti', in *Festschrift for the Journal of Semitic Studies*, ed. Philip Alexander, Andreas Christmann, and Brooke George (Oxford: Oxford University Press, 2005), 279–98, at 282.

[89] For an account involving Badr al-Din al-Hasani, see al-Rifa'i, 'Durus min hayat', no. 4.

[90] 'Al-Shaykh 'Abd al-Karim al-Rifa'i wa masiratuhu', no. 17.

[91] Al-Rifa'i, 'Durus min hayat', no. 4.

[92] Ibid.

[93] On these two figures in Middle Eastern historiography, see Catherine Mayeur-Jaouen (ed.), *Saints et héros du Moyen-Orient contemporain* (Paris: Maisonneuve et Larose, 2002).

(Mawlid) – are considered blameworthy 'innovations' (*bida'*, sing. *bid'a*) by Salafis, who view them as falling under associationism (shirk). However, a large majority within the Syrian religious elite sees them as commendable, or at least acceptable.[94]

The Mawlid, one of the highlights of the religious year, is defended with particular enthusiasm. Proponents of the celebration praise its proselytising qualities, since its festive character attracts to the mosque Muslims who do not usually attend prayers.[95] The carnivalesque 'excesses' – which in Egypt for instance have earned the Mawlid much reformist criticism[96] – are extremely rare in Syria due to the prohibition of most Sunni outdoor religious celebrations.

The supererogatory rituals related to the different Sufi traditions (*turuq*, lit. 'way'; sing *tariqa*), however, remain a source of ongoing debate. The majority of Syrian scholars are now affiliated with the Shadhiliyya Darqawiyya and Naqshbandiyya Khalidiyya.[97] In Damascus, the first of these traditions is represented mainly by the disciples of Sa'id al-Burhani (1894–1967)[98] and 'Abd al-Rahman al-Shaghuri.[99] In Aleppo, its major figures are connected to two rival heirs of 'Abd al-Qadir 'Isa: Ahmad Fathallah Jami, a Kurd who lives in the Turkish city of Ma'rash, and Sa'd al-Din al-Murad, the Jeddah-based son of the Mufti of Hama who was killed during the 1982 siege.[100] The Naqshbandiyya, meanwhile, is virtually monopolised by the Kaftariyya in Damascus and the Nabhaniyya in Aleppo.

Other mystical traditions are dying (Mawlawiyya), or have lost favour with the literate religious elite while persisting in other social settings

---

[94] See for instance al-Rifa'i, 'al-Bid'a'; Wahba al-Zuhayli, fatwa on intercession (www. zuhayli.net, n.d.); Sa'id Ramadan al-Buti, fatwa on intercession and tomb visiting (www.bouti.net, n.d.); on these debates, see Julian Johansen, *Sufism and Islamic Reform in Egypt: The Battle for Islamic Tradition* (Oxford: Clarendon Press, 1996).

[95] 'Al-Shaykh 'Abd al-Karim al-Rifa'i wa masiratuhu', no. 12.

[96] Samuli Schielke, 'On Snacks and Saints: When Discourses of Rationality and Order Enter the Egyptian Mawlid', *Archives de sciences sociales des religions*, no. 135 (2006), 117–40.

[97] On the history of these traditions in Syria, see Weismann, 'The Forgotten Shaykh'; Weismann, 'The Shadhiliyya–Darqawiyya'; Weismann, 'The Hidden Hand'.

[98] His son and designated successor Hisham, Salih al-Hamawi (1932–2009), Rida al-Qahwaji (b. 1932), and Abu al-Nur Khurshid (b. 1935).

[99] Among many others, his designated successors Mustafa al-Turkmani (1924–2006) and Shukri al-Luhafi (b. 1920), 'Abd al-Hadi al-Kharsa (b. 1945), and Muhammad al-Ya'qubi.

[100] The main supporters of the first are Nadim al-Shihabi and the Mufti of al-Bab, Ahmad Na'san, and those of the second are, in Aleppo, Bakri al-Hayyani (b. 1937) and, in Homs, the preacher of the Grand Mosque, Sa'id al-Kahil and prominent preacher 'Adnan al-Saqqa (b. 1942).

(Rifa'iyya, Qadiriyya, Rashidiyya, Sa'adiyya).[101] However, there are notable exceptions to this general picture, since it is the personality of the Sufi master, rather than the tradition to which he belongs, that ultimately determines his relationship with the ulama. For instance, even as eminent a scholar as Abdullah Siraj al-Din was affiliated to the Rifa'iyya.[102] Conversely, whereas his grandfather Muhammad had initiated the greatest scholars of his time into the Naqshbandiyya, the Aleppian sheikh Isma'il Abu al-Nasr (b. 1947) attracts an almost exclusively working-class audience.[103]

Representatives of 'elitist' Sufi traditions produce an apologetic discourse which asserts their superiority in terms of orthodoxy. Shadhilis, for instance, stress the fact that their tradition has been designed for people with a good prior knowledge of the sharia, with the result that it offers quick access to gnostic knowledge.[104] In fact, the spread of the Shadhiliyya among the Syrian ulama is wider than the size of actual Shadhili brotherhoods might suggest, since its masters have initiated, among many others, scholars of the al-Fath institute and of Jama'at Zayd.[105]

Shadhili rituals are not uncontroversial, however: unlike the Naqshbandi dhikr, in which participants remain seated and silent,[106] in the Shadhili dhikr disciples stand, sway, and even jump, and pronounce the name of God out loud, often in an inarticulate way ('Ha!'). All these things are explicitly condemned by leading scholars such as al-Buti,[107] although the latter nevertheless maintains very close relations with major Shadhili figures.[108]

This apparent paradox becomes clear when reading the hagiography he dedicated to his father. Attending such a dhikr, al-Buti's father initially refused to participate, before eventually joining his hosts in abandonment

---

[101] See Pinto, 'Sufism and the Political Economy'; Itzchak Weismann, 'Sufi Brotherhoods in Syria and Israel: A Comparative Overview', *History of Religions* 43 (2004), 303–18.

[102] Interview with Sheikh 'Adil 'Aziza, Aleppo, 21 November 2006.

[103] Observation, Aleppo, 14 May 2006.

[104] Private lesson by Sheikh 'Abd al-Hadi al-Kharsa, 15 April 2007 (observation).

[105] Interview with al-Farfur; interview with an anonymous source, Damascus, June 2006.

[106] Although its followers describe it as the 'orthodox' Sufi tradition par excellence, the Naqshbandiyya is not immune to criticism, particularly because of the *rabita* (bond) – that is, the need for the disciple to focus on the image of his sheikh during meditation. Although a Naqshbandi himself, al-Buti denounced this practice in *Hadha walidi: al-qissa al-kamila li-hayat al-shaykh Mulla Ramadan al-Buti* [This was my father: the full story of the life of Sheikh Mulla Ramadan al-Buti] (Damascus: Dar al-Fikr, 1995), 102–5.

[107] Sa'id Ramadan al-Buti, fatwa on dhikr (www.bouti.net, n.d).

[108] In particular Hisham al-Burhani.

to a trance.[109] This anecdote suggests that there exists a kind of 'mystical state of exception': in normal cases, individuals should observe rules of fiqh to the letter, but they can break free when accessing other forms of understanding as a result of an intense spiritual experience.

This distinction is not always enough to spare Shadhili masters from having to adopt an uncomfortable defensive posture. In the middle of the last decade, Aleppian Sheikh Mahmud al-Husseini, who recruited most of his followers from among students of science faculties, found himself compelled to impose the seated dhikr after the departure of a dozen recalcitrant disciples weakened his brotherhood. At the request of the others, the usual dhikr was restored after a few months – but in an outbuilding of the mosque, with the door closed and lights turned off to protect them from prying eyes.[110]

Sheikh 'Abd al-Hadi al-Kharsa, one of the most assertive opponents of Salafism in Syria, has taken into consideration the reservations raised by the Shadhili dhikr and replaced it with a less controversial 'gathering of prayer for the Prophet' (*majlis al-salat 'ala al-nabi*),[111] a ritual that was established in Damascus in the mid-twentieth century.[112] Participants remain seated and silently repeat 'a hundred thousand times' the formula 'O God pray for our master Muhammad and his family'.[113] Many scholars of Sufi persuasion who do not initiate disciples, such as al-Buti and the sheikh of the Umayyad Mosque, 'Abd al-Razzaq al-Halabi, also adopted this 'orthoprax' ritual to add some spirituality to their exoteric teachings.[114]

Of all the contemporary discourse on the concept of tariqa, the most interesting is that of Zayd, whose line of argument is strictly identical to that of the Nurcu movement in Turkey.[115] 'Abd al-Karim al-Rifa'i was initiated to the Naqshbandiyya by Sheikh Amin al-Zamalkani (1853–1927), and recited its litanies until his death.[116] However, he refused to pass on

[109] Christmann, 'Ascetic Passivity', 292.
[110] Interviews with disciples and observations, Aleppo, November 2006 and July 2007.
[111] Interview with 'Abd al-Hadi al-Kharsa, Damascus, 15 April 2007.
[112] Abaza and Hafiz, *Tarikh 'ulama' Dimashq*, vol. II, 786–8.
[113] 'One hundred thousand' is a theoretical number that is reached by adding the repetitions of each participant.
[114] Observations, al-Buti mosque and Umayyad Mosque, March 2007.
[115] Thierry Zarcone, 'The Transformation of the Sufi Orders (*Tarikat*) in the Turkish Republic and the Question of Crypto-Sufism', in *Cultural Horizons: A Festschrift in Honor of Talat S. Halman*, ed. Jayne Warner (New York: Syracuse University Press, 2001), 198–209.
[116] Al-Rifa'i, 'Durus min hayat', no. 2.

the path to his followers, arguing that 'the age of turuq [was] over': not because they were inherently bad but because they were not suited to the ideological perils of the modern world, which required a focus on the rational dimensions of knowledge.[117]

Al-Rifaʻi did not neglect the spiritual training of his followers, however. In fact, he simply established a new tariqa with rituals more clearly rooted in the scriptures and therefore less vulnerable to Salafi criticisms. Like a Sufi sheikh, he required his disciples to undertake the daily individual recitation of litanies (*awrad*, sing. *wird*). However, instead of transmitting those he had inherited from his own master, he made his own selection of 'authentic hadiths … and sayings of the pious ulama'.[118] Furthermore, in the prayer booklet he set up for that purpose, each litany is followed by its scriptural derivation.[119]

This selection is the basis for a collective dhikr called the 'assembly of purity' (*majlis al-safa'*) held at dawn each Friday in the main Zayd mosques. Again, the practical details of this ritual reflect a clear concern for orthopraxy: participants, whose number may reach several thousand despite the early hour, remain seated and repeat each of the above-mentioned litanies aloud a hundred times, without variation of intensity and without hymns.

September 11 and the Anti-Salafi International

During a visit to his Saudi counterpart ʻAbd al-Aziz Bin Baz, Grand Mufti Kaftaru boasted about having made Sufism compatible with Salafism;[120] such rhetoric reflected the conciliatory stance that was widespread during the last decades of the twentieth century, and it was in the same spirit that Zayd made its amendments to Sufi rituals. Although this policy has not disappeared, it has recently been challenged, as shown above, by an opposing attitude of 'traditionalist revenge' encouraged by the post-September 11 demonisation of Salafism.

It is in this light that one should understand the emergence of an 'anti-Salafi international', in which Syrian ulama play a key role. On going through the layers of this network from Damascus outwards, one first reaches the Jordanian Al al-Bayt Foundation, a think tank headed

---

[117] 'Al-Shaykh ʻAbd al-Karim al-Rifaʻi wa masiratuhu', no. 15.
[118] Ibid.
[119] Al-Rifaʻi, *al-Awrad al-mukhtara*.
[120] Nadaf, *al-Shaykh Ahmad Kaftaru yatahaddath*, 175–6.

by Prince Ghazi,[121] and then the university of al-Azhar, which in 2010 hosted a conference in defence of Ash'ari theology that was attended by al-Buti and Husam al-Din al-Farfur.[122] Syrian clerics also exchanged visits with representatives of the Barelwi school,[123] a South Asian traditionalist current born in the late nineteenth century in reaction to reformism.

In the west of the umma, figures such as al-Buti and al-Ya'qubi have kept in regular contact with prominent neo-traditionalist converts such as Hamza Yusuf Hanson and 'Abd al-Hakim Murad Winter.[124] In the Arabian peninsula, their counterparts have been former Kuwaiti minister Yusuf al-Rifa'i (b. 1936),[125] and the Ba'Alawiyya Yemeni brotherhood. Against 'imported' Salafism, the latter promotes an 'authentic' local religiosity that emphasises the cult of saints and the veneration of the Prophet's descendants.[126]

The Ba'Alawiyya has benefited from a formidable ambassador in the person of al-Habib Ali al-Jifri (b. 1971), one of the most famous 'new preachers' (*al-du'at al-judud*) of the early twenty-first century.[127] Like former Egyptian accountant 'Amr Khalid, al-Jifri owes his fame to satellite channels and to a non-political discourse based on emotion. Born into a wealthy and influential family from South Yemen (his father 'Abd al-Rahman was Vice-President under the Marxist regime), he also maintains close relations with the ruling family of Abu Dhabi.[128]

The Syrian scholars soon realised what benefits they could derive from an alliance with such a charismatic, wealthy, well-connected, and, of course, anti-Salafi figure. While al-Buti joined al-Jifri's European

[121] Thomas Pierret, 'Diplomatie islamique: à propos de la lettre de 138 leaders religieux musulmans aux chefs des Églises chrétiennes', *Esprit*, no. 346 (2008), 161–70, at 163–4.

[122] I thank Stéphane Lacroix for this information.

[123] Alix Philippon, 'Bridging Sufism and Islamism', *ISIM Review* no. 17 (2006), 16–17; interview with al-Husseini; 'Abd al-'Aziz al-Khatib, *Rihla Pakistan* [Journey to Pakistan] (2007) (VCD).

[124] Pierret, 'Diplomatie islamique', 167.

[125] See al-Buti's foreword to his anti-Wahhabi epistle: Yusuf al-Rifa'i, *Nasiha li-ikhwanina 'ulama' Najd* [Advice to our brothers the ulama of Najd] (Kuwait: Dar Iqra', 2000).

[126] Alexander Knysh, 'The Tariqa on a Landcruiser: The Resurgence of Sufism in Yemen', *Middle East Journal* 55, no. 3 (2001), 399–414; Amira Kotb, 'La Tariqa Ba'Alawiyya et le développement d'un réseau soufi transnational', MA thesis, Université Paul Cézanne, 2004.

[127] On al-Jifri, see Kotb, 'La Tariqa Ba'Alawiyya'; Hussam Tammam, 'al-Jifri wa mudat al-du'at al-judud' [al-Jifri and the fashion for the new preachers] (www.islamonline.com, 30 October 2003).

[128] Kotb, 'La Tariqa Ba'Alawiyya', 51, 55.

preaching campaigns at the latter's expense,[129] his colleagues invited the Yemeni preacher to conduct marathon tours of Syrian mosques from 2003 onwards. This was an event of considerable importance, in part because of the tremendous popular success of al-Jifri's performances, but also because, since 1980, the few foreign religious leaders who had made public visits to Syria had done so within the framework of very formal, state-sponsored conventions.

Asked about the reasons for al-Jifri's success, one of his young fans answered, 'We know that God loves him and listens when he asks for something.' Indeed, Syrians witnessed at least one miracle performed by their Yemeni visitor, the creation of an apparent spirit of harmony among the local religious factions. In 2004, the Kaftaru Academy took advantage of his presence to organise a Mawlid which was attended, for the first time, by al-Buti as well as representatives of Zayd and al-Fath.

However, while playing this unifying role, al-Jifri created new fault lines within the Syrian clergy. This dissent demonstrated, if not the discreet pervasiveness of Salafi ideas, at least the attachment of some local ulama to an Islam of the 'middle way' and thus their rejection of the uninhibited traditionalism symbolised by al-Jifri.

Syrian Salafis were convinced – and rightly so – that the tours of the Ba'Alawi preacher were part of a plan mounted against them by the conservative ulama with the blessing of the Syrian security agencies.[130] To their delight, a prominent religious figure in the capital broke the unanimity that had accompanied al-Jifri's first visit to the country.

This was Krayyim Rajih, the Sheikh of the Readers of the Quran, who circulated a letter in which he explained that 'brothers' had warned him, based on footage shot in Yemen, that al-Jifri made frequent use of forged hadiths and promoted ideas characteristic of 'extreme' Sufism such as prayer over the graves of the saints.[131] At a ceremony held at the University of Damascus in 2006, Rajih publicly humiliated the young preacher by reproaching him for his Yemeni accent when quoting Quranic verses.[132] The following year, the Sheikh of the Readers wrote the foreword to a refutation of al-Jifri.[133]

---

[129] Interview with a Belgian Muslim community leader, Brussels, June 2009.

[130] 'Bayna Sufiyya Dimashq'.

[131] Unpublished document, 19 March 2004 (facsimile).

[132] This episode was edited out in the official VCD of the ceremony distributed by the Zayd Centre. It was recounted to me by an eyewitness.

[133] Khaldun Makki al-Hasani, *Ila ayn? Ayyuha al-Habib al-Jifri* [How far, O al-Habib al-Jifri?] (Damascus: al-Bayyina, 2007).

While some scholars, especially those of Zayd, tried to reconcile the two men, others, headed by al-Buti, openly defended the Yemeni.[134] Some traditionalist sheikhs went as far as to accuse Rajih of 'Wahhabism', and prohibited people from praying with him as an imam.[135]

In an apology for al-Jifri, a traditionalist writer expressed his indignation that detractors had not chosen instead to defend Islam against those who seek to undermine its foundations in the name of a 'contemporary reading' of the Quran, of 'women's liberation', or of the 'unity of religions'.[136] This was a means to remind his readers that contemporary religious debates were not only about the traditionalist–Salafi struggle, but also about the challenges addressed by certain reformists to religious precepts agreed upon by partisans of both Ibn 'Arabi and Ibn Taymiyya.

CONTEMPORARY REFORMIST STRATEGIES

The expression 'Islamic reform' is often used to refer to an overhaul of Islamic theology and law; but this is not the purpose of all the people who will be presented here. Some have adopted particular postures (non-reactivity, self-criticism) or commitments (democracy, human rights) that are not necessarily underpinned by reformist doctrines, but nevertheless distinguish them from the wider Syrian religious elite. The following pages will also highlight the complex strategy they use to thread their way between the hammer of the regime and the anvil of the conservative clergy.

Because my focus is on these strategies, I will not dwell here on the famous Muhammad Shahrur (b. 1938), whose arguments have earned him the unanimous opposition of the ulama. The latter unequivocally reject him as being 'secular' (*'ilmani*), a term which, when used by a Syrian cleric, is more or less synonymous with 'atheist'.[137] A successful writer in the 1990s, this Damascene engineer broke with the very notion

---

[134] Sa'id Ramdan al-Buti, monthly editorial (www.fikr.com, May 2004); Jibril Haddad, *Tuhfat al-labib bi-nusrat al-Habib Ali al-Jifri* [The true substance in the defence of al-Habib Ali al-Jifri] (Damascus: Dar Tayyibat al-Gharra', 2007), 15–16.

[135] 'Abd al-Hadi al-Kharsa, 'Shaykh al-qurra' Muhammad Krayyim Rajih laysa wahhabi-yyan' [Sheikh of the Readers Muhammad Krayyim Rajih is not a Wahhabi] (www.abdalhadialkharsa.com, 20 March 2007). Despite its title, this text is an attack against Rajih.

[136] Haddad, *Tuhfat al-labib*, 15.

[137] Andreas Christmann, '73 Proofs of Dilettantism: The Construction of Norm and Deviancy in the Responses to *al-Kitab wa-l-Qur'an: Qira'a Mu'asira* by Mohamad Shahrour', *Die Welt des Islams* 45, no. 1 (2005), 20–73.

of transcendence by claiming that norms are not to be found in sacred texts but in the progress of human reason, with which the Quran necessarily agrees – and that therein lies its miraculous nature.[138] The total ostracism of Shahrur sets him apart from other Syrian reformists, who generally stem from religious circles and maintain ambiguous relations with them.

Muhammad Habash: Fortunes and Misfortunes of Ecumenism

Whether Sunni–Shiite or Christian–Muslim, interfaith dialogue in Syria has always had an important political dimension.[139] During the reign of the first al-Asad it was used to promote national unity, but also to legitimise Shiism – hence the Alawite community – and the regime's alliance with Iran. As is shown by the case of Grand Muftis Kaftaru and Hassun, it has also served to improve the country's image in the West. Given such agendas, it is easy to understand why the Ba'thist regime could only rely here on its most loyal Sunni partners.[140]

The extent of the Syrian ulama's reservations about interfaith dialogue was illustrated by an incident that occurred on the occasion of a symposium organised in 2006 by the al-Fath institute and Hartford Seminary (Connecticut) under the title Common Ground between the Divine Messages. While Krayyim Rajih, a member of al-Fath's scientific committee, boycotted the conference, al-Buti and three other teachers of the institute resigned from their positions, asserting their refusal to compromise in matters of creed.[141]

This anecdote shows how difficult the situation has been for Muhammad Habash (b. 1962), who has transformed religious dialogue into a genuine ecumenical project. A graduate of Abu al-Nur and the husband of the granddaughter of Ahmad Kaftaru, Habash was well positioned to become a major figure within the brotherhood of the Grand Mufti, were it not for his reformist ideas. Indeed, he adopted a highly undogmatic position, asserting that Islam has no monopoly on salvation

[138] Shahrur, Christmann, and Eickelman, *The Qur'an*.

[139] See, respectively, Thomas Pierret, 'Karbala in the Umayyad Mosque: Sunni Panic at the Shiitization of Syria in the 2000s', in *The Dynamics of Sunni–Shia Relationships: Doctrine, Transnationalism, Intellectuals and the Media*, ed. Brigitte Maréchal and Sami Zemni (London: Hurst, 2012), 101–17; Edith Szanto, 'Inter-Religious Dialogue in Syria: Politics, Ethics and Miscommunication', *Political Theology* 9, no. 1 (2008), 93–113.

[140] Böttcher, *Syrische Religionspolitik*, 212.

[141] Krayyim Rajih, 'Interview' (www.islamsyria.net, 10 July 2007); interview with an anonymous source, Damascus, November 2006.

and thus that the gates of Paradise are open to the People of the Book (*ahl al-kitab*) – that is, Jews and Christians.[142]

Habash's arguments were unacceptable to most of his colleagues, who are known for having devoted considerable energy to convincing their flocks that salvation requires not only the embrace of Islam but also commitment to Ash'ari theology. In Bourdieu's terms, Habash aims at depriving his colleagues of the instrument of symbolic violence that is the cornerstone of their power: the threat of eternal damnation.

The Kaftari establishment tolerated Habash until he decided to run for the 2003 legislative elections: concerned that the candidate might appear to be the parliamentary representative of the brotherhood, the Grand Mufti issued a statement denouncing his views as 'deviant, contrary to the rules of sharia, the foundations of exegesis and those of the dogma'.[143] Al-Buti, for his part, rebuked the young reformist in a manner that usually, on the scale of such controversies, immediately precedes excommunication. He described him as 'an individual who reproaches God with reserving eternal happiness for those who have believed in Him, in his Book, in his envoys and in the Hereafter ... This person insists on raising high the banner of heresy [*zandaqa*] in the name of change.'[144] 'Condemning Habash', a friend of the latter quipped, 'is the only thing al-Buti and Kaftaru ever agreed upon.'[145]

With such powerful enemies, the ambitious young 'alim became profoundly dependent on the mukhabarat. In the late 1990s, he began a media career, presenting various radio and television programmes, and was entrusted with the weekly religious section in the newspaper *al-Thawra* – the only religious section in the state-run daily press. In 2001, he was allowed to open the first Syrian religious think tank, the Centre for Islamic Studies (Markaz al-Dirasat al-Islamiyya), which welcomed a stream of foreign delegations.[146] In 2003, he was elected to parliament as an 'independent' deputy. In the middle of the decade, he became an unofficial spokesman for the regime by commenting on political issues in the worldwide media on a daily basis.

Despite being ostracised by what he calls the 'conservatives', Habash refused to break with them completely, making public visits to those

---

[142] Heck, 'Religious Renewal'.
[143] Anwar Warda, *Hiwar ... la shajar* [A dialogue ... not a dispute] (Damascus: Mu'assasat al-Iman, 2003), 13–14.
[144] Ibid., 15–16.
[145] Interview with an anonymous source, Damascus, May 2008.
[146] Böttcher, 'Official Islam', 137.

prominent scholars who agreed to receive him, and showering them with praise in the obituaries he wrote.[147] In addition, he allied himself with the heirs of prestigious religious families, albeit marginal ones: Mahmud Kaftaru and 'Abd al-Latif al-Farfur, the disinherited sons of the late Grand Mufti Ahmad Kaftaru and founder of the al-Fath institute Salih al-Farfur; 'Abd al-Qadir al-Kittani (b. 1945), a reformist-minded son of Makki; and Mundhir al-Daqr (b. 1936), the grandson of Ali.[148]

These contacts assisted Habash within the small Association of Officers of Religious Rites (Jam'iyyat Arbab al-Sha'a'ir al-Diniyya), a fifty-year-old organisation which in 2005 he renamed the Association of Ulama (Jam'iyyat al-'Ulama'). However, his election as chair of this association was not a sign of recognition on the part of the religious establishment, since, according to Habash himself, the membership included none of the 'sheikhs of the jama'at'.[149]

As a member of parliament, a position he filled with a zeal uncommon in Syria, Habash voiced demands that were pleasing to his colleagues: wage increases for mosque personnel, official recognition of the diplomas issued by private sharia institutes, the opening of faculties of sharia at the universities of Aleppo and Deir ez-Zor, the creation of prayer rooms in military bases, and disciplinary measures against military officers who uttered profanities in front of conscripts.

However, Habash's interventions in parliament did not just reflect a desire to redeem himself in the eyes of the senior ulama. True to his reformist convictions, he also promoted causes that were much less popular among his peers, such as the amendment of the Personal Status Law in order to raise the age of children allocated to the custody of the mother after divorce,[150] and increased repression of 'honour crimes'.[151]

At the time that Habash was first elected, his entourage included an unlikely figure: the Kurdish cleric Ma'shuq al-Khaznawi (1957–2005), who was the vice-president of the Centre for Islamic Studies. The heir

[147] *Al-Thawra*, 9 November 2007; *Baladuna*, 24 August 2008.
[148] Heck, 'Religious Renewal', 198–9; interview with al-Daqr.
[149] Interview with Muhammad Habash, Damascus, 9 December 2006.
[150] On that debate, see Souhaïl Belhadj, Baudouin Dupret, and Jean-Noël Ferrié, 'Démocratie, famille et procédure: ethnométhodologie d'un débat parlementaire syrien', *Revue européenne de sciences sociales* 45, no. 139 (2007), 5–44.
[151] Muhammad Habash, *Alf yawm fi majlis al-sha'b* [A thousand days in the People's Council] (Damascus: Nadwat al-'Ulama', 2007). Religious conservatives usually match their denunciation of honour killings with regret that the state does not punish the 'real' cause of these crimes: fornication. See for instance Sa'id Ramadan al-Buti, ''Ayyatuhuma hiya al-jarima?' [Which is the real crime?] (www.naseemalsham.com, 23 October 2008).

of an immensely popular family of Naqshbandi sheikhs from the region of al-Qamishli,[152] al-Khaznawi was a non-conformist who was critical not only of the authoritarian Sufi model promoted by his ancestors, but also of the Ba'thist dictatorship.[153] He participated in Kurdish nationalist rallies,[154] and, in February 2005, secretly met with the leader of the Muslim Brothers, Ali Sadr al-Din al-Bayanuni, in Brussels.[155] The following May, he was kidnapped outside the Centre for Islamic Studies and his tortured corpse was later found near Deir ez-Zor. The authorities spoke of 'bandits'[156] and Habash evoked 'Islamic extremists,'[157] but Murshid al-Khaznawi, the son of the deceased, openly accused the regime before going into exile in Norway.[158]

Habash's association with a personality such as al-Khaznawi highlighted his paradoxical character: a pro-regime cleric, he was at the same time one of the few Syrian men of religion who demanded democratic reforms – as we will see below. A theological reformist, he thus transformed himself into a political one, seeming to forget that such a position is a delicate one for someone so heavily dependent on the good will of the mukhabarat. He would eventually be reminded of that fact.

Jawdat Sa'id, the 'Arab Gandhi'

The case of Jawdat Sa'id (b. 1931), one of the few religious figures who supported Habash,[159] shows that the relationship between reformist and conservative clerics is not merely one of confrontation, especially when well-understood interests are involved. A Circassian from the Golan, Sa'id is an Arabic teacher who received his religious training within the Salafi current before becoming the chief Syrian disciple of Algerian thinker Malek Bennabi (1905–73).[160]

---

[152] Böttcher, 'Official Islam', 146.
[153] Pinto, 'Sufism and the Political Economy', 111; *Christian Science Monitor*, 15 June 2005.
[154] See the photos on www.khaznawi.de/sorat/khaznawi27.jpg.
[155] www.thisissyria.com, 1 June 2005 (dead link).
[156] *Al-Thawra*, 3 June 2005.
[157] *Al-Hayat*, 12 June 2005.
[158] www.thisissyria.com, 23 November 2006 (dead link).
[159] Warda, *Hiwar*.
[160] Interviews with al-Shawish and al-Hawari; Jawdat Sa'id and Malik Bennabi, Foreword, '*Hatta yughayyiru ma bi-anfusihim*': *bahth fi sunan taghyiir al-nafs wa-l-mujtama*' ['As long as they do not change themselves': research on the laws of change of the soul and society] (Beirut: Matba'at al-'Ilm, 1972).

The first pillar of Sa'id's thought is non-violence, a principle that gained popularity in Syria after the disastrous Islamic uprising of 1979–82.[161] This stance is not identical with apoliticism, however: in 2005, for instance, Sa'id was among the first signatories of the opposition manifesto known as the Damascus Declaration for Democratic Change.[162] From Bennabi, Sa'id borrowed the idea of self-criticism – Muslim societies were colonised because they were 'colonisable' – and a humanist project that has ambitions to bring Muslim civilisation back into the movement of universal progress. Although such discourse, being an extension of late nineteenth-century Islamic reformism, might seem devoid of originality, it has nevertheless attracted a relatively large audience in Syria because of its contrast with the dominant religious rhetoric, which is saturated with identitarian reactionism.

Sa'id has not been treated as an enemy by the clergy, despite being on its margins. The first reason for this is that his views are of a philosophical and political nature, rather than theological and legal, and so do not directly compete with the authority of the ulama. A second factor is the personality of Sa'id himself, who is not a polemicist and is happy to focus on the intersections between his ideas and those of conservative authors.[163] The third reason, and perhaps the most important, is the quality of his supporters. They include such influential figures as industrialist 'Adnan Abu Sha'r, the silent partner of many religious institutions, Ghassan al-Nahhas, an independent member of parliament (2003–7), and 'Adnan Salim, the founder and chairman of Dar al-Fikr.[164] The latter is Syria's biggest publishing house, and – even more importantly – the regular publisher of two of the country's most prominent ulama, al-Buti and al-Zuhayli.

The religious elite has been less accommodating towards reformists who have neither the prudence nor the contacts of Sa'id. This was for instance the case for the group founded in the late 1990s by his former disciple 'Abd al-Akram al-Saqqa (b. 1944). A preacher in Dariya, a suburb of Damascus, al-Saqqa attracted the hostility of clerics by his daring

---

[161] See Muhammad al-'Ammar, 'Jawdat Sa'id: kama afhamuhu wa kayfa 'araftuhu' [Jawdat Sa'id: how I understand him and how I met him], in *Buhuth wa maqalat muhaddat ilayhi* [Festschrift in honour of Jawdat Sa'id] (Damascus: Dar al-Fikr, 2006), 47–71, at 48–9.

[162] arraee.com, 16 October 2005 (dead link).

[163] See for instance Jawdat Sa'id, 'al-Duktur al-Buti wa kitab *al-Jihad*' [Dr al-Buti and the book *Jihad*] (www.jawdatsaid.net, n.d.).

[164] In 2006, Dar al-Fikr organised a symposium in honour of Bennabi and Sa'id. On Dar al-Fikr, see Frank Mermier, *Le Livre et la ville: Beyrouth et l'édition arabe* (Paris: Sindbad-Actes Sud, 2005), 102–4.

views on women: he allowed them to attend his lessons in the company of men (rather than in a separate room), told girls that they have the right to choose their husbands, and, before the 2000 lifting of the ban on head-scarves in schools, argued that acquiring knowledge was more important than covering one's hair. On three occasions, Sheikh Usama al-Rifaʻi came to Dariya to put the faithful on guard against such 'deviant' opinions.

Needless to say, the grand ulama had little reason to support the 'group of Dariya' when the mukhabarat swooped on it for its political stance: in 2000, al-Saqqa refused to invoke God for the new President, and then ignored the ban on mosque teaching of which he was subsequently noti-fied. Three years later, he mobilised his followers against the US inva-sion of Iraq, but also against the negligence and corruption of the Syrian authorities: after a peaceful demonstration (an initiative that remained strictly prohibited because of the forty-year-old state of emergency), the residents of Dariya were encouraged to boycott American cigarettes, organise their own waste collection, and refuse to pay bakshish to offi-cials. Al-Saqqa was arrested with twenty-five of his followers, and spent two years behind bars.[165]

The Political Reformists, Heirs of the Muslim Brothers

The individuals we here call 'political reformists' are those who demand structural political change, in particular the restoration of civil liberties and multipartyism. This cause has had few active supporters among the Syrian ulama, who, for reasons that will be expounded in the final chapter, favour a strategy of 'Islamisation of tyranny' – that is, pressuring the regime to provide more room for religious values and practices in public life.

It should be noted here that political reformists do not really differ from the grand ulama on the general principles of the political system for which they yearn: in theory, the two groups agree on the fact that the ruler should be elected and that he should enforce sharia. Those principles are found in the political programme of the Muslim Brothers in exile,[166] and also in the writings of al-Buti, still a pivotal ally of the regime. Indeed,

---

[165] Interview with Radwan Ziadeh, New York, 12 March 2010; interview with a relative of al-Saqqa, Damascus, March 2007; 'Shahada Hasan Khalil al-Kurdi ahad al-muʻtaqilin al-sabiqin fi qadiya sujana' Dariya' [Testimony of Hasan Khalil al-Kurdi, one of the detainees in the affair of Dariya's prisoners] (www.shril-sy.info, 21 May 2005).

[166] Thomas Pierret, 'Le *Projet politique pour la Syrie de l'avenir* des Frères Musulmans', in *La Syrie au présent*, ed. Youssef Courbage, Baudouin Dupret, Mohammed Al-Dbiyat, and Zouhair Ghazzal (Paris: Actes Sud, 2007), 729–38.

according to al-Buti, 'democracy defined as the freedom of people to choose their leaders and the freedom of individuals to express their ideas is a sacred requirement of Islam'.[167]

However, al-Buti continues, *in this particular context* democracy would be 'exploited by the despotic forces of the West to corrupt our values and to turn the fraternal relations that characterise our societies into war and dissension'.[168] In other words, al-Buti's opposition to democratic demands is not based on a political theology that is fundamentally distinct from that of the reformists, but rather on a different assessment of the *appropriateness* of such demands here and now.

Priority to Political Opening

One of the main figures of Islamic political reformism in Syria is Ahmad Muʿadh al-Khatib (b. 1960). An engineer by training, he is one of the few living Damascene sheikhs to come from a leading clerical family of the Ottoman era, his ancestors having occupied the pulpit of the Umayyad Mosque since 1870. Al-Khatib himself inherited this position from his father, Abu al-Faraj (1921–86), in 1990, but two years later his boldness earned him a dismissal, and by 1996 he had been banned from any mosque activity.[169]

Subsequently, in addition to a couple of interventions in the international media,[170] he expressed himself mainly through his website. His criticisms of Baʿthist authoritarianism were unusually frank and direct:

Revolutionary governments that rule the 'eternal Arab nation'[171] have devoured life, religion, dignity and even humanity in the people's souls. [They] have destroyed human rights and dragged human dignity through the mud. [They] have executed, murdered, exiled, robbed, killed, slaughtered, confiscated, nationalised.[172]

Al-Khatib's attacks on the religious establishment were even fiercer, describing it as an essential factor in the perpetuation of the regime, not only because of its complacency but also through its active contribution to the demonisation of the opposition. Deliberately using the classical

---

[167] Saʿid Ramadan al-Buti, 'Alladhina yakiduna li-l-dimuqratiyya bi-ismiha' [Those who conspire for democracy and in its name] (www.bouti.com, February 2000).

[168] Ibid.

[169] Interview with al-Khatib.

[170] Al Jazeera TV, 29 December 2006; *Newsweek* (Arabic), 19 November 2007.

[171] This is an allusion to a slogan of the Baʿth: 'One United Arab Nation Endowed with an Eternal Message'.

[172] Ahmad Muʿadh al-Khatib, 'al-Tawwabun' [The penitents] (www.darbuna.net, 1 February 2007).

legal terminology employed by al-Buti to categorise armed Islamists during the uprising of the early 1980s, he wrote that

certain ulama did not even give the sons of Islam the status of rebels, but said that the Muslim youth should be sentenced to the punishment reserved for those who are guilty of banditry; they dipped their hands in the blood of the umma where the hand of an officer or a pharaoh had never soaked.[173]

Today, he continues, the ulama prey on human rights activists, accusing them of involvement in foreign conspiracies.[174] State-sponsored clerics are such a hindrance to political development, al-Khatib argues, that the priority of any reformist agenda should be to 'separate the state from religion', an inversion of the traditional motto of secularists.[175]

Among the country's religious elite, one of the few figures comparable to al-Khatib was 'Imad al-Din al-Rashid (b. 1965), a professor at the faculty of sharia in Damascus. Although the two men considered each other the leaders of what they called the 'intellectual current of the youth' (*tayyar al-shabab al-fikri*),[176] their strategies were nevertheless different. In contrast to the denunciatory tone of the former preacher of the Umayyad Mosque, Professor al-Rashid preferred a more consensual approach. Aiming, like al-Khatib, to 'recreate the Turkish experience' in Syria,[177] he displayed a willingness to find common ground with the regime in the name of Islamic–nationalist unity against external threats.[178]

To achieve his goals, al-Rashid bet on the exploitation of the – meagre – opportunities offered by the electoral system. During the legislative elections of April 2007, which al-Khatib denounced as a farce,[179] al-Rashid mobilised his faculty in aid of two Islamic-leaning candidates running in the Damascus Countryside governorate (*rif Dimashq*), one of whom (Muhammad Bermu) was elected.[180]

---

[173] Ahmad Mu'adh al-Khatib, 'al-Malik al-'ari wa-l-nassaj al-muhtal' [The naked king and the crafty weaver] (www.darbuna.net, 1 June 2007).

[174] Ahmad Mu'adh al-Khatib, 'al-Hurriyya mahma tal al-tariq' [Freedom, however long the road may be] (www.darbuna.net, 2 April 2007).

[175] Interview in *Newsweek* (Arabic), 19 November 2007.

[176] Interview with al-Khatib.

[177] Interview with a close friend of 'Imad al-Din al-Rashid, Damascus, May 2008; Ahmad Mu'adh al-Khatib, 'Su'ud al-'adala wa-l-tanmiya' [The rise of justice and development] (www.darbuna.net, 4 August 2007).

[178] 'Imad al-Din al-Rashid, *al-Muwatana fi al-mafhum al-islami* [Citizenship in its Islamic conception] (Damascus: Nahwa al-Qimma, 2005), 6–7.

[179] Ahmad Mu'adh al-Khatib, 'Dim'a dimashqiyya' [Damascene tear] (www.darbuna.net, 1 April 2007).

[180] Interview with 'Imad al-Din al-Rashid, Damascus, 29 July 2007.

The Legacy of the Muslim Brothers and Salafism

Despite the very sensitive character of such a claim in Ba'thist Syria, political reformists do not hide the fact that they are intellectually indebted to the Muslim Brothers. Al-Khatib often cites figures such as Mustafa al-Siba'i, the Lebanese Faysal al-Mawlawi (1941–2011), and Yusuf al-Qardawi, whom he defends against al-Buti's attacks.[181] For his part, al-Rashid presents the Muslim Brothers as the source of inspiration for his own reflections on the relationship between Islam and citizenship, and more particularly his call to integrate all citizens, regardless of their confession, into the 'political, cultural and civilisational framework' of the 'Muslim homeland' (*al-watan al-muslim*).[182]

In doctrinal terms, al-Khatib and al-Rashid distinguish themselves from the mainstream ulama by claiming the influence of the 'historical' Damascene Salafism of al-Qasimi and al-Jaza'iri. 'Abd al-Qadir al-Arna'ut, who was one of their masters, was according to them among the heirs of this 'moderate' tradition, whereas al-Albani strayed from it because of his 'literalism'. Adopting a conciliatory stance, they call for a truce between Sufis and Salafis.[183]

Al-Khatib has also worked to revive the Salafi–reformist al-Tamaddun al-Islami association, highlighting its modernist and universalist orientation. After his 2000 election as its chairman, he tried to restore the intellectual role of this lethargic charity, in particular by repeatedly requesting authorisation to relaunch its journal, suspended since 1981 – to no avail.[184]

Between the Ulama and the Independent Islamists

The recent membership of al-Tamaddun al-Islami illustrates the complexity of the relationship between the political reformists and the religious establishment. Notably, al-Khatib had to strike a balance between the wish to recruit like-minded colleagues and the need to 'give some weight' to the association in the eyes of the authorities by involving members of the religious establishment.[185] By 2007, the first category comprised 'Imad al-Din al-Rashid, former fellow travellers of the Muslim Brothers,[186]

---

[181] www.darbuna.net/protocols/text.php?ID=1164, 22 January 2009.
[182] Interview with al-Rashid. On the Islamic state as a civilisational–cultural rather than religious concept, see François Burgat, *L'Islamisme en face* (Paris: La Découverte, 2002), 133–8.
[183] Interviews with al-Khatib and al-Rashid.
[184] See al-Khatib, 'al-Tamaddun al-Islami'.
[185] Interview with al-Khatib.
[186] Judges Murshid 'Abidin (1914–2007) and Sa'di Abu Jib (b. 1932), and Haytham al-Khayyat, a former professor at the faculty of medicine of Damascus who was exiled from 1980 to 2007.

and non-conformist sons of prominent ulama from al-Fath (Suleiman al-Zabibi, b. 1960), al-Gharra' ('Abd al-Hadi al-Tabba', 1968–2009), and Jama'at Zayd (Ahmad Shmays, b. 1954).[187] The second category included the renowned hadith scholar 'Ajjaj al-Khatib (b. 1932), philologist Mazin al-Mubarak (b. 1930),[188] and Abu al-Khayr Shukri (b. 1961), the director of the association funding the Sheikh Badr al-Din al-Hasani institute.

'Imad al-Din al-Rashid also developed a double network of 'olds' and 'moderns' thanks to his connections with Jama'at Zayd, where he had received his early religious training,[189] and in particular thanks to his position at the faculty of sharia. There, he established an apparently unnatural alliance with al-Buti: initially, the relationship between the two men was dreadful, the older scholar reproaching the junior for his 'excessive' rationalism.[190] However, al-Rashid gradually reversed the situation by energetically supporting causes dear to al-Buti, such as the defence of sharia institutes against reform projects, and the denunciation of Shiite proselytising in Syria.[191] For al-Rashid, relying on al-Buti proved beneficial in academic terms (he was appointed head of department when he was barely forty) and provided him with some protection against the mukhabarat.

The young academic found a very receptive audience among the students and young teachers of the faculty, which in recent years has gradually escaped from the domination of conservative scholars such as al-Buti. Al-Rashid himself is a symbol of this shift: in 1999 he was (apart from al-Buti's son Tawfiq) the first student to receive a doctoral degree from that institution. Ten years later, thanks to a recruitment policy that favours internal candidates, holders of doctorates issued by the faculty constituted 40 per cent of its teaching staff and occupied the two positions of vice dean.

By providing a channel of promotion that is independent of traditional clerical networks, this change has favoured a growth in the number of individuals who, like al-Rashid, strongly resemble the figure of the new religious intellectuals imagined in the middle of the twentieth century by al-Siba'i and the other founders of the faculty. They wear suits rather

---

[187] Interviews with al-Khatib, Suleiman al-Zabibi (Damascus, 5 July 2007), and Ahmad Shmays (Damascus, 5 May 2008).
[188] He is the brother of Muhammad al-Mubarak, one of the founding figures of the Muslim Brothers.
[189] Interview with al-Rashid.
[190] E-mail from a friend of al-Rashid, 3 August 2009.
[191] On these two issues, see the final chapter.

than robes, and see themselves less as 'sheikhs' than as 'thinkers' (mufak-kirun) concerned with social and political issues.

In the mid-1990s, reform-minded graduates of the faculty founded the Intellectual Meeting for Innovation (al-Multaqa al-Fikri li-l-Ibda'), which launched a short-lived journal distributed without authorisation, and then a website that published contributions by prominent Arab intellectuals including the Lebanese Ridwan al-Sayyid and the Tunisian Ahmidat Enneifer.[192] Originally, the group was only concerned with religious reform, but two of its members, 'Abd al-Rahman al-Hajj Ibrahim (b. 1970), a researcher in Quran sciences, and Radwan Ziadeh (b. 1976), a dentist, rapidly displayed political ambitions. During the Damascus Spring in 2000–1, they attended the forum of the conservative industrialist and pro-democracy MP Riyad Sayf, who was later sentenced to five years in prison. Ziadeh, who defines himself as a 'liberal conservative' rather than as an 'Islamist', became involved in human rights activism before going into exile in 2007 and becoming one of the most visible figures of the Syrian opposition in Washington.[193]

Ziyadeh asked Mu'adh al-Khatib to give the religious address at his wedding, an invitation which shows that al-Khatib is – to use the terminology of the sociology of social movements – a 'broker': although primarily rooted in the religious field, he has been among the few members of that field to maintain close relations with the political opposition, and especially the laymen of the so-called Independent Islamic Tendency (al-Tayyar al-Islami al-Mustaqill).

Al-Khatib is close to the 'sheikh of defenders of human rights' (*shaykh huquqiyyin*) Haytham al-Malih (b. 1931), a lawyer and former political prisoner,[194] and the physician Yasir al-'Ayti (b. 1968), a former follower of Zayd.[195] 'Independent Islamists' advocate liberal reform of the country's political institutions. According to their representative in Aleppo, Ghassan al-Najjar (b. 1937), an engineer and former political prisoner, their goal is 'a modern civil state based on a multiparty parliamentary system, which considers citizens as equal, separates between the three powers and guarantees respect for human rights'.[196]

---

[192] www.almultaka.net.

[193] Interviews with 'Abd al-Rahman al-Hajj Ibrahim, Damascus, 2005–7, and Ziadeh.

[194] Interviews with al-Khatib and al-Malih.

[195] See al-Khatib's foreword to Yasir al-'Ayti, *Li-'uyunik ya Quds* [For your eyes, O Jerusalem] (Beirut: al-Maktab al-Islami, 2001).

[196] www.thisissyria.net/2007/12/04/syriatoday/04.html, 4 December 2007.

Internationally, the networks of the above lead us, unsurprisingly, into the nebula of the Syrian Islamist opposition. Al-Khatib is a member of the League of the Writers of Sham (Rabita Udaba' al-Sham), an organisation founded in London by Abdullah al-Tantawi, a prominent member of the Muslim Brothers.[197] In 2007, al-Khatib, al-Malih, al-Najjar, and al-'Ayti published numerous articles in the bi-monthly newsletter of the Movement for Justice and Development (Harakat al-'Adala wa-l-Bina'), established in London in 2006 by former Syrian Muslim Brothers inspired by the 'Muslim democrat' model of the Turkish AKP.[198]

A quarter of a century after the siege of Hama, political Islam inside Syria thus gradually ceased to be a ghost and became embodied in a small but tangible movement with visible figures and media channels. However, as will be shown later, the regime was lying in wait.

CONCLUSION

As the first decade of the twenty-first century drew to a close, the Salafi movement was less well represented among the ulama in Syria than in any other country of the Arab East. This situation had undoubtedly resulted from state repression, which had intensified after the millennium, but this was only part of the picture: long before the Salafis had been branded a major security threat, they had been more vulnerable than the conservatives within the authoritarian context due to the weakness of their social roots; in addition, it was not historically the state but the mainstream ulama who were most eager to curtail Salafi influence.

Operating in an individual and elitist mode, the Salafis in the middle of the twentieth century had fewer supporters among the clergy than among the 'modern' intellectual elites. During the pre-Ba'thist era, this social base gave Salafism influence in literary circles, the judiciary, academia, and the administration. However, Salafi-leaning organisations were much less suitable for operating under a police state than the informal, grassroots jama'at of the traditionalist sheikhs: al-Tamaddun al-Islami was a club of notables, whereas the Muslim Brothers, being primarily a political grouping, was logically a priority target for the regime that came to power in 1963.

In the following years, the exodus of much of the Salafi intelligentsia left behind less sophisticated figures such as the hadith scholars

---

[197] www.odabasham.net/member.php.
[198] See Lenfant, 'Les transformations du salafisme', 173.

al-Albani and al-Arna'ut. The former, who scandalised his colleagues with his iconoclastic legal methodology, was at a very early stage subject to intimidation by the religious establishment. In the late twentieth century, 'scholarly Salafis' were hardly perceived as a serious political threat by the regime; rather, its repression of them seemed to be in response to periodic requests from the conservatives who overwhelmingly dominated the country's religious field. This situation changed with September 11: in its aftermath, the scholarly Salafis began to be persecuted in earnest.

Although it is now deprived of any renowned scholars, Syrian Salafism has come to constitute a threatening and invisible enemy in the eyes of mainstream clergymen, since new information technologies allow it to attract an increasing number of young people. For the conservatives, this situation has made it more necessary than ever to develop an apologetic literature, as well as to undertake certain doctrinal and ritual amendments in order to demonstrate their faithfulness to the scriptures. This is the background for the current revival of hadith studies and for the transformation of Sufi discourse and practices. However, as long as certain basic concepts of Islamic mysticism (esotericism, sainthood, tariqa) remain unchanged, addressing Salafi criticism also requires that the ulama resort to a strategy of concealment.

Through their 'moderate' profession of faith, groups such as Zayd and the Kaftariyya have presented themselves as a middle way between 'extreme' Sufism and Salafism. However, by putting the latter in the dock, the attacks of September 11 have encouraged a 'revenge of the Sufis' that has materialised through the formation of an international anti-Salafi trend. The Syrian clergy have been strongly involved in this project of doctrinal reconquest, as evidenced for instance by their warm welcome to the Yemeni Sufi TV preacher al-Habib Ali al-Jifri. However, the controversies that surrounded al-Jifri's visit showed that the scripturalist normative framework that constituted itself in the twentieth century as a result of the Salafi upsurge continues to present strong obstacles to the rise of unabashed traditionalism.

In addition to these modern avatars of the age-old opposition between supporters of Ibn 'Arabi and Ibn Taymiyya, contemporary Syria has also witnessed debates provoked by other brands of reformism. Whereas the conflict between Muhammad Shahrur's positivism and the rest of the Islamic movement was a zero-sum game, other reformists have occupied more ambiguous positions.

Criticised by the grand ulama for his ecumenical positions, Muhammad Habash sought the support of both the mukhabarat and second-rank members of reputable clerical families. Meanwhile, Jawdat Sa'id, an apostle of humanism and non-violence, has enjoyed the support of influential admirers among the pious bourgeoisie and Islamic publishing houses. Political reformists have also been pursuing complex strategies, since they consider the grand ulama to be a pillar of the established order while nevertheless seeking their protection from state harassment.

The old Sunni orthodoxy inherited from the Ottoman era has thus retained its hegemonic character in the early twenty-first century. In terms of social roots, it hardly needs repeating that it was the traditionalist ulama who set up most of the schools and study circles in which tens of thousands of Syrians have received their religious education. These ulama have therefore had access to economic resources beyond comparison with those of their rivals. These resources have not only enabled them to strengthen their domination over the religious field but also, as will be shown in the next chapter, to benefit from the recent economic liberalisation.

4

The Turban and the Chequebook

Political Economy of the Syrian Religious Elite

> The two main values of Damascene society are: to have money, and to have a sheikh.
>
> A Syrian merchant, Damascus, 2007

We have already met Na'im al-'Arqsusi, one of the most popular sheikhs in Damascus despite his relative youth (in the first decade of the new millennium he was still only in his fifties). Due to his popularity, his daily schedule resembles that of a high-ranking state official: he spends much of the day in his office receiving a stream of individuals come to submit various requests. These are sometimes about arbitration of family or business conflicts, a traditional prerogative of clerics,[1] and sometimes about making up for the (formerly) state-run banking system which many Syrians are reluctant to use. A newlywed tells how he turned to al-'Arqsusi in order to obtain a loan to buy a house. The sheikh then contacted his merchant supporters and vouched for the applicant.[2]

While such transactions usually take place in relative secrecy, there are occasions when al-'Arqsusi's qualities of broker between the rich and the needy are displayed openly. During the celebration of the Mawlid, for example, he has organised 'auctions' whose profits are donated to a charitable project called Sunduq al-Mawadda wa-l-Rahma (Fund of love and mercy), which aims to help young people get married by helping to pay the dowry. Responding to the exhortations of the scholar, the faithful

---

[1] See Salwa Ismail, 'Changing Social Structure, Shifting Alliances and Authoritarianism in Syria', in *Demystifying Syria*, ed. Fred Lawson (London: Saqi, 2009), 13–28, at 25.
[2] Interview with an anonymous source, Damascus, May 2007.

raise their hands and indicate with their fingers the number of marriage grants with a value of 50,000 Syrian pounds (about US$1,000) they are willing to pay for. In 2007, 7.5 million pounds were collected in one evening.[3]

As illustrated by this example, men of religion have played a crucial role in the unprecedented growth of private welfare witnessed in Syria from the late 1990s onwards, within a wider context of economic liberalisation and pauperisation.[4] Far from marginalising the ulama, the globalisation of capitalism has provided them with new opportunities to demonstrate their social relevance.

The first part of this chapter deals with the origins of the alliance between the ulama and the private sector. In its current form, this alliance dates back to the colonial and early post-colonial periods. The associations that were created at that time constituted the foundation of the revival of the charitable sector witnessed in the early twenty-first century, after the long interlude of Ba'thist socialism.

Noting that this process has mainly benefited Jama'at Zayd, a group that the regime has long viewed with suspicion, I argue that the success of the financing of Islamic associations is determined by the social capital of the scholars involved, a factor over which the state has little control. In particular, the ulama's fundraising capacity primarily depends on their popularity among small and medium-sized entrepreneurs, sectors which have traditionally provided most of the economic resources of Syrian Islamic charities.

However, through a study of the campaign for the 2007 parliamentary elections, I will show that big businessmen have become increasingly involved in the financing of these charities in order to obtain the public blessing of respected men of religion. Recent economic transformations have thus led to a transformation of state–ulama relations, in part because the proper functioning of the charitable sector requires increased cooperation between the two parties, but also because some of the clergy's new silent partners are intimately associated with the political–military elite.

The final section focuses on the economic ethics of the Syrian ulama, which clearly reflects their relationship with the merchant community and therefore has distinctly bourgeois characteristics.

---

[3] See Pierret and Selvik, 'Limits of "Authoritarian Upgrading"', 595–6.
[4] See ibid.; Laura Ruiz de Elvira, 'L'état syrien de Bachar al-Assad à l'épreuve des ONG', *Maghreb – Machrek*, no. 203 (2010), 41–58.

ROOTS OF THE ULAMA–MERCHANT ALLIANCE

Since the French Mandate, three factors have coincided to give the relationship between the ulama and the merchants its present character: the
accession of merchant ulama to the pinnacle of the religious elite; their
alliance with middle-bourgeois families; and, thanks to the latter's financial support, the spread of Islamic associations.

The Renaissance of Sacred Knowledge and the Emergence of Merchant Ulama

In early twenty-first-century Damascus, some elderly men of religion
could be seen distinguishing themselves from the common people by
wearing a colourful silk scarf tied around a purple tarboosh. Up until
the colonial period, this headgear had been distinctive not of the ulama,
who used to wear turbans, but of the merchants. This semiotic change
reflects the important role played by merchant ulama in the aforementioned sociological renewal of the clergy during the first half of the twentieth century.

Under the Ottomans, the grand ulama drew their revenues from
awqaf, as well as from land ownership and commerce.[5] Members of prestigious houses of knowledge built immense fortunes: Sa'id al-Hamzawi
(1895–1978), the last naqib al-ashraf, for example, participated in the
creation of several joint stock companies;[6] 'Abd al-Qadir al-Khatib
(1874–1932), the preacher of the Umayyad Mosque and Ahmad Mu'adh's
grandfather, was elected as the chairman of the Damascus Chamber of
Commerce in 1914.[7]

In the first chapter I showed how, in the first half of the twentieth century, the old religious elite was gradually replaced by newcomers, many
of whom belonged to a junior class of merchant clerics. Some of them
were medium-sized traders and industrialists, such as Ali al-Daqr and
his partner 'Abd al-Hamid al-Tabba' (1898–1952).[8] Others were humbler craftsmen and shopkeepers: Hasan Habannaka was a binder, Salih
al-Farfur a carpenter, and his associate Ramzi al-Bazam (1917–91) a

---

[5] Schatkowski-Schilcher, *Families in Politics*, 115, 127–9.
[6] Al-Humsi, *al-Du'at*, vol. I, 296.
[7] Abaza and Hafiz, *Tarikh 'ulama' Dimashq*, vol. I, 461.
[8] Ibid., vol. II, 650.

confectioner.[9] In Aleppo, Abdullah Siraj al-Din was the son and grandson of dried-fruit wholesalers.[10]

It is important to understand that mercantile financial support for the sheikhs of the Nahda should not be interpreted as an alliance between two distinct social groups, but rather as cooperation between actors who share much of their social and cultural background. A proof of this symbiosis can be seen in the fact that some merchants did not content themselves with subsidising the founding sheikhs, but also entrusted them with the training of one of their sons. Mustafa al-Bugha, a leading disciple of Habannaka, was the son of the trustee of the butchers,[11] and Jamal al-Sayrawan, one of 'Abd al-Karim al-Rifa'i's closest followers, was the son and grandson of prominent textile manufacturers.[12]

In addition, the people of the souk assiduously attended the lessons of the ulama. Sheikh al-Rifa'i even organised special lessons for them, each week in a different merchant's house. These were simplified and convivial lessons that contrasted with the usually rigid etiquette of religious study circles:

There was a tall man with a beautiful voice named Abu Sayyah al-Sa'd. At the end of the session, he used to sing the glory of the Prophet and the others were repeating each verse after him. At the end of the lesson, everyone was in seventh heaven after drinking the tea, in the preparation of which Abu Sayyah excelled.[13]

Such meetings were designed as much to create social bonds as teach the rudiments of religion. According to al-Rifa'i's hagiographers themselves, the main benefit of all this was to allow the sheikh to raise financial resources in aid of his movement's projects.[14]

The targets of such 'tailor-made da'wa' were not big businessmen, but humbler traders from the city's old neighbourhoods. However, as the popularity of the sheikhs of the Nahda increased, and with it the 'symbolic return' of donations to them, more powerful economic players

---

[9] Abaza, *'Ulama' Dimashq*, 204–6.
[10] Abdullah Siraj al-Din, *Hawla tarjamat al-marhum al-imam al-'allamat al-shahir wa-l-'arif al-kabir fadila sayyidi al-walid al-shaykh Muhammad Najib Siraj al-Din al-Husseini* [Biography of the late imam, the famous savant and great connoisseur of God, His Excellency, my master and father Sheikh Muhammad Najib Siraj al-Din al-Husseini] (Aleppo: Dar al-Falah, 2002), 8.
[11] Al-Sawwaf, *Mu'jam al-usar*, vol. I, 147.
[12] Ibid., 480–1.
[13] 'Al-Shaykh 'Abd al-Karim al-Rifa'i wa masiratuhu', no. 5.
[14] Ibid.

came into the picture. For example, Hasan Habannaka built the new headquarters of his institute in the early 1960s thanks to the support of major figures in international trade (Sultan ʿAjami, ʿIzzat al-Dibs) and industry (Nuri al-Hakim).[15]

Islamic Charities before the Baʿth

Charitable associations (*jamʿiyyat khayriyya*), which began to multiply in Syria from the 1920s,[16] witnessed a golden age in the 1950s. Between 1952 and 1954, for example, their number rose from 73 to 203.[17] Several factors combined to cause this phenomenon: a liberal economic system in which the need for solidarity fell to civil society rather than to the state, a correspondingly flexible system of legislation, and the growing assertiveness of a new generation of religious leaders – the men of the Nahda.

Most of the charities set up after independence operated within a single neighbourhood that was often referred to in their official name: for instance, Sheikh Saʿid al-Burhani founded the Charitable Association of al-ʿUqayba, and his colleague Hasan Habannaka the Charitable Association of Midan Mujtahid. A primary space for sociability and solidarity, the bounds of the neighbourhood usually corresponded to the perimeter of the area within which a local ʿalim was best known and, therefore, most capable of raising funds.

In the 1950s Syrian charities started to coordinate and diversify their activities. The Union of Charitable Associations of Damascus (Ittihad al-Jamʿiyyat al-Khayriyya bi-Dimashq), which was dominated from the start by Islamic-leaning organisations, was founded in 1957.[18]

This process of opening up also took on a national dimension with the growth of the al-Nahdat al-Islamiyya (Islamic renaissance) network, which spread from Hama to the entire country starting from 1954. Al-Nahdat al-Islamiyya was a novelty in two respects: first, local chapters operated at the level of an entire city rather than merely the neighbourhood; second, although each of these sections had its own board of administrators, a national convention was organised every year for all the branches of the network. In order to attract donations city-wide, local sections were sponsored by the most popular ulama of the time, such as

[15] Habannaka, *al-Walid al-daʿiya*, 165.
[16] Reissner, *Ideologie und Politik*, 80–5.
[17] *OFA*, 5–8 January 1952, no. 393, VI; 2–5 April 1955, no. 711, VI.
[18] Al-Humsi, *al-Duʿat*, vol. I, 267.

Muhammad al-Hamid (1910–69) in Hama, 'Abd al-Karim al-Rifa'i in Damascus, and Muhammad al-Nabhan in Aleppo.[19]

Al-Nahdat al-Islamiyya also distinguished itself by a broader conception of social work, which was no longer merely distributive but became productive with the organisation of vocational training and the establishment of workshops.[20] In an instance that tells a great deal about both the margin for manoeuvre enjoyed by the charitable sector in the liberal era and the bourgeois social ethics of the religious elite of that time, al-Nahdat al-Islamiyya set up patrols to chase away beggars on the grounds that 'they were harming the reputation of the city and the rich, who were doing their best to answer the needs of the poor'.[21]

The golden age of the charitable sector ended with the Ba'thist coup of 1963. Although existing Islamic organisations continued to operate and, thanks to al-Asad's limited liberalisation in the early 1970s, were even allowed to receive Saudi funding,[22] launching new projects was now a challenge. In addition to security restrictions, the advent of socialism had made the very principle of charity an anachronism.

In retrospect, however, the first two decades of the Ba'thist era were not all bad for the ulama–merchant nexus. Indeed, given the dismantling of the capitalist class during the 1960s, the first economic opening (*infitah*) carried out by al-Asad in the wake of his takeover certainly benefited a 'new class' (*al-tabaqa al-jadida*) of parasitic businessmen, but also old families from the 'upper merchant middle class' – the traditional silent partners of the mashyakha – who got their hands on large parts of domestic and foreign trade and developed medium-sized industries.[23]

In contrast, the crushing of the Islamist uprising in the early 1980s led to new measures being enacted against the charitable sector, the most spectacular of which was the nationalisation of all the branches of al-Nahdat al-Islamiyya and their transformation into 'social care bureaux'.[24]

---

[19] *OFA*, 29 August–1 September 1959, no. 1141, VII and 28–30 September 1960, no. 1249, V; 'al-Shaykh Muhammad Salim al-Ahdab', (www.islamsyria.com, 23 January 2008); 'al-Shaykh 'Abd al-Karim al-Rifa'i wa masiratuhu', no. 14.

[20] 'Al-Shaykh Muhammad al-Nabhan: min injazatihi' [Sheikh Muhammad al-Nabhan: some of his achievements] (www.alkeltawia.com, 19 December 2007).

[21] Ibid.; interview with al-Malih; 'al-Shaykh 'Abd al-Karim al-Rifa'i wa masiratuhu', no. 14.

[22] *Al-Jazira* (Riyadh), 4 February 1973.

[23] Volker Perthes, *The Political Economy of Syria under Asad* (New York: I. B. Tauris, 1995), 109–15; Philippe Droz-Vincent, *Moyen-Orient: pouvoirs autoritaires, sociétés bloquées* (Paris: PUF, 2004), 240–3.

[24] Interviews with al-Malih and al-Burhani; Pierret and Selvik, 'Limits of "Authoritarian Upgrading"', 602.

BACK TO ECONOMIC LIBERALISM: NEW OPPORTUNITIES,
NEW PARTNERS

In 1986, a severe fiscal crisis set the stage for a second infitah, which greatly enhanced the importance of the private sector. After a pause in the 1990s, economic reforms resumed under Bashar al-Asad. In 2005, the Tenth Regional Congress of the Ba'th officially announced the transformation of Syria into a 'social market economy'.

Although this shift did not entail an outright renunciation of redistributive policies, the Syrian state has nevertheless been overwhelmed by rapid population growth such that by 2004 one-tenth of the population was living on less than two dollars a day.[25] To mitigate the potentially destabilising effects of this impoverishment, the regime liberalised its policy towards the charitable sector, which experienced a marked revival. By providing new opportunities for cooperation between the clergy and private sector, this development put the ulama in contact with economic actors who no longer consisted merely of their traditional partners among the merchant upper middle class.

Renaissance of the Charitable Sector

Between 2004 and 2006, the total number of registered associations in Syria doubled, reaching 1,200. About half had a charitable purpose, and within this category the vast majority were Sunni Muslim. In parallel, a combination of favourable economic factors significantly boosted the means of these charities: between 2002 and 2006, certain associations doubled their expenses every year. Even though no formal statistics were available, there was little doubt that private welfare was benefiting hundreds of thousands by the end of the decade.[26] Surprisingly enough, the major beneficiary of this trend was Jama'at Zayd, a former enemy of the regime.

In 2002, building on the network of neighbourhood associations created by his father, Sariya al-Rifa'i launched the Hifz al-Ni'ma (Preservation of grace) project, which collects and distributes food, medicine, clothing, and furniture to thousands of needy families. Meanwhile, Zayd took control of the Union of Charitable Associations of Damascus, after businessmen from among its following were elected to leading positions within

---

[25] Pierret and Selvik, 'Limits of "Authoritarian Upgrading"', 601.
[26] Ibid., 601–2.

the board of directors. In this way, the movement found itself at the helm of two major projects launched by the Union in the late 1990s: Sunduq al-'Afiya (Health fund), which covers the cost of surgical operations, and the already-mentioned Sunduq al-Mawadda wa-l-Rahma.[27]

The rise of Zayd in the charitable sector was not the choice of the regime, but the result of a capacity to raise private funds that could not be matched by more quiescent clerical networks. By the admission of its own director, Salah al-Din Kaftaru, the al-Ansar association, which funds the activities of the Kaftaru Academy, has been extremely vulnerable to fluctuations in donations from the United Arab Emirates and Kuwait – a source of funding, incidentally, which remained strictly forbidden to other Islamic groups.[28] Another telling example: in trying to acquire land to build its new headquarters, the al-Fath institute raised only 20 million pounds out of the 150 million needed. According to the journalist Sha'ban 'Abbud, the management of al-Fath was therefore constrained to ask for help from Zayd, which mobilised its many donors in support of the cause.[29] This imbalance became even more marked throughout the decade as Zayd reportedly managed to 'take' merchant supporters from other groups. As the president of an Islamic charity explains, 'merchants were looking for a guide [*murshid*] and found it in Sariya al-Rifa'i'.[30]

The popularity of Zayd among the bourgeoisie of the capital is based on factors that are not within state control: its relatively independent political stance, and the outreach work the movement has carried out for decades. Da'wa has thus been the cause, not the consequence, of Zayd's successful charitable projects; and these projects have apparently not been used as a recruitment tool by the group, which has remained firmly rooted in the sociological milieu of its origin.[31]

Elections and the Ulama's Rapprochement with 'Crony Capitalism'

One should not ignore the religious aspect of the donations made by merchants to Islamic associations: many of them are genuine devotees who sincerely believe that this is one of the keys to the salvation of their souls. However, it would be naive not to insist on the functional dimension of this transaction as well. In exchange for the entrepreneurs' management

---

[27] Ibid., 603–4.
[28] Stenberg, 'Préserver le charisme', 70; *al-Thawra*, 2 February 2007.
[29] *Al-Nahar*, 19 June 2006.
[30] Interview with an anonymous source, Damascus, April 2008.
[31] Pierret and Selvik, 'Limits of "Authoritarian Upgrading"', 607.

skills and financial support (donations in the strict sense, but also back-handers for lubricating the wheels of state bureaucracy and the mukhaba-rat in favour of religious and charitable activities),[32] the ulama help to maintain or improve the reputation of their silent partners by being seen in their company.

Donors are particularly honoured during the celebration of the Mawlid: the greater their generosity, the closer to the sheikh they sit.[33] Wealthy businessmen also frequently invite Muslim scholars to the 'pri-vate' Mawlids they organise in their *mezra'a* ('farm', in fact a luxurious country house with gardens) in the presence of several hundred guests.[34] In the early twenty-first century, this symbolic resource was widely used by businessmen running for parliamentary elections.

The reader might be surprised to find here an account of the role of the ulama in electoral campaigns, since this topic falls, one would think, within the realm of politics in the strict sense. In fact, the properly polit-ical importance of Syrian parliamentary elections under the Ba'th has been somewhat limited given that the so-called People's Council (Majlis al-Sha'b) is a rump parliament, of which only one-third of the members, the so-called 'independents', are elected. From the point of view of this book, the real importance of parliamentary elections is that they are one of the most dramatic illustrations of the rapprochement between the ulama and parasitic capitalism, which is itself heavily dependent on the political–military elite.

The opening of the Syrian parliament to 'independent' deputies in the early 1970s was designed, with corporatist intent, to allow for the rep-resentation of certain interest groups – in particular the private sector,[35] and, to a much lesser extent, the clergy. Whereas some non-conformist figures – such as the aforementioned Riyad Sayf – emerged during the 1990s among the businessmen–MPs, the ulama who were elected after the (comparatively open) elections of 1973 were mainly members of the Kaftariyya and Nabhaniyya and enjoyed strong support from the mukhabarat.

Since independent candidates were not allowed to create parties and, being a minority in the People's Council, could not seriously pretend to

---

[32] Interviews with the chairmen of two Damascene Islamic charities, June 2007 and April 2008.

[33] Observation, Damascus, 2006–8.

[34] For a description of one such party, attended by all of Damascus's most influential clerics, see Pierret and Selvik, 'Limits of "Authoritarian Upgrading"', 600.

[35] Perthes, *The Political Economy of Syria*, 167.

have a programme they wished to implement, the campaign was over-whelmingly dominated by notables – and especially by businessmen, the latter being the only group with the financial means to afford an expensive propaganda machine, to make the generous donations necessary to gain the favour of certain influential social elites (I will illustrate this in the case of the clergy), and, more simply, to buy votes.

Their 'natural' electoral base being conservative, these candidates had to enhance their reputation by portraying themselves as pious men. In April 2007, Qa'imat al-Sham (the al-Sham list) of tycoon Hashim al-'Aqqad vowed to 'preserve the identity of Syria and the values of the prophets who have enriched the history of our civilisation'.[36] The posters of 'Umar al-Hallaq, a spice merchant of the souk and an administrator of al-Fath, bore the slogan 'God protects Syria, watches over it, and enriches it'. Other posters had the Umayyad Mosque as a background picture, and telecoms magnate Muhammad Hamshu's al-Fayha' ('the Vast', a nickname for Damascus) list opted for a more subliminal approach by printing all of its publicity on an emerald green that everyone recognised as the colour of Islam.

Other candidates stressed their family ties with respected men of religion. Halbuni Street, which is home to Damascus's Islamic bookshops, was covered with placards for Anas al-Bugha, presented there as 'Anas Mustafa al-Bugha' so that everyone would know he was the son of the famous disciple of Hasan Habannaka. More explicitly, in Aleppo, banners called people to vote for the brother of the local mufti by presenting him as "Abd al-Rahman al-Salqini, the son of Sheikh Muhammad'.[37]

An even better electoral proposition was to include an 'alim in the list. In Damascus, both of the main coalitions of businessmen had recruited a sheikh: 'Abd al-Salam Rajih (b. 1969), one of the deans of the Kaftaru Academy and the son of Ahmad Rajih, a leading disciple of the late Grand Mufti, joined al-Fayha', which came out on top with six members of parliament, whereas the reformist Muhammad Habash rallied to al-Sham, which ranked second with five. In terms of individual votes, the big winners were Rajih and his running-mate Muhammad Hamshu, with 80,000 votes each, who had enjoyed the more or less enthusiastic support of the main factions of the local clergy.

To the delight of independent candidates, the campaign in 2007 coincided with the season of the Mawlid, which provided multiple

---

[36] www.vote4Sham.com, April 2007 (dead link).
[37] Observations, April 2007.

opportunities for electoral propaganda. Al-Fayha' candidates, in particular, invited themselves to the ceremonies organised by the religious institutions they had funded over the years.

The Mawlid of the Kaftaru Academy was 'serendipitously' held just one week before the polls in the presence of distinguished guests such as the ambassadors of Indonesia and Sudan and, most importantly, Hamas's politburo head Khalid Mish'al. The 'green list' was doubly welcome in this prestigious event, both because one of its members was a local sheikh and because Hamshu was such an important donor to the institution that he had been appointed to the supervisory committee of the Academy after the death of Ahmad Kaftaru in 2004.[38] Inviting, by name, the six candidates of al-Fayha' to come and sit in places of honour, master of ceremonies Salah al-Din Kaftaru straightforwardly announced in colloquial Arabic: 'I'll be the first to vote for you … after I vote for the National Progressive Front.' This was the only openly electoral speech of the evening, but candidate Rajih, in a turban, was later called to the pulpit to evoke the outstanding morality of the Prophet.[39]

The scenario was slightly different at the 'Ammar bin Yasir mosque (Baramke district) – which had just been lavishly rebuilt, according to a marble epigraph, at the expense of 'Hajj Muhammad Sabir Hamshu'. Most of the ulama present were affiliated to the al-Tawba mosque and the al-Fath institute.[40] There was no explicit electoral slogan that evening, the master of ceremonies limiting himself to greeting the visit of a 'delegation of members of the People's Assembly' – a 'delegation' that was, in fact, the complete al-Fayha' list. In his capacity as a man of religion (although this time he was wearing a three-piece suit), 'Abd al-Salam Rajih was once again invited to deliver a panegyric of Muhammad in front of the crowd.[41]

As for Jama'at Zayd, it also contributed to the campaign of Hamshu and his running-mates, but more discreetly. Attending a Mawlid held in the Bab Srije souk under the patronage of Sariya al-Rifa'i, the candidates were not invited to speak, nor were they even mentioned in the exhortations, but the audience could nevertheless see the affectionate welcome embrace given by al-Rifa'i to the visitors.[42]

---

[38] *Mujamma' al-shaykh Ahmad Kaftaru*, 29.
[39] Observation, Damascus, 15 April 2007.
[40] Al-Fath was represented in the campaign by two young sheikhs (Muhammad Dahla and Bassam Difda'), who unsuccessfully ran as candidates in the Damascus Countryside governorate.
[41] Observation, Damascus, 9 April 2007.
[42] Mawlid of Souk Bab Srije, 4 April 2007 (DVD).

The members of the list were probably received in a similar way on many other occasions, given their generosity in all directions. For instance, Hamshu had funded the reconstruction of the Lala Pasha mosque (100 million pounds), and two of his fellow candidates, Baha' al-Din Hasan and 'Adnan Dakhakhni, were donors and members of the al-Fath and Sheikh Badr al-Din al-Hasani associations.[43]

For many average Syrians, this exchange of material and symbolic gifts was nothing but the quintessence of Pharisaism. What was important, however, was that through this process, the main components of the clergy were publicly displaying their alliance with businessmen who were no longer the, medium-sized, 'respectable' entrepreneurs who had for decades been their traditional supporters, but now were also prominent representatives of 'crony capitalism' and, through them, with the political–military elite. Hamshu, for instance, is the brother-in-law and frontman of Mahir al-Asad, Bashar's brother and the head of the Republican Guard. A newcomer in the business community, he was unknown before his sudden emergence a few years prior to his first election in 2003.[44]

In Aleppo, only one list, Halab al-Shahba' ('Aleppo-the-Grey'), enjoyed the support of the authorities and therefore won all the seats in the constituency. Its composition was similar to that of al-Fayha', with big businessmen (Salih al-Mallah, president of the Chamber of Commerce, Khalid 'Alabi, a founding member of al-Sham holdings) and a pro-regime sheikh, 'Abd al-'Aziz al-Shami. Due to specific features of the local context, however, the list also included two Christian notables and a tribal leader from the al-Barri family of Bab al-Nayrab.

Whereas in the capital the main factions of the clergy supported al-Fahya', the situation in Aleppo was more complex. Indeed, the Friends of Aleppo (Muhibbi Halab), a list composed of scions of old urban families, was supported by the independent-minded mufti Ibrahim al-Salqini, whose brother 'Abd al-Rahman, a deputy under the previous legislature, was removed from the Halab al-Shahba' list by the mukhabarat. The Friends of Aleppo also enjoyed the support of Ghassan al-Najjar, the

---

43 *Al-Thawra*, 23 February 2007; 'Qa'ima a'da majlis idara jam'iyyat al-fath al-muntakhabun sana 2005' [List of the members of the board of the al-Fath association who were elected in 2005] (www.alfatihonline.com, n.d.); *Jam'iyyat al-muhaddith al-akbar al-shaykh Badr al-Din al-Hasani* [Association of the supreme hadith scholar Sheikh Badr al-Din al-Hasani] (Damascus: n.p., 2007), 3.

44 Caroline Donati, *L'Exception syrienne: entre modernisation et résistance* (Paris: La Découverte, 2009), 232; interview with a businessman, Damascus, June 2007.

local leader of the Independent Islamic Tendency,[45] which probably confirmed the decision of the mukhabarat to prevent the Friends of Aleppo
from taking any seat.

A similar scenario had occurred in 2003 with the candidacy of Hala
al-Za'im, the daughter of the aforementioned conservative businessman
Hamdi al-Za'im, who also enjoyed the support of al-Salqini but finally
had to pull out under official pressure.[46] The two first legislative elections
of Bashar al-Asad's era thus demonstrated that the old urban elite of
Aleppo had not given up resisting the grip of the regime's privileged partners; but these elections also showed that this resistance was apparently
too weak to be anything other than a rearguard action.

THE ULAMA'S BOURGEOIS ETHICS

Besides the fact that, unlike Catholicism, the dominant Sunni tradition
has never problematised wealth,[47] the distinctly bourgeois ethics of the
Syrian ulama derives directly from their material conditions of life. The
modern Sunni religious elite of the country was born in the souk, and the
state never offered them the resources that would have enabled them to
become independent from the merchant community.

In the following section, I analyse the economic discourse of the Syrian
ulama on three different issues: the relation between the men of religion,
work, and money; the wealth of laymen; and the overall organisation of
the economy.

The Virtues of Independence

The Syrian ulama now enjoy sources of income other than trade, such as
to a minor extent the Awqaf bureaucracy, and, more meaningfully, public
and private educational institutions. But they nonetheless remain closely
related to the private sector: via the businessmen who finance their institutions and, in a country that had no stock exchange before 2009, still
grow their assets by linking them with their own investments; via those

---

[45] Ghassan al-Najjar, 'Law yuthbitu nazahatahum!' [If at least they could establish their
probity] (www.annidaa.org, 14 April 2007).

[46] [Ghassan al-Najjar], www.thefreesyria.org/f-s-1/kadaia-3011.htm, 4 December 2008.

[47] Éric Chaumont, 'Pauvreté et richesse dans le Coran et dans les sciences religieuses musulmanes', in *Pauvreté et richesse dans le monde musulman méditerranéen*, ed. Jean-Paul
Pascual (Paris: Maisonneuve et Larose, 2003), 17–38, at 26; Denis Gril, 'De l'usage sanctifiant des biens en islam', *Revue d'histoire des religions* 215, no. 1 (1998), 59–89.

among their children who opt for business careers, which is extremely common; and because many Muslim scholars, especially second-rank ones, continue to engage in trade.

As a reflection of this social reality, self-employment (*al-'amal al-hurr*, lit. 'free work') is at the top of the ulama's scale of values in economic matters. For a man of religion, making a living in this way is considered foremost as evidence of disinterestedness in the pursuit of one's sacred mission. The hagiography of Ramzi al-Bazam, one of the founders of the al-Fath institute, underlines that his time 'was divided between da'wa and trade, so that he carried out da'wa in order to please God, not to draw any money or prestige'.[48] Second, self-employment guarantees lawful income (*al-kasb al-halal*). As Sheikh Hisham al-Burhani explains to his students, 'self-employment is by far the best occupation because when you work for the state, you can never be sure that your salary does not include money of illicit origin', such as taxes on alcohol.[49]

Finally, according to a long-standing Sunni ideal, self-employment is praised because it preserves the political independence of the 'alim.[50] Usama al-Rifa'i expresses this view by praising the attitude of Sheikh Ali al-Daqr who, during the Mandate, objected to the state's decision to pay clerics a salary because he feared this would allow the government to 'dictate his actions and words'. Under heavy pressure from the administration, al-Daqr eventually accepted this salary but refrained from using it for himself: 'When the official came to give him his salary, the sheikh used to show him a box and tell him to put the money there. Then when the needy came asking for help, the sheikh used to say: "Open this box and take what you need."'[51]

Accordingly, al-Rifa'i encourages his contemporaries to officiate in mosques as a volunteer (*hisbatan*).[52] However, even those who can afford it sometimes prefer to accept the state salary because not being 'true' functionaries makes them more vulnerable in the face of the administration. Like Sheikh al-Daqr seventy years ago, they often pay this 'impure' money into their mosques' funds.[53]

---

[48] 'Tarjamat al-'alim al-shaykh Ramzi al-Bazam' [Biography of the 'alim Sheikh Ramzi al-Bazam] (www.alfatihonline.com, n.d.).

[49] Observation, Damascus, 5 May 2006.

[50] For the Middle Ages, see Daphna Ephrat, *A Learned Society in a Period of Transition: The Sunni 'Ulama' of Eleventh Century Baghdad* (Albany: SUNY Press, 2000), 131–5.

[51] Al-Rifa'i, 'Durus min hayat', no. 3.

[52] Ibid.

[53] Interviews with two Damascene preachers, May and July 2007.

'The Hand That Gives Is Better Than the Hand That Receives' (Hadith)

Among the Syrian ulama, asceticism (*zuhd*) is a respected but not mandatory lifestyle. Evidence of this is the exceptionality of a figure such as the Grand Reader of the Quran and Shadhili master Shukri al-Luhafi (b. 1920), who dresses in rags and serves coffee to his disciples.[54] Many other scholars, including prominent representatives of the same Sufi tradition (Hisham al-Burhani in Damascus, Mahmud al-Husseini in Aleppo, 'Adnan al-Saqqa in Homs), display a comfortable way of life. This is not perceived as a contradiction by their followers as long as that wealth is 'purified' through charitable donations.[55]

In any case, a broad consensus exists to encourage laymen to enrich themselves based on the principle that 'the Umma needs rich and generous men'.[56] The merchant's piety is presented not only as the cause of his prosperity,[57] but also as its consequence. In an exhortation he pronounced at the Mawlid celebration in the Bab Srije souk, Sariya al-Rifa'i warned against giving up the 'love of money' because, he insisted, 'it is when you work in the souk that you worship God'.[58]

Conversely, the attitude of the same al-Rifa'i towards the poor (whom he helps with his charitable projects) would place him, in a Western context, alongside right-wing hardliners. In one of his sermons he denounced the beggars who, according to him, earn in a week the monthly salary of a graduate functionary. Given this situation, the 'Sheikh of the Merchants' promised the faithful, who were probably very concerned that their generosity might be benefiting such impostors, to replace redistributive associations with a workfare system:

I have requested from the Ministry of Social Affairs ... that it sees to it that in the future, charitable help would be given to a family only in exchange for productive work. A disabled woman who cannot move or walk is perfectly able to work with her hands ... Let the woman work, and let the man work instead of pretending they are sick! For even a sick man can work, from his bed if necessary![59]

---

[54] Observations, Damascus, 2006–8.
[55] Interviews, Aleppo, November 2006, Homs, July 2007. On the Shadhiliyya's rejection of excessive intra-mundane asceticism, see Éric Geoffroy, *Une voie soufie dans le monde: la Shadhiliyya* (Paris: Maisonneuve et Larose, 2005).
[56] 'Al-Shaykh 'Abd al-Karim al-Rifa'i wa masiratuhu', no. 17.
[57] Ibid., no. 20.
[58] Pierret and Selvik, 'Limits of "Authoritarian Upgrading"', 607.
[59] Friday sermon, 1 December 2006 (www.sadazaid.com, 2 December 2006).

From Socialism to Islamic Finance

The Syrian ulama's exaltation of work and prosperity has long been echoed in their liberal approach to the organisation of the national economy. After independence, leading ulama such as Muhammad al-Hamid and Hasan Habannaka rejected, on the basis of the sanctity of private property, the Muslim Brothers' 'Islamic socialism' – which was in fact a very moderate social-democratic programme they had adopted for the purposes of being relevant to the political debate of that time.[60]

A fortiori, the Syrian clergy roundly rejected Ba'thist socialism. In 1965, Sheikh Krayyim Rajih, who in company with the other members of Habannaka's group was one of the most vocal critics of nationalisation, reportedly expounded his point of view to a Ba'thist officer, who was surprised at the anti-socialist stance of this man of humble extraction. In his diatribe, Rajih mixed liberal arguments with concerns about nationalisation strengthening state control over society:

Socialism scares away capital holders and those with an entrepreneurial spirit. It deprives the individual of any motivation to work. It imposes on workers a servitude that prevents them from aspiring to become their own boss, and it leaves them with no refuge if they are victims of injustice, since all authority is now in the hands of the state.[61]

The Syrian ulama's advocacy of economic liberalism was never tantamount to a formal endorsement of capitalism, even after the latter triumphed over its socialist rival at the end of the last century. To capitalism's 'tyranny of materialism', they have continued to counterpose the 'humanism' of Islam, which contains legal and ethical principles that are supposed to ensure the harmonious coexistence of social classes.[62]

Because it is presented as an alternative both to socialism, which has long guided the economic policies of the Ba'thist regime, and to capitalism, which has been an increasingly central component of the Syrian 'social market economy', Islamic economics might appear to be a subversive topic. In reality, however, it has been the subject of lectures given

---

[60] Reissner, *Ideologie und Politik*, 300–15; Muhammad al-Hamid, [On Mustafa al-Siba'i's *Socialism of Islam*], in *Hadarat al-Islam* 3, no. 10 (1963), 1128–31; Zarzur, *Mustafa al-Siba'i*, 146–7.

[61] Habannaka, *al-Walid al-da'iya*, 248.

[62] See for instance Sariya al-Rifa'i, 'al-Iqtisad bayn insaniyyat al-islam wa tughiyan al-maddiyya' [The economy between the humanism of Islam and the tyranny of materialism] (www.sadazaid.com, 4 November 2008).

by such arch-official religious leaders as the Minister of Awqaf and the Grand Mufti.[63]

If the regime is so little disturbed by the ulama's enthusiasm for Islamic economics, it is because clerics have settled for a capitalist version of it. Indeed, in its drive to attract Gulf money and encourage private savings, the government gave the green light to the opening of Islamic banks and insurance companies in 2005.

That Islamic finance is one of the vectors of capitalist globalisation, rather than a real alternative to it,[64] is not a concern for the ulama given that the development of this sector has constituted both a symbolic victory and a new opportunity to demonstrate their social relevance in the twenty-first century.[65] Indeed, in their quest for legal expertise and, even more importantly, for prestige, the recently created Syrian Islamic banks have invited renowned scholars to sit on their sharia boards: the famous Gulf-based Aleppian expert 'Abd al-Sattar Abu Ghudda (b. 1940), the nephew of the late 'Abd al-Fattah Abu Ghudda, as well as Wahba al-Zuhayli, Sa'id Ramadan al-Buti, and Mufti of Damascus 'Abd al-Fattah al-Bazam. The latter two are not really specialists in Islamic banking, but were clearly recruited for the purposes of advertising.[66]

CONCLUSION

Being themselves for the most part merchants and craftsmen, the ulama of the Nahda allied with the merchant upper-middle class, which financed the sharia institutes, mosques, and charities that multiplied after independence.

Whereas this nexus functioned smoothly during the liberal age, under the Ba'th new political restrictions and economic policies severely curtailed the possibilities of ulama–merchant cooperation. However, because it was only superficially bureaucratised, the clergy remained strongly dependent on the private sector. In addition, the elimination of big capitalism in the

---

[63] *Al-Thawra*, 30 November 2007; Syrian National Television, 29 August 2007.

[64] Charles Tripp, *Islam and the Moral Economy: The Challenge of Capitalism* (Cambridge: Cambridge University Press, 2006), 133–49.

[65] Monzer Kahf, 'Islamic Banks: The Rise of a New Power Alliance of Wealth and Shari'a Scholarship', in *The Politics of Islamic Finance*, ed. Clement Henry and Rodney Wilson (Edinburgh: Edinburgh University Press, 2004), 17–36.

[66] 'Al-Hay'a al-shar'iyya li-l-bank' [The sharia board of the bank] (www.chambank.com, [2007]); 'Hay'a wa jihaz al-riqaba al-shar'iyya' [Sharia board and audit apparatus] (www.siib.sy [2007]).

1960s and the subsequent waves of economic liberalisation favoured the medium-sized entrepreneurs who had been the traditional silent partners of the clergy.

From the late 1990s, the ulama spearheaded the revival of the charitable sector, stimulated by the combined effects of pauperisation and economic liberalisation. Jama'at Zayd emerged as a leading actor in that process, because, despite the movement's momentary eclipse after the uprising, state-backed religious networks had proved unable to conquer its merchant support base. Zayd's charitable empire thus stands on solid pillars, since decades of da'wa have allowed it to establish intimate relations with an unparalleled number of small and medium entrepreneurs in the capital.

In addition to their traditional silent partners, the various factions of the clergy have more recently been courted by representatives of crony capitalism, who have financed religious institutions in order to use them as an electoral springboard. The arrival of new opportunistic partners has transformed not only the decades-old ulama–merchant nexus but also the position of the clergy within the political order, by making religious institutions more dependent on businessmen who often act as fronts for members of the military establishment.

In this context, the Syrian ulama have less reason than ever to abandon a bourgeois ethics that exalts self-employment, enrichment, and economic liberalism. From their point of view, the Syrian economy's gradual shift away from socialism is all the more valuable in that it has been accompanied by the recruitment of Muslim scholars to the sharia boards of the newly created Islamic banks.

The economic transformations that are under way in Syria have therefore reinforced a coalition of elites – political–military, economic, and religious. This coalition is of course characterised by a profound imbalance in favour of the political–military element, but nevertheless allows for the growth of each of these elites' respective endeavours. Independent Islamist Yasir al-'Ayti denounced this alliance as a 'destructive triad' that guarantees the perpetuation of the regime:

The sheikh thinks that by allying with the state official, he protects his jama'a, and that by joining forces with the merchant, he ensures he gets money for his charity. The state official thinks that through his alliance with the sheikh, he keeps the situation under control and that through his alliance with the merchant, he makes sure he takes a dividend in return for the green light he gives for the merchant's illegal practices. As for the merchant, he believes that through his alliance with the state official, he ensures the necessary support to continue violating the law, and that through his alliance with the sheikh, he assures himself a place in the afterlife, because his mentality of corruptor leads him to believe that just as he was able to buy off the state official who condoned his offenses, he can bribe God with the donations he grants to the sheikh.[67]

This pamphlet thus highlights a set of pragmatic transactions that have ensured the solidarity of Syrian elites, however intense the distrust and contempt that persists between them. This was probably key to the amazing resilience of the Syrian regime during the foreign policy crisis of 2004–6, which had led some observers to proclaim the imminent fall of the al-Asad family. We will return to this episode in the next chapter.

---

[67] Yasir al-'Ayti, 'al-Thulathi al-mudammir: al-shaykh – al-tajir – rajul al-dawla' [The destructive triad: the sheikh – the merchant – the state official] (www.annidaa.org, 26 March 2007).

5

Ulama and Islamists in the Political Field

This chapter does not deal with the Syrian ulama's conception of the ideal political order. On this issue, I refer the reader to classical authors such as al-Ghazali and al-Mawardi, who are frequently cited by Sunni clerics as references in that realm. Instead, I am concerned here with concrete political *practices* enacted in particular historical contexts.

Can any particular feature of the ulama's political behaviour be picked out as properly unique and essential to them? Adopting a schema on which their supposed 'quietism' is set in contrast to the oppositional stance of Islamic activists would certainly be overly simplistic and reductive, as has been demonstrated by previous authors and as is illustrated earlier in this book by figures such as Sheikh Habannaka.[1]

Does this mean that from a political point of view the ulama–Islamist dichotomy is not relevant to framing our understanding of the Syrian Islamic field, and that it would be more appropriate simply to distinguish between Islamic 'opponents' and 'loyalists'? The answer here is no, since, as will be shown in this chapter, the political behaviour of the ulama presents features that set them apart from lay Islamic activists, and this is the case *regardless* of the quality of their relations with the state.

The ulama's approach to politics should not principally be characterised as 'moderate', 'subservient', or 'society-centred' (as opposed to state-centred), but is first and foremost 'sectoral', in the sense that it aims to influence state policies on issues that are seen as crucial from the point of view of a particular sectoral elite; in this their approach resembles that

---

[1] See Zeghal, *Gardiens de l'islam*; Zaman, *The Ulama*.

of businessmen.[2] For the ulama, the relevant sectoral issues include the expansion of religious institutions, the preservation of orthodoxy against 'deviant' ideas, and public morality (which they invariably assimilate to female modesty). However, clerical demands are not merely corporatist and society-centred, since the ulama are no less concerned than Islamic activists with the implementation of sharia and the status of Islam in the constitution. In addition to examples that will be presented in this chapter, one might mention the fact that in 1955, the president of the Association of Ulama of Aleppo, Muhammad Balanku (1897–1991), called for the establishment of a committee of scholars to check on the Islamic character of all laws passed by the parliament.[3] More recently, in a best-seller published in 1984 by the country's largest publisher, leading faqih Wahba al-Zuhayli wrote:

> The future belongs to Islam, its fiqh and its legislation. If some people postpone the benefit we could draw from this system by maintaining positive imported laws, then I want to explain the rules of fiqh, because *such postponement is a temporary apostasy* which cannot be prolonged on any account.[4]

Although they generally sympathise with all of these issues, the Islamists adopt a different strategy, prioritising structural changes in the political system: their aim is to modify the *central* principles of the monopoly on legitimate violence, changing those controlling this monopoly, the rules governing to whom the power may be devolved, and the general limits of its application – in the case of Syria, for instance, they demand free elections, respect for human rights, and the end of the single-party system. The difference thus runs deeper than the obvious fact that, unlike political activists, religious specialists do not seek political power for themselves: it also implies that, in routine contexts – that is, outside periods of crisis – they display little interest in issues that Islamists view as absolutely crucial.

The fact that this dichotomy is witnessed in Syria is particularly interesting in view of the fact that this country is devoid of the factors that are frequently invoked to account for the ulama's particular political stance,

---

[2] The use of the term 'sectoral' in this context is borrowed from Stéphane Lacroix's *Awakening Islam: Religious Dissent in Contemporary Saudi Arabia* (Cambridge, MA: Harvard University Press, 2011). However, I give it a somewhat different meaning: whereas Lacroix refers to the ulama and lay Islamists as two different 'sectors', I restrict the use of this adjective to non-primarily political, functionally specialised elites such as, in this case, the ulama.

[3] *OFA*, 2–4 February 1955, no. 694, V.

[4] Zuhayli, *al-Fiqh al-islami*, vol. I, 7–8 (my emphasis).

such as their incorporation into state institutions, which as we know has remained very limited, or the existence of distinct channels of intellectual socialisation. Although until the 1970s it was still possible to distinguish between a 'traditional' mashyakha trained in study circles and a 'modern' effendiyya produced by the nascent universities, the situation was complicated by the modernisation, albeit partial, of the training of clerics, and the integration of graduates of secular faculties into traditional patterns of religious authority by groups such as Zayd.

I argue that the diverging political practices of the clerics and Islamist 'politicos' should be seen as the logical outcome of discrete defining daily practices: the former owe their social identity to religious work in the strict sense (Max Weber's 'the management of the goods of salvation') and consequently use politics as a means to maximise their influence in that realm, whereas the latter are defined by political activism and therefore prioritise the quest for relevance in that field. This analysis is inspired by Stéphane Lacroix's study of Islamist mobilisations in Saudi Arabia, which shows that individuals belonging to the same activist current, the Sahwa (Awakening), adopt different patterns of political behaviour depending on their vocation, either as an 'alim or as a lay intellectual (*muthaqqaf*).[5]

In the following pages, I analyse the Syrian ulama's forms of organisation and political intervention since the 1930s. This historical perspective allows one to observe their behaviour in very different contexts, each of them requiring specific responses. However, it will also highlight a number of constants that reflect their specific patterns of politicisation.

FROM FRENCH MANDATE TO INFISAL (1930–1963)

The Syrian ulama entered the political fray as soon as the Ottoman armies withdrew from Damascus in 1918. Under King Faysal, clerics from the merchant middle class led by the reformist sheikh Kamil al-Qassab joined the 'popular committees' that challenged the legitimacy of the regime in the name of radical Arab nationalism.[6] In 1920, they took part in the battle of Maysalun, which ended with the defeat of the Syrian fighters and marked the beginning of a quarter of a century of French occupation. Five years later, many of them reappeared on the occasion of the Great Revolt.[7]

---

[5] Lacroix, *Awakening Islam*.
[6] James Gelvin, *Divided Loyalties: Nationalism and Mass Politics in Syria at the Close of Empire* (Berkeley: University of California Press, 1998), 108–9.
[7] Ibid., 115–16; Weismann, 'The Invention', 135.

Conversely, scholars of higher social status collaborated with the colonial regime – for example, Taj al-Din al-Hasani (1890–1943), Badr al-Din's son, who was Prime Minister (1928–31) and President of the Republic (1941–43),[8] and former judge of Medina Suleiman al-Jukhdar (1868–1957), Minister of Justice from 1933 to 1934.[9] At the same time, the ulama set up their own political organisations while trying their hand at the electoral game.

Federative Experiences

In addition to educational and charitable associations, the Mandate witnessed the creation of structures aimed at federating the religious elite in order to make its voice heard in the public sphere. Whereas educational associations were seeking to counter diffuse cultural threats, the new advocacy organisations aimed directly at influencing the government, which, being subject to the will of the coloniser, was perceived as a threat to the country's Islamic identity.

The first association of this kind, al-Hidayat al-Islamiyya (Islamic guidance), was founded in Damascus in 1930 on the model of the Egyptian association of the same name.[10] Reflecting the sociological changes being experienced by the Syrian religious elite at that time, most of its founders were renowned but newcomer ulama such as Naqshbandi master Abu al-Khayr al-Midani (1875–1961), merchant Kamil al-Qassar (1906–95), and eminent faqih Salih al-'Aqqad (1892–1970). The association issued numerous communiqués, principally about religious education (it requested the establishment in Syria of a 'little al-Azhar') and the 'deterioration' of public morals symbolised by the fashion for unveiling.[11]

Al-Hidayat al-Islamiyya was still in existence in 2011, although now merely a charity. Its heyday in the 1930s was brief, and it rapidly gave way to more representative organisations.

The Association of Ulama and the Congress of 1938

The Association of Ulama (Jam'iyyat al-'Ulama') was founded in 1937 by reformist sheikh Kamil al-Qassab, who had just returned from seventeen

---

[8] Abaza and Hafiz, *Tarikh 'ulama' Dimashq*, vol. II, 576–8. Understandably, the hagiographers of the Supreme Hadith Scholar do not dwell on the political career of his son.

[9] Ibid., vol. II, 693–4.

[10] Al-Tantawi, *Dhikrayat*, vol. I, 265–7.

[11] Basil al-Rifa'i, 'al-Jam'iyyat al-diniyya fi Suriyya: al-Hidayat al-Islamiyya' [Religious associations in Syria: al-Hidayat al-Islamiyya] (www.islamysria.com, 7 June 2008).

years in exile. Within this organisation, al-Qassab united members of the Salafi-leaning al-Tamaddun al-Islami with conservatives from al-Hidayat al-Islamiyya and al-Tahdhib wa-l-Ta'lim, the educational association of Ali al-Daqr's former associate Hashim al-Khatib.[12] The Association of Ulama nevertheless suffered from a lack of representativeness, in that it had no representative of al-Gharra', Damascus's most powerful Islamic association. The reason for this was the personal rivalry that set Ali al-Daqr in opposition to both president Kamil al-Qassab and his vice-president, who was none other than the aforementioned al-Khatib.[13]

Despite this, the Association of Ulama was responsible for two major achievements. In 1942, it convinced President Taj al-Din al-Hasani, who was on good terms with al-Qassab, to create the first public Islamic seminary in Damascus, the (secondary) Faculty of Sharia. Four years earlier, it had organised Damascus's first Congress of Ulama, which brought together a hundred clerics from Syria, Lebanon, Palestine, and Iraq.[14] The meeting also scored a notable success in that its participants included Ali al-Daqr as well as young activists who were about to found the Syrian branch of the Muslim Brothers.[15] Accordingly, the final communiqué of the congress emphasised the need to 'strengthen ties between the ulama, the Islamic associations and the organisations of the educated youth'[16] – the latter being, of course, the proto-Muslim Brothers associations.

The intergenerational alliance established during the congress was not only the result of al-Qassab's talents as a cultural broker, but also of shared concerns about the intentions of the French. In addition to calls for the development of religious education and the strengthening of censorship, including of 'street language' (!), the final communiqué lambasted official policies such as the rampant nationalisation of awqaf and the introduction of civilian judges into religious courts. Delegates also denounced the strategy of sectarian division adopted by the coloniser, which was accused of raising the spectre of 'religious fanaticism ... and shedding hypocrite's tears over the fate of what it calls the minorities, claiming to protect them to better dominate us all'. The communiqué

---

[12] Abaza and Hafiz, *Tarikh 'ulama' Dimashq*, vol. II, 657–67. Elizabeth Thompson describes the Association of Ulama as the organ of the old religious elite (Thompson, *Colonial Citizens*, 108). In reality, however, it included very few members of the old clerical families.

[13] Al-Tantawi, *Dhikrayat*, vol. VII, 75.

[14] *Bayan mu'tamar al-'ulama'*.

[15] Mustafa al-Siba'i, Mustafa al-Zarqa, Ma'ruf al-Dawalibi, and Muhammad al-Hamid.

[16] *Bayan mu'tamar al-'ulama'*.

countered such 'colonialist propaganda' using modern terminology that probably owed much to al-Qassab's reformist orientations, stressing the 'Islamic principles of equality between Muslims and other citizens'.[17]

Since the beginning of the Mandate, the 'protection of minorities' had served as a rationale for projects of reform of the Personal Status Law, all of which had been abandoned due to the outcry they aroused among the Syrian elites. At the very moment the ulama were holding their congress of 1938, the French High Commissioner was secretly negotiating a new project of reform with the ruling National Bloc (moderate nationalists). In November of that year, the government promulgated a decree known as the 'Law of Communities' (*qanun* or *nizam al-tawa'if*), whose terms were particularly intolerable to the Muslim clergy. In particular, it allowed for the recognition of civil marriages contracted abroad, and created a high jurisdiction in charge of arbitrating conflicts between civil law and the personal status law of each religious community, which theoretically gave the state the right to abolish or amend the provisions of the sharia. The ulama responded by sending petitions and encouraging massive demonstrations that convinced the Syrian and French authorities to withdraw the decree.[18]

At the Crossroads: The League of Ulama and the Muslim Brothers

By the time the ageing Sheikh al-Qassab died in 1954, his Association of Ulama had become something of an empty shell. This was because after the French withdrawal in 1946, both the mashyakha and the 'educated youth', two categories he had aspired to unite, had set up their own political arms: the League of Ulama (Rabitat al-'Ulama') and the Muslim Brothers.

Although there were certainly a handful among the leaders of the Muslim Brothers who were ulama by training, these were exceptions. With his elegant three-piece suits and thin moustache, his involvement in publishing and politics, his modern essays, and his non-conformist ideas, the founder, Mustafa al-Siba'i, was not the embodiment of a 'sheikh' but rather that of a *da'iya* (preacher), that is to say, an Islamist intellectual and activist. The Hama section was founded by a much more traditional scholar, Muhammad al-Hamid, but he retired from the organisation

---

[17] Ibid.
[18] Benjamin Thomas White, *The Emergence of Minorities in the Middle East: The Politics of Community in French Mandate Syria* (Edinburgh: Edinburgh University Press, 2011), 185–92. Habannaka, *al-Walid al-da'iya*, 213–18.

in the 1950s in favour of a predominantly lay leadership. Conversely, the upper echelons of the movement ordered Hamid's disciple Sa'id Hawwa, a graduate of the faculty of sharia in Damascus, to resign from the Hama Association of Ulama in order 'to avoid any ambiguity'.[19] As for the Aleppian hadith specialist 'Abd al-Fattah Abu Ghudda, he was appointed as the Muslim Brothers' superintendent three times (1955, 1973, and 1986), but always during periods of internal crisis where his moral authority was called for to strengthen one faction against another. Moreover, he obviously accepted this position with reluctance, since he completed only the last of his three terms.[20]

The League of Ulama, for its part, was clearly dominated by traditional clerics, such as its presidents Abu al-Khayr al-Midani (1946–61) and Makki al-Kittani (1961–3). The only notable representatives of the Salafi and reformist currents were Bahjat al-Bitar and Ahmad Mazhar al-'Azma, the president of al-Tamaddun al-Islami. The League never included any member of the Muslim Brothers, and it was only in 1955 that the latter were granted an observer seat.[21]

The League of Ulama was more representative than al-Qassab's Association. It was not the instrument of particular networks, but a federative body bringing together all of the most influential sheikhs of the post-independence era, such as al-Daqr's son Ahmad, Habannaka, al-Farfur, al-Rifa'i, Kaftaru, and the Shadhili masters Muhammad al-Hashimi and Sa'id al-Burhani.[22]

At the same time, the League was just as Damascene as the Association. 'Associations' and 'leagues' of ulama had also been established in the other cities of the country from the 1940s,[23] but they were related to their Damascene sister-organisation only by very loose coordination mechanisms such as the granting of observer seats to provincial muftis.[24] The pervasiveness of local identities among the mashyakha was probably the

---

[19] Hawwa, *Hadhihi tajribati*, 91–2. On al-Hamid and Hawwa, see Itzchak Weismann, 'Sa'id Hawwa: The Making of a Radical Muslim Thinker in Modern Syria', *Middle Eastern Studies* 29, no. 4 (1993), 601–23.

[20] *OFA*, no. 728, 11–4 June 1955, VII, no. 752, 10–3 September 1955, VII; Barut, 'Suriyya', 271–3, 303–5.

[21] Interview with al-'Attar.

[22] Abaza and Hafiz, *Tarikh 'ulama' Dimashq*, vol. II, 725.

[23] In Aleppo, its first president was Raghib al-Tabbakh, the reformist-leaning moderniser of the Khusrawiyya. Muhammad Balanku succeeded him when he died in 1951 (*OFA*, 26–29 April 1957, V).

[24] 'Abd al-Qadir al-Kittani, 'al-'Allamat al-imam al-mujahid al-sayyid Makki al-Kittani' [The savant, imam, combatant, and descendant of the Prophet Makki al-Kittani], *al-Thawra*, 16 March 2007.

main factor responsible for this situation, since during the period of parliamentary rule that lasted from 1946 to 1949 and from 1954 to 1958, no political obstacle would have prevented the creation of a nationwide league of ulama. It was not until the end of 1962 and the growing threat of a takeover by the Nasserites and Ba'thists that the president of the Damascene League of Ulama, Makki al-Kittani, launched a project for a national federation composed of delegates elected by their peers in each governorate.[25] The reform was under way when it was abruptly interrupted by the coup of March 1963, which put an end to the existence of the League.

From the start, there was a contrast between the regional fragmentation of the ulama's political organisations and the national vision of the early Muslim Brothers. The latter movement was legally established in May 1946, one month after the French withdrawal,[26] through the merger of reformist associations that had emerged across the country in the 1930s, such as al-Shubban al-Muslimun in Damascus, Dar al-Arqam in Aleppo, and the Muslim Brothers in Hama.[27] This difference is probably best explained in terms of worldviews: whereas the parochial conservative sheikhs had no obvious reason to look seriously for partners outside their respective cities, the much more mobile (and sometimes cosmopolitan) effendis of the Muslim Brothers were part of not only pan-Syrian but also pan-Islamic networks of reformist-minded activists.

Public Interventions in the Liberal Era: The Primacy of Moral and Religious Themes

The League of Ulama functioned in a manner very different to the Muslim Brothers. It was not a party-like structure aimed at mobilising grassroots membership on a permanent basis and winning positions in the political field, but merely a syndicate of clerics. In this period of rapid cultural change, the ulama's main concern was to pressure policymakers in aid of a conservative, primarily moral and religious, agenda.

Moral, religious, and educational demands constituted no less than 82 per cent of 104 public interventions by the Syrian ulama (petitions, press

---

[25] *OFA*, 12–14 September 1962, no. 1443, V.

[26] *Al-Tamaddun al-Islami* 12, no. 17, June 1946, 264 (from al-Khatib, 'al-Tamaddun al-Islami', 82).

[27] Reissner, *Ideologie und Politik*, 58–63; 'Adnan Sa'd al-Din, *al-Ikhwan al-muslimun fi Suriyya: ma qabla al-ta'sis wa hatta 'am 1954* [The Muslim Brothers in Syria: from before the foundation to 1954] (Amman: Dar 'Ammar, 2006), 55–123.

releases, delegations sent to government officials) recorded between 1948 and 1963 in the OFA press survey. In the realm of morals (31 per cent), their chief concern was the popularisation of new forms of entertainment (radio, cinema, illustrated magazines, amusement parks), which they saw as vehicles of moral corruption and therefore requested their prohibition or censorship by committees placed under the control of the ulama.[28] Clerics were also deeply disturbed by the changing status of women, who were indulging in 'indecent' activities such as sports, public dances, and beauty pageants. They were not hostile to the schooling of girls, but requested that schools and universities be segregated.[29]

Just as important (30 per cent of the interventions) was the defence of orthodoxy against 'heresies' and blasphemy. The former were embodied in local cults (including a reportedly nudist group in the village of Harasta near Damascus),[30] and, more importantly, the 'Qadiyani discord' (*al-fitnat al-qadiyaniyya*),[31] a fierce controversy which in the second half of the 1950s set the ulama against the Ahmadi preachers based in a mosque of the Damascene neighbourhood of al-Shaghur.[32] Such was the context that led Grand Mufti 'Abidin to claim for himself the right to legislate directly against heresies – despite the fact that, by definition, muftis only issue non-binding opinions.[33] With respect to blasphemy, clerics occasionally mobilised to stigmatise the writings of 'irreligious' intellectuals and journalists of a progressive stripe.[34] They also opposed various practices that they saw as contrary to dogma, such as the erection of a statue of Yusuf al-'Azma, the Minister of War under King Faysal who was killed while fighting French invaders.[35]

After morals and orthodoxy came the defence of corporatist interests (13 per cent), such as the status of mosque personnel and the expansion of waqf administration, which the ulama tried to slow in some cases and to orient in a favourable direction in others. In 1950, in order to 'preserve

---

[28] *OFA*, 25–28 June 1955, no. 732, V.

[29] See for instance al-Tantawi, *Dhikrayat*, vol. V, 109.

[30] *OFA*, 20–22 January 1960, no. 1180, V.

[31] 'Qadiyaniyya' is the name Sunni heresiologists give to the Ahmadiyya, an Islamic movement founded in India by the self-proclaimed messiah Mirza Ghulam Ahmad (1835–1908).

[32] *OFA*, 16–19 January 1954, no. 592, V; 19–21 January 1955, no. 690, V; 9–12 June 1956, no. 825, V.

[33] *OFA*, 21–23 August 1957, no. 92, V.

[34] *OFA*, 25–27 April 1951, no. 322, V; 2–4 March 1954, no. 702, V; 11–14 June 1955, no. 728, V.

[35] *OFA*, 1–5 January 1951, no. 290, V.

the social status of the ulama with respect to the problems related to the exercise of their official duties', the religious elite created the Association of Officers of Religious Rites (the organisation that half a century later was chaired by reformist MP Muhammad Habash), whose first chairman was the Shadhili sheikh Muhammad al-Hashimi.[36]

Less than 20 per cent of the recorded interventions were concerned with more strictly political issues such as voting instructions, the Islamisation of law, and foreign policy. In this, the ulama clearly differentiated themselves from the Muslim Brothers, who were generally supportive of the demands of the clergy,[37] but also took a formal stance on many other topics, such as economic policy and foreign affairs.[38] Once again, the reason for this contrast is obvious: as a sectoral elite, the ulama were making their voice heard only on issues directly related to their particular area of activity; as professional politicians, the Muslim Brothers had to position themselves within every debate deemed important in the political field.

Another remarkable feature of the ulama's political discourse of that time was that, even under parliamentary rule, it made few criticisms of the country's political leadership despite the fact that the latter was rarely receptive to clerical demands. Apart from the introduction of religious courses and daily prayers in public schools (1954–5),[39] the ulama only received satisfaction on minor issues such as the prohibition of alcohol advertising in cinemas (1950) and the removal of alcoholic drinks from official receptions (1955).[40] On such fundamental – from their point of view – problems as the 'Qadiyani cult' and the state regulation of prostitution, the ulama had to wait until the advent of the United Arab Republic to win their case, as will be shown later.

The real cause of the ulama's moderate stance towards the men in power during the liberal era was the strategic alliance they had established with bourgeois politicians from the Mandate onwards. In the 1930s, the politicians had relied on the sheikhs to attract support in popular neighbourhoods.[41] Although this partnership experienced severe tensions during the subsequent decade, as will be shown below, it was reinstated

---

[36] *Qanun jam'iyyat arbab al-sha'a'ir al-diniyya al-asasi* [Statutes of the Association of Officers of Religious Rites] (Damascus: Dar al-Taraqqi, 1950), 2.

[37] *OFA*, 11–14 September 1948, no. 51, VI; 14–17 October 1950, no. 267, VI.

[38] Reissner, *Ideologie und Politik*, 163 ff.; Joshua Teitelbaum, 'The Muslim Brotherhood and the "Struggle for Syria", 1947–1958: Between Accommodation and Ideology', *Middle Eastern Studies* 40, no. 3 (2004), 134–58.

[39] *OFA*, 3–6 July 1954, no. 637, V; 26–28 October 1955, no. 765, V.

[40] *OFA*, 14–17 October 1950, no. 268, VII; 26–28 October 1955, no. 765, V.

[41] Khoury, 'Syrian Urban Politics', 526.

in the 1950s in the face of al-Shishakli's 'enlightened despotism' and the rise of progressive political forces.

The alliance between the ulama and bourgeois politicians was symbolised by the cordial relations uniting the leading figures of the clergies of Damascus and Aleppo, Hasan Habannaka and Muhammad al-Nabhan, with, respectively, Shukri al-Quwwatli (National Party) and Rushdi Kikhiya (People's Party).[42] After the fall of al-Shishakli in 1954, Habannaka took part in the delegation that travelled to Alexandria to invite al-Quwwatli, who had lived in exile since his overthrow in 1949, to return to Syria.[43] As for al-Nabhan, he justified his membership in the People's Party by the 'desire to serve the public interest and to safeguard religion and morals'.[44] Some of his colleagues tried to achieve these goals by running for parliamentary seats themselves.

In the Maze of Parliamentary Politics

The Syrian ulama's encounter with modern politics was a painful experience. Elected as a deputy for Hama in 1947, Sheikh Mahmud al-Shuqfa (1898–1979) abandoned his office a few months later, a decision he justified in the following verses:

> I saw the sharia of Islam crying
> I said, 'What does the Pure One sorrow for?'
> She said, 'How could I help crying when my own people
> Threw me down and had me bitten by a snake?'[45]

First Disappointments

In 1943, the merchant–'alim 'Abd al-Hamid al-Tabba', Ali al-Daqr's right-hand man, was elected to parliament. In accordance with the alliance that had been established between al-Gharra' and the National Bloc in the 1930s,[46] al-Tabba' had been included on the electoral ticket of al-Quwwatli. Once in power, however, the latter quickly forgot his promises to support the conservative agenda of his running-mate, who thus

[42] Habannaka, *al-Walid al-da'iya*, 221–4; interviews with al-Hawari and Ali Sadr al-Din al-Bayanuni.
[43] Habannaka, *al-Walid al-da'iya*, 196–7.
[44] *OFA*, 12–15 March 1955, no. 705, VII.
[45] Sulayman al-Sali'i, 'al-Shaykh al-'allamat al-shahid Mahmud 'Abd al-Rahman al-Shuqfa' [The savant and martyr Sheikh Mahmud 'Abd al-Rahman al-Shuqfa] (www.ghrib.net, 11 October 2007).
[46] Abaza, *al-Shaykh Ali al-Daqr*, 111.

resorted to the street. In May 1944, the ulama asked the Damascus police to ban a charity ball involving unveiled Muslim women. Faced with a refusal, they organised demonstrations that degenerated into riots.[47]

The ulama learnt their lesson, and in the elections of 1947 ran against al-Quwwatli alongside the Muslim Brothers. But this second electoral experience proved to be a new disappointment: despite a campaign marked by police pressures and fraud, the Muslim Brothers won several seats, but all of the ulama's candidates for Damascus and Aleppo failed.[48] A similar scenario occurred during the elections for the constituent assembly in November 1949, al-Tabba' being the only unsuccessful candidate of the Islamic Socialist Front set up by al-Siba'i's movement.[49] Parliamentary politics thus did not turn out well for the ulama, who were losing ground to the effendis as chief representatives of the Islamic trend. They were faced with an even greater disappointment during the battle for the new constitution.

Against the Muslim Brothers' Pragmatism: The 1950 Constitutional Crisis

Prior to the elections for the constituent assembly, the League of Ulama had announced that, in addition to its own candidates, it would support anyone who vowed to work for a constitution stipulating that Islam is the state religion (*din al-dawla*).[50] Consequently, they stood firmly behind al-Siba'i who, as a member of the Preparatory Committee, obtained in April 1950 a vote on a draft constitution in accordance with their wishes.[51] In July, however, the fierce criticisms of the project expressed by secularist parties and Christian Churches convinced the parliamentary majority to replace the contentious clause with the formulas 'The religion of the President of the Republic is Islam' and 'Islamic Fiqh is the main source of legislation'.

Whereas the League of Ulama stubbornly rejected this compromise, the deputies of the Muslim Brothers eventually voted for the text, which al-Siba'i described as 'a model constitution for a Muslim

[47] Reissner, *Ideologie und Politik*, 166–74.
[48] Ibid., 175–88; Fawzi 'Ayntabi and Najwa 'Uthman, *Halab fi mi'a 'am* [Aleppo through one hundred centuries] (Aleppo: Ma'had al-Turath al-'Ilmi al-'Arabi, 1993), 234.
[49] *OFA*, 16–18 November 1949, no. 172, VII.
[50] Gordon Torrey, *Syrian Politics and the Military 1945–1958* (Columbus: Ohio State University Press, 1964), 148.
[51] On this episode, see Reissner, *Ideologie und Politik*, 338–54; Zarzur, *Mustafa al-Siba'i*, 241–73.

state'.[52] According to Johannes Reissner, this sudden shift resulted from purely political considerations: the Brothers wanted to avoid a political crisis that would lead to new elections because they expected they would fare poorly and thus lose their minister in the government.[53] The ulama were angered by this tactical retreat.[54] 'Arif al-Taraqji, a physician representing Ahmad Kaftaru in the parliamentary group of the Islamic Socialist Front, left the group in protest.[55] A couple of months later, when the Front sought to rally conservative independent deputies, the League of Ulama rejected its request for a formal statement of support, saying it was unwilling 'to be involved in [its] political activities'.[56]

The dispute between the ulama and the Muslim Brothers about the constitution was not an ideological one, since both sides agreed that Islam should be the religion of the state. Instead, it had its roots in the discrete social practices that define each group. The former, as theologians, jurisconsults, and models of virtue, were showing themselves to be all the more faithful to their vocation as principled men, given that their previous electoral failures had placed them outside the parliamentary game. The Muslim Brothers, on the other hand, being engaged in a process of political professionalisation, were literally 'trapped' in those games.

Once bitten, twice shy. In the elections held after the fall of al-Shishakli in 1954, the League of Ulama did not present candidates of its own, and merely called, without further detail, for people to vote for those who 'practise and defend Islam'.[57] The Hanbali Mufti of Damascus, 'Abd al-Ra'uf Abu Tawq, who had individually decided to run for a seat, was the only 'alim in parliament during the next four years.[58] Surprisingly enough, it was the return of authoritarianism on the occasion of Syria's union with Nasserite Egypt in 1958 that stimulated a brief but remarkable revival of the ulama's interest in representative politics. Again, however, the experiment was hardly encouraging.

---

[52] Barut, 'Suriyya', 258.
[53] Reissner, *Ideologie und Politik*, 351–4.
[54] Hawwa, *Hadhihi tajribati*, 18.
[55] *OFA*, 14–16 December 1950, no. 180, VII.
[56] *OFA*, 20–22 December 1950, no. 286, VII; 27–29 December 1950, no. 288, VII.
[57] *OFA*, 18–22 and 22–24 August, nos. 657–8, VII.
[58] *OFA*, 2–5 July 1955, no. 734, V. Going through serious internal strife, the Muslim Brothers also refrained from participating in the polls, except for Muhammad al-Mubarak, who ran as an independent and was elected (Barut, 'Suriyya', 259–60).

The United Arab Republic (1958–1961): A Brief Moment of Enthusiasm

In the early years of his rule, Nasser was not popular among religious-minded Syrians. Because of his crackdown on the Muslim Brothers and the decision to abrogate religious courts, he was seen as a secularist dictator cast in the same mould as al-Shishakli.[59] In 1956, however, the Suez crisis turned him into the hero of the Arab nation. In solidarity with Egypt, and in order to defend itself against a possible attack by Turkey, a member of the British-led Baghdad Pact, Syria set up a 'Popular Army' for which the country's leading scholars volunteered and took part in shooting exercises.[60]

Beyond anti-imperialism, the main reason why Syrian conservative opinion swung behind Nasser was that he was seen as a bulwark against the growing influence of the radical left – that is, the Communist Party and the Ba'th.[61] The situation was all the more worrying in that progressive forces were gaining supporters within unexpected social sectors. In the 1954 elections the Communists had made a remarkable breakthrough in the conservative Midan neighbourhood, thanks to the support of Sheikh Muhammad al-Ashmar (1892–1960). A hero of the anti-colonial revolt of 1925 and a volunteer fighter during the 1936 Arab revolt in Palestine, this sheikh–mujahid was the target of a campaign of seduction on the part of the Soviet Union, which invited him to receive the International Stalin Award for Peace.[62]

In this context, Syrian ulama carried out several official visits to Cairo in 1956–7.[63] When the United Arab Republic was established in February 1958, they resonated with the general enthusiasm, all the more so given that the new regime promised to satisfy their conservative demands and closed the Ahmadi mosque in al-Shaghur.[64]

Thus it was during the short-lived Syrian–Egyptian union that the ulama's participation in electoral politics reached its highest level ever. Dozens of them – including representatives of Hasan Habannaka (Hussein

---

[59] Barut, 'Suriyya', 261; *OFA*, 8–11 October 1955, no. 760, V.

[60] See the photos in Nadaf, *al-Shaykh Ahmad Kaftaru*, 386.

[61] Hawwa, *Hadhihi tajribati*, 54.

[62] *OFA*, 2–5 December 1950, no. 281, VII; *al-Mujahid al-samit, shaykh Muhammad al-Ashmar: siratuhu wa jihaduhu* [The silent combatant, Sheikh Muhammad al-Ashmar: his life and jihad] ([Beirut]: [al-Maktab al-Islami], 2002), 197–210.

[63] Habannaka, *al-Walid al-da'iya*, 200–1; interview with al-'Attar.

[64] *OFA*, 12–14 February 1958, no. 990, V; 28–30 January 1959, no. 1083, V; 4–6 February 1959, no. 1085, V.

Khattab), Salih al-Farfur (Ramzi al-Bazam), Ahmad Kaftaru (Marwan Shaykhu), 'Abd al-Karim al-Rifa'i (Fu'ad Shmays), Sa'id al-Burhani (his son Jihad), and Muhammad al-Nabhan (Muhammad al-Shami, Hasan Farfuti) – ran in the June 1959 elections to the organs of the single party, the Nationalist Union (al-Ittihad al-Qawmi). At least fifteen were elected, of whom five were appointed to parliament, then called the Council of the Nation (Majlis al-Umma).[65]

The first reason for this unprecedented involvement in formal politics was the legitimacy of the regime, rooted in its unionist agenda and anti-Communist orientation. The second was the nature of the Nationalist Union: it was not a Leninist, ideological party like the Ba'th, but an inclusive structure designed to rally a broad range of political sensibilities in support of the regime.[66] Third, the three-level electoral system based on small constituencies (the people elected village or neighbourhood councils, which designated members of district councils, which in turn appointed the members of governorate councils) favoured local notables, who in addition were freed from the competition of the parties, which had spontaneously disbanded in the aftermath of the union.

The United Arab Republic thus seemed to inaugurate a genuine revolution in the ulama's relationship with electoral politics. However, the elected councils were deprived of any actual power, and in any case the honeymoon was extremely brief. In the summer of 1961, the clergy opposed the regime's policy of nationalisations as well as its project of authoritarian modernisation of religious institutions, to the extent that Grand Mufti 'Abidin was dismissed from his position. Therefore, in spite of the abolition of regulated prostitution, a long-standing clerical demand, the ulama were bound to support the *infisal* (secession) carried out in September 1961 by conservative politicians and military officers.[67] The projected reform of the Awqaf Ministry was immediately suspended, and 'Abidin was reinstated.[68]

---

[65] Interview with al-'Attar; Muhammad Shakir As'id, *al-Barlaman al-suri fi tatawwurihi al-tarikhi* [The Syrian parliament in its historical development] (Damascus: al-Mada, 2002), 363–5. On the Nationalist Union, see *OFA*, 2–5 May 1959, no. 1108, VII; Samir 'Abduh, *Hadatha dhat marra fi Suriyya: dirasa li-l-siyasat al-suriyya–al-'arabiyya fi 'ahday al-wahda wa-l-infisal 1958–1963* [It happened in Syria: a study of Syrian–Arab politics during the union and the secession] (Damascus: Dar 'Ala' al-Din, 1998), 64–7.

[66] Illiga Harik, 'The Single Party as a Subordinate Movement: The Case of Egypt', *World Politics* 26, no. 1 (1973), 80–105.

[67] *OFA*, 16–18 August 1961, no. 1336, V; 4–6 October 1961, no. 1350, V; 18–20 October 1961, no. 1354, V.

[68] *OFA*, 30 August–1 September 1961, no. 1340, VI; 9 September–3 October 1961, no. 1349, V, 28–31 October 1961, no. 1357, V.

The Paradoxes of Infisal (1961–1963)

The post-secession context was more than favourable from the clergy's point of view: Syria's new strongman, General 'Abd al-Karim al-Nahlawi, was a conservative; the parliament that was elected in November 1961 included about fifteen Islamic-leaning deputies, a third of whom were ulama;[69] within a few months, Syria had experienced a government headed by Ma'ruf al-Dawalibi, a sympathiser of the Muslim Brothers, and another, that of Khalid al-'Azm, which included four Islamist ministers.

The ulama took advantage of this context to ask again for the constitutional recognition of Islam as the state religion.[70] Concerned about the rise of leftist forces, they also opposed the restoration of parties in the name of preserving 'the country's creed, morals and unity'.[71] Although neither of these demands was met, the ulama, encouraged by the – once again very pragmatic – Muslim Brothers, decided not to press the issue in order not to destabilise a friendly regime threatened by the left-wing elements in the military.[72]

In this context of great anxiety came the first serious attempt at uniting the ulama and the Muslim Brothers within a single political framework. An 'Islamic Congress' had been established in 1955 with this end in view, but its purpose consisted merely in organising demonstrations in support of Arab people under colonial occupation.[73] In 1961, Makki al-Kittani, the notoriously pro-Saudi president of the League of Ulama (who was at that time involved in the establishment of the Muslim World League),[74] worked to set up a broad organisation, the Islamic Front, in order to counter the Nasserite–Ba'thist trend. The manoeuvre was particularly aimed at shifting the Muslim Brothers from their ambiguous position vis-à-vis the regime: although critical of Nasser's dictatorship and, as we have just seen, concerned about the preservation of the post-infisal arrangement, they had been among the few political forces to refuse to sign the statement of support for secession. Likewise, they declined al-Kittani's invitation.[75]

---

69 For Damascus: 'Abd al-Ra'uf Abu Tawq, Bashir Ramadan, Hussein Khattab; for Aleppo: 'Abd al-Fattah Abu Ghudda, Mustafa al-Zarqa; for Homs: Muhammad Ali Mish'al (As'id, *al-Barlaman al-suri*, 377–83).

70 *OFA*, 15–17 November 1961, no. 1362, V.

71 *OFA*, 15–17 August 1962, no. 1435, VII.

72 'Al-Shaykh al-shahid al-'allama Muhammad al-Shami' [The martyr and savant Sheikh Muhammad al-Shami] (www.alkeltawia.com, 24 September 2008).

73 Interview with al-'Attar; *OFA*, 22–28 February 1957, nos. 895–6, V.

74 Kittani, 'al-'Allamat al-imam al-mujahid'.

75 Barut, 'Suriyya', 263–5; interview with al-'Attar.

The Islamists' paradoxical attitude was due to the popularity of Nasser among their social base, the youth of the Sunni conservative urban middle class. The Islamists feared that, if they took up the cause of the secessionists too vocally, many of their supporters might defect to the Nasserites. Indeed, in Syria and Iraq, the latter were 'the meeting point of right-wing forces in the covert struggle between them ... and the increasingly radical trends arising in the Ba'th Party'.[76] Accordingly, in the early 1960s, alliances between the Brothers and the Nasserites in the elections of student unions were common, as were cases of members of the former movement switching to the latter.[77]

Thus, ten years after the crisis over the constitution, the ulama and the Muslim Brothers had again taken different positions on a political issue of paramount importance, and had done so less for ideological reasons than because of different priorities. As a sectoral elite chiefly concerned with the preservation of the status quo, the ulama granted their support to the most conservative political forces; the Brothers, meanwhile, behaved as a political party whose foremost objective is not to defend a particular social order but to retain its members and voters.

The Muslim Brothers' procrastinations did not last. On 8 March 1963, a military coup put an end to Syria's parliamentary experience, and inaugurated the long rule of the Ba'th. The ulama and the Muslim Brothers had no other choice than to join together on the side of what the new masters of the country called the 'reactionary forces'.

UNDER THE BA'TH'S IRON RULE (1963–2000)

The advent of the Ba'th entailed a profound change in the relative importance of the ulama and the Muslim Brothers as representatives of the Islamic trend. Until that point, even under Nasser, enough leeway had been left to the Brothers to allow for the emergence of charismatic figures such as Mustafa al-Siba'i and his successor 'Isam al-'Attar. After 1963, however, although the movement pursued its activities in a semi-underground fashion, most of its leading figures went into exile. In such circumstances, the ulama monopolised the symbolic leadership of the Islamic opposition,

---

[76] Georges Corm, *Le Proche-Orient éclaté, 1956–2003* (Paris: Gallimard, 2003), 284.

[77] The most famous defectors were 'Abd al-Majid al-Trabulsi, from Homs, who later became the Minister of Awqaf (1987–96), and 'Abd al-Rahman 'Utba, a prominent figure of the opposition in Aleppo. See Hawwa, *Hadhihi tajribati*, 31; Barut, 'Suriyya', 263–5; interview with Ali Sadr al-Din al-Bayanuni.

sometimes playing the agitator, but never despairing of finding friendly contacts inside the regime.

The Crisis of 1964: Between Radical Islamists and Moderate Ba'thists

During its first three years in power, Michel 'Aflaq's party did not implement a truly anti-religious policy. Of course, Makki al-Kittani was placed under house arrest, while Grand Mufti 'Abidin was definitively removed from his office, but these measures were targeted less at the clergy as a whole than at two of the staunchest supporters of the late secessionist regime.[78] The policy of appointment to official religious positions was still relatively consensual. 'Abd al-Razzaq al-Humsi, 'Abidin's interim successor, was not a creature of the Ba'th, having been known in the 1950s as the favourite preacher of President Shukri al-Quwwatli.[79] The Ministry of Awqaf, one remembers, was entrusted to al-Nabhan's legal counsellor Ahmad Mahdi al-Khudr. Hasan Habannaka himself was still on relatively good terms with the authorities, since his son 'Abd al-Rahman was appointed as the head of the religious education department at the Ministry of Awqaf.[80]

One should not forget here that, at this point, the party's civilian old guard was still in control of leading executive positions. For instance, the co-founder of the Ba'th, Salah al-Din al-Bitar, was Prime Minister four times between 1963 and 1966: despite his ideological choices, the social background of this descendant of a venerable Sunni Damascene family was closer to that of the ulama than to the young officers of the party's military wing, who were generally of rural origin and belonged to religious minorities. These officers' hostility to the traditional urban order was well known, and their radical socialist and secularist convictions were deeply worrying for the religious elite.[81]

In April 1964, merchant strikes against nationalisations convinced two young executives of the Hama branch of the Muslim Brothers, Sa'id Hawwa and Marwan Hadid, to organise an uprising in their city. Although this initiative started as a campaign of civil disobedience, it soon turned to guerrilla warfare as a result of the brutal response by the regime.[82] The besieged insurgents surrendered or fled after a month, without having

---

[78] Interview with al-Kittani.
[79] Abaza and Hafiz, *Tarikh 'ulama' Dimashq*, vol. II, 814–15.
[80] *OFA*, 20–23 July 1963, no. 1526, V.
[81] Hawwa, *Hadhihi tajribati*, 72.
[82] Ibid., 69–78.

succeeded in carrying with them the Damascene and Aleppian branches of the Brothers, which condemned their adventurism.[83] The ulama did not follow either. Sheikh Muhammad al-Hamid, the spiritual father of Hama's Islamic militants, reportedly tried to discourage his disciples from their project. Riding through the streets of the city aboard an official car equipped with a loudspeaker, he later called on the population to end the uprising and negotiated an amnesty for the prisoners.[84]

In Damascus, the clerics had also remained calm. At this time the socialist reforms were still focused on big business rather than on the petty and middle bourgeoisie associated with the clergy. In addition, the government was careful to deprive capitalists of the weapon of the 'defence of Islam' by refraining from any anti-religious provocation, and even by assigning a generous grant to Sheikh Habannaka's institute.[85]

In these troubled times, the ulama found an understanding partner at the head of the regime, President Amin al-Hafiz. At first an ally of the radical faction of the Ba'th, this Aleppian Sunni gradually distanced himself from it, notably by showing some benevolence towards the Islamic trend. During the troubles in Hama, where Ba'thist hardliners were pushing for a purely military solution, he reportedly negotiated the end of the uprising with Sheikh al-Hamid.[86]

Habannaka's biographer also portrayed al-Hafiz in a positive manner, as illustrated for example by the story of an encounter between the two men in the presence of the Maoist-leaning officer Ahmad Suwaydan. Referring to a recent incident between the latter and himself, the 'alim said to the President: 'I want to carry a weapon in order to defend myself if one of them threatens me again with his pistol.' Laughing, the head of state held his own service weapon out to Habannaka.[87]

In the aftermath of the Hama uprising, the regime pledged good will towards the religious community. Salah al-Din al-Bitar took up the post of Prime Minister, which he had left in November 1963, while the Awqaf portfolio changed hands but remained occupied by a member of a renowned religious family, the grandson and namesake of famous Aleppian reformist 'Abd al-Rahman al-Kawakibi, who promised to establish sharia

---

[83] Ibid., 81.
[84] Ibid., 73–9; Khalid al-Ahmad, 'mi'dhana wa dabbaba' [A minaret and a tank] (www.islamysria.com, 21 April 2007).
[85] OFA, 25–27 March 1964, no. 1594, V; Steven Heydemann, *Authoritarianism in Syria: Institutions and Social Conflict, 1946–1970* (Ithaca: Cornell University Press, 1999), 189.
[86] Rabinovich, *Syria under the Ba'th*, 111; al-Ahmad, 'Mi'dhana'.
[87] Habannaka, *al-Walid al-da'iya*, 253.

high schools in every governorate.[88] At the same time, family allowances were granted to mosque personnel.[89] A couple of months later, however, a sudden left-turn on the part of the regime inaugurated a period of deep crisis in state–clergy relations.

On a Collision Course (1965–1967)

By the time that a new permanent Grand Mufti was appointed in October 1964, the government was no longer headed by al-Bitar but by the Alawite general Muhammad 'Umran, who personally ensured that the selection committee chose Kaftaru over Habannaka.[90] From then on, the unsuccessful candidate led the clerical resistance to the regime. Every week, he brought together a sort of small League of Ulama composed of his most faithful allies: 'Abd al-Karim al-Rifa'i, Ahmad al-Daqr, Mulla Ramadan al-Buti (Sa'id's father), and Amin al-Masri (1917–79), a Salafi who had recently left the Muslim Brothers.[91]

Al-Masri, whose 'modern' intellectual profile contrasted with that of his colleagues – he had a Ph.D. in Islamic studies from a British university – gave inflammatory sermons in which he called for the establishment of Islamic rule through military jihad.[92] His disciples formed a secret organisation called the Phalange of Muhammad (Kata'ib Muhammad), which took action following a new wave of nationalisations in January 1965. By targeting small and medium-sized companies,[93] and hence the clergy's economic interests, socialist reforms were now offering a rare opportunity for convergence between the Islamists and the ulama. While preachers gave fiery sermons, the Phalanges of Muhammad organised an insurrectional meeting at the Umayyad Mosque. Senior clerics such as Habannaka were supposed to attend but were barred from getting there by the police. The way was thus clear for the army, which stormed the mosque and killed several inside.[94]

---

[88] *OFA*, 10–13 October 1964, no. 1649, V.

[89] *OFA*, 12–14 August 1964, no. 1632, V.

[90] Habannaka, *al-Walid al-da'iya*, 66–8.

[91] Ibid., 230–1.

[92] Ibid., 229–30; 'al-Shaykh al-duktur Muhammad Amin al-Masri' (www.odabasham.net, 13 December 2003).

[93] Rabinovich, *Syria under the Ba'th*, 140; Perthes, *The Political Economy of Syria*, 38–40.

[94] Habannka, *al-Walid al-da'iya*, 228–35; interviews with al-Malih, al-Hawari, and al-Khatib.

In the weeks that followed the 'events of the Umayyad Mosque' (*ahdath al-umawi*), the regime was still hesitating between conciliation and strong-arm tactics: on the one hand, a new understanding with Amin al-Hafiz resulted in the swift release of the prisoners;[95] on the other, as mentioned in the prologue, the prerogatives of official clerical councils were transferred to the government, and Amin al-Masri had to go into exile in Saudi Arabia while Habannaka and his most prominent followers were banned from preaching.[96]

It took more than this to discourage the sheikh of the Midan from remaining at the forefront of the protest, however. Two factors encouraged him in adopting that stance: first, the acceleration after 1965 of the exodus of the Muslim Brothers' executives, which more than ever made the ulama the most credible candidates for the leadership of the Islamic opposition; second, the ideological radicalisation of the regime following the coup carried out in February 1966 by the Neo-Ba'th of Salah Jadid against Amin al-Hafiz and the old guard.

In the meantime, Habannaka had challenged the state by returning to the minbar without due authorisation.[97] In the months that followed, the sheikh was at the height of his popularity: in March 1967, returning from the pilgrimage to Mecca, during which he was officially received by King Faysal – one of the 'reactionary monarchs' for whose overthrow the Neo-Ba'thists were overtly calling[98] – the scholar was welcomed in Damascus by a jubilant crowd.[99]

This plebiscite in favour of a sheikh who embodied hostility to the regime occurred one month prior to the publication in the army magazine of the aforementioned article calling for religion to be put in the museum of history. The following Friday, fiery sermons were followed by demonstrations. Although the author of the contentious article was briefly placed in custody as a sop to conservative opinion,[100] the regime reacted with firmness by arresting Habannaka and other leading ulama; in Aleppo, Tahir Khayr Allah was incarcerated, while the city's mufti, Muhammad Balanku, was retired.[101]

---

[95] Interview with al-Hawari.
[96] Habannaka, *al-Walid al-da'iya*, 268.
[97] Ibid., 269.
[98] Joseph Mann, 'The Syrian Neo-Ba'th Regime and the Kingdom of Saudi Arabia, 1966–70', *Middle Eastern Studies* 42, no. 5 (2006), 761–76.
[99] Habannaka, *al-Walid al-da'iya*, 272.
[100] Petran, *Syria*, 197–8.
[101] Habannaka, *al-Walid al-da'iya*, 279–87; interview with al-Hawari.

The release of the prisoners the following June did not result from the strike by the merchants of the Midan, which was easily stopped by the police, but from the crushing defeat of the Syrian army in the Six-Day War, which badly weakened the regime and made it unable to keep such popular figures in jail. Habannaka paid dearly for his attitude, however, since the authorities permanently shut down his institute.

The Crisis of the Constitution (1973)

Three years after the loss of the Golan, a more favourable era seemed to begin for the ulama with the coming to power of Hafiz al-Asad. Despite being the first non-Sunni President in Syrian history, his Corrective Movement was seen in conservative circles as a welcome break with the left-wing policies of the previous leadership.[102] Al-Asad's first years in power were marked by limited economic liberalisation, but also by a measure of political opening. In 1972, governorate councils were formed through relatively open elections that witnessed the success of conservative candidates supported by the Muslim Brothers.[103]

In foreign policy, more flexible inter-Arab diplomacy led to a rapprochement with Saudi Arabia as well as a new project of union with Egypt and Libya called the Tripartite Federation.[104] At that time, the new rulers of the two latter countries, Anwar al-Sadat and Mu'ammar al-Qaddafi, were inclined to reassert the value of Islamic references. The new Syrian President himself adopted a comparable stance, declaring to the ulama that 'the Corrective Movement is necessary to preserve the Islamic identity of the country' against previous Marxist 'deviances'.[105]

In this context, the disappointment of the clergy was all the greater when the draft of a 'permanent' constitution of secular orientation was released in February 1973.[106] The ulama and the Muslim Brothers coordinated their opposition to the text, but the crisis highlighted their profound differences with respect to strategy.

---

[102] Hawwa, *Hadhihi tajribati*, 99.

[103] Ibid., 107; interview with Ali Sadr al-Din al-Bayanuni; Seale, *Asad of Syria*, 176.

[104] Sonoko Sunayama, *Syria and Saudi Arabia: Collaboration and Conflicts in the Oil Era* (London: I. B. Tauris, 2007), 37–41; Seale, *Asad of Syria*, 186–7.

[105] Habash, *al-Shaykh Ahmad Kaftaru*, 294; Sa'id Ramadan al-Buti, lecture at the University of Aleppo, 4 April 2007 (observation).

[106] Provisional constitutions had been enacted in 1964 and 1969. See Rabinovich, *Syria under the Ba'th*, 118.

Unlike the constitution of 1950, the draft did not specify that the President should be a Muslim. It also subjected freedom of worship to the requirements of 'public order', a provision that gave a constitutional basis to the de facto ban on Sunni outdoor religious celebrations that had been in force since 1963. Finally, unlike the draft constitution of the Tripartite Federation, it did not mention that the purpose of education is to raise 'generations of believers'. At the political level, the infamous Article No. 8 enshrined the quasi-single-party system in the constitution by stating that the Ba'th 'leads the state and society'.[107]

In Hama, Sa'id Hawwa immediately understood that the draft constitution provided the Muslim Brothers with a unique opportunity to mobilise (and shield themselves behind) both the ulama, on religious grounds, and secular opposition parties, which were de jure marginalised by Article No. 8:

> When I read the constitution, I thought we had to take action, and that we had to do so in the name of the ulama. I also thought that many parties would join the movement [such as] the Nasserites, [Akram al-Hawrani's] Socialists, and even the group of Salah Jadid ... Given that the movement would be in the name of the ulama, it would appear as an entirely Islamic phenomenon ... I thought that we, the Muslim Brothers, had to get people to take action while remaining under cover.[108]

In other words, Hawwa's goal was to exploit the religiously driven anger of the clergy in pursuit of an eminently political endeavour, the destabilisation of the regime. In order to do so, he drafted a statement denouncing the constitution and attached a fatwa calling for the boycott of the referendum scheduled for 8 March. However, obtaining the signatures of the ulama was no mere formality because, as Hawwa pointed out, they are 'cautious by nature'.[109] To succeed, he needed a lever, a prestigious personality who would encourage his peers by being the first to sign.

This personality was Sheikh Muhammad al-Nabhan, whom Hawwa approached through his right-hand man, Muhammad al-Shami. The Muslim Brother was aware of al-Shami's close relations with the authorities and suspected him of favouring an action of limited scope enjoying the tacit approval of some high-ranking officials.[110] However, he thought

---

[107] John Donohue, 'The New Syrian Constitution and the Religious Opposition', *CEMAM Reports*, no. 1 (1973), 81–96, at 81–3.
[108] Hawwa, *Hadhihi tajribati*, 111.
[109] Ibid., 110.
[110] Ibid., 112.

he could use him to initiate the first phase of the process, which needed to appear exclusively as the initiative of the ulama. With this purpose in mind, he did not make contact with the clerics of Aleppo on behalf of the Muslim Brothers, but, being himself a graduate in sharia, as a representative of Hama's men of religion. Nevertheless, he bypassed the latter as much as he could, as illustrated in his memoirs by an episode where he waits, in company with the ulama of Hama, for a delegation of their Aleppian colleagues with whom they will discuss the draft petition:

The delegation of Aleppo was a long time coming; our sheikhs waited for a long time, then they got tired and announced they wanted to retire to bed ... I looked forward to their departure because it gave me the freedom to speak on behalf of the sheikhs of Hama and granted me more flexibility in the discussion.[111]

When Hawwa's petition came back from Aleppo with the signatures of the city's leading scholars,[112] their colleagues in Hama found the text too harsh. They therefore decided to write another draft and to leave it to Sheikh Habannaka to choose between the two. However, the ulama of Homs regretted both the harshness of the Aleppian version and the half-heartedness of the Hamawi one. Consequently, they wrote a third draft which Hawwa eventually submitted, with the two previous ones, to Habannaka. The latter showed little enthusiasm for the initiative, proving difficult to convince and eventually choosing the most moderate of the three drafts. His signature paved the way for many leading scholars of the capital to follow.[113] The first phase of the operation was thus a major success since, as Hawwa noted, 'for the first time in Syria's recent history, the ulama of all the governorates adopted a common position of a rebellious nature'.[114]

In reality, however, although the aforementioned scholars did indeed sign a petition, it was not exactly the one that was eventually released, Hawwa having hardened the text somewhat in the mean time.[115] Of the two slightly different petitions that were published in the Lebanese newspaper *al-Hayat* on 23 and 24 February 1973,[116] none answered

[111] Ibid., 113.
[112] In addition to al-Nabhan and al-Shami, the list included Ahmad al-Bayanuni, Muhammad Abu al-Nasr's son 'Abd al-Basit, Tahir Khayr Allah, Adib Hassun and Muhammad al-Salqini, Ibrahim's father (*al-Hayat*, 23 and 24 February 1973).
[113] Among others: Mulla Ramadan al-Buti and his son Sa'id, the former deputy and Hanbali mufti 'Abd al-Ra'uf Abu Tawq, Jama'at Zayd's new leader Muhammad 'Awad (al-Rifa'i was dying), and Muhammad al-Zu'bi.
[114] Hawwa, *Hadhihi tajribati*, 116.
[115] Interview with al-Hawari.
[116] Plausibly, the publication of two petitions with different lists of signatories was aimed at obscuring the unique origin of the initiative – that is, Hawwa.

Habannaka's concern for moderation: the first described the authors of the constitution as 'an enemy backed by colonialism' and the second called on Muslims to 'fight the partisan and sectarian domination'.

The difference between the text he had been given to read and the one that was finally released might be the reason why Habannaka refrained from explicitly taking responsibility for his signature.[117] Such a stance, which was tantamount to sinking the petition, was perhaps also related to the timing of its publication in the press, which seems to have gone against the desires of the clergy. On 20 February al-Asad had asked parliament to take into account 'the wishes of the people' by restoring the article stating that the religion of the head of state is Islam.[118] In Aleppo, Muhammad al-Shami informed Hawwa that he was satisfied with this symbolic victory and was unwilling to push the campaign further. In Damascus, the President received Habannaka, former Grand Mufti ʿAbidin, and delegations of notables, and obtained the cancellation of a merchant strike.[119]

The possible reservations of his elders regarding the decision to publish the petition after the President had made an important concession was of little concern for Hawwa, who had a broader plan in mind. In parallel, indeed, he had distributed an anonymous leaflet calling for the 'fall of the Alawite power'.[120] The document was written in a way that gave the impression that its author was a group that enjoyed support within the military and, as such, was on the verge of carrying out a coup. The objective here was to make opposition parties believe that a window of opportunity had opened. In Hama, the operation was entirely 'successful', with Nasserites and followers of Akram al-Hawrani joining riots that resulted in dozens of casualties. However, apart from the troubles that were witnessed in Homs until April, things went no further.

One of the reasons for the failure of this initiative by the Muslim Brothers of Hama was their inability to rally the rest of the Islamic trend. As we have just seen, the ulama were limited to strictly religious concerns, with the result that they were content to win the most important battle, the clause stipulating that the President must be a Muslim, if nothing more ambitious seemed feasible. Al-Asad certainly was a despot, but unlike his radical left-wing predecessors, he was one with whom it was

[117] Hawwa, *Hadhihi tajribati*, 116.
[118] Donohue, 'The New Syrian Constitution', 85.
[119] Ibid.
[120] Ibid., 89; Hawwa, *Hadhihi tajribati*, 114–15.

possible to engage: until his death in 1978, Habannaka would be regularly received for consultation at the presidential palace.[121]

On the contrary, it was for very political reasons that, as in 1964, the national leadership of the Muslim Brothers, now based in Aleppo after the north–south schism, rejected the insurrectional strategy of the Hama section.[122] Eager to exploit the opportunities offered by the timid process of political liberalisation, the Aleppo branch was preparing for the legislative elections of May 1973. During those elections they supported the successful campaigns of four conservative candidates, including Ibrahim al-Salqini and Zayn al-'Abidin Khayr Allah, the brother of Sheikh Tahir and the president of the union of Syrian physicians.[123] Their parliamentary experience was short-lived, however, since the Brothers, following in this the rest of the opposition, boycotted the next elections in 1977.[124] The political atmosphere then deteriorated continuously until the launch of the insurgency in 1979.

Uprising and Holy Alliance: The Islamic Front

In January 1980, the regime was still trying to defuse the crisis by showing some signs of good will, such as the release of Islamist prisoners and the formation of a new government which included members of old Sunni Damascene families such as Prime Minister 'Abd al-Ra'uf al-Kasm (b. 1932), the son of the late Mufti of Damascus 'Ata' Allah al-Kasm (1844–1938).[125]

In parallel, the authorities tried to prevent an alliance between the ulama and the Islamists by playing on the former's sectoral streak. In order to 'reinforce the values and principles of Islam', the new Minister of Awqaf, Muhammad al-Khatib, promised the creation of a 'Higher Islamic Council' to the grand ulama, who had been deprived of any representative organ since the 1960s.[126] The project was rapidly abandoned in view

---

[121] Habannaka, *al-Walid al-da'iya*, 303–10.

[122] Interviews with al-Hawari and Ali Sadr al-Din al-Bayanuni.

[123] Interview with Ali Sadr al-Din al-Bayanuni.

[124] Yahya Sadowski, 'Ba'thist Ethics and the Spirit of State Capitalism: Patronage in Contemporary Syria', in *Ideology and Power in the Middle East*, ed. Peter J. Chelkowski and Robert Pranger (Durham: Duke University Press, 1988), 160–84, at 175–6; Zuhayr Salim, 'Safha min tarikh al-ikhwan al-muslimin fi Suriyya' [A page from the history of the Muslim Brothers in Syria] (www.levantnews.com, 19 September 2010).

[125] Batatu, *Syria's Peasantry*, 272.

[126] John Donohue, 'Religion and Politics in Syria', *CEMAM Reports*, no. 7 (1980), 157–77, at 161.

of the deterioration of the political situation, but in the meantime the Minister had also had time to make preparations for a reform of the curricula of religious institutes.[127] By entrusting a genuinely representative committee of ulama with this task, the government displayed its desire to take into account the views of the religious elite.[128] The committee never met, however: no sooner had it been set up, in March 1980, than an arrest warrant was issued against one of its members, Abu al-Nasr al-Bayanuni, who took refuge in Jordan.

In Damascus, the regime succeeded in maintaining a facade of harmony with the ulama until the following year. In June 1980, al-Asad could still appear on the front page of *al-Ba'th* newspaper in company with Damascus's most prominent religious leaders, even if – though of course, the organ of the party did not breathe a word about it – it was on the occasion of a stormy reception during which the President blamed his visitors for the involvement of their disciples in armed groups.[129]

The situation was radically different two years later when, following the bloody siege of Hama in February 1982, and in the presence of the Minister of Awqaf, another delegation of clerics signed a statement condemning the 'crimes of the Gang of the Criminal Brothers' (*'isabat al-ikhwan al-mujrimin*).[130] This delegation, however, was no prestigious learned assembly, but – excepting Grand Mufti Kaftaru – a collection of obscure figures brought in for the occasion from all over the country.

Meanwhile, on the side of the opposition, the Islamic Front in Syria (al-Jabha al-Islamiyya fi Suriyya) was established in Saudi Arabia in October 1980. This was the most successful attempt at uniting ulama and lay Islamists in a single political framework that had yet been seen. The Front comprised the Muslim Brothers, who unsurprisingly were behind the initiative, and about a hundred exiled scholars. The latter came for the most part from Aleppo, in part because natives of this city constituted the largest proportion of exiled Syrian ulama, but also because they had the closest relations with the (Aleppian) national leadership of the Brothers. Both the president and secretary-general of the Front were from Aleppo: respectively, former superintendent of the Muslim Brothers 'Abd al-Fattah Abu Ghudda, and Abu al-Nasr al-Bayanuni, Abi Dharr's leader

[127] Ibid.
[128] The committee included representatives of Kaftaru and al-Farfur but also leading disciples of Habannaka and members of Zayd, in addition to Abi Dharr's leader, Abu al-Nasr al-Bayanuni. See Böttcher, *Syrische Religionspolitik*, 129–30.
[129] *Al-Ba'th*, 9 June 1980; Sharbaji, 'Mudawwinat', no. 19.
[130] *Al-Thawra*, 11 March 1982.

and the brother of one of the main leaders of the Islamist movement. However, the Front also included prominent ulama from all over the country,[131] including, for Damascus, the exiled leaders of Jama'at Zayd and Hisham al-Burhani.[132]

The Islamic Front was also the first Syrian clerical organisation to adopt a detailed political programme, the Charter of the Islamic Front in Syria, which was published in January 1981. It was largely based on the *Declaration of the Islamic Revolution in Syria*, a document released in November 1980 by the Muslim Brothers which advocated the establishment of a relatively liberal Islamic state.[133]

At first glance, the unprecedented nature of this coalition constituted a serious challenge to the regime. However, the initiative was seriously weakened by the paradoxical strategy of its initiators. Although the leadership aimed to emphasise the importance of the role played by the ulama within the Front by making Abu al-Nasr al-Bayanuni its most visible figure, the non-publication, for security reasons, of the names of the other affiliated clerics deprived this move of most of its symbolic weight.

Moreover, after the fall of Hama in 1982, the Front experienced tensions due to the differences of approach on the part of its political and religious components: when the Muslim Brothers turned towards the secular opposition to form the National Alliance for the Liberation of Syria, a group of ulama led by Tahir Khayr Allah left the organisation.[134] The platform eventually disbanded in the middle of the decade following a new split within the Muslim Brothers, which, from 1986, saw the Aleppo wing of Abu Ghudda and Ali Sadr al-Din al-Bayanuni, supported by the Egyptian mother-organisation, in opposition to the pro-Iraqi Hama faction of 'Adnan Sa'd al-Din.[135]

BASHAR AL-ASAD'S FIRST DECADE IN POWER: THE ULAMA'S FAILED POLITICAL COMEBACK

During the dark years that followed the uprising, no 'alim, except for privileged figures such as al-Buti, would dare to address controversial

[131] For Aleppo: Muhammad al-Hajjar, the famous exegete Muhammad Ali al-Sabuni, Tahir Khayr Allah, 'Abd al-Qadir 'Isa (represented by one of his disciples); for Homs: 'Adnan al-Saqqa, Muhammad Ali Mish'al; for Hama: Sa'd al-Din al-Murad, Bashir al-Shuqfa.
[132] Interview with Ali Sadr al-Din al-Bayanuni.
[133] See Abdallah, *The Islamic Struggle*, 128–87.
[134] 'Abd al-Hakim, *al-Thawra al-islamiyya*, 106.
[135] Chris Kutschera, 'L'éclipse des Frères Musulmans syriens', *Cahiers de l'Orient*, no. 7 (1987), 121–33; Barut, 'Suriyya', 302–7.

political issues in public. It was not until the crises of the first years of the twenty-first century that this situation changed significantly, and clerics once more had the opportunity to position themselves on the problem of political reform – thereby displaying, once again, the depth of their strategic differences with Islamic activists.

Islamic–Liberal Offensive (2004–2005)

Although the Damascus Spring, an attempt by mostly secular intellectuals to recreate a public sphere after the death of Hafiz al-Asad in 2000, had been stifled without a shot being fired,[136] only three years later the Syrian regime was destabilised by the fall of Saddam Hussein. In its vociferous condemnations of the British–American invasion the regime was of course perfectly in tune with public opinion, and especially with the men of religion who, following the example of Grand Mufti Kaftaru, called for jihad against coalition forces.[137] However, the new regional order paved the way for external pressures (Israeli bombardment of a Palestinian camp near Damascus in October 2003, followed by US military and economic sanctions in May 2004 and resolution 1559 on Lebanon in September of the same year) that emboldened the opposition. In the spring of 2004, human rights activists organised an unprecedented sit-in in front of the parliament, while an uprising was violently suppressed in the Kurdish regions. In December, the now London-based Muslim Brothers released their first detailed political programme since 1980, in which they advocated both the establishment of a 'civil' (*madani*) democratic state and the Islamisation of laws.[138]

For the regime, the situation was all the more worrying in that its ranks were divided between the al-Asad clan and the allies of Lebanese Prime Minister Rafiq al-Hariri, Vice-President 'Abd al-Halim Khaddam and the former chief of Syrian mukhabarat in Lebanon, Ghazi Kana'an.[139]

Following the assassination of Hariri in February 2005, the 'Beirut Spring', and the Syrian withdrawal from Lebanon, hopes for democratisation in the Arab world were at their highest. Many in Syria, including

---

[136] See Alan George, *Syria: Neither Bread nor Freedom* (London and New York: Zed Books, 2003), 30–63.
[137] AFP, 27 March 2003.
[138] Pierret, 'Le *Projet politique*'.
[139] Nicholas Blanford, *Killing Mr Lebanon: The Assassination of Rafik Hariri and Its Impact on the Middle East* (London: I. B. Tauris, 2006), 54–6.

Ba'th members, were convinced that the regime had no alternative but to reform or perish.[140]

Among the Islamic trend, the liberal demands of the Muslim Brothers were relayed by 'Independent Islamists' such as Haytham al-Malih,[141] but also by a handful of young ulama. In 2004, the sheikh–engineer Mu'adh al-Khatib proposed the creation of the Union of Ulama, Imams and Preachers' (Ittihad al-'Ulama' wa-l-A'imma wa-l-Du'at). This project was reminiscent of Kamil al-Qassab's Association of Ulama, of which al-Khatib's father had been a member in the early 1950s: using his status of broker, the former preacher of the Umayyad Mosque aspired to unite clerics (*'ulama', a'imma*) and lay activists (*du'at*).[142]

The project was greeted with very little enthusiasm on the part of the grand ulama, in particular because the agenda of the projected union was too overtly political. Among the basic demands in its draft charter were the '[restoration of] public liberties ... the release of political prisoners, the repeal of emergency laws, special courts and arbitrary arrests, the abolition of the single-party system'.[143] Yet, as this section will show, most of the religious elite were unwilling at that time to address the problem of authoritarianism.

Similar demands were voiced by two other young clerics who – unlike al-Khatib, a long-standing rebellious figure – were known to be close to the regime. Both were heirs of the now-defunct Grand Mufti Kaftaru: his son Salah al-Din, the director of the Academy, and his grandson-in-law the ecumenist MP Muhammad Habash. Given 'the total failure of secular Arab governments' and the impending 'tsunami of American hawks', Kaftaru and Habash asked the Syrian leadership to 'accelerate the pace of reforms' in order to prevent 'a very difficult future'.[144] The required reforms were eminently political: lifting the state of emergency, authorising 'faith-oriented' (i.e. moderate Islamic) parties on the Turkish model, and responding positively to the exiled Muslim Brothers' offers of dialogue.[145]

---

[140] Joshua Landis, 'The Jasmine Revolution?' (www.joshualandis.com, 3 May 2005).

[141] *Al-Sharq al-Awsat*, 22 October 2004.

[142] Interview with al-Khatib.

[143] Ahmad Mu'adh al-Khatib, 'Musawwada Ittihad al-'Ulama' wa-l-A'imma wa-l-Du'at' [Draft project for the Union of Ulama, Imams and Preachers], (www.darbuna.net, 8 May 2006).

[144] Quotations from, respectively, Kaftaru (*Washington Post*, 23 January 2005 and 27 May 2005), Habash (*al-Ra'i al-'Amm*, 23 October 2005), and Kaftaru (*Washington Post*, 27 May 2005).

[145] On the relations between the Muslim Brothers and the regime before 2002, see Zisser, 'Syria, the Ba'th Regime', 52–7.

In addition, Kaftaru established an ostensible relationship with leading opponent Riyad Sayf after his release from prison in 2006.[146]

By calling for democratic reforms and positioning themselves as possible mediators between the government and the opposition, Kaftaru and Habash were seeking to strengthen their contested personal legitimacy. The former, it must be recalled, was a mere administrator with no proper religious training who could not claim to have inherited the spiritual aura of his father, while the latter's theological positions were anathema to many of his colleagues. Both were also aware of the fact that if a process of 'democratisation' was to be set in motion, it would be tightly controlled and would therefore tend to favour the traditional clients of the regime – that is to say, themselves.

In 2004, the regime showed some signs of good will by resuming indirect contacts with the Syrian Muslim Brothers through the Egyptian branch of the organisation (Damascus's ambassador to Cairo attended its Ramadan fast-breaking reception) and foreign Islamist leaders such as Yusuf al-Qardawi and Faysal al-Mawlawi.[147] However, by the spring of 2005, it had come to the conclusion that the best way to ensure its survival was not liberalisation but the reaffirmation of the old red lines, starting with the prohibition of any relationship with the Muslim Brothers. In May, independent Islamist Ali Abdullah was arrested after reading out a letter from Ali Sadr al-Din al-Bayanuni during a meeting at the Jamal al-Atasi Forum for Democratic Debate.[148] At the same time, Kurdish sheikh Ma'shuq al-Khaznawi, who had secretly met with the superintendent of the Muslim Brothers, was found murdered. In June, the Tenth Regional Congress of the Ba'th ruined any hope for democratisation, and speakers accused the Muslim Brothers of collusion with the United States.[149]

Despite the rupture of the truce between the regime and the Brothers, the domestic opposition continued its rapprochement with the latter, which officially supported the Damascus Declaration for Democratic Change published in October 2005.[150] At first glance, this document was a serious blow to the regime in that it brought together a wide array of opponents, including Islamic-leaning ones such as the Muslim Brothers, Haytham

---

[146] Interview with a European diplomat, Damascus, May 2008.
[147] Al-Bayanuni, 'Ziyara khassa'; *al-Sharq al-Awsat*, 22 October 2004.
[148] www.thisissyria.com (dead link), 16 May 2005.
[149] *Al-Hayat*, 10 June 2005.
[150] Joshua Landis and Joe Pace, 'The Syrian Opposition', *The Washington Quarterly* 30, no. 1 (2007), 45–68, at 55.

al-Malih, and the champion of non-violence Jawdat Saʻid. Moreover, it was released a few days before the first report by UN-appointed judge Detlev Mehlis on al-Hariri's assassination, which unofficially pointed a finger at the Syrian regime.[151]

Nonetheless, by mid-October 2005, the window of opportunity was already closing for Syrian oppositionists. A popular uprising being very unlikely, their only chance was to take advantage of intra-regime dissent. Yet throughout the month that followed al-Hariri's killing, his main partners in Damascus were eliminated: Khaddam resigned during the June 2005 Baʻth Congress and went into exile in Paris, and Kanaʻan committed suicide in October. By the end of the year, al-Asad had managed to return to the fore and brush aside the threat of regime change – not least because the country's leading Muslim scholars had proved loyal to his shaky regime.

Suriyya Allah Hamiha! ('Syria, God Is Her Protector!')

In the autumn of 2005, the regime responded to Mehlis's accusations by launching an impressive campaign of nationalist propaganda. Mass demonstrations took place and cities were covered with Syrian flags. Although organised from above, the campaign received some genuine popular support, in part because the regime allowed the display of symbols that expressed a Syrian-centred and religious identity rather than secular pan-Arabism. The usually omnipresent flag of the Baʻth Party almost completely disappeared during that period while, following the Iraqi fashion, the regional (*qutri*) – that is, Syrian – flag sometimes bore the words 'Syria, God is its Protector!' (*Suriyya Allah hamiha!*) between its two green stars. This slogan had become popular after it was used by the President to finish an address in November 2005.[152] Unsurprisingly, al-Asad's unusual religious rhetoric sounded pleasant to the ulama: so much so that, in a mosque lesson given in November 2005, Sheikh al-Buti expressed his delight at the fact that 'the President paid tribute to this country in the language of the Quran'.[153]

[151] Blanford, *Killing Mr Lebanon*, 179.
[152] Syrian National Television, 10 November 2005.
[153] Saʻid Ramadan al-Buti, 'Qadiyat al-Hariri wa ʻalaqatuha bi-mukhattat al-qada' ʻala al-Islam' [The Hariri affair and its relation to the plan to destroy Islam] (www.bouti. com, December 2005).

Sheikh al-Buti's Bargain

One remembers that al-Buti had been somewhat marginalised after the advent of Bashar al-Asad, who did not grant him the long private meetings that had been customary with his father. For the Kurdish scholar, the crisis was therefore an opportunity to return to the front of the stage.

In the sermons he had delivered during the weeks following al-Hariri's assassination, al-Buti had remained deliberately vague, repeatedly saying that 'coming back to God' was the key to victory against foreign enemies.[154] In his lesson of November 2005, however, he proposed a deal to the regime, lending it full support against 'foreign conspiracies' in exchange for the fulfilment of three main requests.

According to al-Buti, al-Hariri's assassination and the subsequent UN enquiry were nothing but a US–Israeli conspiracy against Syria, which was being targeted because its steadfastness on foreign policy issues constituted the last obstacle to complete Western–Zionist hegemony over the Arab world, an objective that was itself part of a wide-ranging plan 'to destroy Islamic civilisation'.[155] In the face of such a threat, al-Buti told the faithful, the duty of the Syrian people was to 'strengthen national unity'. Tackling the very sensitive issue of Islamist exiles and prisoners, he asked their families to put their anger aside in consideration of the challenges facing the nation:

People come crying and say: 'One of my parents has lived abroad for years and has not been allowed to come back.' Another says: 'One of my parents is in prison, he served his sentence but he was not released.' I answer: 'I understand, but you have to wipe the slate clean on your personal interest in aid of the umma.'[156]

In order not to give the enemy the opportunity to exploit such distress, al-Buti expressed his first demand not by laying claim to (civil and political) *rights* but by begging the regime to be 'lenient'. 'National unity cannot be realised by the people only', he said; 'I am forced to say: pronounce an amnesty.'

Al-Buti's second request concerned the clergy's traditional pet hate: feminists. In the weeks that preceded al-Buti's lesson, the Syrian ulama had been infuriated by a campaign by women's rights associations in favour of a secular reform of the sharia-inspired Personal Status Law (balancing the rules of inheritance in women's favour, abolition of polygamy).[157]

---

[154] See for instance 'Hanat sa'at al-'awda ila Allah' [The time has come to return to God] (www.bouti.net, 18 March 2005).

[155] Al-Buti, 'Qadiyat al-Hariri'.

[156] Ibid.

[157] See 'Qanun al-ahwal al-shakhsiyya bayn al-jam'iyyat wa fatawa rijal al-din' [The Personal Status Law between the associations and the fatwas of the men of religion]

Two events had particularly scandalised the men of religion: a conference organised in the grand lecture hall of the University of Damascus, during which a book entitled *Down with the Veil!*[158] had been promoted; and a survey conducted among Damascene women by the feminist Association for Social Initiative. According to al-Buti, such activities were nothing but Western scheming against Syria:

Foreign conspiracies cannot succeed without another plan at the domestic level. What is this plan? It consists in dismantling the umma's social fabric ... For that reason, we notice today – in the perilous times we are going through – suspect activities that were not existing yesterday ... new associations, new names: 'Association for Social Initiative', 'Women of Syria', people who organise conferences in hotel lobbies. That is odd! ... Where were these activities two years ago?[159]

The third demand by the Kurdish scholar was the creation of a higher Islamic council, forty years after official clerical councils were deprived of their prerogatives, and a quarter of a century after the Minister of Awqaf promised to re-establish such an organ.

Al-Buti's offer was received acrimoniously by the Islamist proponents of political liberalisation. From Saudi Arabia, the chair of the Muslim Brothers' Consultative Council, Munir al-Ghadban (b. 1942), directed this philippic at him: 'You are the protector of the tyrants, the one who legitimises their oppressive rule. You are the one who calls his own people to submit to slavery.' Making it clear that for him the criterion for political alliance was opposition to dictatorship, not the defence of 'Islam' at the expense of change, al-Ghadban continued by praising 'our non-Muslim and secularist brothers' who were 'fighting against oppression ... at the risk of being tortured and jailed'.[160]

Although he was speaking from inside Syria, Muhammad Habash reacted no less fiercely to al-Buti's statement – the latter having been, in preceding years, a notable detractor of his theological views. In a resounding address given at the Military Academy in March 2006,

(www.tahawolat.com, 8 April 2006). In this context, Usama al-Rifa'i launched a series of no fewer than sixty sermons under the theme of the 'defence of the Muslim woman'. See also this sermon of 9 December 2005 by Mufti of Aleppo Ibrahim al-Salqini: 'al-Hujum 'ala al-ahwal al-shakhsiyya' [The attack against personal status] (www.dr-salkini.com).

[158] This was an Arabic translation of a French book published in 2003 by French-Iranian Chahdortt Djavann.

[159] Al-Buti, 'Qadiyat al-Hariri'.

[160] Munir al-Ghadban, 'Sidi al-shaykh: la takun zahiran li-l-mujrimin' [My sheikh, don't be the auxiliary of the criminals] (www.arraee.com, 2 January 2006).

Habash derided 'those clergymen who went as far as to display their emotion and cry bitterly on television screens', an obvious reference to the widely commented-on tears shed by al-Buti during Hafiz al-Asad's funeral. The Islamist MP then denounced the 'hypocritical' strategy that had been adopted by these figures since the 1980s, 'expressing total support for state policies and justifying it as mere dissimulation necessary to the achievement of some of the religious class's demands'. Such an obsequious – and, although he did not use the word, sectoral – posture, he continued, did nothing to bring about change.[161]

With the spectacular rise of Islamic forces in neighbouring countries, and in the face of new 'challenges' from the exiled opposition – the Muslim Brothers and ex-Vice-President Khaddam had just announced the creation of the National Salvation Front – another way had to be pursued: the time had come to reform the law on parties in order to 'give the Islamic trend its chance' – that is, to authorise Islamic parties.[162]

Habash did not hide the fact that, according to 'echoes' coming from the Ba'th Party, his call would probably fall on deaf ears. Neither was he unaware of the fact that proponents of democracy were hopelessly isolated among the clergy: while Syria was witnessing an 'Islamic Spring', the country's most prominent Muslim scholars were aligning themselves with al-Buti's sectoral strategy.

Syria's 'Islamic Spring'

In the first weeks of 2006, the triumph of Hamas in the Palestinian parliamentary elections filled the religiously minded sections of the Syrian public with enthusiasm. However, bitter disappointment immediately followed as the West refused to recognise the new government. Resentment was soon exacerbated by the Danish cartoons affair: the regime gave free rein to popular expressions of discontent, including parades with flags bearing Islamic slogans – which had not been seen in Damascus for decades – and the burning of the Danish and Norwegian embassies on 4 February 2006. As a reaction to the affair, the celebration of the Mawlid was extremely public by local standards.[163]

Such an atmosphere was highly beneficial to the regime, whose support for Hamas – the latter's politburo head Khalid Mish'al regularly

---

[161] Muhammad Habash, 'Suriyya fi muwajahat al-tahaddiyat: risalat al-shari' al-islami [Syria facing challenges: the message of the Islamic street] (all4syria.info, 28 March 2006).

[162] Ibid.

[163] Observations.

addressed the crowds in Damascus's mosques[164] – was praised by senior ulama, including figures traditionally much less compliant than al-Buti. Among them was Krayyim Rajih, Habannaka's main spiritual heir. During a celebration of the Mawlid in April 2006, Rajih stated that

God's enemies must know that Damascus and Syria will be the vanguard of the jihad that will brush them aside ... Our brothers from Hamas have been elected freely ... now they are fought by all the enemies of God ... But Syria stands firmly against these unbelievers! Neither Syria nor its President pay attention to what is said against the Truth; actually, they are the very ones who say the Truth![165]

One better understands the importance of such statements for the regime when one remembers that Rajih's great popularity rests precisely on his outspokenness. Indeed, few scholars dare, as he did during a religious ceremony attended by thousands of spectators, overtly to mock the regime as a police state:

I was told I had to shorten my speech but it does not matter because you said you wanted a long speech. It is the audience that is in command. Who is the president today? The audience! [with feigned confusion, smiling] I'm sorry, I meant at this level, I ask God for forgiveness! [the crowd laughs] There are people from the mukhabarat here, I ask God for forgiveness, it's a scary issue. [more laughter in the crowd][166]

During the same spring, in 2006, other prominent religious leaders were not only ignoring the issue of democratisation but were openly delegitimising it, if not in principle then at least because of Western 'double standards'. According to Usama al-Rifa'i, if democracy was what had been witnessed in Palestine, then Muslims would be better off without it:

Elections in Palestine were fair but now they impose a tyrannical embargo on the Palestinians in order to bring down the government that was established on the very basis of this democracy which they advocate.[167]

With democracy being a mere tool of imperialism, the sheikh continued, its proponents in Syria were nothing but traitors: '[Westerners] impose

[164] Observations, 1 December 2006, 15 April 2007, 6 July 2007.
[165] Celebration of the Mawlid at the Sheikh Ali al-Daqr mosque, Damascus, 12 April 2006 (VCD).
[166] *Al-Hafl al-takrimi al-awwal li-kibar al-shuyukh al-qurra' – hafl jami' al-shaykh 'Abd al-Karim al-Rifa'i* [First tribute to the Grand Readers of the Quran – ceremony at the Sheikh 'Abd al-Karim al-Rifa'i mosque], 14 March 2006 (Damascus: Markaz Zayd, 2006) (VCD).
[167] Exhortation given on the occasion of the Mawlid, Zayd bin Thabit mosque, Damascus, 26 April 2006 (VCD).

this democracy on us, they pressure our leaders. *They rely on the hypocrites among the Muslims to spread democracy.*[168]

The grand ulama's readiness to use such language cannot be explained by the regional context alone. It also owed much to the regime's decision to build upon previous measures of relaxation on public religiosity in response to clerical requests, some of which had been expressed by al-Buti the previous November.

The first measures concerned women's rights activism. Following a demand formulated by al-Buti and al-Rifa'i, copies of the controversial *Down with the Veil!* were removed from bookshops.[169] The following March, the authorities allowed al-Rifa'i's movement to organise the first 'Tribute to the Grand Readers of the Quran of Damascus' in the university's grand lecture hall – that is, in the very place that five months earlier had hosted the aforementioned feminist conference.

Other decisions aimed at satisfying the religious establishment included the quadrupling of the number of sharia high schools between 2005 and 2008,[170] the appointment of the highly respected Ibrahim al-Salqini as Mufti of Aleppo, the opening of a faculty of sharia in that latter city (September 2006),[171] a 50 per cent salary rise for mosque personnel, and authorisation for the Qubaysiyyat to operate in mosques after forty years underground.[172] However, the most symbolic event of this 'Islamic Spring' was the acceptance by the regime of al-Buti's demand for the re-establishment of a representative council of ulama.

The League of Ulama of Bilad al-Sham

In his aforementioned Mawlid exhortation, Usama al-Rifa'i did not merely denounce the 'conspiracies' hatched in the name of democracy, but also invited the regime to respect the principle of consultation (*shura*): 'Consultation is a pillar of Islam ... However wise, pious, sincere or committed the commander of the Umma, he cannot abandon consultation, and no military defeat justifies doing so.'[173]

By the time the leader of Zayd made this exhortation, the regime had already proved willing to accept some progress in the realm of

---

[168] Ibid. (my emphasis).
[169] Interviews with anonymous sources, Damascus, March 2006 and April 2008.
[170] *Al-Majmu'a al-ihsa'iyya*, 2009, 329.
[171] *Al-Thawra*, 26 January 2006.
[172] *Al-Hayat*, 3 May 2006.
[173] Exhortation given on the occasion of the Mawlid of the Zayd bin Thabit mosque, Damascus, 26 April 2006 (VCD). This is an obvious allusion to the maintenance of the state of emergency under the pretext of the Israeli occupation of the Golan since 1967.

'consultation'. Needless to say, what was on the agenda was not the opening up of political competition, but a narrowly sectoral approach to the exclusive benefit of the ulama.

The idea of restoring a representative organ of Syrian clerics was based on the examples of past local experiences (the Association and League of Ulama) and of recently created foreign organisations such as Yusuf al-Qardawi's World Union of Ulama (2004),[174] and the Iraqi Committee of Ulama (2003).[175] The latter in particular had strongly impressed the Syrian ulama, who had received its leader, Harith al-Dari, several times.[176]

In January 2006, the ulama of Aleppo were authorised to set up a consultative committee in order to manage the religious activities of the city in a collegial way.[177] Of much greater importance, however, was the founding congress of the League of Ulama of Bilad al-Sham (Rabita 'Ulama' Bilad al-Sham), which was held in Damascus on 19 April 2006. This event marked nothing less, as Minister of Awqaf Ziyad al-Ayyubi made clear in the address he gave on that occasion, than the 'return' of the famous League of Ulama that had been dissolved four decades earlier.[178]

Like its ancestor, the new League was legally established as a non-governmental organisation. This status had been achieved despite serious official reservations, which the ulama had managed to overcome by suggesting that the League be constituted as a regional organisation covering Bilad al-Sham. Such a proposal was perfectly in tune with Damascus's hegemonic ambitions in the Levant, but it also required the granting of formal independence to the League because it would have been problematic for foreign men of religion to become members of an official Syrian organ.[179] The regime eventually agreed, which allowed for the inclusion in the league of the Mufti of Palestine and Jordan's Supreme Judge (*qadi al-qudat*), the highest religious authority of the Hashemite Kingdom. However, given the tense relations between Syria and Lebanon,

---

174 See Bettina Gräf, 'In Search of a Global Islamic Authority', *ISIM Review*, no. 15 (2005), 47.

175 See Roel Meijer, 'The Association of Muslim Scholars in Iraq', *Middle East Report*, no. 237 (2005), 12–19.

176 See for instance 'Nashatat al-mujamma'' [Activities of the (Kaftaru) Academy] (www.abunour.net).

177 Interview with al-Husseini.

178 Extracts of speeches given during the inaugural session are taken from the report published in the Jordanian newspaper *al-Ra'i al-'Amm* of 28 April 2006.

179 Interview with one of the founders of the League, Damascus, June 2007.

the latter was represented by members of pro-Syrian groups such as the Beirut branch of the Kaftariyya and the Tripoli-based al-Tawhid movement.

Otherwise, the 'new' league was remarkably similar to the 'old', starting with the fact that it was not the instrument of a particular faction but a genuinely representative body, at least as far as the Damascene clergy was concerned. Indeed, although the Kaftaru Academy hosted the meeting and was proclaimed the 'permanent headquarters' of the organisation, the congress was attended by representatives from all the other major clerical groups (al-Fath, Zayd, al-Midan, the al-Tawba mosque) in addition to the three leading 'media sheikhs' – Wahba al-Zuhayli, who was elected as president of the League, Ratib al-Nabulsi, and, of course, al-Buti.

The restoration of the League thus reflected a dramatic rapprochement between the clerics and the regime, as evidenced by the remarks made by an enthusiastic Krayyim Rajih during the inaugural session. According to the Sheikh of the Readers of the Quran, the page of the dark years had been turned for good in favour of genuine cooperation:

Gone are the years where, when we held such meetings … reproachful eyes were looking at us. Now we meet and we see … that the president is with us and said, 'Go ahead, the state is with you … we lack Islam and we want to walk in its shadow'.… We do not have the right to back down, and we won't.

Of all the speeches pronounced that day, the most important was, unsurprisingly, that of al-Buti. For the seventy-seven-year-old scholar, the creation of the League was a kind of crowning achievement, and he repeated several times that the moment had been long awaited. After twenty-five years of playing the *éminence grise*, he was about to be endowed with formal authority, not as a senior religious official or as a party leader – two options he had always rejected – but in the framework of an 'independent' clerical body where, as one of the Arab world's most famous Muslim scholars, his primacy would necessarily be recognised by his peers.

In line with the organisation's statutes, which assigned to it the mission to 're-establish the role of the ulama in the guidance of the Islamic awakening', al-Buti clearly defined the League as the tool of a sectoral strategy. The League should become an authoritative point of reference (*marjaʿiyya*) responsible for protecting Islam against external ideological threats, but also, and more importantly, against inner differences of opinion which 'impoverish more than they enrich'. Accordingly, it would fight 'the hurly-burly of contradictory fatwas', especially those inspired by 'the obsession of modernity'. In exchange for the 'full prerogatives' necessary for the achievement of this mission, al-Buti stated, the League would constitute 'the single voice of the *umma* that expresses its sentiments and its attachment to its rulers in a peaceful way'.

The Kurdish-born scholar was thus defining the political role of the ulama in a typically sectoral fashion: the aim of the League was not to influence *the general policies* of the state but to strengthen the hold of senior Muslim scholars over the religious field at the expense of reformist trends. In other words, the League was conceived as a 'Church' – that is, an institution that claims a monopoly on the definition of orthodoxy.

Although a major symbolic event, the League's founding session had barely any consequences. A follow-up meeting was planned within two months, but factional rivalries concerning the election of the board meant it was never held: the Kaftaris wanted regulations that would have guaranteed their domination over the League, whereas the members of Zayd were advocating an elective system that would have advantaged them given their broader support base among the clergy.[180]

The following year, Grand Mufti Hassun attempted to make up for this failure by establishing the Council of Ulama of Syria (Majlis 'Ulama' Suriyya), whose composition was more or less similar. However, the initiative also came to a sudden end after just two meetings, again because of internal disagreements.[181]

The aborted renaissance of the League of Ulama served at least as a vivid illustration of the sectoral nature of the ulama's involvement in politics. One might observe, of course, that the authoritarian context gave them little choice. However, a similar pattern of behaviour was adopted by another Syrian clerical organisation which acted outside the Ba'thist straitjacket.

The League of Ulama of Syria (Rabita 'Ulama' Suriyya, later renamed the League of Syrian Ulama (Rabitat al-'Ulama' al-Suriyyin)) was founded in Amman in the same spring, 2006, by former members of the Islamic Front – that is to say, exiled clerics associated with the northern branch of the Syrian Muslim Brothers: its initiator Majd Makki (b. 1957), president Muhammad Ali al-Sabuni and general secretary Faruq al-Batal (b. 1936) were all from Aleppo. In this regard, it is revealing that the

---

[180] Ibid.
[181] Interview with a Damascene cleric, April 2008.

historical precedent claimed here was not the League of Ulama of 1946, but the Association of Ulama of Kamil al-Qassab, which, one remembers, advocated cooperation between the clergy and proto-Muslim Brothers associations.[182] In addition, the organisation officially declared itself a member of al-Qardawi's World Union of Ulama.[183]

However, the new 'League of Brothers' was not merely designed to rally the men of religion behind the Islamist movement. In fact, its main declared purpose was to strengthen the ties between the numerous ulama of the Syrian diaspora,[184] via a very rich website and the biennial journal *Basha'ir al-Islam* (Messages of Islam). Both of these media provided essentially religious content, and the League issued only a handful of political statements between its inception and the 2011 uprising.

Against Secularist 'Conspiracies'

For the Syrian regime, the 2005–6 flirtation with the clergy proved a double-edged sword: not because the ulama expressed any political ambition in the strict sense – as opposed to sectoral ambitions – but because their closer partnership with the state dramatically emboldened them in their fight against their secularist enemies. The latter, however, did not merely consist in women's rights associations, but also included certain state agencies.

In his numerous sermons devoted to the 'defence of the Muslim woman', Usama al-Rifa'i denounced the cooperation of the Syrian government with UN agencies on birth control, which he deemed a 'Western conspiracy', or on AIDS prevention, which he described as 'management of fornication'.[185] Official media were not spared: in July 2006, Zayd's spiritual leader excoriated the official newspaper *al-Thawra* for denouncing the transformation of the public park of Kafr Suse into a garden reserved for women and children.[186] His brother Sariya also condemned

[182] Mustafa al-Tayyib, 'Rabita 'ulama' Suriyya ... sab'un 'aman min al-intizar' [The League of the Ulama of Syria ... seventy years of waiting] (www.islamsyria.com, 15 June 2006).

[183] Majd Makki, 'Rabita 'Ulama' Suriyya nashat da'ib' [The League of the Ulama of Syria, a long-drawn-out job], (www.islamsyria.com, 13 September 2006).

[184] Ibid.

[185] Usama al-Rifa'i, 'Qadaya al-mar'a fi al-mu'tamarat al-dawliyya' [Women's issues in international conferences] (www.sadazaid.com, 1 April 2008); *al-Thawra*, 2 June 2006.

[186] Friday sermon, 7 July 2006, quoted by www.jaml.com, 9 July 2006; *al-Thawra*, 28 June 2006.

al-Thawra's secularist 'bias' after the newspaper published an article in which the Quranic descriptions of Hell were presented as 'inventions'.[187]

The fact that the latter criticism was published in the pages of the Ministry of Awqaf's official journal reminds us that the secular–religious cleavage does not set 'society' in opposition to the 'state', but extends *inside* the state apparatus. Another example of this is that Minister of Awqaf Ziyad al-Din al-Ayyubi echoed al-Rifa'i's arguments against feminist activism, birth control, and AIDS prevention.[188]

The Kaftariyya, once regarded as the epitome of pro-regime Islam, was no exception. In 2007, Salah al-Din Kaftaru was forced to apologise to Minister of Media Muhsin Bilal for delivering a sermon in which he expressed his hope that Bilal 'does not stay long at his post' because of his refusal to broadcast the Friday prayer on television.[189] That same year, *al-Ijtima'iyya* (The social journal), a bi-monthly launched in early 2006 by the brotherhood, was banned after the editor invited his readers to 'urinate' on secularist intellectual Nabil Fayyad.[190]

Although the last two examples show that the Alawite-dominated mukhabarat have been often favourable to secularists, they could not systematically ignore the demands of Sunni clerics, especially when the need was felt to strengthen the home front in times of crisis. This has already been illustrated with the case of the book *Down with the Veils!*, which was impounded despite the imprimatur granted by the Ministry of Information.

The same scenario was repeated in January 2007 in a context of sectarian tensions that had been fed for several months by swelling rumours of Shiite proselytising in Syria, and exacerbated by the execution of Saddam Hussein at the hands of Shiite militiamen on the Sunni 'Id al-Kabir.[191]

On the same day that al-Buti appeared on national television to denounce the hanging of the former Iraqi dictator as an American–Zionist conspiracy aimed at dividing Muslims, the government withdrew the authorisations of two feminist associations: the Social Initiative, which had organised the poll that had infuriated the sheikhs, and an organisation linked to the loyalist branch of the Communist Party.[192]

---

[187] Sariya al-Rifa'i, 'Risala min *Nahj al-Islam* ila *al-Thawra*' [Message from *Nahj al-Islam* to *al-Thawra*], *Nahj al-Islam*, no. 107 (2007), 20–2.

[188] Ziyad al-Din al-Ayyubi, 'al-'Awlama wa mu'tamar al-sukkan' [Globalisation and the conference on population], lecture given in Cairo, 9 April 2006 (www.mow.gov.sy).

[189] www.champress.net/index.php?q=ar/Article/view/14585, 8 June 2007; *al-Rayat al-Qatariyya*, 2 November 2007.

[190] *Al-Rayat al-Qatariyya*, 24 October 2007.

[191] See Pierret, 'Karbala'.

[192] www.asharqalarabi.org.uk/ruiah/b-sharq-0612.htm, 11 February 2007.

Thus, secular–religious tensions put the regime in an uncomfortable position where it had to arbitrate between antagonistic social sectors whose loyalty was indispensable. Preserving political stability thus implied preventing such skirmishes from degenerating into open confrontation through tight control of the public sphere. In June 2006, however, things came very close to getting out of control when the ulama's struggle against 'secularist conspiracies' reached unprecedented levels of organisation and boldness.

The previous month, the government had issued a decree abolishing the preparatory level (first three years) of sharia high schools and institutes in order to extend the compulsory core curriculum of general education. This decision was not inspired by the mukhabarat, which at that time posed no obstacle to the proliferation of Islamic schools, but by senior officials in the Ministry of Education, a bastion of secularism. In the first move of this kind since the 1973 petition, forty leading ulama reacted by secretly sending President al-Asad a letter of protest.[193]

The list of signatories was extremely impressive: in addition to al-Buti, the author of the text, it included most of the members of the recently founded League of Ulama and well-respected elders such as the Sheikh of the Umayyad Mosque, 'Abd al-Razzaq al-Halabi, the 'Imam of usul al-fiqh' Mustafa al-Khann, the former Maliki Mufti Fatih al-Kittani, and six of the seven members of the Council of the Grand Readers of the Quran. The letter was also signed by Usama al-Khani, the director of the department of religious education at the Ministry of Awqaf, former Minister of Awqaf Muhammad al-Khatib, and two MPs, businessman Hashim al-'Aqqad and former Islamic activist Ghassan al-Nahhas.

In their letter, the ulama addressed the head of state respectfully and treated him as an ally. 'We are convinced', they wrote, 'that you are not less concerned than we are about the religion of this umma.' By contrast, the Ministry of Education was overtly accused of scheming against Islam: 'What would happen if we revealed, by relying on the testimony of some officials in the Ministry, the outlines of the secret conspiracy that aims at the abandonment of the religion of the umma?'

The June 2006 petition could be seen as a move aimed merely at defending one of the ulama's core sectoral interests – Islamic schooling; this is probably how it was perceived by most of the signatories. Among the signatories, however, were also political reformists such as

---

[193] For the text, see www.asharqalarabi.org.uk/huquq/c-huquq-mawaqif13.htm, 30 June 2006.

Mu'adh al-Khatib and 'Imad al-Din al-Rashid, who played a discreet but decisive role in the launch and publicisation of the initiative.[194] These pro-democracy figures had not simply climbed on al-Buti's bandwagon as the Middle East's aborted 'democratic moment' was drawing to a close. For instance, none of them had agreed to join the League of Ulama of Bilad al-Sham, which al-Khatib dismissed as a mere toy of the regime.[195]

For al-Khatib and al-Rashid, the letter to the President was not only about the fate of religious schools: it also constituted a rare occasion to exploit the grand ulama's symbolic weight in order to disrupt the political status quo. In 2004, al-Khatib had encouraged al-Buti to mobilise his colleagues against a decree (which ultimately was not applied) forbidding Syrian Islamic institutes to admit foreign students, a decision that had been taken following the arrest in Turkey of alumni of the Kaftaru Academy with suspected ties to al-Qaeda. At the time, al-Buti had objected that the ulama should not make trouble for the regime when the US–Israeli stranglehold was closing on Syria.[196] In June 2006, however, al-Khatib was determined not to miss the opportunity.

While it remained secret, the ulama's move was tolerated by the regime. Al-Asad even assured a delegation of the signatories that although he refused to formally cancel the decree, he would not implement it either – a promise he has, to date, kept.[197] However, things turned sour in the last days of June, when major Arab media (*al-Nahar* and *al-Hayat* newspapers, Al Arabiya TV) uncovered the affair after it was leaked to the London-based Movement for Justice and Development, whose ties with Syria-based Independent Islamists have been mentioned earlier.[198] In early July, the Minister of Awqaf dismissed Sheikh Usama al-Khani from his position of national director of Islamic teaching because he refused to endorse the decision of the government.[199]

The rumour spread that General Asif Shawkat, the feared military intelligence director, had vowed to 'hang the signatories one by one'.[200] This story reflects, albeit perhaps in a hyperbolic way, the intense displeasure of the security establishment, which mobilised its favourite religious

---

[194] E-mail from a Syrian intellectual, 27 June 2009.
[195] Interview with al-Khatib.
[196] Ibid.
[197] Interview with a member of the delegation.
[198] Interview with an anonymous source, Damascus, November 2006.
[199] www.champress.net/index.php?q=ar/Article/view/8414, 10 July 2006.
[200] Interview with an anonymous source, Damascus, November 2006.

partners to nip the 'plot' in the bud. Intervening on satellite TV channels, Muhammad Habash openly supported the planned reform and condemned the ulama's letter as 'a betrayal of Syria's civilisational and developmental project'.[201] He also claimed that al-Buti had withdrawn his signature, which was somewhat absurd given that the Kurdish scholar was the author of the text. However, although not disavowing the move, al-Buti nevertheless worked to limit its consequences. For instance, he personally called one of the signatories to prevent him from appearing on Al Jazeera TV to comment on the petition. Unlike the political reformists, the old sheikh's only concern was to defend Islamic schools, not to shake the political system.[202]

No one will ever know whether al-Buti's manoeuvres would have sufficed to put an end to the crisis. On 12 July, war broke out between Israel and Hizbullah. With an armed conflict next door, and one in particular that set the nation's deadly foe against one of Syria's closest strategic allies, the requirement for unity took precedence over all considerations of domestic politics.

The Political Reformists Abandoned to Their Fate

In addition to the reform of religious institutes, the war of July 2006 also led to the bracketing off of an issue that in previous months had seriously impinged on regime–clergy relations: Shiite 'proselytising'.[203]

Since the 1970s, Twelver Shiite institutions had developed in Syria thanks to al-Asad's alliance with the Iraqi opposition, and later the Islamic Republic of Iran. After the overthrow of Saddam Hussein in 2003, the rise of sectarian tensions in the Middle East translated in Syria into rumours of a 'Shiitisation' (*tashayyu'*) of the country. From the spring of 2006, influential ulama such as al-Buti and Mahmud al-Husseini publicly denounced the 'intrigues' of Imami missionaries.

After Hizbullah's 'divine victory' in the summer of 2006, the Syrian opposition and Arab regimes hostile to Damascus launched a large-scale propaganda campaign on Shiite proselytising in Syria. In late 2007, the wrath of the ulama even led the regime to yield to their demand that Iranian ambassador Hassan Ikhtari be replaced – the diplomat having been accused of orchestrating the Shiite missionary enterprise in Syria.

---

[201] Al Arabiya TV, 3 July 2006.
[202] Interview with one of the signatories, Damascus, November 2006.
[203] On this issue, see Pierret, 'Karbala'.

Because of its sectarian dimension, the panic over 'Shiitisation' transcended the sectoral cleavages between the Sunni ulama and political activists, as illustrated by Haytham al-Malih and 'Imad al-Din al-Rashid's interventions on that issue in the pan-Arab media.[204] However, this joint mobilisation around the defence of communal identity was a mere tactical alliance: when the state turned against the Independent Islamists in early 2008, the ulama did not take the risk of publicly supporting them.

In August 2006, although weakened by the recent arrest of its founder, Michel Kilo, the Damascus Declaration set up a General Secretariat headed by the recently released former MP Riyad Sayf.[205] In December 2007, a 'national council' composed of 167 activists met at Sayf's house and appointed a new General Secretariat. The poll revealed the influence of the Independent Islamic Tendency, which had three members elected.[206]

The regime responded to this act of defiance by arresting a dozen leaders of the Damascus Declaration, including Riyad Sayf and five Independent Islamists.[207] While pro-regime columnists branded the oppositional platform a fundamentalist outfit, announcing the death of the 'Kandahar Declaration',[208] the only Muslim scholars to publicly denounce the crackdown were the Mufti of Aleppo, Ibrahim al-Salqini,[209] who was a personal friend of Independent Islamist Ghassan al-Najjar, and Professor 'Imad al-Din al-Rashid from the faculty of sharia, whose house had been searched during the crackdown and who demanded 'the immediate release of the patriots of the Damascus Declaration and first of all those of the Islamic Tendency'.[210] As a result, al-Rashid himself was imprisoned, but thanks to pressure by his peers on the authorities he was released after only three days.[211] The members of the Damascus Declaration who had been arrested were not so lucky: in October 2008, they were each sentenced to two-and-a-half years in prison.[212]

[204] Ibid.
[205] *Bulletin of the Movement for Justice and Development*, no. 6 (August 2006), 1.
[206] Yasir al-'Ayti, Ghassan al-Najjar, and dentist Ahmad Tu'mat al-Khudr from Deir ez-Zor (www.thisissyria.net/2007/12/04/syriatoday/04.html, 4 December 2007).
[207] www.thisissyria.net/2008/02/04/syriatoday/01.html, 28 January 2008.
[208] Nidal Na'isa, 'I'lan Dimashq fi dhimmat Allah' [The Damascus Declaration, RIP] (www.champress.com, 22 January 2008).
[209] www.thisissyria.net/2007/12/24/syriatoday/09.html, 24 December 2007.
[210] 'Imad al-Din al-Rashid, 'Li-l-sabr hudud wa li-l-hikma hudud' [Patience has its limits, wisdom has its limits] (www.dctcrs.org/s3637.htm, 1 February 2008).
[211] Interview with an anonymous source, Damascus, 26 April 2008.
[212] www.thisissyria.net/2008/10/29/syriatoday/04.html, 29 October 2008.

With hindsight, the silence of the ulama regarding the fate of the Damascus Declaration was not surprising. Why would they have jeopardised sectoral interests in aid of civil society activists who were often critical of the mashyakha? In addition, as the next chapter will show, in early 2008 the regime was still apparently willing to flatter the clergy.

CONCLUSION

During recent decades, the constraints, opportunities, and issues specific to each political context have entailed different responses on the part of the ulama. Under colonial rule and after independence, priority was given to the fight against moral corruption, the defence of Islamic legal institutions against secular modernisation, and the establishment of representative bodies for the clergy. With the advent of the United Arab Republic, clerics enthusiastically rallied to a regime that promised to save them from communism, before supporting the secession as a result of Nasser's centralism and socialist radicalisation. From then on, the religious elite worked towards the survival of the conservative Infisal regime threatened by left-wing political forces.

After the Ba'th takeover in 1963, the ulama first tried to establish a modus vivendi with the new regime's moderate figures, in particular President Amin al-Hafiz. When the latter was supplanted by secularist hardliners in 1966, the clergy itself radicalised, as illustrated by Hasan Habannaka's rebellious stance. Despite the ulama's anger at the regime's final attempt to enshrine secularism in the constitution in 1973, state–ulama relations subsequently relaxed somewhat thanks to Hafiz al-Asad's more pragmatic policies. This fragile détente was brought to an end by the 1979–82 Islamic uprising. Dozens of Muslim scholars went into exile and overtly called for an 'Islamic revolution' in their homeland, while their colleagues who had stayed in Syria faced unprecedented levels of repression, and consequently entered a period of near-total political paralysis which lasted two decades.

In the first years of the twenty-first century, a severe foreign policy crisis convinced the regime to give freer rein to the religious elite in order to secure its loyalty. Most of the ulama exploited these new political opportunities in pursuit of the struggle against secularist and Shiite 'conspiracies' and the reconstruction of a sectoral representative body.

Despite the huge differences between these contexts, it is nevertheless possible to make some general observations concerning the Syrian ulama's modes of politicisation, which have evolved according to two main variables: first, the presence or absence of issues perceived as requiring direct pressure on political authorities (institutional reforms, 'intolerable' degrees of moral corruption in society); and second, the extent of the latitude granted by the state for political mobilisation.

Beyond such short-term variables, however, the political behaviour of the ulama is structurally determined by the intrinsic qualities of their social category. Their political involvement is an extension of their sectoral activity – that is, the management of the goods of salvation – rather than being an end in itself. Such is the reason for their focus on issues with direct relevance to religion and morals – and they maintain this focus, under ordinary circumstances, *regardless of their degree of proximity to the state.*

Only in very exceptional contexts of crisis have the ulama moved away from this sectoral approach to politics: it happened when they fiercely opposed the nationalisations of January 1965, a stance that is easily explained by the fact that socialist reforms were directly affecting the economic base of the clergy; as for the participation of many religious scholars in the revolutionary Islamic Front in 1980, this resulted from a situation that was very close to civil war. This pattern confirms the analysis of political scientist Michel Dobry, according to which one of the defining features of political crises is precisely the fact that sectoral boundaries are temporarily blurred, and therefore that social actors no longer behave according to sectoral logics.[213]

Another characteristic of the ulama's political behaviour is their combination of strategic rigidity and tactical flexibility: strategic rigidity because, due to their vocation as men of faith, it is difficult for them to compromise on the religious principles they are supposed to defend; and tactical flexibility because they can enter the political arena when the context is propitious, but it is also easy for them to fall back on their primordial social identity as clerics when circumstances change – for example, with the advent of an authoritarian regime.

Lay Islamists are characterised, conversely, by a combination of strategic (or ideological) flexibility and tactical rigidity. Because of the absence of a sectoral position to which they could retreat in difficult political contexts, they are effectively imprisoned in the political field. This was obvious, for example, in the Muslim Brothers' support for the 'semi-secular' constitution of 1950, and in their adoption of the 'socialist' label, two decisions they took that contrasted with the opinions of the ulama.

---

[213] Michel Dobry, *Sociologie des crises politiques: la dynamique des mobilisations multisectorielles* (Paris: Presses de la Fondation nationale des sciences politiques, 1986).

Such conflicting approaches to politics have generally shattered the efforts of 'brokers' such as Kamil al-Qassab, Saʿid Hawwa, and Muʿadh al-Khatib to engender political convergence between the ulama and the Islamists. From this point of view, it is significant that, in the second half of the twentieth century, only the bloodbath of 1979–82 succeeded in creating such convergence in an organised form, with the creation of the Islamic Front.

The secondary nature of politics in the ulama's social practice has also influenced the form of their political interventions. Even in liberal contexts, these interventions consisted less in types of routinised involvement than in occasional irruptions through petitions and delegations, two modes of action that are characteristic of social actors who do not consider themselves part of the political arena. Likewise, the ulama's leagues and associations have never been 'parties' in the sense of permanent structures for mobilisation, but elite federations. Such a model reflects the clergy's ideal of Islamic unity, but it is also, as employers' unions illustrate, the favourite organisational structure of sectoral elites in the political realm. Indeed, such elites share common sectoral interests that transcend the rivalries that otherwise divide them.

The ulama's sectoral approach to politics helps explain why they adapted more easily than the Muslim Brothers to Baʿthist authoritarianism, despite the fact that the clergy was more radically hostile to the ideology of the regime than the Islamist movement, which in the preceding decade had integrated elements of socialism and nationalism into its discourse.[214] The ulama have been mostly concerned with the preservation and enlargement of the room to manoeuvre conceded by the state for religious activities, a task that has been made increasingly easier by the regime's gradual retreat from militant secularism. Meanwhile, Islamist activists have been totally barred from entering the political arena because of the regime's refusal to countenance even a facade democracy in the mould of Mubarak's Egypt.

In other words, although both the ulama and lay Islamists aim to Islamicise society and state, they tend to pursue different – and even antagonistic – practical goals. In early twenty-first-century Syria, whereas Islamists called for Turkish-style political liberalisation that would open party politics to religious forces, senior Muslim scholars worked instead for a pre-revolutionary-Egypt-style system combining enduring authoritarianism with an empowered clergy.

[214] Reissner, *Ideologie und Politik*.

6

Reforms and Revolution

In early 2008, the replacement of the Kaftari Minister of Awqaf, Ziyad al-Ayyubi, with the Mufti of Tartus, Muhammad al-Sayyid (b. 1958), whose father 'Abd al-Sattar had taken on the same portfolio in the 1970s,[1] was followed by renewed attempts at seducing the ulama. Al-Buti was appointed as the preacher and director of the Umayyad Mosque,[2] and he reorganised the teachings to replace Kaftari lecturers with sheikhs from Zayd and the Midan.

From July 2008, however, following orders from the Ba'th's National Security Bureau, al-Sayyid implemented a sudden change, promising the 'end of anarchy'.[3] One recalls that in previous years the regime's rapprochement with the clergy had been encouraged by the foreign policy crisis; this time it was the dramatic improvement of Syria's international position (the takeover of West Beirut by pro-Syrian militias in May 2008, Bashar al-Asad's invitation to attend the 14 July ceremonies in Paris that same year) that allowed the regime to enact this reversal.

THE END OF 'INDIRECT RULE'

In September 2008, the death of seventeen civilians in a car bombing near a mukhabarat facility in Damascus gave the authorities an opportunity

---

[1] *Al-Thawra*, 9 December 2007.

[2] Until then, preaching at the Umayyad Mosque had usually been organised according to a rota system involving several preachers, among which there would be one of the muftis of Damascus as well as members of the al-Khatib family.

[3] www.champress.net/index.php?q=ar/Article/view/26584, 28 August 2008; for a more detailed discussion of this shift and of the subsequent reforms, see Pierret, 'The State Management of Religion in Syria'.

to expand the scope of the measures announced a few weeks earlier. The televised confessions (doubtful, of course) of the alleged perpetrators, who were presented as members of the formerly Tripoli-based jihadi group Fath al-Islam, did indeed highlight the role of two kinds of religious institutions that had already been singled out in al-Sayyid's summer statements: sharia institutes, with one of the detainees claiming to have been influenced by the 'many radical Arab students' he had met during his studies at al-Fath; and charities, some of which had served as a 'cover' for raising funds in aid of the terrorist cell.[4]

Until this point, the authorities had never tried to exploit the few incidents attributed to jihadi militants to put the religious elite into a difficult situation. This would have been absurd when the regime was seeking the support of the ulama, but times had changed.

Although the Minister of Awqaf initially presented his reforms as designed to 'purify Islamic thought from the stains of Wahhabism',[5] he later revealed that the real objective was, in contrast to the religious policy followed so far, to reinforce the integration of the ulama into the state administration. Clerics, lamented the Minister, 'consider that they are not part of any institution',[6] their sense of belonging going first and foremost to 'the jama'a of Sheikh So-and-So, or the Tariqa So-and-So'.[7] Such was the problem that, in the words of the Minister, convinced the state of the need to 'get its hands on the institutes [of sharia]'[8] by nationalising them, except for the higher studies sections of the Kaftaru Academy and al-Fath.[9]

An even more striking illustration of the regime's renunciation of the strategy of indirect rule it had pursued since the 1960s was the establishment of the first state-run non-university post-secondary Islamic institutes in the history of the country,[10] as well as a centre of further education for clerics.[11] Meanwhile, the Ministry of Awqaf underwent unprecedented bureaucratic expansion with a massive increase in human resources, the

[4] *Al-Thawra*, 7 November 2008.
[5] www.champress.net/index.php?q=ar/Article/view/28473, 6 November 2008.
[6] *Tishrin al-Iqtisadi*, 1 September 2009.
[7] www.champress.com, 28 August 2008.
[8] Ibid.
[9] www.champress.com, 6 November 2008.
[10] The Middle Institute for Religious and Arabic Sciences (al-Ma'had al-Mutawassit li-l-'Ulum al-Shar'iyya wa-l-'Arabiyya) and the International Institute for Religious and Arabic Sciences (al-Ma'had al-Dawli li-l-'Ulum al-Shar'iyya wa-l-'Arabiyya), destined for foreign students. See *Nahj al-Islam*, no. 114 (May 2009), 81–3, 86–7.
[11] Centre for the Empowerment of Preachers and for Personal Development (Markaz Ta'hil al-Du'at wa-l-Tanmiya al-Bashariyya). See *Nahj al-Islam*, no. 117 (March 2010), 81.

Minister aiming to bring the number of statutory civil servants to 1,500, a 1,500 per cent rise compared to the year 2000.[12]

Alongside institution building, the regime continued to use repressive means to rein in the religious elite. In order to reduce the influence of the ulama over charities, religious figures were ordered to resign from the boards of benevolent associations.[13] Clerics were also barred from leaving the country without the approval of the Ministry of Awqaf.[14]

In early 2009, the regime grew even more confident because of the political capital it had gained by vocally supporting Hamas during the Gaza war. After the closure of the satellite channel al-Da'wa, recently launched by Sariya al-Rifa'i,[15] and the Centre for Islamic Studies of Muhammad Habash, who was dismissed from his Friday pulpit,[16] several prominent members of the Islamic trend were arrested: human rights activist Haytham al-Malih spent one year in jail;[17] 'Abd al-Rahman al-Kawki, a young sheikh of Zayd, was imprisoned for several weeks after he took part in a debate on Al Jazeera TV where he denounced Sheikh al-Azhar Sayyid al-Tantawi's criticisms of the face-veil;[18] and most notably, Salah al-Din Kaftaru, the son of the former Grand Mufti and the head of the largest Syrian Islamic institute, was imprisoned for one year for embezzlement, misuse of company assets, and 'inciting sectarian hatred', a reference to his – private but hardly discreet – criticisms of Shiite proselytising.[19]

Through this latest arrest, the authorities actually supported a 'coup' carried out by a faction of influential Kaftari scholars who had turned against the son of their master, accusing him of venality, disregard for the clerical etiquette, and excessive love of the media.[20] The eviction of Kaftaru Junior allowed the regime to kill two birds with one stone: first, it got rid of an unruly partner; second, it reinforced the control of the government over the (still formally private) Kaftaru Academy, whose new board was appointed by the Ministry of Awqaf, with a Kaftari official of the Ministry, Sharif al-Sawwaf (b. 1970), as its chair.[21]

[12] *Nahj al-Islam*, no. 115 (August 2009), 82.
[13] Pierret and Selvik, 'Limits of "Authoritarian Upgrading"', 609.
[14] Ibid.
[15] all4syria.info/content/view/11978/113/, 30 July 2009.
[16] all4syria.info/content/view/31843/113/, 8 September 2010.
[17] www.thisissyria.net/2009/10/15/syriatoday/02.html, 21 October 2009.
[18] all4syria.info/content/view/16151/113/, 25 October 2009.
[19] all4syria.info/content/view/11194/113/, 8 July 2009.
[20] Ghassan al-Jabban, Abu al-Khayr Fatima, and Bassam al-Sabbagh (all4syria.info/content/view/11301/113/, 11 July 2009).
[21] www.nohr-s.org/new/2009/07/page/2/, 9 July 2009.

In parallel to the subduing of the religious elite, measures were taken to roll back the influence of the Islamic trend in various social sectors. Following statements by officials, including Bashar al-Asad himself, about the need to 'preserve secularism',[22] prayer-rooms in shopping-malls were closed;[23] the myriad religious symbols displayed on cars were prohibited in order to curb the expression of sectarian identities;[24] three judges and ten members of the Damascus Governorate Council – including three out of the ten members of the Executive Bureau – were dismissed because of their proximity to the ulama;[25] wearing of the niqab was banned in universities and more than a thousand face-veiled public-school teachers were transferred to administrative positions;[26] and women-only parks were reopened to men.

Thus, on the eve of the Arab revolutions, state–ulama relations had hit a new low. During Ramadan 2010, for the first time in decades, no fast-breaking banquet was held by the President in honour of the religious elite. Meanwhile, al-Buti suffered a personal affront when his call for censoring a TV series he deemed offensive to Muslims was rejected following a decision taken 'at a high level',[27] and the President publicly honoured Syrian TV directors, including the author of the contentious series.[28]

In support of his demand for censorship of television, al-Buti had evoked a 'vision' he had had in a dream, that of 'devastating divine wrath filling the horizon'.[29] In December 2010, the Kurdish scholar stated that he had found the confirmation of this prediction in the fact that winter rains had still not come, further aggravating the severe drought that had affected the country for three years. When the government announced the organisation of a national rogation prayer, al-Buti publicly objected that this ritual would not be valid as long as 'injustices' were committed against Islam.[30] Unfortunately for the old sheikh, the elements were not on his side: in response to the official rogation prayer, the Almighty covered Damascus with an unprecedentedly thick blanket of snow.

---

[22] Al-Asad's interview with Charlie Rose on PBS TV, 27 May 2010.

[23] www.thisissyria.net/2009/08/14/syriatoday/03.html, 14 August 2009.

[24] *Al-Quds al-'Arabi*, 13 October 2010.

[25] all4syria.info/content/view/27236/113/, 3 June 2010; all4syria.info/content/view/28638/113/, 1 July 2010.

[26] all4syria.info/content/view/28048/113/, 17 June 2010.

[27] The series was Najdat Anzur's *Ma malakat aymanukum* [What your right hand possesses]: see *al-Akhbar*, 19 August 2010; *al-Watan*, 14 September 2010.

[28] all4syria.info/content/view/32340/113/, 20 September 2010.

[29] all4syria.info/content/view/30699/113/, 14 August 2010.

[30] Mosque lesson, 6 December 2010 (mp3).

Thus, by late 2010, a combination of foreign policy successes, heavy-handed reforms, repression, and auspicious weather had allowed Bashar al-Asad to domesticate the ulama. However, westerly winds were now rising and pushing revolutionary clouds eastward. The Tunisian, Egyptian, and Libyan examples soon inspired Syrians: in mid-March 2011, demonstrations broke out in the southern plain of Hauran, then gradually spread, driven by bloody repression, and became transformed into a nationwide uprising.

THE PROVINCIAL ULAMA: SIDING WITH THE REVOLUTION

In the rebellious cities that were soon occupied by the army's armoured units, the most prominent ulama joined the protest – and sometimes became its key figures. In Der'a, the first seat of the movement, such was the case for Ahmad al-Sayasne, the imam of the al-'Umari Grand Mosque, and Rizq Aba Zayd, the Mufti of the city.[31] Following the recapture of Der'a by the army in May and the execution of al-Sayasne's son, the two clerics were blackmailed into appearing on television in order to describe the uprising as an 'armed rebellion' inspired by a 'foreign conspiracy'.[32] Al-Sayasne eventually escaped to Jordan in January 2012.

Top clerics also turned against the regime in Latakia. One of the opposition's strongholds was the Sufan mosque, whose preacher, Hasan Sari, was the city's most respected scholar. The eighty-one-year-old Sari was placed under house arrest for allegedly 'assaulting' a policeman. The director of the city's Awqaf administration, Fahd Ra'i, was also relieved of his duties for his lack of discipline.[33] In the nearby town of Banyas, the very first demonstrations were led by Sheikh Anas 'Ayrut (b. 1971), the son of the renowned Shadhili master 'Abd al-Rahman (d. 1996).[34] When the army moved in, 'Ayrut went into hiding before reappearing in Istanbul as a member of the Syrian National Council that represented the exiled opposition from the autumn of 2011.

In the governorate of Idlib, where the regime lost several districts to the armed opposition in the autumn of 2011, collective resignations of

---

[31] See for instance al-Sayasne's account on his meeting with President al-Asad on 14 April (www.youtube.com/watch?v=cXTNKqEeq74) and Aba Zayd's speech after his resignation on 23 April (www.youtube.com/watch?v=KNE3jC_DbEg).
[32] Al-Ikhbariyya al-Suriyya TV, 10 May 2011; Duniya TV, 26 May 2011.
[33] Ministry of Awqaf, Decision no. 1051, 25 January 2012.
[34] www.champress.net/index.php?q=ar/Article/view/90367, 16 May 2011.

clerics were broadcast on YouTube.[35] In Homs, which rapidly became the 'capital of the revolution', the majority of Muslim scholars also sided with the revolutionaries. Since the local religious elite had been decimated as a result of the previous uprising, most of the charismatic preachers who rose to prominence during the demonstrations and funerals of 2011 were clerics in their forties such as Mahmud al-Dalati, Sahl Junayd, and also Anas Suwayd, who was among the founders of Homs's Revolutionary Council.[36] These figures denounced the sectarian violence that had brought bloodshed to the city, both in their Friday sermons and in a joint statement released by Sunni and Alawite men of religion.[37]

As had happened thirty years earlier, the local religious elite was severely hit by state repression: Sheikh Abu Tayyib al-Atasi, the son of the former Mufti of Homs, was killed by a sniper, al-Dalati and Junayd escaped assassination attempts, and death threats forced Suwayd to leave the country. In this he was following the grand Sufi master 'Adnan al-Saqqa, who had returned only eleven years earlier from two decades of exile in Saudi Arabia.[38]

DAMASCUS AND ALEPPO: A DIVIDED RELIGIOUS ELITE

Things were more ambiguous for the ulama of Damascus and Aleppo. Despite several demonstrations, especially in the capital, neither city experienced open insurrection during the first year of the uprising.[39] This relative 'calm' resulted partly from stringent security measures, but also, in a context of recent economic liberalisation, from the Sunni bourgeoisie's lack of enthusiasm for this distinctly popular uprising.

The relatively low intensity of the crisis in Damascus and Aleppo enabled local scholars to choose from within a wide spectrum of responses, ranging from loyalty to dissent. This diversity of views reflected two trends that have been analysed throughout this book: on the one hand, the establishment of a partnership between the Ba'thist regime and

---

[35] On 30 January (http://www.youtube.com/watch?v=6rsW8yVvFeo) and 9 February 2012 (http://www.youtube.com/watch?v=XuZH74zlsdM).

[36] Interview with journalist Nir Rosen, by phone, 2 February 2012.

[37] Ibid.; Mahmud al-Dalati, Friday sermon, 4 November 2011 (mp3); 'Bayan li-'ulama' al-muslimin (al-sunna wa-l-'alawiyyin) fi Homs yuharrim al-qatl wa-l-khatf' [A communiqué by the Muslim (Sunni and Alawite) scholars of Homs proscribes killings and kidnappings] (new-syria.com, 20 November 2011).

[38] E-mail sent to the author by a preacher from Homs, 2 February 2012.

[39] As far as Damascus is concerned, this is true only for the city's central neighbourhoods, not for the suburbs.

influential religious figures; on the other, the survival or re-emergence of pockets of political independence among the clergy.

On the loyalty side, despite some initial hesitations, Grand Mufti Hassun unsurprisingly did what the regime expected of him,[40] branding popular unrest as 'discord' (*fitna*) inspired from abroad by 'seditious satellite channels' (i.e. Al Arabiya and Al Jazeera) in order to 'break national unity'.[41] Following the assassination of his son Sariya in October 2011, for which the regime and the opposition traded mutual accusations, Hassun even threatened that any foreign attack against Syria would entail a wave of suicide bombings in Western countries.[42]

Less predictable was the position of al-Buti, whose relations with the regime had turned sour in the previous months. The sheikh was all the more emboldened to clarify his stance given that his personal authority was directly challenged by the events: indeed, it was at the end of his 18 March sermon at the Umayyad Mosque that one of the first demonstrations witnessed in Damascus broke out in front of him.

From the very first days, al-Buti branded the uprising a foreign conspiracy. In a televised interview, moving his fingers like tentacles, he asserted that 'a hand has sneaked into our society in the name of reform'. This conspiracy, which 'very likely' involved 'Zionist fingers',[43] not only aimed at the fall of the regime, but also, like the assassination of al-Hariri six years earlier, sought 'the fall of Islam'.[44]

Growing state repression did not lead al-Buti to reconsider his positions, but to radicalise. When an Internet user asked him to issue a fatwa condemning security operatives who force prisoners to blaspheme by saying 'Bashar is my Lord', al-Buti gave this amazing answer: 'Why do you ask me about the result rather than about the cause? Isn't the cause of this the fact that this person took part in demonstrations?'[45] In February 2012, al-Buti's only reaction to the army's shelling of Homs with heavy artillery was to denounce the 'Israeli war against Syria'.[46]

[40] In April 2011 Hassun visited the southern town of Sanamayn, where twenty demonstrators had just been shot dead by the police. During his speech, the Grand Mufti addressed the President and said, speaking of the demonstrations: 'This is not terrorism, and this is not about bread; it is about dignity' (www.youtube.com/watch?v=teQj_1aSRbg, 18 April 2011).

[41] Al-Ikhbariyya al-Suriyya TV, 24 March 2011.

[42] www.youtube.com/watch?v=8yRoQ6Sagtw, 11 October 2011.

[43] Al-Ikhbariyya al-Suriyya TV, 24 March 2011.

[44] all4syria.info/web/archives/20494, 31 July 2011.

[45] Fatwa no. 14658, 7 July 2011 (www.naseemalsham.com/ar/Pages.php?page=readFatwa& pg_id=14658&back=8928).

[46] www.youtube.com/watch?v=Ia4z3cFFaVM, 12 February 2012.

Why did the most influential Syrian cleric jeopardise his popularity (his books were publicly burnt during a demonstration in Deir ez-Zor)[47] by insisting on defending a beleaguered regime, as he had done in 1979 and 2005? When senior colleagues visited him to try to convince him to change his mind, al-Buti told them he would never do so because his stance was dictated by 'godly inspiration' (*ilham ilahi*).[48] There might also have been more mundane considerations, however.

It should be emphasised that, regardless of the tensions witnessed in 2010, al-Buti was more closely related to the state in 2011 than at any other moment in his career. First, three decades of intimate relationships with political and security agencies had probably generated their share of 'dirty secrets' whose disclosure could forever tarnish his reputation, thereby endangering one of the things an 'alim cares about the most: his future hagiography. In addition, since 2008 al-Buti had been given increasing responsibilities within the religious administration. After he was appointed the head of the Umayyad Mosque, the Ministry of Awqaf relied heavily on his reputation to bolster its reforms, in particular by entrusting him with the supervision of the new state-designed curriculum for sharia institutes.[49]

Nor should one exclude the importance of psychological factors, namely al-Buti's well-known obsession with conspiracy theories, his outright elitism, and his hubris, which was hurt twice at the start of the crisis: once by the demonstrations in 'his' Umayyad Mosque after his sermon, and then by the criticisms levelled by Yusuf al-Qardawi, an enthusiastic supporter of the Syrian revolution, at the 'negative ulama' (*'ulama' al-su'*) – that is, the apologists for oppressive regimes.[50]

Al-Buti and al-Qardawi had a long-standing rivalry, both of them nurturing 'pontifical' ambitions over Sunni Islam.[51] The 'feud' manifested itself, for instance, during the Gaza War in January 2009. On this occasion, al-Qardawi visited Bashar al-Asad at the head of a delegation of the World Union of Ulama. This was a slap in the face for his Syrian colleague, who had not been received at the presidential palace since the death of Hafiz al-Asad. In his following Friday sermon, al-Buti derided the initiative by al-Qardawi's organisation, which he encouraged to focus on its duty of religious guidance rather than

---

[47] Demonstration, 22 July 2011 (www.youtube.com/watch?v=YReM9oXRfWE).
[48] Interview with a Damascene scholar, by phone, October 2012.
[49] *Nahj al-Islam*, no. 114 (May 2009), 86; *Tishrin al-Iqtisadi*, 1 September 2009.
[50] Friday sermon, 1 April 2011, on Al Jazeera TV.
[51] Pierret, 'Diplomatie islamique', 169.

'gesticulating from pillar to post in the political realm, thus competing with its specialists'.[52]

Three years later, the Arab Spring revived this 'war of the minbars', with al-Buti responding to al-Qardawi's criticisms by advising him to 'follow the rules, teachings and good manners of religion … instead of adjusting to circumstances and partisan [i.e., the Muslim Brothers'] interests, keeping silent when they require to do so, and calling to revolution when they change'.[53]

By defending the regime, al-Buti also sought to preserve for himself a political role, which a democratic system would probably not grant him without requiring that he first acquire electoral legitimacy. It was indeed through al-Buti that, in early April, the regime announced the imminence of a second presidential address aimed at 'clarifying' al-Asad's reformist intentions after the bellicose address the President gave on 30 March before the People's Council.[54]

By taking on such a role, al-Buti could once again portray himself as a broker rather than as a mere sycophant. Reforms were necessary, he said, because the current unrest was the actual materialisation of the 'divine wrath' he had seen in his dream the previous year.[55]

The reforms announced by al-Buti included the lifting of the Law of Emergency, the end of the one-party system, and 'the establishment of many freedoms'. So far the Law of Emergency has been replaced with a no less restrictive 'Anti-Terrorist Law', and the draft constitution released in February 2012 – after almost a year of bloodshed – failed to convince anyone among the opposition.

By contrast, other decisions announced by al-Buti were much more concrete and, in some cases, were immediately implemented. They were designed to play on the sectoral sensibility of the clergy: reinstatement of face-veiled teachers and Islamic-leaning members of the Governorate Council of Damascus, launching of the Islamic satellite channel Nur al-Sham (broadcasts started on 1 August), closing of the recently opened casino in Damascus,[56] creation of a sharia high school for girls named after Sheikh Hasan Habannaka, and the establishment of the al-Sham

---

[52] Friday sermon, 9 January 2009 (www.naseemalsham.com/ar/Pages.php?page=read Speech&pg_id=123&bk_id=42).

[53] Mosque lesson, 5 April 2011 (www.youtube.com/watch?v=x9ZjlQLljmo).

[54] Ibid.

[55] Ibid.

[56] This measure was not publicly announced by al-Buti, but it was implemented on the day of his statement (all4syria.info/web/archives/2210, 6 April 2011).

Higher Institute for Religious Sciences (Ma'had al-Sham al-'Ali li-l-'Ulum al-Shar'iyya), which would issue university degrees up to doctorate level.

The al-Sham Institute was constituted by nationalising and federating three formerly private institutions: the Kaftaru Academy, the al-Fath institute, and the Shiite Hawza of Sayyida Ruqqaya.[57] The move was remarkable in several respects. Besides the fact that it established what was probably the first Sunni–Shiite academic institution in modern history, it completed the nationalisation of specialised Islamic education, three years after the takeover of secondary seminaries. It also answered some clerical concerns, by putting an end to the situation of non-recognition of the diplomas issued by formerly private structures, and by strengthening 'traditional' Islamic education in the face of the increasingly 'reformist' faculty of sharia.

Other measures helped secure the loyalty of long-standing religious allies. In Damascus, relations between the authorities and the disciples of Ahmad Kaftaru had been endangered by the dismissal of Minister al-Ayyubi in 2007, and the imprisonment of Salah al-Din Kaftaru two years later. Shortly after the first demonstrations of 2011, the Kaftari sheikh 'Adnan Afiyuni (b. 1954) was appointed as the Mufti of Damascus Countryside, a post that had been vacant for years.[58]

Three months before the start of the uprising, the regime had reversed a decision that could have undermined its hold on Aleppo had it been maintained. Among the numerous reforms undertaken by the Ministry of Awqaf during the previous years, one was to break with one of the pillars of the regime's religious policy in the city – the alliance with the Kiltawiyya institute. Addressing the local clerics in 2009, Minister al-Sayyid caused outrage by claiming that the fight against extremism meant close monitoring of the graduates from this institute,[59] who as we know constitute a relative majority of Aleppo's mosque personnel.

Shortly afterwards, the government appointed the Shadhili sheikh Mahmud al-Husseini, whose relations with the Kiltawiyya were notoriously bad, as the director of the local Awqaf administration.[60] Although he had enjoyed the support of Suhayb al-Shami at the time the latter was the supreme ruler of Aleppian Islam, al-Husseini turned against the symbol of clerical corruption and dismissed several of al-Shami's clients.[61]

---

[57] Decree no. 48, 4 April 2011 (*al-Thawra*, 5 April 2011).
[58] *Al-Thawra*, 26 May 2011.
[59] www.shukumaku.com/PDA/Content.php?id=6427&s=3&c=&t=0, 19 August 2009.
[60] www.syria-news.com/readnews.php?sy_seq=107797, 12 January 2010.
[61] Interview with an anonymous source, Aleppo, July 2010.

Al-Husseini had misapprehended the balance of power, however: after less than a year, al-Shami indirectly recaptured the local religious administration by engineering the replacement of his former friend with his ally Ahmad 'Isa Muhammad, the Mufti of Manbij and the head of the Kiltawiyya's sister institute in that city.[62] The new director of Aleppo's Awqaf administration was also a member of the Madjadme clan, a prominent chief of which was reportedly hired by the mukhabarat to suppress the protests in the al-Raqqa region.[63] This was part of a broader policy of recruitment of tribal clans – including those in Nabhaniyya's cradle, Bab al-Nayrab – in order to set up auxiliary groups of *shabbiha* (pro-regime thugs) in northern Syria, which is almost devoid of Alawites.

The quiescence of certain ulama was also ensured by the process analysed in the fourth chapter of this book: the deepening of the tripartite alliance between the clergy, the business community, and the political–military elite. An interesting case was that of the Aleppian sheikh Abu al-Fath al-Bayanuni.

Many expected that as a former exile, heir of an Islamic group that had been exterminated in the early 1980s (Abi Dharr), and brother of the former head of the Muslim Brothers, al-Bayanuni would adopt a critical stance. In fact, although he did not go as far as al-Buti and Hassun in his condemnation of the opposition, he repeatedly prohibited demonstrations on the basis that they could be 'exploited' by ill-intentioned people, and even reproached his outspoken colleagues for spreading 'discord' (fitna).[64] It is probably not irrelevant here to remember that whereas in the late 1970s the al-Bayanuni family was tied to merchant interests that had been undermined by socialist policies, by 2011 they had considerably benefited from a decade of economic liberalisation. As already mentioned, al-Bayanuni's son Bashar had sizeable investments in one of Aleppo's shopping-centres. Like many of the city's businessmen, he adopted a vocally pro-regime discourse during the uprising, to the extent that rumours spread that he was financing the local shabbiha.[65]

[62] all4syria.info/content/view/35727/113/, 2 December 2010.

[63] Unauthenticated letter from the head of the intelligence service in Raqqa to the governor of Raqqa, n.d. (facsimile (digitised document sent via e-mail)).

[64] 'Tawdihan li-bayan 'ulama' Halab' [Clarifying the communiqué of the ulama of Aleppo] (www.asdaaalwatan.net/, 8 August 2011); Abu al-Fath al-Bayanuni, 'Kuntu u'jabu … fa-sartu a'jabu' [I was appreciative … then I became sceptical] (www.beyanouni.com/, 25 August 2011).

[65] Survey of Facebook status updates, July 2011 to February 2012.

All of this was not enough to guarantee the support of all of the upper clergy, however. Beside the fact that influential ulama openly expressed dissent, as will be shown later, the mere fact that most of them were silent – including such official figures as Mufti of Damascus 'Abd al-Fattah al-Bazam – was sometimes embarrassing for the regime. When the Ministry of Awqaf issued statements denouncing the repeated support for Syrian demonstrators expressed by al-Qardawi's World Union of Ulama, it was forced to publish them in the name of the 'Grand Ulama of Syria', an indication that too few renowned figures had agreed to sign these documents.[66] Nor did any individual signature appear at the bottom of the statement published by the Ministry in February 2012 condemning the assassination of the young Damascene sheikh Ahmad Sadiq (b. 1975). The second pro-regime religious figure to perish in such circumstances after Hassun's son, Sadiq was widely perceived as an arch-collaborator responsible for the arrest of opposition activists.[67] He was also among the very few scholars who agreed to parrot state propaganda and to show up at the numerous press conferences organised by Minister al-Sayyid to denounce 'the exploitation of religion for political ends'.[68]

In August 2011, a great deal of pressure had to be applied to assemble a decent panel of ulama for the President's Ramadan banquet. The atmosphere was tense, as al-Asad tried hard to deny that the army had used anti-aircraft guns against minarets in Homs and Deir ez-Zor, despite video evidence to the contrary. Just as unconvincing was the head of state's assertion that reports of forced blasphemy in detention centres merely reflected 'isolated cases'.[69]

Some apparently pro-regime statements by senior ulama were so half-hearted that they could just as well imply support for the opposition. When he was pressured into appearing on television to call on young people not to demonstrate, Sariya al-Rifa'i offered a masterpiece of ambiguity:

To the extent that there are suspicions about the presence of infiltrated elements [*mundassin*] in the demonstrations, I encourage young people to stay home.

[66] These communiqués were released on the website of the Ministry (www.mow.gov.sy) on 18 April 2011 and 8 February 2012.

[67] Thomas Pierret, 'Assassinat d'un "cheikh du pouvoir" à Damas', blogs.mediapart.fr/, 16 February 2012.

[68] See for instance *al-Thawra*, 27 July 2011.

[69] www.youtube.com/watch?v=TZsB9I70A5c, 26 August 2011; for the shelling of the minarets, see www.youtube.com/watch?v=xDGmbjeMMDQ, 10 August 2011 and www.youtube.com/watch?v=22ZUbGAvxSI, 18 October 2011.

However, if such elements were not present, I would call on everyone to demonstrate until the complete disappearance of corruption in this country.[70]

A few months later, however, al-Rifa'i openly joined the ranks of Damascus's rebellious clerics. The latter belonged to three main categories: political reformists, former allies of the regime who had recently suffered from marginalisation, and independent-minded grand ulama.

Political reformist sheikhs were unsurprisingly very active during the first months of the uprising. Mu'adh al-Khatib toured the wakes organised for the victims of demonstrations in the suburbs of Damascus and called on the crowds to continue the fight for freedom while stressing the need for peacefulness and interfaith unity:

All of us are one same body. I say to you: the Alawites are much closer to me than many people. I know their villages, their impoverished villages where they live under oppression and toil. We speak for the freedom of every human being in this country, for every Sunni, every Alawite, every Ismailite, every Christian, every Arab and every member of the great Kurdish nation.[71]

Al-Khatib also signed several pro-democracy petitions in company with members of the Independent Islamic Tendency,[72] which had called for demonstrations as early as 29 January,[73] as well as with apostle of non-violence Jawdat Sa'id and leading figures of the Damascus Declaration such as Michel Kilo and Riyad Sayf.[74]

Al-Khatib was rapidly silenced through temporary imprisonment. A similar fate befell his friend 'Imad al-Din al-Rashid, who eventually fled to Jordan and became a leading figure in the exiled opposition. In company with Islamist-leaning lawyer Haytham al-Malih, who also left the country, he was among the organisers of the National Salvation Congress that took place in Istanbul in July 2011.[75] The following month, both of them joined the Syrian National Council (SNC) that was established in the Turkish metropole.

With twelve members of the SNC and more than twenty activists based inside Syria, al-Rashid founded the Syrian National Movement

[70] Duniya TV, 31 March 2011.
[71] Speech in Duma, 5 April 2011(www.youtube.com/watch?v=yAbBrpC8bWE).
[72] www.levantnews.com/index.php?option=com_content&view=article&id=6954:-q-q-q-q&catid=81:syria-politics-headlines&Itemid=55, 23 March 2011.
[73] See Ghassan al-Najjar's communiqué, www.sooryoon.net/?p=16589, 30 January 2011.
[74] www.aljazeera.net/NR/exeres/79CD59F6-EB36-4572-8443-0D89348A27B2.htm, 29 March 2011.
[75] all4syria.info/web/archives/16202, 3 July 2011.

(al-Tayyar al-Watani al-Suri) in December 2011. The movement included Islamists of different persuasions ('liberal Islamists', that is, members of the Independent Islamic Tendency and followers of Jawdat Sa'id, members of mosque networks such as Zayd, and Salafis) and secular opponents who recognise Islam as Syria's principal cultural and civilisational reference (marja'iyya). The movement was explicitly created as the main Islamist rival of the Muslim Brothers within the SNC. As a comparative advantage, it stressed the fact that, unlike the Brothers, it was not a group of old exiles cut off from Syrian realities, but a network of relatively young activists (most leaders were in their forties) with a significant presence inside their homeland.[76]

The ranks of the opposition also welcomed religious figures who had first been elevated and then later discarded by the authorities. Two cases were most spectacular. The first was that of Mahmud al-Husseini, the recently dismissed director of Aleppo's Awqaf administration. After the assault on Hama, the Shadhili sheikh blamed the regime for 'crossing all the red lines' and took refuge in Turkey, while some of his close disciples were arrested.[77]

The second case was that of Ihsan al-Ba'darani (b. 1947), a former counsellor of Hafiz al-Asad on religious affairs and one of the late President's favourite preachers. Under Bashar al-Asad, al-Ba'darani fell from grace as a result of the regime's rapprochement with more popular religious figures such as the sheikhs of Zayd and the Midan.

In the first weeks of the uprising, al-Ba'darani's critical tone led to him being barred from preaching. After he addressed the crowd during wakes organised for victims of state repression,[78] he was assaulted by pro-regime thugs, and subsequently left for Turkey. There, the cleric established close relations with military defectors and even countersigned an agreement between two initially rival groups of officers, the Free Syrian Army and the Supreme Military Council.[79]

The recently marginalised Islamic MP Muhammad Habash also defected from the regime, although in a gradual way. During the first year of the uprising, he portrayed himself as a moderate opponent by founding the Movement for a Third Way (Tayyar al-Tariq al-Thalith). However, his refutation of state propaganda concerning the role of

[76] Thomas Pierret, 'Le Courant National Syrien, un concurrent pour les Frères Musulmans?', blogs.mediapart.fr/, 7 February 2012.
[77] Facebook status update, 27 August 2012.
[78] www.youtube.com/watch?v=zJPSE8_URdQ&feature=related, 26 August 2011.
[79] *Mithaq 'ahd wa-sharaf* [Charter of covenant and honour], 13 January 2012 (facsimile).

'foreign conspiracies' in the uprising turned him into the pet hate of certain loyalist media.[80] In the spring of 2012, Habash eventually moved to Dubai and called on al-Asad to resign from the presidency.[81]

A much more serious threat to the regime's legitimacy came from the criticisms levelled by heavyweight ulama. Whereas it was only to be expected that loyalists would be found among the long-standing partners of the regime, rebellious clerics were figures who had only recently become part of the religious establishment. Such rebellious figures included Muhammad al-Ya'qubi, the lecturer in theology at the Umayyad Mosque, and the more senior Sheikh of the Readers of the Quran Krayyim Rajih, as well as the leaders of Jama'at Zayd, Usama and Sariya al-Rifa'i. By September 2011, all of them had been banned from preaching.[82] Al-Ya'qubi fled the country, following in this the example of popular radio-preacher Ratib al-Nabulsi, who did not formally go into exile but engaged in an extended tour abroad in order to escape security pressures.

The outspokenness of Usama al-Rifa'i and Krayyim Rajih, in particular, turned their mosques into the main hotbeds of protest in the central districts of the capital. Even – mostly secular – artists chose Rajih's mosque as the starting-point of the demonstration they organised in June 2011. This was highly symbolic, since the two places of worship had been named after the most prominent figures of clerical resistance to the early Ba'thist regime: 'Abd al-Karim al-Rifa'i and Hasan Habannaka.

Like al-Buti, the rebellious ulama claimed to provide the ruler with 'benevolent advice' (*nasiha*); however, they imparted a very different meaning to this concept. In his first sermon after the start of the demonstrations, al-Rifa'i kept stressing sectoral demands such as the reinstatement of face-veiled schoolteachers.[83] We know, however, that sectoral logics rarely survive crises of such severity. Indeed, al-Rifa'i rapidly gave up religious issues for more strictly political ones. In the following weeks, he asserted the legitimacy of democratic demands, rejected official allegations of a foreign-inspired 'armed insurgency', and made it

---

[80] www.syriandays.com/?page=show_det&select_page=68&id=26930#.Tg9kimv_sCl. facebook, 2 July 2011; Al Jazeera TV, 19 December 2011.

[81] all4syria.info/web/Archive/45769, 23 June 2012.

[82] The list of the preachers who were dismissed in the capital also included 'Abd al-Qadir al-Khatib, Mu'adh's brother, and Ziyad al-Jaza'iri (b. 1963), a popular sheikh in the neighbourhood of Mezze.

[83] Friday sermon, 25 March 2011 (www.youtube.com/watch?v=qAAXNPDkPO4).

clear that popular unrest could not be contained in the absence of actual
political reforms:

Nothing changes, oppression remains the same as it has been for more than forty
years ... no demand has been satisfied, no reform was implemented; in such conditions, how can we ask people to stay calm? ... I call on the regime in general,
and on security forces in particular: if you want to restore stability in this country,
the responsibility for that lies with you, and none else.[84]

A similar tone was adopted by Krayyim Rajih. Now almost ninety years
old, he was a remnant of the Midan's rebellious spirit once embodied
by his master Habannaka – photomontages associating Habannaka and
Rajih multiplied on the Internet in the spring of 2011.

Brandishing a folded sheet of paper in order to display his contempt
for the sermon guidelines coming from the Ministry,[85] Rajih bluntly
denounced Ba'thist tyranny:

We ask for nothing more than freedom and dignity. We want people to sleep without feeling fear in their heart. [We want] no one [to] be forced to go to an office
of the mukhabarat unless the Attorney General tells him to do so. [Not like what
we see] today: 'Let's go!', that's it. [The prisoner] goes, but where, we don't know,
and nobody can get any information about it ... I do not want violence on your
part, but I do not want it either on the part of those who have been given absolute
power over the bodies of the Syrians.[86]

Our people that demonstrates at the risk of being beaten or killed is not seeking to usurp power, but to recover rights that were stolen from him forty, fifty
years ago.[87]

Asking al-Asad to open a 'new page' in order to break with a 'dark
past', Rajih derided the President's attempt to reassert his legitimacy by
addressing the nation amid the ovations of the deputies: 'Please don't tell
us about the parliament and its applause, all of this has no value ... These
people are a bunch of ....'[88]

Having become the starting-point for demonstrations of several thousand people, the al-Hasan mosque was soon subject to special security measures, the police prohibiting entry to potential agitators while
encouraging the massive presence of members of pro-regime 'popular

---

[84] Friday sermon, 10 June 2011 (www.naseemalsham.com/ar/Pages/showVideo.php?file=../
Component/video/Usama/Friday_Speak/2011/20110610_0.flv).
[85] Friday sermon, 1 April 2011 (www.youtube.com/watch?v=oito-uIOBOQ).
[86] Ibid.
[87] Friday sermon, 22 April 2011 (www.youtube.com/watch?v=T8RS1FaVv1k).
[88] Friday sermon, 1 April 2011.

committees'. In protest, Rajih publicly announced his resignation, before changing his mind after receiving a – false – promise that this situation would cease.[89]

Although he did not name him, Rajih also addressed his colleague al-Buti in an exhortation that was dedicated to 'the ulama and the merchants'. 'If you cannot say the word of truth', he insisted, 'at least do not say the word of delusion.'[90]

As in 1973 and 2006, the ulama also made their voices heard through petitions. The first was signed in April 2011 by such respected figures as Rajih, the al-Rifa'i brothers, Ratib al-Nabulsi, Hisham al-Burhani, the sheikh of the al-Tawba mosque, and Mufti of Aleppo Ibrahim al-Salqini, in addition to famous clerics from Homs and Latakia. The initiative was a failure since its release was foiled by the mukhabarat, reportedly after al-Buti informed upon his colleagues' project. The document is interesting, nevertheless, because it showed that at the early stage of the uprising, the depth of the crisis had already led the ulama to break completely with sectoral logics. Indeed, the petition did not reflect any religious agenda, but formulated distinctly liberal demands such as the establishment of the rule of law, respect for civil and political rights, and the abrogation of Article No. 8 of the constitution according to which the Ba'th leads the state and society.[91]

In August 2011, a second petition was released by the rebellious Damascene ulama and Independent Islamists (Mu'adh al-Khatib, Jawdat Sa'id) condemning the offensive conducted by the army to put an end to the mass demonstrations in Hama and Deir ez-Zor. The crackdown was all the more shocking for many Syrians in that it coincided with the beginning of the month of Ramadan, and it targeted a highly symbolic city whose people had been martyred by Hafiz al-Asad in 1982.

The tone of the document, which held the Syrian leadership 'entirely responsible' for the violence,[92] displeased the authorities so much that that they published a falsified version of it that put the blame on 'armed gangs'.[93] The situation was all the more worrying for the regime in that even the relatively quiescent ulama of Aleppo released a similar

---

[89] Friday sermons, 20 May 2011 (www.youtube.com/watch?v=Fd9mPfc2nnk); www.syria-news.com/readnews.php?sy_seq=133087, 27 May 2011.

[90] 3 July 2011 (www.youtube.com/watch?v=qQgDJupuZoc).

[91] *Risala maftuha min 'ulama' Suriyya* [Open letter from the ulama of Syria], 24 April 2011 (facsimile)

[92] *Risala min 'ulama' al-Sham* [Letter from the ulama of Damascus], 1 August 2011 (facsimile).

[93] all4syria.info/web/archives/21020, 4 August 2011.

communiqué, in which they also denounced the use of thugs to suppress demonstrations. The list of signatories was particularly impressive since it included such senior religious officials as the two Muftis of the city, Ibrahim al-Salqini and Mahmud 'Akkam, Fatwa Secretary Muhammad al-Shihabi, Mufti of al-Bab Ahmad Na'san, in addition to eminent hadith scholar Nur al-Din 'Itr, Shadhili master Nadim al-Shihabi, the Mas'ud brothers, Zakariya and Abdallah (non-Nabhani Naqshbandi sheikhs), and even the very cautious Abu al-Fath al-Bayanuni.[94]

In previous months, although a handful of outspoken second-rank preachers had been arrested in Aleppo, there had been no high-profile dissenter among the local clergy except for Mahmud al-Husseini, who had stopped preaching after he lost the directorship of the Awqaf. This situation possibly resulted from the weakness of the religious elite, as the results of the repression of the early 1980s were still tangible, but it was also due to the influence of the local bourgeoisie, whose economic situation had considerably improved under Bashar al-Asad as compared with the decades during which the city had been marginalised by the government of Damascus.

When, in April 2011, Aleppian intellectuals published an open letter to the President calling for democratic reforms, the ulama were absent except for al-Husseini, Bilal Safi al-Din, the former dean of Aleppo's faculty of sharia, and Mahmud al-Masri, the upright director of the Awqaf Library.[95] A delegation of the city's religious scholars presented demands for reforms to the President, but it was in a secret meeting that was heard about only through a leak.[96]

As we have seen, the notoriously independent Mufti of Aleppo, Ibrahim al-Salqini, had signed the failed April 2011 open letter by the ulama, but his stance could in no way be compared to that of Rajih and al-Rifa'i. His boldest statement had been to say in a press interview that 'anyone who thinks that Aleppo is calm is wrong' – a way of implying that, in the absence of reforms, the apparent apathy of the city might not last.[97] However, he turned a deaf ear to his friend Ghassan al-Najjar, the head of the Independent Islamic Tendency in Aleppo, when he called on him to resign from his position.[98] Likewise, when al-Salqini's name appeared at

---

[94] *Bayan 'ulama' Halab* [Communiqué of the ulama of Aleppo], 7 August 2011 (facsimile).
[95] 'Nidâ' min ajl Halab' [A call for Aleppo] (all4syria.info, 12 April 2011).
[96] www.sooryoon.net/?p=21723, 21 April 2011.
[97] www.asdaaalwatan.net/news/4174/, 21 May 2011.
[98] www.alhakaek.com/news.php?action=vfc&id=20666, 25 April 2011.

the bottom of the call to hold the July 2011 National Salvation Congress, al-Salqini forcefully denied that he had anything to do with the initiative.[99] Last but not least, the Mufti of Aleppo and other signatories of the petition released in the aftermath of the offensive on Hama and Deir ez-Zor endeavoured to dampen the subversive character of the text, which they did with a conviction that suggested that they were not merely obeying official orders.'[100]

Al-Salqini was clearly walking a fine line between the opposition, the state, and the lukewarm Aleppian bourgeoisie when he suddenly died in September 2011. Opponents claimed that his health had deteriorated as a result of harassment by the security forces, and his funeral turned into an anti-Asad demonstration.[101] However, religious scholars who could by no means be described as regime stooges asserted that he became seriously ill after a heated discussion with radical opponents.[102]

In Damascus, Ramadan had seen the rebellious ulama following the opposite course, as they backed their communiqué with unprecedentedly harsh criticisms of the regime, which eventually led to a spectacular showdown.

In an exhortation, Sariya al-Rifaʻi commented on the Hama offensive by saying: 'I could not imagine that the crimes of our military, which used to defend the people, would reach the point where it turns its rifles and tanks against the sons of our dear homeland, all of this during the sacred month of Ramadan.'[103] As for Ratib al-Nabulsi, he issued the following statement: 'It is unacceptable … that for five decades, a nation has suffered from economic difficulties because of what it spent on its military in order to be protected by it … and that this military aims its lethal weapons at citizens who demonstrate.'[104]

These statements came in a context of renewed popular protests in the capital. Jamaʻat Zayd was at the forefront of the movement, for instance when the funeral of one of the group's young members who had been killed in a demonstration turned into an anti-regime rally.[105] In the

---

[99] 'Tawdihan li-bayan ʻulamaʼ Halab'.

[100] Ibid.; 'Interview with Sheikh Nadim al-Shihabi', www.asdaaalwatan.net/, 6 October 2011.

[101] Yasir al-Najjar, 'Communiqué', 6 September 2011; www.youtube.com/watch?v=SiLQy2–8QYo&feature=related, 6 September 2011.

[102] E-mail from an Aleppian scholar, 19 November 2011. See also Abu al-Fath al-Bayanuni, 'Zalamuka ya shaykhuna hayyan wa mayyitan' [They have been unfair to you, O our sheikh, in your life and in your death] (www.beyanouni.com/, 7 September 2011).

[103] www.youtube.com/watch?v=dGwRjt2J7V4, 1 August 2011.

[104] The statement was released on al-Nabulsi's personal website on 3 August 2011, but the sheikh was rapidly bullied into removing it.

[105] www.youtube.com/watch?v=RPZPdBCoguQ&NR=1, 4 August 2011.

following weeks, pressure was exerted on Sariya al-Rifaʿi through the arrest, torture, and even murder of his disciples.[106]

The last act of that summer's confrontation between Zayd and the regime occurred in late August during Laylat al-Qadr. When the crowd shouted anti-regime slogans inside the al-Rifaʿi mosque, the shabbiha surrounded the place. Sheikh Usama al-Rifaʿi reportedly called business-man Muhammad Hamshu in the hope that he could use his close ties with Mahir al-Asad to facilitate the withdrawal of the thugs,[107] but in vain: in the early morning, the shabbiha stormed the mosque, killed one of the faithful, and injured Usama al-Rifaʿi. A few hours later, a picture of the scholar lying on a hospital bed in a bloodstained robe was circulated on the Web.

Many opponents thought that such sacrilege would prove fatal to the regime, since widespread anger would allow the mobilisation of many more people than the usual few thousand. Calls were issued for mass demonstrations that would turn ʿId al-Fitr (the celebration of the end of Ramadan) into the 'earthquake of Damascus' (*zilzal al-sham*). In fact, the 'earthquake' proved to be a mere tremor. Imposing demonstrations did occur in the suburbs, where popular mobilisation had been strong for months, but almost nothing happened in the central neighbourhoods of the capital.

The weakness of the popular reaction to the aggression against al-Rifaʿi had given the lie to the famous saying 'the flesh of the ulama is poisoned'. After months of hesitation, the regime therefore felt con-fident enough to bar the al-Rifaʿi brothers and Krayyim Rajih from preaching.

In order to explain their failure, the closest disciples of al-Rifaʿi might have invoked the unprecedented security deployment witnessed in Damascus in the last days of Ramadan. What they stressed, how-ever, was rather the 'cowardice' of the Damascenes. One of them wrote: 'O Sheikh Usama ... your disciples betrayed you ... the people of Damascus betrayed you'.[108] Another one gave this revealing account of the hours that followed the assault on the al-Rifaʿi mosque:

We were thinking that the Damascenes would rise in droves, that the Kafr Suse roundabout would be covered with thousands of people who would expel the

---

[106] Thomas Pierret, 'Syrie: les prêcheurs relaient la révolution malgré la répression', blogs. mediapart.fr/, 8 September 2011.

[107] all4syria.info/web/archives/29708, 27 September 2011.

[108] Imad Lm, 'Kalam yakhruj min qalb mahruq li-ahad tullab al-shaykh Usama' [Words that come out of the burning heart of a disciple of Sheikh Usama] (www.facebook.com, 1 September 2011).

security and the regime thugs ... Calls were issued for people to gather in front of the al-Andalus hospital in order to rescue Sheikh Usama, because we were afraid that the regime's henchmen would go for him again. Indeed, thousands walked from the countryside until bullets fell on them like the rain ... But what about the people of Damascus? Unfortunately, they were seeking refuge in invocations ... A friend of mine who called me from the hospital asked: 'Where are the supporters of the sheikh?' ... No more than one hundred people gathered in front of the hospital! Where were the sheikh's thousands of disciples, and those who claim his authority?[109]

What this account reveals is the class dimension of the Syrian uprising. The so-called countryside refers in reality to former villages that have become lower-class suburbs of the capital (Zamalka, Harasta, Saqba, al-Hamuriyya). Their inhabitants demonstrated in support of al-Rifa'i although many of them had never attended any of his lessons. On the contrary, the middle- and upper-class districts that were home to most of al-Rifa'i's supporters remained calm. Apart from some of the youth, whose determination had been eroded by months of repression, there was a clear lack of enthusiasm for the revolution among the well-off.

The lukewarm response of the Damascenes was further demonstrated by the dramatic drop in the audience for the Friday sermon of Krayyim Rajih, before he was dismissed, and of Usama al-Rifa'i's son Bilal, when he replaced his father after the Laylat al-Qadr incident. For many, even simply showing up in a 'revolutionary' mosque was deemed too adventurous. Equally revealing of the bourgeoisie's cautiousness was the fact that members of the Qubaysiyyat announced their defection from the (upper-class) female movement because of its leadership's hostility to the revolution.[110]

This situation did not escape the attention of the exiled ulama, who tried to awaken the pious bourgeoisie through video messages. The head of the League of Syrian Ulama, Sheikh Muhammad Ali al-Sabuni, admonished the people of his native city of Aleppo. By standing idly by, he said, they were helping the tyrant in his crimes, and therefore laying themselves open to 'divine vengeance'.[111] In an equally threatening tone, the Damascene scholar Muhammad al-Ya'qubi scolded the people of the capital, and more particularly privileged social categories: 'Are

---

[109] Ahmad B., 'Hal qat'tum sha'ra Mu'awiya baynakum wa bayna 'ulama'ikum alladhi qata'aha al-nizam al-ghashim?' [Did you cut Mu'awiya's hair between your Ulama and you, as did this brutal regime?] (www.facebook.com, 10 September 2011).

[110] www.youtube.com/watch?v=iWRgu7sVEkg, 18 December 2011.

[111] www.youtube.com/watch?v=kPLHzpW-ehc, 8 October 2011.

you among those who love God ... or do you fear for your business or your position? ... On the Day of Judgement, everything will be worthless except for jihad in the path of God and the defence of the truth.'[112] These calls hardly had any impact.

Rajih and the al-Rifaʻi brothers were thus faced with a lack of support from their traditional social base, and from their own clerical factions. During the Ramadan crisis, Jamaʻat Zayd had not presented a united front: most of its sheikhs abstained from echoing the critical discourse of the al-Rifaʻis, and one of them, Nadhir Maktabi, even attended the infamous presidential banquet. And whereas the ulama of Aleppo released a communiqué to condemn the aggression against Usama al-Rifaʻi,[113] their Damascene colleagues did not react.

Thus, by September 2011, all of the oppositional ulama of the capital had retreated into silence,[114] a posture that badly damaged the image of the whole clergy among opposition activists. Tellingly, a fake 'communiqué of the ulama' was circulated on the Internet, which was completely blank except for the following explanation: 'This communiqué is empty because the honourable ulama fear the tyrant Bashar and his henchmen more than God.'

Although the ulama did react to the dramatic developments of early 2012, the content of their intervention only demonstrated the weakness of their position. When battles erupted between al-Asad's forces and the Free Syrian Army in the eastern suburbs of Damascus, Sariya al-Rifaʻi, who had resumed his lessons in the mean time, wearily told his audience that whatever he could say would be useless: 'Nobody listens to us, neither the army, nor the Free Syrian Army.'[115]

In February, the brutal shelling of Homs by the army was met with new clerical communiqués, but although the episode was much bloodier than the attack on Hama six months earlier, the ulama's verve had faded in the mean time. The Aleppian communiqué was by far the weaker of the two since it limited itself to a call to provide the inhabitants of Homs with humanitarian aid.[116] As for the five pillars of the independent Damascene

---

[112] www.youtube.com/watch?v=a3UYdDbFgyo, 15 October 2011.

[113] *Nida al-'ulama' wa-tullab al-'ilm fi Halab hawla intihak al-hurumat wal-shaʻa'ir al-diniyya* [Call of the ulama and religious students in Aleppo concerning the violation of sanctities and religious rites], 1 September 2011 (facsimile).

[114] The only exception was an audio message released by Rajih on 20 December 2011 in which he describe the regime's repressive strategy as 'folly'.

[115] E-mail from an attendant, 27 January 2012.

[116] *Nida li-ighathat al-mutadarririn* [Call to rescue the victims], 9 February 2012 (facsimile).

religious elite (Rajih, the al-Rifaʿi brothers, al-Nabulsi, and al-Burhani), they limited themselves to regretting the 'continuation of repression' and to 'demand' that soldiers not take part in the shelling of the rebellious cities.[117] But even this was more than the regime could stand, and new threats were directed at the three signatories who were still based in Syria (al-Nabulsi and al-Burhani had left), for instance through the ransacking of Sariya al-Rifaʿi's country house.[118]

In spite of such pressures, second-rank members of the capital's clerical jamaʿat kept on publicly criticising the regime,[119] as did their elders: during the funeral of the famous Hanafi faqih ʿAbd al-Razzaq al-Halabi, one of the speakers politely reminded the remaining grand ulama of the al-Fath institute that the time had come for them to break their silence.[120]

In the summer of 2012, warfare reached the central quarters of both Damascus and Aleppo, as the Free Syrian Army's advance was met with fierce counter-offensives by loyalist forces. By that time, all of the capital's rebellious clerics had gone into exile, whereas their Aleppian colleagues remained more silent then ever.

THE VIRTUAL COMEBACK OF THE EXILED ULAMA

For decades, public discussion of political issues by members of the Syrian clergy had been the prerogative of the handful of grand ulama of Damascus and Aleppo mentioned in the previous pages. Religious figures of lesser importance generally avoided sensitive topics, as did most of the exiled scholars – as shown, in the fifth chapter, by the extreme cautiousness of the League of Syrian Ulama. Such an attitude was dictated by a will to avoid jeopardising both the possibility of being allowed to come back to the homeland and the security of relatives and friends living in the country.

With the uprising, the circle of Syrian clerics addressing the political situation expanded well beyond the usual figures. Thanks to forms of media that were non-existent during the 'events' of 1979–82 (YouTube, satellite channels), Syrians were literally brought face to face with a

---

[117] *Risala maftuha min ʿulama' al-Sham* [Open letter from the ulama of Damascus], 8 February 2012 (facsimile).

[118] Facebook status update by al-Rifaʿi's son ʿAmmar, 13 February 2012.

[119] Friday sermon by Nizar al-Kurdi, a member of Jamaʿat Zayd, www.youtube.com/watch?v=TCAcU571YaE&feature=youtu.be, 24 February 2012.

[120] Speech of Sheikh Ismaʿil al-Zabibi, www.youtube.com/watch?v=RccBrmpapEU&feature=youtu.be, 12 February 2012.

profusion of men of religion who were praising their 'blessed revolution' and vilifying pro-regime ulama such as al-Buti and Hassun.

Some of the virtual preachers were recently exiled prominent scholars such as al-Ya'qubi and al-Husseini, but others were lesser-known preachers from provincial towns who had distinguished themselves by leading demonstrations (Anas 'Ayrut from Banyas, Muti' al-Batin from Der'a), or long-standing exiles whom Syrians knew only by name or, at best, had encountered during a stay in the Arabian peninsula. The latter group included men such as Jamal al-Sayrawan and Nur al-Din Qarh Ali, two leading disciples of 'Abd al-Karim al-Rifa'i who had left Syria in the early 1980s; Bashir Haddad, the son of one of Muhammad al-Nabhan's right-hand men; and Mahmud al-Hamid, the son of the late grand sheikh of Hama, Muhammad al-Hamid.

In organisational terms, the League of Syrian Ulama displayed an increasingly political profile, as its president, Muhammad Ali al-Sabuni, participated in an opposition meeting organised in Istanbul in April,[121] before visiting a camp of Syrian refugees in southern Turkey.[122] As had happened three decades earlier, the revolutionary situation inside Syria led to attempts at coordinating the efforts of the exiled ulama and lay Islamist activists. In July 2011, the League held a meeting in Istanbul in the presence of Haytham al-Malih and leading figures of the Muslim Brothers.[123]

A further attempt at formalising cooperation between the two main components of the Islamic trend occurred in October of the same year with the organisation of the first Syrian Islamic Meeting (al-Multaqa al-Islami al-Suri) in Istanbul. The conveners elected a hybrid figure as their permanent spokesman: 'Abd al-Karim Bakkar (b. 1951), a Saudi-based native of the Homs region, had a doctorate from al-Azhar and was the author of very popular essays inspired by theories of personal development.[124]

Despite these efforts, no unified organisation similar to the Islamic Front of the early 1980s had been set up by February 2012. This was probably rooted in the nature of the relations between the Islamists and the secular opposition. For most of the previous uprising, the Muslim Brothers had refrained from allying with secular forces (the National Alliance for the Liberation of Syria was founded *after* the 1982 Hama

---

[121] www.ikhwanonline.com/new/Article.aspx?ArtID=83304&SecID=211, 27 April 2011.
[122] Al Jazeera TV, 19 June 2011.
[123] Al Jazeera TV, 12 July 2011 (www.youtube.com/watch?v=P7Dcf5ufDVE).
[124] *Al-Bayan al-khatimi li-l-multaqa al-islami al-suri* [Final communiqué of the Syrian Islamic Meeting] (www.islamsyria.com, 22 October 2011).

massacre), and therefore had no choice, if they were willing to bolster their representativity, than to find allies *within* the Islamic trend, hence their partnership with the ulama. Things were completely different thirty years later, since as early as May 2011, Islamists were meeting with secular opponents in Antalya. This was only three months before both sides took part in the establishment of the SNC, which made it less urgent for lay Islamists to seek a formal alliance with the clerics. Moreover, several of the latter subsequently joined the SNC, following the examples of Anas 'Ayrut, Muti' al-Batin, and Muhammad Bashir Haddad.

The new media also allowed for the involvement of actors who over recent decades had been excluded from the Syrian religious debate by the combined efforts of the state and the religious elite: the Salafis. By far the most prominent of this group was 'Adnan al-'Ar'ur (b. 1948), a Hama-born, Saudi-based TV sheikh who had made a name for himself over the previous five years with his anti-Shiite programmes. As soon as demonstrations started in Der'a, al-'Ar'ur reoriented his media effort to support the uprising with the programme *With Syria Until Victory* (Ma'a Suriya hatta al-nasr) on al-Wisal channel.

Al-'Ar'ur rapidly acquired considerable popularity among the protesters: he was frequently praised by crowds during demonstrations,[125] and his call on Syrians to defy the forces of repression by shouting 'God is great' from their rooftops at night was highly successful.[126] Key to this success was the preacher's populist, informal style, which stood in sharp contrast to the solemn attitude of his colleagues. He used both (very simple) classical Arabic and the Syrian dialect, and his tone alternated between laughter and tears, calm and anger. Especially striking was the cheering smile he wore when dealing with one of the main concerns of an audience regularly faced with live fire: death and martyrdom.

Al-'Ar'ur's imprecations were not reserved for the regime and its allies among the clergy, but also targeted the Syrian National Council. Although initially supportive of the organisation he gradually turned against it, accusing its members of being more concerned with sharing its seats between them than with practical support for the revolutionaries. By February 2012, al-'Ar'ur was calling on exiled defector officers to set up a body that would constitute an alternative political leadership for the revolution.[127]

---

[125] In Der'a: www.youtube.com/watch?v=LTugTKSqoNE, 27 April 2011; in Homs: www.youtube.com/watch?v=f4EI5xeuZ58&feature=related, 4 June 2011.

[126] www.youtube.com/watch?v=4P2mYyl2Hpo, 25 May 2011.

[127] www.youtube.com/watch?v=7fki-nWPfTs, 27 January 2012; www.youtube.com/watch?v=zaQsXWJrZNU, 20 February 2012.

For a regime eager to portray the revolution as a fanatical Sunni movement, the fact that a Salafi preacher was one of the most prominent media figures of the opposition was a godsend. Official and semi-official media presented al-'Ar'ur as the mastermind of the uprising,[128] with some success, since al-'ara'ira (lit. 'the 'Ar'urs') became a common nickname for opponents among regime supporters.

The 'star' of *With Syria Until Victory* was demonised and portrayed as a bloodthirsty sectarian agitator whose programmes were said to consist of hate-filled diatribes and fatwas ordering the murder of the Alawites and the rape of their womenfolk. The reality was somewhat different. During the first year after the beginning of the uprising, al-'Ar'ur made only one really controversial statement concerning the Alawites, and it was one in which he specifically targeted those who had 'violated sanctities', a probable reference to the rape of women:

The problem resides in the fact that the regime has succeeded in seducing a small number of minorities into supporting it ... I would like to mention in particular the Alawite community: no harm will be done to those who remained neutral [during the revolution]; as for those who supported the revolution, they will be with us ... however, those who violated sanctities, [here he rises from his chair and points a threatening finger to the camera], we will chop their flesh and feed them to dogs.[129]

This gruesome statement had such a negative impact among Alawites that it largely overshadowed al-'Ar'ur's references to the 'noble' Alawites who were opposing the regime,[130] as well as his endorsement of an open letter addressed to the religious community of the president by the Muslim Brothers and the League of Syrian Ulama, in which it was stated that 'none would be condemned on the basis of his communal identity' after the revolution.[131]

By early 2012, al-'Ar'ur's popularity looked likely to continue to rise among Syrian revolutionaries because of a lack of competitors: the grand ulama living inside Syria were either pro-regime, silent, or pathetically helpless, and their exiled non-Salafi colleagues had failed to set up such

[128] See for instance 'Istijabatan li-da'wat al-'Ar'ur ... ighlaq al-mahal al-tijariyya fi Hama bi-quwwat al-tahdid' [In response to the call of al-'Ar'ur ... closing of shops under threat in Hama] (www.champress.com, 16 July 2011).

[129] www.youtube.com/watch?v=DnJyqrMngC8, 26 June 2011.

[130] See for instance this dialogue with an Alawite opponent: www.youtube.com/watch?v=JZsMNU8ZEYI, 16 September 2011.

[131] Thomas Pierret, 'Des islamistes syriens tendent la main à la communauté alaouite', blogs.mediapart.fr/, 4 October 2011.

powerful media outlets as *With Syria Until Victory*. Moreover, internal rivalries were badly damaging the credibility of the Syrian National Council, whereas the brigades of the Free Syrian Army, of which al-'Ar'ur was a vocal supporter, were now seen by many as the true depositories of revolutionary legitimacy.

Conclusion

Three words could summarise the challenges faced by the Syrian ulama in the twentieth century: autonomy, relevance, and flexibility. Autonomy from the state had to be preserved in the realms of administrative control, specialised religious education, and economic resources. Resisting the embrace of the state administration was probably less acute a problem in Syria than in other Muslim countries. The young Syrian republic did not inherit deep-rooted official Islamic institutions, and the political instability of the first two decades after independence defeated attempts to replicate the religious policies of Mustafa Kemal and Nasser. In the 1960s, the Ba'th's revolutionary stance translated into the exclusion of 'reactionary' ulama from the state apparatus. From then on, the religious field would be managed by strong mukhabarat and a weak administration. This trend took an even more radical form after the 1979–82 Islamic uprising, following which the regime engineered the decay of the Ministry of Awqaf, while outsourcing the management of the religious field to loyal private networks (the Kaftariyya, the al-Farfur family, the Nabhaniyya).

The ulama also maintained significant autonomy with respect to the training of junior clerics. Indeed, the twentieth-century institutionalisation of specialised religious teaching has not entailed the disappearance of the mechanisms of social reproduction that, in the traditional informal system, have allowed scholars to appoint their successors from among their children and favourites. The first reason for this is that a significant proportion of the Syrian men of religion have been trained in private institutes that offer the advantages of modern education – that is to say, the ability to produce literate elites on an unprecedented scale – while preserving the advantages of the master–disciple relationship. Second, even graduates of the state-run faculty of sharia tend in parallel to follow a 'free' curriculum in order to accumulate, through their association with venerable scholars, the symbolic capital that is necessary for their admission into the religious elite. Third, it has remained possible to reach the summit of the Syrian religious elite by attending only informal study circles – that is, without having a formal diploma in religious sciences.

Two main factors explain the persistence of ancient conceptions of religious authority. On the one hand, being suspicious of its own faculty of sharia, the Ba'thist regime has shown little enthusiasm for the development of state-run specialised Islamic education, thus renouncing the challenge of wresting the training of clerics away from conservative jama'at. On the other hand, the traditional system of knowledge transmission has been not only preserved but expanded by groups such as Jama'at Zayd, which have relied on halqat to provide religious training to the students of secular faculties.

As for the economic autonomy of the ulama, this survived thanks to several factors: the merchant background of many of the founding figures of the Nahda; and their early alliance with the small and medium-sized entrepreneurs of the private sector, who assumed the financial burdens related to their educational and charitable activities. The ulama's reliance on merchants was maintained because, in accordance with its strategy of 'indirect rule', the Ba'th never fully bureaucratised the religious elite.

No less important than the challenge of autonomy was that of maintaining relevance in a rapidly changing society. To begin with, the ulama needed to be relevant from the point of view of their own criteria for legitimacy – that is to say, they needed to be part of a scholarly genealogy. However, especially in Damascus, the disappearance of the old houses of knowledge in the first half of the twentieth century left the senior positions in the local clergy filled, for the most part, by newcomers. These newcomers and their heirs have bolstered their legitimacy by developing a heroic tale of their origins that revolves around the Nahda brought about by the disciples of Sheikh Badr al-Din al-Hasani, a figure who symbolises both continuity and change.

More fundamental was the need to demonstrate the functional relevance of the ulama in the modern world. The various attempts to find a solution to this problem gave rise to the jama'at that structure Syria's religious scene today, providing their members with a collective identity relying on the memory of a founding sheikh, a neighbourhood of origin, and a particular method of action.

General education being almost monopolised by the post-colonial state, the ulama turned to the establishment of Islamic seminaries. By training clerics on a large scale, such initiatives allowed them to strengthen clerical supervision over society and, since the state tolerated them, they provided the religious elite with institutional strongholds.

Other Muslim scholars were anxious about the fact that focusing on the training of religious specialists might lead them to lose touch with laymen. Rather than seeing the students of secular education as potential rivals or mere consumers of the goods of salvation, these ulama invited them to spend their free time in mosques. They provided them with informal religious education in order to allow them to play an active role in the process of re-Islamisation – both as 'preachers' and, for the most knowledgeable, as genuine religious scholars. This strategy of cooptation took advantage of the resources offered by traditional conceptions of the transmission of knowledge (study circles, master–disciple relationship), which provided an organisational framework that was both flexible and cohesive. It not only resulted in the neutralisation of potential rivals in the struggle for religious authority: it also turned the ulama into the spiritual leaders of a significant part of the educated youth that spearheaded the Islamic 'awakening' of the 1970s – and then, with well-known disastrous consequences, the insurrection that broke out at the end of the decade.

Other ulama reached out to the new literate audiences on a much wider scale thanks to the modern media. With his widely read essays, Sa'id Ramadan al-Buti demonstrated that an Azharite scholar was just as capable as a secularly trained intellectual of refuting modern Western ideologies. Other examples show that the development of the mass media has not occurred at the expense of 'traditional' religious authorities. In the early twenty-first century, the fact that Syrian Muslims, like many of their fellow Arabs, had a passion for the televised sermons of former Egyptian accountant 'Amr Khalid did not prevent them from diligently following the daily radio programme of Sheikh Ratib al-Nabulsi.

The social relevance of the Syrian ulama has been further reinforced by Syria's recent neo-liberal turn. Indeed, they have emerged as the actors most capable of raising funds from the private sector in order to develop private welfare in a context of growing inequality. This capability was not only based on the ulama's decades-old relationship with the small and medium-sized merchants, but also on their gradual rapprochement with famous figures of crony capitalism who sought to improve their reputation by gaining the imprimatur of key men of religion in exchange for generous donations. It was also the ulama's symbolic capital, rather than their mere legal expertise, that led the newly created Islamic banks to include them in their sharia boards.

The ability of the Syrian ulama to survive the transformations of the twentieth century is both a cause and a consequence of the success they have encountered in their struggle to preserve the relevance of their defining feature – their knowledge. The main challenge in this realm came from the Salafi trend, which critically reassessed the scholarly corpus in order to expurgate late 'innovations'. Although Salafis always remained a small minority among the ulama themselves, from the Mandate period their discourse appealed to a growing number of modern-educated intellectuals who occupied influential positions in the political, judicial, academic, and literary realms.

The Salafi ulama, who were already exposed to the hostility of their colleagues, greatly suffered from Ba'thist repression against the Muslim Brothers, which deprived them of powerful allies. The situation further worsened at the turn of the century, when clerical pressures and the September 11 attacks led the regime to actively pursue the partisans of Ibn Taymiyya, whether quietist – as were the majority – or militant. Although bereft of any prominent figure after the death of 'Abd al-Qadir al-Arna'ut in 2004, the Syrian Salafi trend has continued to exert growing social influence, in particular thanks to new information technologies. This phenomenon has alarmed the defenders of the old orthodoxy, who have reacted, among other things, by reviving the study of hadith and, before that, by making Sufi beliefs and practices more acceptable from a scripturalist point of view.

As for the other reformist trends, except perhaps for Muhammad Shahrur's theistic positivism, they have not really undermined the authority of conservative clerics. Indeed, the repeated attempts of Syrian Islamic reformists to build alliances with members of the religious establishment demonstrates the enduring centrality of the very people whose conservatism and political cowardice they denounce.

After autonomy and relevance, the third challenge the ulama overcame in the twentieth century was that of political flexibility. This quality was particularly necessary in the face of a regime that has repeatedly shown that it would stop at nothing to ensure its survival. Flexibility is a natural tendency for these men of religion. Although their vocation is to embody intangible principles, which translate into displays of ideological rigidity, the ulama are nevertheless characterised by a high level of tactical flexibility.

The ulama are a sectoral elite whose political behaviour is driven by their desire to protect their 'turf' – that is, the management of the goods of salvation. Therefore, whatever its authoritarian nature, a regime is only properly intolerable to them when, as the Neo-Ba'th of the 1960s did, it actively works to transform society in a way that clashes with the clergy's worldview and interests. Faced with more pragmatic regimes, the ulama generally preferred to exchange obedience for sectoral advantage. Outside insurrectionary contexts (1979–82, 2011 onwards), they were careful not to undermine the fragile process of religious liberalisation by following the lead of the political opposition, whose project of democratisation was too low a priority for the ulama to justify the correlative risks.

The reforms of official religious institutions launched in 2008 were intended to break with the policy of indirect rule that the Ba'th had implemented since the 1960s. This strategy had obvious limitations, in particular the fact that it allowed the state to influence neither the distribution of symbolic capital, which tended to concentrate among the most politically independent ulama, nor that of economic capital, since groups such as Zayd have relied on an elusive myriad of small and medium-sized business owners.

'Erasing' the recalcitrant elements of the clergy proved an effective option in Aleppo, which after 1982 remained subject to the hegemony of the regime's favourites. However, such an option was conceivable only in exceptional circumstances, such as the Islamic uprising. By contrast, having been lighter-handed in Damascus, the authorities could not prevent the reconstitution of Zayd from the 1990s, and all the more so because this group relies on informal networks rather than on formal institutions that could be closed. In other words, resorting to violence has not always sufficed to offset the infrastructural weakness of the Ba'thist regime, which should certainly not be seen as an omnipotent force.

The developments outlined above should also lead us to reconsider the idea that the Syrian regime only ensured the loyalty of social elites, including conservative Sunnis, by maintaining an atmosphere of terror. In saying this, I certainly do not deny the importance of repression in the longevity of Ba'thist authoritarianism; rather, I aim to emphasise the transactional dimension of the relationship between government and clergy, the latter exchanging loyalty for sectoral benefits.

Although the outcome of the Syrian revolution was still uncertain one year after its inception in March 2011, there was little doubt that if the regime was eventually to fall, the country's religious scene would change dramatically. In particular, the hegemony of the grand ulama of Damascus and Aleppo would be irremediably damaged by the pro-regime stance adopted by some of them, the ineffective, even if courageous, opposition of a minority of their colleagues, and the silence of the majority.

Of course, the traditionalist ulama, and in particular the most independent among them, would certainly continue to play an important role in a post-Ba'thist Syria, partly because of their deep anchorage among urban middle and upper classes. However, the scholars studied in this book would probably be forced to reckon with new forces: Salafis, with 'Adnan al-'Ar'ur as their most probable strongman; political groups such as the Muslim Brothers, the Syrian National Movement, and the Islamic Liberation Party; third-rank clerics from the suburbs and provincial towns, some of whom were playing a prominent role within local coordination committees and opposition militias; and, more worrying, jihadi militants, who were beginning to establish a foothold within Syria thanks to the growing brutality of the regime.

Bibliography

Publications in European Languages

Abdallah, Umar. *The Islamic Struggle in Syria* (Berkeley: Mizan Press, 1983).

Ardito, Aurelia. 'Les cercles féminins de la Qubaysiyya à Damas', *Le Mouvement Social*, no. 231 (2010), 77–88.

Batatu, Hanna. 'Syria's Muslim Brethren', *Merip Reports*, no. 110 (1982), 12–20.

Syria's Peasantry, the Descendants of Its Lesser Rural Notables, and Their Politics (Princeton: Princeton University Press, 1999).

Bein, Amit. *Ottoman Ulema, Turkish Republic: Agents of Change and Guardians of Tradition* (Stanford: Stanford University Press, 2011).

Belhadj, Souhaïl, Dupret, Baudouin and Ferrié, Jean-Noël. 'Démocratie, famille et procédure: ethnométhodologie d'un débat parlementaire syrien', *Revue européenne de sciences sociales* 45, no. 139 (2007), 5–44.

Ben Achour, Yadh. *Aux fondements de l'orthodoxie sunnite* (Paris: PUF, 2008).

Berger, Maurits. 'The Shari'a and Legal Pluralism: The Example of Syria', in *Legal Pluralism in the Arab World*, ed. Baudouin Dupret (The Hague: Kluwer Law International, 1999), 113–24.

Berkey, Jonathan. *The Transmission of Knowledge in Medieval Cairo: A Social History of Islamic Education* (Princeton: Princeton University Press, 1992).

Blanford, Nicholas. *Killing Mr Lebanon: The Assassination of Rafik Hariri and Its Impact on the Middle East* (London: I. B. Tauris, 2006).

Botiveau, Bernard. 'La formation des oulémas en Syrie: la faculté de shari'a de l'Université de Damas', in *Les intellectuels et le pouvoir: Syrie, Égypte, Tunisie, Algérie*, ed. Gilbert Delanoue (Cairo: CEDEJ, 1986), 67–91.

'Le mouvement de rationalisation du droit en Syrie au cours de la première moitié du XXe siècle', *Bulletin d'études orientales* 35 (1983), 123–35.

Böttcher, Annabelle. 'Au-delà des frontières: réseaux soufis au Moyen-Orient' (naqchbandi.org, n.d.).

'Official Islam, Transnational Islamic Networks, and Regional Politics: The Case of Syria', in *The Middle East and Palestine: Global Politics and Regional Conflict*, ed. Dietrich Jung (New York: Palgrave Macmillan, 2004), 125–50.

Syrische Religionspolitik unter Asad (Freiburg im Breisgau: Arnold-Bergstraesser-Institut, 1998).

Bourdieu, Pierre. 'Genèse et structure du champ religieux', *Revue française de sociologie* 12(1971), 295–334.

Brown, Jonathan. *The Canonization of al-Bukhari and Muslim: The Formation and Function of the Sunni Hadith Canon* (Leiden: Brill, 2007).

Burgat, François. *L'Islamisme en face* (Paris: La Découverte, 2002).

Carré, Olivier. *La Légitimation islamique des socialismes arabes: Analyse conceptuelle combinatoire des manuels scolaires égyptiens, syriens et irakiens* (Paris: FNSP, 1979).

Carré, Olivier and Michaud, Gérard. *Les Frères musulmans: Égypte et Syrie, 1928–1982* (Paris: Gallimard, 1983).

Chamberlain, Michael. *Knowledge and Social Practice in Medieval Damascus, 1190–1350* (Cambridge: Cambridge University Press, 1994).

Chaumont, Éric. 'Pauvreté et richesse dans le Coran et dans les sciences religieuses musulmanes', in *Pauvreté et richesse dans le monde musulman méditerranéen*, ed. Jean-Paul Pascual (Paris: Maisonneuve et Larose, 2003), 17–38.

Cheikh, Mériam. 'Pour une histoire de l'émigration syrienne vers l'Amérique latine. Le cas du Qalamoun: territoire d'émigration, lieu de mémoire', master's thesis, Université de Provence, 2005.

Chih, Rachida. 'Sainteté, maitrise spirituelle et patronage: les fondements de l'autorité dans le soufisme', *Archives des Sciences Sociales des Religions* 49 (2004), 79–98.

Christmann, Andreas. '73 Proofs of Dilettantism: The Construction of Norm and Deviancy in the Responses to al-Kitab wa-l-Qur'an: Qira'a Mu'asira by Mohamad Shahrour', *Die Welt des Islams* 45, no. 1 (2005), 20–73.

'Ascetic Passivity in times of Extreme Activism: The Theme of Seclusion in a Biography by al-Buti', in *Festschrift for the Journal of Semitic Studies*, ed. Philip Alexander, Andreas Christmann, and Brooke George (Oxford: Oxford University Press, 2005), 279–98.

'Les cheikhs syriens et l'Internet', in *La Syrie au présent*, ed. Youssef Courbage, Baudouin Dupret, Mohammed Al-Dbiyat and Zouhair Ghazzal (Paris: Actes Sud, 2007), 421–8.

'An Invented Piety? Subduing Ramadan in Syria State Media', *Yearbook of the Sociology of Islam* 3 (2001), 243–63.

'Islamic Scholar and Religious Leader: A Portrait of Muhammad Sa'id Ramadan al-Buti', *Islam and Christian–Muslim Relations* 9, no. 2 (1998), 149–69.

'Transnationalising Personal and Religious Identities: Muhammad Sa'id Ramadan al-Buti's Adaptation of E. Xani's "Mem u Zin"', in *Sufism Today: Heritage and Tradition in the Global Community*, ed. Catharina Raudvere and Leif Stenberg (London: I. B. Tauris, 2009), 31–46.

Chukri, Abu al-Kheir. 'Un Soufi dans le siècle: autobiographie du cheikh Abu al-Kheir Chukri', *Maghreb – Machrek*, no. 198 (2008), 75–8.

Commins, David Dean. *Islamic Reform: Politics and Social Change in Late Ottoman Syria* (New York: Oxford University Press, 1990).

'Wahhabis, Sufis and Salafis in Early Twentieth Century Damascus', in *Guardians of Faith in Modern Times: 'Ulama' in the Middle East*, ed. Meir Hatina (Leiden: Brill, 2009), 231–46.

Corm, Georges. *Le Proche-Orient éclaté, 1956–2003* (Paris: Gallimard, 2003).

Deguilhem, Randi. 'Idées françaises et enseignement ottoman: l'école secondaire Maktab 'Anbar à Damas', *Revue des mondes musulmans et de la Méditerranée*, no. 52–3 (1990), 199–206.

'Le *waqf* en Syrie indépendante', in *Le Waqf dans le monde musulman contemporain (XIXe–XXe siècles)*, ed. Faruk Bilici (Istanbul: Institut Français d'Études Anatoliennes, 1994), 123–44.

de Jong, Frederick. 'Les confréries mystiques musulmanes du Machreq arabe: centres de gravité, signes de déclin et de renaissance', in *Sufi Orders in Ottoman and post-Ottoman Era in Egypt and the Middle East* (Istanbul: ISIS Press, 2000), 197–234.

Delanoue, Gilbert. 'L'enseignement religieux musulman en Égypte du XIXe au XXe siècle: orientations générales', in *Madrasa: la transmission du savoir dans le monde musulman*, ed. Nicole Grandin and Marc Gaborieau (Paris: Arguments, 1997), 93–100.

Dobry, Michel. *Sociologie des crises politiques: la dynamique des mobilisations multisectorielles* (Paris: Presses de la Fondation nationale des sciences politiques, 1986).

Donati, Caroline. *L'Exception syrienne: entre modernisation et résistance* (Paris: La Découverte, 2009).

Donohue, John. 'The New Syrian Constitution and the Religious Opposition', *CEMAM Reports*, no. 1 (1973), 81–96.

'Religion and Politics in Syria', *CEMAM Reports*, no. 7 (1980), 157–77.

Droz-Vincent, Philippe. *Moyen-Orient: pouvoirs autoritaires, sociétés bloquées* (Paris: PUF, 2004).

Eickelman, Dale. 'The Art of Memory: Islamic Education and Its Social Reproduction', *Comparative Studies in Society and History* 20, no. 4 (1978), 485–516.

Knowledge and Power in Morocco (Princeton: Princeton University Press, 1985).

Eickelman, Dale and Anderson, Jon. *New Media in the Muslim World: The Emerging Public Sphere* (Bloomington: Indiana University Press, 2003).

Ephrat, Daphna. *A Learned Society in a Period of Transition: The Sunni 'Ulama' of Eleventh Century Baghdad* (Albany: SUNY Press, 2000).

Feillard, Andrée. *Islam et Armée dans l'Indonésie contemporaine: les pionniers de la traditions* (Paris: L'Harmattanand Association Archipel, 1995).

Gaborieau, Marc and Zeghal, Malika (eds.). 'Autorités religieuses en islam', *Archives de sciences sociales des religions* 49, no. 125 (2004), 5–210.

Gaulmier, Jean. 'Note sur l'état présent de l'enseignement traditionnel à Alep', *Bulletin d'études orientales* 9 (1942), 1–27.

Gelvin, James. *Divided Loyalties: Nationalism and Mass Politics in Syria at the Close of Empire* (Berkeley: University of California Press, 1998).

Geoffroy, Éric. *Le Soufisme en Égypte et en Syrie sous les derniers Mamelouks et les premiers Ottomans: orientations spirituelles et enjeux culturels* (Damascus: IFEAD, 1995).

'Soufisme, réformisme et pouvoir en Syrie contemporaine', *Egypte/Monde arabe*, no. 29 (1997), 11–21.

Une voie soufie dans le monde: la Shadhiliyya (Paris: Maisonneuve et Larose, 2005).

George, Alan. *Syria: Neither Bread nor Freedom* (London and New York: Zed Books, 2003).

Gonnella, Julia. *Islamische Heiligenverehrung im urbanen Kontext am Beispiel von Aleppo (Syrien)* (Berlin: Klaus Schwarz, 1995).

Gräf, Bettina. 'In Search of a Global Islamic Authority', *ISIM Review*, no. 15 (2005), 47.

Gräf, Bettina and Skovgaard-Petersen, Jakob. *Global Mufti: The Phenomenon of Yusuf al-Qaradawi* (New York: Columbia University Press, 2009).

Graham, William. 'Traditionalism in Islam: An Essay in Interpretation', *Journal of Interdisciplinary History* 23, no. 3 (1993), 495–522.

Gril, Denis. 'De l'usage sanctifiant des biens en islam', *Revue d'histoire des religions* 215, no. 1 (1998), 59–89.

Haddad, Jibril Fu'ad. *Albani and His Friends: A Concise Guide to the Salafi Movement* (n.p.: Aqsa Publications, 2004).

Harik, Illiga. 'The Single Party as a Subordinate Movement: The Case of Egypt', *World Politics* 26, no. 1 (1973), 80–105.

Hartung, Jan-Peter. 'Standardising Muslim Scholarship: The Nadwat al-Ulama', in *Assertive Religious Identities: India and Europe*, ed. Satish Saberwal and Mushirul Hasan (New Delhi: Manohar, 2006), 121–44.

Viele Wege und ein Ziel: Leben und Wirken von Sayyid Abu l-Hasan 'Ali al-Hasani Nadwi (1914–1999) (Würzburg: Ergon, 2004).

Hatina, Meir (ed.). *Guardians of Faith in Modern Times: 'Ulama in the Middle East* (Leiden: Brill, 2009).

Heck, Paul. 'Religious Renewal in Syria: The Case of Muhammad al-Habash', *Islam and Christian–Muslim Relations* 15, no. 2 (2004), 185–207.

Heydemann, Steven. *Authoritarianism in Syria: Institutions and Social Conflict, 1946–1970* (Ithaca: Cornell University Press, 1999).

Hinnebusch, Raymond. *Authoritarian Power and State Formation in Baathist Syria* (Boulder: Westview Press, 1990).

Syria: Revolution from Above (London: Routledge, 2001).

Hivernel, Jacques. 'Bab al-Nayrab, un faubourg d'Alep, hors la ville et dans la cité', *Études rurales*, no. 155–6 (2000), 215–37.

Houot, Sandra. 'Le Cheikh al-Bouti: exemple d'une éthique de la médiation aux fins de résolution du conflit', *Maghreb – Machrek*, no. 198 (2009), 53–64.

'Culture religieuse et média électronique: le cas du cheikh Muhammad al-Buti', *Maghreb – Machrek*, no. 178 (2003), 75–87.

'De la religion à l'éthique: esquisse d'une mediation contemporaine', *Revue du monde musulman et de la Méditerranée*, no. 85–6 (1999), 31–46.

Ismail, Salwa. 'Changing Social Structure, Shifting Alliances and Authoritarianism in Syria', in *Demystifying Syria*, ed. Fred Lawson (London: Saqi, 2009), 13–28.

Johansen, Julian. *Sufism and Islamic Reform in Egypt: The Battle for Islamic Tradition* (Oxford: Clarendon Press, 1996).

Kahf, Monzer. 'Islamic Banks: The Rise of a New Power Alliance of Wealth and Shari'a Scholarship', in *The Politics of Islamic Finance*, ed. Clement Henry and Rodney Wilson (Edinburgh: Edinburgh University Press, 2004), 17–36.

Kalmbach, Hilary. 'Social and Religious Change in Damascus', *British Journal of Middle Eastern Studies* 35, no. 1 (2008), 37–57.

Kedar, Mordechai. *Asad in Search of Legitimacy: Message and Rhetoric in the Syrian Press under Hafiz and Bashar* (Brighton: Sussex Academic Press, 2005).

Kepel, Gilles. 'Les oulémas, l'intelligentsia et les islamistes en Égypte: Système social, ordre transcendantal et ordre traduit', *Revue française de science politique* 35, no. 3 (1985), 424–45.

Keshavarzian, Arang. 'Turban or Hat, Seminarian or Soldier: State Building and Clergy Building in Reza Shah's Iran', *Journal of Church and State* 45, no. 1 (2003), 81–112.

al-Khatib, Ahmad Mouaz. 'al-Tamaddun al-Islami: passé et présent d'une association réformiste damascène', *Maghreb – Machrek*, no. 198 (2008), 79–92.

Khoury, Philip. 'Syrian Urban Politics in Transition: The Quarters of Damascus during the French Mandate', *International Journal of Middle East Studies* 16, no. 4 (1984), 507–40.

Knysh, Alexander. 'The Tariqa on a Landcruiser: The Resurgence of Sufism in Yemen', *Middle East Journal* 55, no. 3 (2001), 399–414.

Kotb, Amira. 'La Tariqa Ba'Alawiyya et le développement d'un réseau soufi transnational', MA thesis, Université Paul Cézanne, 2004.

Krämer, Gudrun and Schmidtke, Sabine. *Speaking for Islam: Religious Authorities in Muslim Societies* (Leiden: Brill, 2006).

Kutschera, Chris. 'L'éclipse des Frères Musulmans syriens', *Cahiers de l'Orient*, no. 7 (1987), 121–33.

Lacroix, Stéphane. *Awakening Islam: Religious Dissent in Contemporary Saudi Arabia* (Cambridge, MA: Harvard University Press, 2011).

'Between Revolution and Apoliticism: Nasir al-Din al-Albani and His Impact on the Shaping of Contemporary Salafism', in *Global Salafism: Islam's New Religious Movement*, ed. Roel Meijer (New York: Columbia University Press, 2009), 58–80.

Landis, Joshua. 'Syria: Secularism, Arabism and Sunni Orthodoxy', in *Tailor-Made Islam: Religion, Identity and Nation in Middle Eastern Schoolbooks*, ed. Eleanor Doumato and Gregory Starrett (Boulder: Lynne Rienner, 2006), 177–96.

Landis, Joshua and Pace, Joe. 'The Syrian Opposition', *The Washington Quarterly* 30, no. 1 (2007), 45–68.

Lazarus-Yafeh, Hava. 'Muhammad Mutawalli al-Sha'rawi: A Portrait of a Contemporary 'Alim in Egypt', in *Islam, Nationalism and Radicalism in Egypt and the Sudan*, ed. Gabriel Warburg and Uri Kupferschmidt (New York: Praeger, 1983), 281–97.

Leder, Stefan. *Spoken Word and Written Text: Meaning and Social Significance of the Institution of Riwaya* (Tokyo: University of Tokyo, 2002).

Lenfant, Arnaud. 'Les transformations du salafisme syrien au XXe siècle', in *Qu'est-ce que le salafisme?*, ed. Bernard Rougier (Paris: PUF, 2008), 161–78.

Lobmeyer, Hans Günter. *Opposition und Widerstand in Syrien* (Hamburg: Deutsches Orient-Institut, 1995).

Mahmood, Saba. *Politics of Piety: The Islamic Revival and the Feminist Subject* (Princeton: Princeton University Press, 2005).

Mann, Joseph. 'The Syrian Neo-Ba'th Regime and the Kingdom of Saudi Arabia, 1966–70', *Middle Eastern Studies* 42, no. 5 (2006), 761–76.

Ma'oz, Moshe. 'The Ulama and the Process of Modernisation in Syria during the Mid-Nineteenth Century', *Asian and African Studies*, no. 7 (1971), 77–88.

Mardin, Serif. *Religion and Social Change in Modern Turkey: The Case of Bediuzzaman Said Nursi* (Albany: State University of New York Press, 1990).

Mariani, Ermete. 'Les oulémas syriens à la recherche d'une audience virtuelle', in *La société de l'information au Proche-Orient*, ed. Yves Gonzalez-Quijano (Lyons: Gremmo, 2007), 93–116.

Mayer, Thomas. 'The Islamic Opposition in Syria, 1961–1982', *Orient* 24, no. 4 (1983), 589–609.

Mayeur-Jaouen, Catherine (ed.). *Saints et héros du Moyen-Orient contemporain* (Paris: Maisonneuve et Larose, 2002).

Meijer, Roel. 'The Association of Muslim Scholars in Iraq', *Middle East Report*, no. 237 (2005), 12–19.

Meijer, Roel (ed.). *Global Salafism: Islam's New Religious Movement* (New York: Columbia University Press, 2009).

Mermier, Frank. *Le Livre et la ville: Beyrouth et l'édition arabe* (Paris: Sindbad-Actes Sud, 2005).

Mitchell, Richard. *The Society of the Muslim Brothers* (London: Oxford University Press, 1969).

Mouline, Nabil. *Les Clercs de l'islam: autorité religieuse et pouvoir politique en Arabie saoudite, XVIIIe–XXIe siècle* (Paris: PUF, 2011).

O'Fahey, Rex and Radtke, Berndt, 'Neo-Sufism Reconsidered', *Der Islam*, no. 70 (1993), 52–87.

Perthes, Volker. *The Political Economy of Syria under Asad* (New York: I. B. Tauris, 1995).

Petran, Tabitha. *Syria* (London: Ernest Benn, 1972).

Philippon, Alix. 'Bridging Sufism and Islamism', *ISIM Review*, no. 17 (2006), 16–17.

Pierret, Thomas. 'Assassinat d'un "cheikh du pouvoir" à Damas', blogs.mediapart.fr/, 16 February 2012.

'Le Courant National Syrien, un concurrent pour les Frères Musulmans?', blogs.mediapart.fr/, 7 February 2012.

'Diplomatie islamique: à propos de la lettre de 138 leaders religieux musulmans aux chefs des Églises chrétiennes', *Esprit*, no. 346 (2008), 161–70.

'Des Islamistes syriens tendent la main à la communauté alaouite', blogs.mediapart.fr/, 4 October 2011.

'Karbala in the Umayyad Mosque: Sunni Panic at the Shiitization of Syria in the 2000s', in *The Dynamics of Sunni–Shia Relationships: Doctrine, Transnationalism, Intellectuals and the Media*, ed. Brigitte Maréchal and Sami Zemni (London: Hurst, 2012), 101–17.

'Le *Projet politique pour la Syrie de l'avenir* des Frères Musulmans', in *La Syrie au présent*, ed. Youssef Courbage, Baudouin Dupret, Mohammed Al-Dbiyat, and Zouhair Ghazzal (Paris: Actes Sud, 2007), 729–38.

'Staging the Authority of the Ulama: The Celebration of the Mawlid in Urban Syria', in *Ethnographies of Islam*, ed. Paulo Pinto, Thomas Pierret, Kathryn Spellman, and Baudouin Dupret (Edinburgh: Edinburgh University Press, 2012), 93–104.

'The State Management of Religion in Syria: The End of Indirect Rule?', in *Comparing Authoritarianisms: Reconfiguring Power and Regime Resilience in Syria and Iran*, ed. Steven Heydemann and Reinoud Leenders (Palo Alto: Stanford University Press, 2012), 83–106.

'Sunni Clergy Politics in the Cities of Ba'thi Syria', in *Demystifying Syria*, ed. Fred Lawson (London: Saqi, 2009), 70–84.

'Syrie: les prêcheurs relaient la révolution malgré la répression', blogs.media-part.fr/, 8 September 2011.

Pierret, Thomas and Selvik Kjetil. 'Limits of "Authoritarian Upgrading" in Syria: Private Welfare, Islamic Charities, and the Rise of the Zayd Movement', *International Journal of Middle East Studies* 41, no. 4 (2009), 595–614.

Pinto, Paolo. 'Bodily Mediations: Self, Values and Experience in Syrian Sufism', in *Veränderung und Stabilität: Normen und Werte in Islamischen Gesellschaften*, ed. Johann Heiss (Vienna: Österreichischen Akademie der Wissenschaften, 2005), 201–24.

'Mystical Bodies: Ritual, Experience and the Embodiment of Sufism in Syria', Ph.D. thesis, Boston University, 2002.

'Performing Baraka: Sainthood and Power in Syrian Sufism', *Yearbook of Sociology of Islam* 5 (2004), 195–214.

'Sufism and the Political Economy of Morality in Syria', *Interdisciplinary Journal of Middle Eastern Studies* 15 (2006), 103–36.

Rabinovich, Itamar. *Syria under the Ba'th, 1963–66: The Army–Party Symbiosis* (Jerusalem: Israel Universities Press, 1972).

Rafeq, Abdul-Karim. 'The Syrian University and the French Mandate (1920–1946)', in *Liberal Thought in the Eastern Mediterranean: Late 19th Century until the 1960s*, ed. Christoph Schumann (Leiden: Brill, 2008), 75–98.

Reissner, Johannes. *Ideologie und Politik der Muslimbrüder Syriens: Von den Wahlen 1947 bis zum Verbot unter Adib ash-Shishakli* (Freiburg im Breisgau: Klaus Shwarz, 1980).

Ritzer, George and Ryan, J. Michael (eds.), *The Concise Encyclopedia of Sociology* (Chichester and Malden, MA: Wiley-Blackwell, 2011).

Robinson, Francis. 'Technology and Religious Change: Islam and the Impact of Print', *Modern Asian Studies* 27, no. 1 (1993), 229–51.

Rougier, Bernard. *L'Oumma en fragments: contrôler le sunnisme au Liban* (Paris: PUF, 2011).

Rougier, Bernard (ed.). *Qu'est-ce que le salafisme?* (Paris: PUF, 2008).

Ruiz de Elvira, Laura. 'L'état syrien de Bachar al-Assad à l'épreuve des ONG', *Maghreb – Machrek*, no. 203 (2010), 41–58.

Sadowski, Yahya. 'Ba'thist Ethics and the Spirit of State Capitalism: Patronage in Contemporary Syria', in *Ideology and Power in the Middle East*, ed. Peter J. Chelkowski and Robert Pranger (Durham: Duke University Press, 1988), 160–84.

Schatkowsky-Schilcher, Linda. *Families in Politics: Damascene Factions and Estates of the 18th and 19th Centuries* (Wiesbaden: Steiner, 1985).

Schielke, Samuli. 'On Snacks and Saints: When Discourses of Rationality and Order Enter the Egyptian Mawlid', *Archives de sciences sociales des religions*, no. 135 (2006), 117–40.

Seale, Patrick. *Asad of Syria: The Struggle for the Middle East* (Berkeley: University of California Press, 1989).

The Struggle for Syria: A Study of Post-war Arab Politics, 1945–1958 (London: Oxford University Press, 1965).

Shahrur, Muhammad, Christmann, Andreas, and Eickelman, Dale F. *The Qur'an, Morality and Critical Reason: The Essential Muhammad Shahrur* (Boston: Brill, 2009).

Skovgaard-Petersen, Jakob. *Defining Islam for the Egyptian State: Muftis and Fatwas of the Dar al-Ifta* (Leiden: Brill, 1997).

Starrett, Gregory. *Putting Islam to Work: Education, Politics, and Religious Transformation in Egypt* (Berkeley: University of California Press, 1998).

Stenberg, Leif. 'Préserver le charisme: les conséquences de la mort d'Ahmad Kaftaro sur la mosquée-complexe Abu al-Nur', *Maghreb – Machrek*, no. 198 (2008), 65–74.

'Young, Male and Sufi Muslim in the City of Damascus', in *Youth and Youth Culture in the Contemporary Middle East*, ed. Jørgen Bæck Simonsen (Aarhus: Aarhus University Press, 2005), 68–91.

Sunayama, Sonoko. *Syria and Saudi Arabia: Collaboration and Conflicts in the Oil Era* (London: I. B. Tauris, 2007).

Szanto, Edith. 'Inter-Religious Dialogue in Syria: Politics, Ethics and Miscommunication', *Political Theology* 9, no. 1 (2008), 93–113.

Talhamy, Yvette. 'The Fatwas and the Nusayri/Alawis of Syria', *Middle Eastern Studies* 46, no. 2 (2010), 175–94.

Tapiéro, Norbert. *Les Idées réformistes d'al-Kawakibi, 1265–1320=1849–1902: contribution à l'étude de l'Islam moderne* (Paris: Les Editions Arabes, 1956).

Teitelbaum, Joshua. 'The Muslim Brotherhood and the "Struggle for Syria", 1947–1958: Between Accommodation and Ideology', *Middle Eastern Studies* 40, no. 3 (2004), 134–58.

Thompson, Elizabeth. *Colonial Citizens: Republican Rights, Paternal Privilege, and Gender in French Syria and Lebanon* (New York: Columbia University Press, 2000).

Torrey, Gordon. *Syrian Politics and the Military 1945–1958* (Columbus: Ohio State University Press, 1964).

Tripp, Charles. *Islam and the Moral Economy: The Challenge of Capitalism* (Cambridge: Cambridge University Press, 2006).

Valter, Stéphane. *La Construction nationale syrienne* (Paris: CNRS éditions, 2002).

Volpi, Frédéric and Turner, Bryan (eds.). 'Authority and Islam', *Theory, Cultures & Society* 24, no. 2 (2007), 1–240.

Weber, Max. *Economy and Society: An Outline of Interpretive Sociology* (Berkeley: University of California Press, 1978).

Wedeen, Lisa. *Ambiguities of Domination: Politics, Rhetoric, and Symbols in Contemporary Syria* (Chicago: University of Chicago Press, 1999).

Weismann, Itzchak. 'Democratic Fundamentalism? The Practice and Discourse of the Muslim Brothers Movement in Syria', *The Muslim World* 100 (2010), 1–16.

'The Forgotten Shaykh: 'Isa al-Kurdi and the Transformation of the Naqshbandi–Khalidi Order in Twentieth Century Syria', *Die Welt des Islams* 43 (2003), 273–93.

'The Hidden Hand: The Khalidiyya and the Orthodox–Fundamentalist Nexus in Aleppo', *Journal of the History of Sufism* 5 (2007), 41–58.

'The Invention of a Populist Islamic Leader: Badr al-Din al-Hasani, the Religious Educational Movement and the Great Syrian Revolt', *Arabica* 52, no. 1 (2005), 109–39.

'The Politics of Popular Religion: Sufis, Salafis, and Muslim Brothers in 20th-Century Hamah', *International Journal of Middle East Studies* 37, no. 1 (2005), 39–58.

'Sa'id Hawwa: The Making of a Radical Muslim Thinker in Modern Syria', *Middle Eastern Studies* 29, no. 4 (1993), 601–23.

'The Shadhiliyya–Darqawiyya in the Arab East', in *La Shadhiliyya: une voie soufie dans le monde*, ed. Éric Geoffroy (Paris: Maisonneuve et Larose, 2004), 255–70.

'Sufi Brotherhoods in Syria and Israel: A Comparative Overview', *History of Religions* 43 (2004), 303–18.

'Sufi Fundamentalism between India and the Middle East', in *Sufism and the 'Modern'*, ed. Martin van Bruinessen and Julia Howell (London: I. B. Tauris, 2007), 115–28.

Taste of Modernity: Sufism, Salafiyya, and Arabism in Late Ottoman Damascus (Leiden: Brill, 2001).

White, Benjamin Thomas. *The Emergence of Minorities in the Middle East: The Politics of Community in French Mandate Syria* (Edinburgh: Edinburgh University Press, 2011).

Zaman, Muhammad Qasim. *The Ulama in Contemporary Islam: Custodians of Change* (Princeton: Princeton University Press, 2002).

Zarcone, Thierry. 'The Transformation of the Sufi Orders (*Tarikat*) in the Turkish Republic and the Question of Crypto-Sufism', in *Cultural Horizons: A Festschrift in Honor of Talat S. Halman*, ed. Jayne Warner (New York: Syracuse University Press, 2001), 198–209.

La Turquie moderne et l'islam (Paris: Flammarion, 2004).

Zeghal, Malika. *Gardiens de l'islam: les oulémas d'Al Azhar dans l'Egypte contemporaine* (Paris: Presses de la Fondation nationale des sciences politiques, 1996).

Zisser, Eyal. 'Syria, the Ba'th Regime and the Islamic Movement: Stepping on a New Path?', *The Muslim World*, no. 95 (2005), 43–65.

Publications in Arabic

Abaza, Nizar. *al-Shaykh Ali al-Daqr: Rajul ahya Allah bihi al-umma* [Sheikh Ali al-Daqr: the man through whom God reawakened the umma] (Damascus: Dar al-Fikr, 2010).

'Ulama' Dimashq wa a'yanuha fi al-qarn al-khamis 'ashar al-hijri (1401–1425) [The ulama and noteworthy people of Damascus in the fifteenth century AH (1980–2004)] (Damascus: Dar al-Fikr, 2007).

Abaza, Nizar and al-Hafiz, Muti '. *Tarikh 'ulama' Dimashq fi al-qarn al-rabi' 'ashar al-hijri* [History of the ulama of Damascus in the fourteenth century AH] (Damascus: Dar al-Fikr, 1986–91).

'Abd al-Hakim, 'Umar (aka Abu Mus'ab al-Suri). *al-Thawra al-islamiyya al-jihadiyya fi Suriyya* [The jihadi Islamic revolution in Syria] (n.p.: n.p., n.d.).

'Abduh, Samir. *Hadatha dhat marra fi Suriyya: dirasa li-l-siyasat al-suriyya–al-'arabiyya fi 'ahday al-wahda wa-l-infisal 1958–1963* [It happened in Syria: a study of Syrian–Arab politics during the union and the secession] (Damascus: Dar 'Ala' al-Din, 1998).

'Absu, Fayyad. 'al-Madrasa al-Sha'baniyya' (www.alkeltawia.com, 2 August 2008).

al-Ahmad, Khalid. 'Mi'dhana wa dabbaba' [A minaret and a tank] (www.islamysria.com, 21 April 2007).

'Akkam, Mahmud. *Min maqulat al-fikr al-islami* [On the philosophical categories of Islamic thought] (Aleppo: Fussilat, 2002).

al-'Alawna, Ahmad. *Dhayl al-a'lam* [Continuation of the great men] (Jeddah: Dar al-Manara, 1998).

al-Albani, Nasir al-Din. *al-Radd 'ala al-Ta'aqqub al-hathith li-l-Shaykh Abdullah al-Habashi* [Refutation of *The Winged Monitoring* of Sheikh Abdullah al-Habashi] (Damascus: al-Tamaddun al-Islami, 1958).

al-'Ali, Ibrahim Muhammad. *Muhammad Nasir al-Din al-Albani: muhaddith al-'asr wa nasir al-sunna* [Muhammad Nasir al-Din al-Albani: hadith scholar of the century and defender of the Sunna] (Damascus: Dar al-Qalam, 2001).

al-'Ammar, Muhammad. 'Jawdat Sa'id: kama afhamuhu wa kayfa 'araftuhu' [Jawdat Sa'id: how I understand him and how I met him], in *Buhuth wa maqalat muhaddat ilayhi* [Festschrift in honour of Jawdat Sa'id] (Damascus: Dar al-Fikr, 2006), 47–71.

'Arrabi, Nizar. *Murafa'at wa ahkam* [Pleadings and judgments] (Damascus: Dar Tlass, 2007).

As'id, Muhammad Shakir. *al-Barlaman al-suri fi tatawwurihi al-tarikhi* [The Syrian parliament in its historical development] (Damascus: al-Mada, 2002).

al-Atasi, Ali. 'al-Faqih wa-l-sultan: Shaykh al-Buti namudhijan' [The faqih and the sultan: the example of Sheikh al-Buti] (www.arraee.com, 19 November 2004).

al-Atasi, Basil. *Tarikh al-usra al-atasiyya wa tarajim mashahiriha* [History of the al-Atasi family and the biographies of its famous men]. Unpublished document, undated.

'Ayntabi, Fawzi and 'Uthman, Najwa. *Halab fi mi'a 'am* [Aleppo through one hundred centuries] (Aleppo: Ma'had al-Turath al-'Ilmi al-'Arabi, 1993).

al-'Ayti, Yasir. *Li-'uyunik ya Quds* [For your eyes, O Jerusalem] (Beirut: al-Maktab al-Islami, 2001).

Barut, Jamal. 'Suriyya: usul wa ta'arrujat al-sira' bayn al-madrasatayn at-taqlidiyya wa al-radikaliyya' [Syria: origins and twists and turns of the conflict between the traditional and radical schools], in *al-Ahzab wa-l-harakat wal-jama'at al-islamiyya* [Islamic parties, movements, and groups], ed. Jamal Barut and Faysal Darraj (Damascus: Arab Center for Strategic Studies, 2000), 255–324.

al-Ba'th al-shi'i fi Suriyya 1919–2007 [The Shiite renaissance in Syria] (n.p.: n.p., 2008).

Bayan mu'tamar al-'ulama' al-awwal al-mun'aqad bi-Dimashq 11–13 rajab 1357 [Communiqué of the First Congress of Ulama Held in Damascus, 6–8 September 1938] (www.islamsyria.com, 1 May 2006).

al-Bayanuni, 'Abd al-Majid. *Ahmad 'Izz al-Din al-Bayanuni: al-da'iya al-murabbi (1913–1975)* [Ahmad 'Izz al-Din al-Bayanuni: the preacher and educator (1913–1975)] (Damascus: Dar al-Qalam, 2006).

al-Bayanuni, Ahmad 'Izz al-Din. *al-Iman bi-l-llah* [Faith in God] (Cairo: n.p., 1987).

al-Bayanuni, Ali Sadr al-Din. 'Ziyara khassa', al-Jazira, 26 November 2005.

'Bayna sufiyya Dimashq wa sufiyya Dar al-Mustafa bi-Tarim, wa lu'bat al-salibi-yyin al-judud bi-tawatu' wa qasd ma'a al-mutasawwifa' [Between the Sufis of Damascus and the Sufis of Dar al-Mustafa in Tarim, and the game of the new Crusaders with the voluntary complicity of the Sufis] (www.alsoufia. org [2003])

al-Bayruti, Mahmud. *al-Shaykh Muhammad Badr al-Din al-Hasani wa athr majalisihi fi al-mujtama' al-dimashqi* [Sheikh Muhammad Badr al-Din al-Hasani and the influence of his teachings on Damascene society] (Damascus: Dar al-Bayruti, 2009).

al-Buti, Sa'id Ramadan. *al-'Aqidat al-islamiyya wa-l-fikr al-mu'asir* [The Islamic creed and contemporary thought] (Damascus: University of Damascus, 1982).

'al-Asha'ira wa-l-maturidiyya' [The Ash'aris and the Maturidis] (www.bouti. net, 3 December 2004).

Fiqh al-sira al-nabawiyya [Fiqh of the life of the Prophet] (Damascus: Dar al-Ghazali, 1968).

Hadha ma qultuhu amama ba'd al-ru'asa' wa-l-muluk [Here is what I said in front of some presidents and kings] (Damascus: Dar al-Farabi, 2002).

Hadha walidi: al-qissa al-kamila li-hayat al-shaykh Mulla Ramadan al-Buti [This was my father: the full story of the life of Sheikh Mulla Ramadan al-Buti] (Damascus: Dar al-Fikr, 1995).

'Hakadha nasha'at al-qawmiyya' [This is how nationalism was born], *Hadarat al-Islam* 3, no. 6 (1963); reprinted in *Shawqi Abu Khalil: buhuth wa maqalat muhaddat ilayhi* [Festschrift in honour of Shawqi Abu Khalil] (Damascus: Dar al-Fikr, 2004), 169–82.

Ila kull fatat tu'min bi-llah [To every girl who believes in God] (Damascus: Dar al-Farabi, 1973).

al-Jihad fi al-islam: kayfa nafhamuhu wa kayfa numarisuhu [Jihad in Islam: How we understand it, how we practise it] (Damascus: Dar al-Fikr, 1993).

'Kayfa sarat ma'rifati li-l-ustadh al-duktur Wahba al-Zuhayli' [How I met Dr Wahba al-Zuhayli', in *Wahba al-Zuhayli buhuth wa maqalat muhaddat ilayhi* [Festschrift in honour of Wahba al-Zuhayli] (Damascus: Dar al-Fikr, 2003), 24–43.

Kubra al-yaqiniyyat al-kawniyya [The great convictions of the universe] (Damascus: Dar al-Fikr, 1969).

al-La madhhabiyya: akhtar bid'a tuhaddid al-shari'a al-islamiyya [Anti-madhhabism: the dangers of an innovation that threatens sharia] (Damascus: Dar al-Fikr, 1970).

'Laysat al-mushkila ghiyab al-hadatha innama al-mushkila ghiyab al-hawiya' [The problem is not the absence of modernity but that of identity] (www. sadazaid.com, 8 August 2008)

Min al-fikr wa-l-qalb: fusul al-naqd fi al-'ulum wa-l-ijtima' wa-l-adab [From thought and heart: chapters of critique in the realms of sciences, society, and literature] (Damascus: Dar al-Farabi, 1972).

Naqd awham al-jadaliyya al-maddiyya al-diyaliktikiyya [Refutation of the illusions of dialectical materialism] (Damascus: Dar al-Fikr, 1986).

'Qadiyat al-Hariri wa 'alaqatuha bi-mukhattat al-qada' 'ala al-Islam' [The Hariri affair and its relation to the plan to destroy Islam] (www.bouti.com, December 2005).

al-Salafiyya; marhala zamaniyya mubaraka la madhhab islami [Salafiyya: a blessed historical period, not a school of fiqh] (Damascus: Dar al-Fikr, 1991).

Shakhsiyyat istawqafatni [People who attracted my attention] (Damascus: Dar al-Fikr, 1999).

al-Dawalibi, Ma'ruf. *Mudhakkirat* [Memoirs] (Riyadh: 'Ubaykan, 2006).

Habannaka, 'Abd al-Rahman. *al-Walid al-da'iya al-murabbi al-shaykh Hasan Habannaka al-Midani* [My father the preacher and educator Sheikh Hasan Habannaka al-Midani] (Jeddah: Dar al-Bashir, 2002).

Habash, Muhammad. *Alf yawm fi majlis al-sha'b* [A thousand days in the People's Council] (Damascus: Nadwat al-'Ulama', 2007).

al-Shaykh Ahmad Kaftaru wa manhajuhu fi al-tajdid wa-l-islah [Sheikh Ahmad Kaftaru and his method for renewal and reform] (Damascus: Dar Abu al-Nur, 1996).

Haddad, Jibril. *Tuhfat al-labib bi-nusrat al-Habib Ali al-Jifri* [The true substance in the defence of al-Habib Ali al-Jifri] (Damascus: Dar Tayyibat al-Gharra', 2007).

Hadid, Marwan. 'Nida' ila al-'ulama' al-'amilin wa-l-muslimin al-mukhlisin wa-l-jama'at al-islamiyya' [Call to the active scholars, the sincere Muslims, and the Islamic groups] (www.almaqdese.net [written in 1975]).

al-Hafiz, Muti'. *Dar al-Hadith al-Ashrafiyya bi-Dimashq: dirasa tarikhiyya wa tawthiqiyya* [Dar al-Hadith al-Ashrafiyya in Damascus: a historical and documentary study] (Damascus: Dar al-Fikr, 2001).

al-Hajj Ibrahim, 'Abd al-Rahman. 'al-Shaykh 'Abd al-Qadir al-Arna'ut' (www. islamweb.net, 20 March 2002).

al-Hakami al-Fifi, Yahya. 'Muhammad Krayyim Rajih' (www.islamsyria.com, 10 July 2007).

al-Hamid, Muhammad. [On Mustafa al-Siba'i's *Socialism of Islam*], in *Hadarat al-Islam* 3, no. 10 (1963), 1128–31.

Hassun, Adib. *Ala' al-rahman 'ala al-'arif al-Nabhan* [Benedictions of the merciful upon the knower of God al-Nabhan] (Aleppo: n.p., n.d.).

Hawwa, Sa'id. *Hadhihi tajribati … wa hadhihi chahadati* [This is my experience … this is my testimony] (Cairo: Maktaba Wahba, 1987).

al-Humsi, Hasan. *al-Du'at wa-l-da'wa al-islamiyya al-mu'asira al-muntaliqa min masajid Dimashq* [The preachers and contemporary Islamic call stemming from the mosques of Damascus] (Damascus: Mu'assasat al-Iman, 1991).

al-Humsi, Lina. *al-Muftun al-'ammun fi Suriyya* [The Grand Muftis in Syria] (Damascus: Dar al-'Asma', 1996).

Ibrahim, al-Tahir. '*al-Jama'at al-islamiyya bayn al-ihtiwa' wa-l-ilgha'* [Islamic groups between restraint and self-effacement], *Majallat al-'Asr*, 28 June 2007.

'Itr, Nur al-Din. *Safahat min hayat al-imam shaykh al-islam al-shaykh Abdullah Siraj al-Din al-Hussayni* [Pages from the life of the Imam Sheikh of Islam, Sheikh Abdullah Siraj al-Din al-Husseini] (Aleppo: Dar al-Ru'ya, 2003).

Jam'iyyat al-muhaddith al-akbar al-shaykh Badr al-Din al-Hasani [Association of the supreme hadith scholar Sheikh Badr al-Din al-Hasani] (Damascus: n.p., 2007).

al-Janabi, Abdullah. '*al-Shaykh Najib Salim*' (www.islamsyria.com, 7 April 2007).

al-Jarrah, 'A'ida. *'Abd al-Rahman Hasan Habannaka al-Midani, al-'alim al-mufakkir al-mufassir: zawji kama 'araftuhu* ['Abd al-Rahman Hasan Habannaka al-Midani, the scholar, thinker, and exegete: my husband as I have known him] (Damascus: Dar al-Qalam, 2001).

al-Jibali, Mundhir. '*al-Da'iya al-shaykh Shawkat al-Jibali*' [The sheikh and preacher Shawkat al-Jibali] (www.sadazaid.com, 19 April 2008).

Ka'ayyid, Ahmad Taysir. *Mawsu'at al-du'at wa-l-a'imma wa-l-khutaba' fi Halab (al-'asr al-hadith)* [Encylopaedia of the imams and preachers in Aleppo (the modern period)] (Aleppo: Dar al-Qalam al-'Arabi, 2008).

Kallas, Ahmad. '*Tarjamat al-'allamat al-murabbi al-zahid al-faqih al-shaykh Muhammad Adib Kallas*' [Biography of the savant, educator, ascetic, and *faqih*, Sheikh Muhammad Adib Kallas] (www.alfatihonline.com, 2007).

Katibi, 'Adnan. *al-Ta'lim al-shar'i wa madarisuhu fi Halab fi al-qarn al-rabi' 'ashar al-hijri* [Religious teaching and its schools in Aleppo in the fourteenth century AH] (Aleppo: n.p., 2006).

Tarikh al-ifta' fi Halab al-shahba' [History of *ifta'* in Aleppo-the-Grey] (Aleppo: Maktabat al-Turath, n.d.).

'Ulama' min Halab fi al-qarn al-rabi' 'ashar [Ulama from Aleppo in the fourteenth century AH] (Aleppo: n.p., 2008).

al-Khatib, Ahmad Mu'adh. '*al-Imam al-mazlum, nasir al-sunna al-'allama 'Abd al-Qadir al-Arna'ut*' [The oppressed imam, the defender of Sunna, the savant 'Abd al-Qadir al-Arna'ut] (www.darbuna.net, 3 November 2006).

'*Musawwada Ittihad al-'Ulama' wa-l-A'imma wa-l-Du'at*' [Draft project for the Union of Ulama, Imams and Preachers] (www.darbuna.net, 8 May 2006).

al-Kittani, 'Abd al-Qadir. '*al-'Allamat al-imam al-mujahid al-sayyid Makki al-Kittani*' [The savant, imam, combatant, and descendant of the Prophet Makki al-Kittani], *al-Thawra*, 16 March 2007.

al-Majmu'a al-ihsa'iyya [Statistical yearbook] (Damascus: Central Bureau of Statistics, 1962–78).

Makki, Majd. 'Hussein Khattab: shaykh qurra' al-Sham' [Hussein Khattab: sheikh of the Quran readers of Damascus] (www.islamsyria.com, 10 July 2007).

'al-Shaykh Ahmad Raf'at Ikbazli Zadeh' (www.odabasham.net, 22 January 2011).

'al-Shaykh Muhammad al-Hajjar' (www.islamsyria.com, 25 January 2007).

'al-Shaykh Muhammad Raghib al-Tabbakh' (www.islamsyria.com, 24 July 2007).

Makki al-Hasani, Khaldun. *Ila ayn? Ayyuha al-Habib al-Jifri* [How far, O al-Habib al-Jifri?] (Damascus: al-Bayyina, 2007).

Mardini, Raghda'. 'Rahil al-'allama al-mawsu'a al-duktur 'Abd al-Karim al-Yafi' [Death of the eminent scholar, the encyclopaedia Dr 'Abd al-Karim al-Yafi] (www.odabasham.net, 18 October 2008).

Mastu, Muhi al-Din Dib. *Mustafa Sa'id al-Khann: al-'alim al-murabbi wa shaykh 'ilm usul al-fiqh fi bilad al-Sham* [Mustafa Sa'id al-Khann: the scholar, educator, and sheikh of usul al-fiqh in Bilad al-Sham] (Damascus: Dar al-Qalam, 2001).

Mubayyid, 'Amir Rashid. *Mi'a awa'il min Halab* [One hundred prominent figures from Aleppo] (Aleppo: Dar al-Rifa'i, 2004).

al-Mujahid al-samit, shaykh Muhammad al-Ashmar: siratuhu wa jihaduhu [The silent combatant, Sheikh Muhammad al-Ashmar: his life and jihad] ([Beirut]: [al-Maktab al-Islami], 2002).

Mujamma' al-shaykh Ahmad Kaftaru [Sheikh Ahmad Kaftaru Academy] (Damascus: Kaftaru Academy, 2006).

al-Mun'im al-Badawi, Usama Muhammad. *al-Nafahat al-rabbaniyya fi hayat al-qutb sayyidi al-shaykh Yahya al-Sabbagh al-dimashqi* [Divine inspirations in the life of the Pole, my master Sheikh Yahya al-Sabbagh the Damascene] (Damascus: n.p., n.d.).

al-Nabhan, Faruq. *al-Shaykh Muhammad al-Nabhan: shakhsiyyatuhu – fikruhu – atharuhu* [Sheikh Muhammad al-Nabhan: his personality – his thought – his influence] (Aleppo: Dar al-Turath, 2004).

al-Nabulsi, Ratib. *Mawsu'at al-i'jaz al-'ilmi fi al-qur'an wa-l-sunna* [The encyclopaedia of scientific miracle in the Quran and Sunna] (Damascus: Dar al-Maktabi, 2007).

Nadaf, 'Imad 'Abd al-Latif. *al-Shaykh Ahmad Kaftaru yatahaddath* [Sheikh Ahmad Kaftaru speaks] (Damascus: Dar al-Rachid, 2005).

al-Nadwi, Abu al-Hassan Ali. *Mudhakkirat sa'ih fi al-sharq al-'arabi* [Memories of a tourist in the Arab East] (Beirut: Dar Ibn Kathir, 1975).

Qanun jam'iyyat arbab al-sha'a'ir al-diniyya al-asasi [Statutes of the Association of Officers of Religious Rites] (Damascus: Dar al-Taraqqi, 1950).

al-Qudmani, Muhammad Yasir. *Muhammad Fawzi Fayd Allah* (Damascus: Dar al-Qalam, 2002).

al-Rashid, 'Imad al-Din. *al-Muwatana fi al-mafhum al-islami* [Citizenship in its Islamic conception] (Damascus: Nahwa al-Qimma, 2005).

al-Rifa'i, 'Abd al-Karim. *al-Awrad al-mukhtara* [Selected litanies] (Damascus: al-Ghazali, 1992).

al-Ma'rifa fi bayan 'aqidat al-muslim [Knowledge in the statement of the doctrine of the Muslim] (Damascus: al-Ghazali, 1990).

al-Rifa'i, Basil. 'al-Jam'iyyat al-diniyya fi Suriyya: al-Hidayat al-Islamiyya' [Religious associations in Syria: al-Hidayat al-Islamiyya] (www.islamysria. com, 7 June 2008).

al-Rifa'i, Sariya. 'Min fiqh al-da'wa' [From fiqh of da'wa] (www.sadazaid.com, 10 May 2006).

'al-Qidwat al-rabbaniyya asas al-da'wat al-islamiyya' [The rabbanian model is the foundation of da'wa] (www.sadazaid.com, 5 April 2008).

'Risala min *Nahj al-Islam* ila *al-Thawra*' [Message from *Nahj al-Islam* to *al-Thawra*], *Nahj al-Islam*, no. 107 (2007), 20–2.

al-Rifa'i, Usama. 'Ba'd al-masa'il allati hiya mathar jadal ma'a al-ikhwa al-salafiyyin' [Some questions that are a source of controversy with our Salafi brothers] (www.sadazaid.com, 4 November 2008).

'al-Bid'a bayn al-salafiyya wa ahl al-sunna wa-l-jama'a' [Innovation between the Salafis and the Sunnis](www.sadazaid.com, 27 August 2008).

'Durus min hayat al-shaykh 'Abd al-Karim al-Rifa'i' [Lessons from the life of Sheikh 'Abd al-Karim al-Rifa'i] (www.sadazaid.com, 17 April 2008).

'al-Salafiyya wa ahl al-sunna wa-l-jama'a' [The Salafis and the Sunnis] (www. sadazaid.com, 4 June 2008).

al-Rifa'i, Yusuf. *Nasiha li-ikhwanina 'ulama' Najd* [Advice to our brothers the ulama of Najd] (Kuwait: Dar Iqra', 2000).

al-Sabbagh, Muhammad Lutfi. 'Muhammad Amin al-Masri', *Majallat al-Jami'at al-Islamiyya fi al-Madinat al-Munawwara* 39 (n.d.), 17.

Sa'd al-Din, 'Adnan. *al-Ikhwan al-muslimun fi Suriyya: ma qabla al-ta'sis wa hatta 'am 1954* [The Muslim Brothers in Syria: from before the foundation to 1954] (Amman: Dar'Ammar, 2006).

Sa'id, Jawdat and Bennabi, Malik. Foreword, '*Hatta yughayyiru ma bi-anfusihim*': *bahth fi sunan taghyiir al-nafs wa-l-mujtama*' ['As long as they do not change themselves': research on the laws of change of the soul and society] (Beirut: Matba'at al-'Ilm, 1972).

al-Sali'i, Sulayman. 'al-Shaykh al-'allamat al-shahid Mahmud 'Abd al-Rahman al-Shuqfa' [The savant and martyr Sheikh Mahmud 'Abd al-Rahman al-Shuqfa] (www.ghrib.net, 11 October 2007).

Salim, Zuhayr. 'Safha min tarikh al-ikhwan al-muslimin fi Suriyya' [A page from the history of the Muslim Brothers in Syria] (www.levantnews.com, 19 September 2010).

al-Sawwaf, Sharif. *Mu'jam al-usar wa-l-a'lam al-dimashqiyya* [Dictionary of Damascene families and notables] (Damascus: Bayt al-Hikma, 2004).

al-Sayyid al-Lahham, Badi'. 'Juhud 'ulama' Dimashq fi al-hadith fi al-qarn al-rabi' 'ashar al-hijri Habashi' [The efforts of the ulama of Damascus in the realm of hadith in the fourteenth century AH]' (www.alfatihonline.com, n.d.).

Wahba al-Zuhayli: al-'alim al-faqih al-mufassir [Wahba al-Zuhayli: the 'alim, the faqih, the exegete] (Damascus: Dar al-Qalam, 2001).

al-Sharbaji, Ayman. 'Mudawwinat' [Log book] (www.sooryoon.net, November 2010).

'al-Shaykh 'Abd al-Karim al-Rifa'i wa masiratuhu al-da'wiyya' [Sheikh 'Abd al-Karim al-Rifa'i and his journey through da'wa] (www.sadazaid.com, 5 April 2008).

Siraj al-Din, Abdullah. *Ad'iyat al-sabah wa-l-masa'* [Invocations of the morning and evening] (Aleppo: Dar al-Falah, n.d.).

Hawla tarjamat al-marhum al-imam al-'allamat al-shahir wa-l-'arif al-kabir fadila sayyidi al-walid al-shaykh Muhammad Najib Siraj al-Din al-Husseini [Biography of the late imam, the famous savant and great connoisseur of God, His Excellency, my master and father Sheikh Muhammad Najib Siraj al-Din al-Husseini] (Aleppo: Dar al-Falah, 2002).

al-Salat 'ala al-nabi: ahkamuha, fada'iluha, fawa'iduha [The prayer for the Prophet: its rules, its virtues, its benefits] (Aleppo: Dar al-Falah, 1990).

al-Tabba', Iyyad Khalid. *'Abd al-Ghani al-Daqr* (Damascus: Dar al-Qalam, 2003).

Tammam, Hussam. 'al-Jifri wa mudat al-du'at al-judud' [al-Jifri and the fashion for the new preachers] (www.islamonline.com, 30 October 2003).

al-Tantawi, Ali. *Dhikrayat* [Memories] (Jeddah: Dar al-Manara, 1989).

al-Thaqafat al-islamiyya li-l-nashi'a [Islamic culture for the youth] (Damascus: Dar Zayd bin Thabit, 2007).

al-Uwaysi, 'Abd al-Rahman. *Nukhba min a'lam Halab al-shahba' min anbiya' wa 'ulama' wa awliya'* [Elite of the great figures of Aleppo-the-Grey among the prophets, the ulama and the saints] (Aleppo: Dar al-Turath, 2003).

Warda, Anwar. *Hiwar ... la shajar* [A dialogue ... not a dispute] (Damascus: Mu'assasat al-Iman, 2003).

Zaghlul, Anas. 'al-'Ilmaniyya: mafhumuha wa haqiqatuha' [Secularism: concept and reality] (www.sadazaid.com, 16 August 2007).

al-Zarqa, Mustafa. *al-Fiqh al-islami wa madarisuhu* [Fiqh and its schools] (Damascus: Dar al-Qalam, 1995).

Zarzur, 'Adnan. *Mustafa al-Siba'i: al-da'iya al-mujaddid* [Mustafa al-Siba'i: the preacher and renovator] (Damascus: Dar al-Qalam, 2000).

al-Zuhayli, Wahba. *al-Fiqh al-islami wa adillatuhu* [Fiqh and its scriptural evidences] (Damascus: Dar al-Fikr, 1984).

al-Mujaddid Jamal al-Din al-Afghani wa islahatuhu fi al-'alam al-islami [The renewer Jamal al-Din al-Afghani and his reforms in the Islamic world] (Damascus: Dar al-Maktabi, 1998).

'Na'am li-tajid al-fikr la li-tajdid al-fiqh' [Yes to the renewal of thought, no to the renewal of fiqh] (www.islammemo.cc, 19 October 2006).

Ta'aththur al-da'wat al-islamiyya bi-da'wat al-shaykh Muhammad bin 'Abd al-Wahhab [The influence of the da'wa of Sheikh Muhammad bin 'Abd al-Wahhab over Islamic da'wa] (Riyadh: n.p., 1994).

Interviews

Mahmud 'Akkam, Aleppo, 20 November 2006
'Isam al-'Attar, Aachen, 29 September 2007.
'Adil 'Aziza, Aleppo, 21 November 2006
Abu al-Fath al-Bayanuni, Aleppo, 20 April 2008

Ali Sadr al-Din al-Bayanuni, London, 15 April 2009
Hisham al-Burhani, Damascus, 4 August 2007
Mundhir al-Daqr, Damascus, 7 February 2007
Husam al-Din al-Farfur, Damascus, 28 June 2006
Muhammad Habash, Damascus, 9 December 2006
Muhammad al-Hawari, Aachen, 11 August 2008
Mahmud Abu al-Huda al-Husseini, Aleppo, 9 March 2006
'Abd al-Rahman al-Hajj Ibrahim, Damascus, 2005–7
'Abd al-Hadi al-Kharsa, Damascus, 15 April 2007
Ahmad Mu'adh al-Khatib, Damascus, 23 April 2008
'Abd al-Qadir al-Kittani, Damascus, 12 February 2007
Haytham al-Malih, Damascus, 13 May 2008
Qasim al-Nuri, Damascus, 29 November 2006
'Imad al-Din al-Rashid, Damascus, 29 July 2007
'Ammar al-Rifa'i, Damascus, 17 June 2007
Usama al-Rifa'i, Damascus, 5 March 2007
Zuhayr al-Shawish, Beirut, 23 February 2006
Nadim al-Shihabi, Aleppo, 22 November 2006
Ahmad Shmays, Damascus, 5 May 2008
Muhammad Khayr al-Tarshan, Damascus, 13 April 2008
Suleiman al-Zabibi, Damascus, 5 July 2007
'Abd al-Qadir al-Za'tari, Aleppo, 9 November 2005
Radwan Ziadeh, New York, 12 March 2010
Muhammad al-Zu'bi, Damascus, 8 May 2007

Index

List of Books in the Series